ANSELM
COMPANION TO
THE BIBLE

Editor Acknowledgments

During the development of this text, I have had the privilege to work with an esteemed group of scholars. I also want to acknowledge the fine editors at Anselm Academic, who came to me with the initial idea for the collection, and helped me shepherd this through to completion. Their support, especially that of Maura Hagarty and Paul Peterson, has been invaluable to this book's overall quality. Finally, I want to thank those scholars who served as reviewers for the material, Carolyn Osiek, Amy-Jill Levine, and Margaret Odell. The process of completing this book was itself a model of interreligious and ecumenical dialogue.

Publisher Acknowledgments

The publisher thanks Carolyn Osiek, RSCJ, for her service as academic consultant throughout the development of this text. Dr. Osiek holds a doctorate in New Testament and Christian Origins from Harvard University and is Charles Fischer Professor of New Testament emerita at Brite Divinity School. The publisher also thanks the following scholars who reviewed the work in progress.

Amy-Jill Levine
Vanderbilt University, Nashville, Tennessee

Margaret Odell
St. Olaf College, Northfield, Minnesota

ANSELM COMPANION TO THE BIBLE

WITH NRSV TRANSLATION

Corrine L. Carvalho, editor

Created by the publishing team of Anselm Academic.

Cover images

Top left: Aphik, Golan. Architectural components from a fourth or fifth-century synagogue. Candelabra (menorah) carved in the local basalt stone. © Zev Radovan / *www.biblelandpictures.com*

Top middle: Torah scroll. © *www.istockphoto.com*

Top right: Hamat Tiberias, fourth or fifth-century synagogue. Detail of the mosaic floor depicting the Holy Ark surrounded by two large candelabra and other ceremonial objects. © Zev Radovan / *www.biblelandpictures.com*

Center background: © *www.istockphoto.com*

Bottom left: Italy, Friuli-Venezia Giulia region, Aquileia, mosaic representing the good shepherd at the Patriarchal Basilica of Aquileia. © De Agostini Picture Library / A. Dagli Orti / The Bridgeman Art Library

Bottom middle: Biblical text. © *www.istockphoto.com*

Bottom right: The monastery of St. Martyrius at Ma'ale Adumim, east of Jerusalem. Architectural details with Christian symbols. © Zev Radovan / *www.biblelandpictures.com*

Contents

Introduction

Corrine L. Carvalho

The Bible is part of the fabric of North American culture. In the United States, early European settlers were often seeking a haven for religious freedom: not freedom from religion, but rather the freedom to practice their religion without state control or cultural harassment. The waves of settlers included Christians—Puritans, Quakers, Lutherans, Presbyterians, Moravians, Catholics, and Baptists among them—but also a sizable Jewish population. As a result, biblical images and traditions became imbedded in the cultures of the United States. To be an educated member of United States society, then, necessitates at least some knowledge of the sacred texts of Jews and Christians.

The chapters in this companion to the Bible are geared for those new to the study of the Bible in an academic setting. The use of the term *companion* in the title is a deliberate effort to convey that this text is meant to be read alongside biblical texts. Although the authors quote the New Revised Standard Version of the Bible, students can use this companion profitably with any modern scholarly translation.

Because this companion introduces readers to academic study— rather than to faith-based exploration—of biblical texts, the authors presume an audience of people of a variety of faiths, including readers who do not view the Bible as sacred. However, because many people view some or all of the Bible as sacred, the authors' approaches are sensitive to this reality. In classrooms around the country, especially in courses with students who are members of different Christian churches or adherents of different religions, these chapters aim to foster dialogue that is ecumenical (among Christians of various denominations) and interreligious (among people of different faiths). The process of completing this book was itself a model of interreligious and ecumenical dialogue as it brought together Christian scholars of various denominations, as well as Jewish and Muslim scholars.

The authors and reviewers that contributed to this companion are leading biblical scholars from across North America. Together, they have created an excellent introduction to contemporary biblical study. The contributors were chosen not just for their scholarly expertise, however, but also for their ability to make material accessible to college students.

Part 1, "Introduction to Biblical Studies," addresses foundational topics such as the formation and translation of the Bible; methods of biblical interpretation; biblical geography and archeology; the role of the Bible in the United States; Christian, Jewish, and Muslim understandings of sacred texts; the interpretation of biblical art; and theological reading of biblical texts. Part 2, "The Old Testament," explores topics such as the social world and religions of ancient Israel and Jewish biblical interpretation and provides introductions to the Pentateuch and to the Historical, Wisdom, and Prophetic books. Part 3, "The New Testament," discusses the social and historical context of the Greco-Roman world, the understandings of Jesus presented by the biblical texts, and early Christian apocrypha, and provides introductions to the Synoptic Gospels, Acts of the Apostles, the Johannine literature, the Pauline Letters, the Catholic Epistles, Hebrews, and Revelation. The written material is complemented by full-color captioned images that aim to further the reader's learning. The chapters include study questions that reinforce comprehension of the material and serve as a springboard to discussion. They also include a short bibliography for those wanting to know more about a topic or begin a research paper. The companion also includes a part titled "Additional Study Aids," which provides a time line of biblical history, maps, and charts, and concludes with a full index.

The many contributors to this volume were drawn together by a passion for the academic study of the Bible. It is my hope that this companion will give students a taste of this passion.

Part 1

Introduction to Biblical Studies

The Formation of the Bible

James Chukwuma Okoye, CSSp

Introduction

The word "Bible" comes from the Greek *ta biblia* ("the books"), for the Bible is a library of books that Christians regard as inspired by God, a collection that spans many centuries. Jews more often call the collection the Miqra, meaning "a reading," or Tanak, an acronym of the letters TNK, representing the three divisions of the collection: Torah (Law), Nevi'im (Prophets), and Kethuvim (Writings). Jews and Christians believe that God's people first transmitted God's word orally. These oral traditions were eventually put into writing, adapted, or expanded, in order to reflect the communities' fresh experiences of God. The term "Scripture" is also sometimes used for such writings.

Another term sometimes applied to this collection is "canon" (from the Greek, *kanōn*). The word means a rule or measuring cane, and it is used also for lists of works that set the standard in literature or art. In reference to the Bible, the canon is "a fixed collection of Scriptures that comprise [the] authoritative witness for a religious body."[1] Although the notion of a canon implies a stable collection, a canon may allow tensions to stand. In the New Testament canon, for example, letters bearing Paul's name but written by others stand alongside authentic letters of Paul. A more striking example of tension is found in Exodus 20:5–6 and Deuteronomy 7:10. The former says that the punishment for crimes committed by fathers will fall

---

1. Lee Martin McDonald and James A. Sanders, introduction to *The Canon Debate*, ed. Lee Martin McDonald and James A. Sanders (Peabody, MA: Hendrickson, 2002), 3–20, at 11.

upon their children. The latter, however, asserts that God "repays with destruction *those who hate him*; he does not delay with those who hate him, but makes *them* pay for it" (NABRE; italics added)—rejecting trans-generational retribution for individual retribution.

Canons also differ among and even within traditions. This is seen especially in the various collections of Jewish Scriptures. For example, the Hebrew Bible contains thirty-nine books arranged in tripartite form (Torah, Prophets, and Writings). The ancient Greek version, called the "Septuagint" (discussed below), had about fifty books in a fourfold arrangement: Pentateuch (Law), Historical Books, Poetic Books, and Prophets. In the various Christian traditions, the books of the Old Testament follow the divisions of the Septuagint. The Protestant Old Testament has the same number of books as the Hebrew Bible (thirty-nine), while the Roman Catholic has forty-six, the Greek Orthodox has forty-eight or nine, and the Ethiopian Orthodox has fifty. For Jews, Torah is the center of revelation and the books of Judges–2 Kings are "prophets." For Christians, Judges–2 Kings (with the addition, in many denominations, of certain books from the Septuagint) are "history."

The picture is much simpler with regard to the New Testament. All Christians now accept the same twenty-seven books.

The Hebrew Bible—Christian Old Testament

While the Jewish Tanak and the Christian Old Testament contain many of the same books, they remain distinct collections. "Old Testament" is a Christian term. Paul referred to the Scriptures of Israel as the "old covenant" (2 Cor. 3:14), and in Luke 22:20 Jesus proclaimed a "new covenant." The Septuagint rendered the Hebrew word for covenant (*berit*) with a word more often translated as "testament" (*diathēkē*). Irenaeus of Lyon (130–200 CE) was the first to speak of an "Old Testament" and a "New Testament." Today, some Christian scholars prefer to speak of the "First Testament" in order to avoid the implication that the Hebrew Scriptures are outmoded or obsolete; rather, they are the foundational revelation for understanding the New Testament.

No matter which collection is the focus of study, the Tanak or the Christian Bible, these collections are the end product of a long history of, first, composition; second, collation into a collection; and third, acceptance as sacred texts. While some of that history is the same for Jews and Christians, the formation of the Christian Bible is more complex.

The Pentateuch

Some of the poetic pieces of the Pentateuch appear to be as early as the twelfth century BCE (Exod. 15:1–18 [the Song of Moses] and Deut. 33). Outside the Pentateuch, Judges 5, and Psalm 29 also seem quite ancient, with parallels in non-Israelite writings dating from the fourteenth to twelfth centuries BCE. Such early examples of poetry, which is generally transmitted orally, remind us that pre-literate communities generally preserve communal history through oral tradition. Gerhard von Rad believed that Genesis, Exodus, Leviticus, Numbers, Deuteronomy, and Joshua grew out of a "cultic credo" (Deut. 26:5–9) recited in the central shrines of Gilgal and Shechem, with the following broad themes: Exodus from Egypt, entry into the promised land, patriarchal stories, wilderness wanderings, and Sinai and covenant.[2] These credos would have been expanded into written historical units by various writers at different stages in Israel's history. The prevailing theory of Julius Wellhausen (1878), called the Documentary Hypothesis, posits four writers over a period from the tenth century BCE until about 400 BCE.

The Documentary Hypothesis: J E D P

Scholars have long noticed repetitions, contradictions, and inconsistencies throughout the Pentateuch. These can best be explained by thinking of the composition of these texts as occurring over centuries, first through gathering oral traditions, and later by editing and adding to these traditions to address new situations in Israel's history.

(continued)

2. Gerhard von Rad, "The Form-Critical Problem of the Hexateuch," in *The Problem of the Hexateuch and Other Essays,* trans. E. W. Trueman Dicken (New York: McGraw-Hill, 1966), 1–78.

The Documentary Hypothesis: J E D P *(continued)*

Although specific theories about the formation of the Pentateuch are quite varied, the model proposed by Wellhausen provided the vocabulary for this history until recently, but is increasingly being challenged. These written traditions are called "sources." This chart[3] summarizes the main features of these four sources as proposed by Wellhausen.

	Yahwist (J)	Elohist (E)	Deutero-nomist (D)	Priestly Writer (P)
Date	United monarchy	Divided monarchy	Reign of Josiah (Judah alone)	End of the exile
Place	Southern kingdom	Northern kingdom	Southern kingdom	Judah
Divine Name	Uses *Yahweh* throughout the Pentateuch.	Uses *Elohim* exclusively until the divine name is introduced in Exodus.	Not applicable	Uses *Elohim* exclusively until the divine name is introduced in Exodus.
Religious Features	Sacrifice is offered in different locations. Priests and heads of household offer sacrifices.	Sacrifice is offered in different locations. Priests and heads of household offer sacrifices.	Only the Levites can make sacrifices in the one place God chooses.	Only the offspring of Aaron can make sacrifices. A single place of sacrifice is assumed.
Literary Features	Lively narrative and anthropomorphic view of God.	Lively narrative and anthropomorphic view of God.	Sermonic, with characteristic phrases.	Preserves traditions, such as genealogies, precise locations, and ages. Regal view of God.

3. Corrine L. Carvalho, *Encountering Ancient Voices* (Winona, MN: Anselm Academic, 2010), p. 34.

More recent evaluation of the sources of the Pentateuch has challenged parts of this model. Some scholars postulate that Israel's national and religious traditions in the Pentateuch were transmitted primarily in oral form in twin traditions (the P-composition and the D-composition) that merged during the exile. Whatever the precise details of the formation of the Pentateuch, it was in a form close to what is in the Bible today before 300 BCE, evidenced by the fact that the Samaritans, who split from Judea about that time, retained a Pentateuch (the Samaritan Pentateuch) close in form to the Hebrew Torah, but with multiple variations.

The Historical Books

Another significant collection of material is found among the historical books. How this collection came together and then eventually was combined with the Pentateuch is a matter of speculation. Many scholars believe that the Deuteronomistic History (Deuteronomy–2 Kings) was first composed either under King Hezekiah (716–687) or King Josiah, and was later supplemented during the exile. At some point, this historical collection was combined with Genesis–Numbers. Others propose that the corpus of Deuteronomy–2 Kings was the work of an exilic editor. Deuteronomy was later detached from this corpus and attached to Genesis–Numbers to close the period of Mosaic revelation. Still other scholars propose a Primary History (Genesis to Kings) which was the Bible of the exiles. What is clear is that many of these books bear the stamp of an exilic redaction or composition.

The Prophets

Outside of the Pentateuch and the Deuteronomistic History, the biblical books tend to be discrete texts, each with its own history of composition. The history of the collation of these discrete books into other larger collections is obscure. For example, it is clear that many of the prophetic books passed through an oral stage before being written down. Already in the eighth century, Isaiah recorded and sealed an apparently unfulfilled prophecy (Isa. 8:16). Jeremiah wrote down all his prophecies and repeated the exercise after King Jehoiakim burned the first scroll (Jer. 36).

The book of Isaiah offers a classic example of a prophetic book passing through many different stages. The historical prophet, Isaiah of Jerusalem, delivered his oracles primarily in prophetic speeches, the oral stage of the material. These oracles were eventually written down, but this written stage led to further expansions and development. The book of Isaiah now contains oracles related to three diverse contexts: Isaiah 1–39 (largely the eighth century), 40–55 (the exilic context, 586–539 BCE),[4] and 56–66 (the postexilic context, around the fifth century BCE). Even within that broad sweep, more recent material can be found; Isaiah 24–27 (called the Isaiah Apocalypse) was probably added in the third century BCE.

This complex process of composition is found in other prophetic books as well. For example, the book of Jeremiah exists in at least two versions: a Hebrew version preserved in the Jewish canon (sometimes called the "Masoretic Text") and the Septuagint version, based on a different Hebrew version, which is one-eighth shorter. In contrast to Isaiah and Jeremiah, however, the book of Ezekiel may have originated as a written collection, although even that written form developed over time with significant variations found in various ancient manuscripts.

Although the shorter prophetic books each have their own history of composition, they were eventually brought together to form a fixed list of twelve minor prophets. Within the Jewish tradition, they are counted as one "book," perhaps because they were often written on one scroll. Many scholars agree that the collection started with the books of Hosea and Amos. Beyond this, no consensus exists.[5] The Septuagint included Daniel among the prophets, although the Hebrew Bible places it among the Writings. Some collections of the prophets were stabilized by the first century BCE/CE.

---

4. H. G. Williamson, *The Book Called Isaiah: Deutero-Isaiah's Role in Composition and Redaction* (Oxford: Clarendon Press, 1994), 241. "In order to locate his message in relation to the earlier and continuing ways of God with Israel [Deutero-Isaiah] included a version of the earlier prophecies with his own and edited them in such a way as to bind the two parts of the work together" (240–41).

5. For one influential reconstruction, see James Nogalski, *Literary Precursors to the Book of the Twelve* (Berlin: Walter de Gruyter, 1993), 282.

The Septuagint

There are versions of the Hebrew Bible in various ancient languages, such as Aramaic, Syriac, Latin, and Coptic, but the most important is the ancient Greek translation, call the Septuagint, which became the basis for the Christian Old Testament. The *Letter of Aristeas* (between 130 and 70 BCE) narrated the myth of seventy-two translators, six from each of the twelve tribes, summoned from Palestine to Alexandria by the Hellenistic king, Ptolemy II Philadelphus (285–246), to produce a Greek version of the Torah. This translation came to be called the Septuagint, meaning "Seventy" (abbreviated LXX). At first only the Torah (Genesis–Deuteronomy) was translated, suggesting that it was the only part of the Hebrew Bible to have reached some fixity at that time. By the second to early third centuries CE, "Septuagint" referred to a Greek translation of the entire Bible. It also seems to have been the Bible used by the first Christians: when the New Testament authors quote the First Testament, more than 90 percent of the time they use the Septuagint.[6]

The Dead Sea Scrolls

The Dead Sea Scrolls were discovered in the Judean wilderness around a site called Qumran, near the Dead Sea, from 1947 to 1956. These scrolls, dating from around the mid-second century BCE to around 70 CE, attest to the fluid state of the text of the Old Testament at that time. Among the scrolls were found Hebrew and Aramaic copies of scriptures that would be excluded from the Hebrew Bible but would be preserved in Greek translation in the Septuagint, such as Sirach, Tobit, Psalm 151, and the Letter of Jeremiah (in Hebrew and Greek).[7] The six Jeremiah fragments from Qumran belong to two different text types: a shorter text resembling that of the Septuagint (4Q Jer^b and 4Q Jer^d),

---

6. Lee Martin McDonald, *The Biblical Canon: Its Origin, Transmission, and Authority* (Peabody, MA: Hendrickson, 1995), xvii, 35.

7. Further evidence of the circulation of Greek translations of the Scriptures in Palestine at that time is offered by fragments of a Greek version of the book of the Twelve Prophets (dating from ca. 50–100 CE), at Muraba'at near Bethlehem.

Fragments of the original Hebrew text of Sirach have been found among the Dead Sea Scrolls and in the Cairo Geniza, the source of the fragment shown here. Sirach did not become part of the Hebrew Bible, but was included in the Septuagint and Vulgate.

and a longer one resembling the Masoretic Text (4Q Jer[a] and 4Q Jer[c]).[8]

The group who hid these texts also preserved other Jewish texts, some of which may or may not have been considered sacred, such as *1 Enoch, Jubilees*, and the *Temple Scroll*.[9] The variations found among documents that would eventually be included in the Bible show that the text was not yet fixed. One mid-second-century BCE sectarian text (4QMMT) yields some evidence of an emerging canon when it speaks of blessings and curses "in the book of Moses [and] in the book[s of the Pr]ophets and in Davi[d and in the events] of ages past."[10] This suggests a canon of Torah and Prophets, possibly an emerging third section (indicated by "David," that is, the Psalms), and maybe even a fourth section that covers historical writings (similar to the four divisions of the Septuagint).

---

8. Cf. James VanderKam and Peter Flint, *The Meaning of the Dead Sea Scrolls* (San Francisco: HarperSanFrancisco, 2002), 134.

9. Ibid., 177–79; see also James C. VanderKam, "Questions of Canon Viewed through the Dead Sea Scrolls," in *Canon Debate*, ed. McDonald and Sanders, 91–109, at 108.

10. VanderKam and Flint, *The Meaning of the Dead Sea Scrolls*, 170.

The Canonization of the Hebrew Bible—Christian Old Testament

Before discovery of the Dead Sea Scrolls, the consensus among scholars was that the collection of Torah closed by about 400 BCE, Prophets by 200 BCE, and the Writings around 90 CE. Now it is clear that the process of canonization was longer and more complicated, and that it varied within both Judaism and Christianity. The "praises of famous men" in Sirach 44–50, written ca. 182 BCE, follows the order of the Pentateuch (the five books of Moses), Joshua–2 Kings, Isaiah, Jeremiah, Job, the Twelve Prophets, and Nehemiah. The foreword to the Greek translation of Sirach, which was written slightly later (ca. 117 BCE), refers to apparently closed sections of "Law and Prophets" and an indeterminate third section, referred to as "the rest of the books," and "the others that followed them."

In Luke 24:44, Jesus speaks of "the law of Moses, the prophets, and the psalms," with "psalms" perhaps representing an emerging section. In the late first century, Josephus (*Against Apion* 1.37–42) was the first to list the books of a Hebrew canon. This list numbered twenty-two books, the number of the Hebrew alphabet: five books of Moses, the prophets in thirteen books covering Israelite history, then four books of hymns and "instructions."[11] In the extra-biblical *4 Ezra* 14:23–28 (ca. 100 CE), Ezra dictated ninety-four books, twenty-four for everybody (corresponding to the Hebrew numbering of the current Hebrew canon) and seventy reserved for the wise.

Jewish texts like the Mishnah and the Talmud give further evidence of how the canon developed in Jewish tradition.[12] *Mishnah Yadayim* 3:5 (the Mishnah dates to 200 CE) reports a discussion at Jamnia (Hebrew: *Yabneh*) toward the end of the first century CE about whether Qohelet (Ecclesiastes) and the Song of Songs "defile the hands," that is, are sacred Scripture. A passage in the Talmud that contains discussions between rabbis at the end of the second century CE lists by name the current twenty-four books of the Hebrew Bible in its three sections (*B. Baba Batra* 14b).

---

11. Barclay suggests this refers to wisdom texts like Proverbs and Ecclesiastes; *Flavius Josephus: Translation and Commentary*, ed. Steve Masonvol, vol. 10, *Against Apion*, trans. by John M. G. Barclay (Leiden and Boston: Brill, 2007), 30.

12. See chapter 7, "Christians, Jews, and Muslims: People of the Book."

The New Testament

The formation of the New Testament canon was also a complex process. Christians regard Jesus Christ as the center of God's revelation. So the sayings of Jesus and traditions about him from witnesses who knew him were of paramount importance to the early believers, but at first these circulated in oral form only. Until about the end of the second century CE, "Scripture" for the early church meant the Greek Old Testament. First Corinthians seems to refer to the words of Jesus as having some normative force as well (see 7:10, 25; 9:14). Additional sayings continued to circulate, some of them later collected in the *Gospel of Thomas*.[13] Joachim Jeremias compiled a list of 266 sayings of Jesus found in texts outside of the New Testament.[14] Together, these show that there was a vibrant oral stage to the formation of early Christian texts, some of which became part of the New Testament.

The Greek word for "gospel," *euangelion*, originally referred to oral preaching about Jesus Christ, and occurs in that sense throughout Paul's letters, the authentic letters of Paul being the first known Christian literature. As Christian communities spread throughout the Roman Empire and began to be established and the apostles and eye-witnesses of Christ's ministry began to die, the Christian movement needed written records of this gospel. The first such written Gospel was that of Mark, possibly written between 66 and 70 CE, when the Temple was destroyed. Other written Gospels followed, Matthew and Luke around 80–85 CE and John around 90 CE.

The collection of these texts as sacred or canonical Scripture, however, varied among different groups. Marcion (early second century), the first author known to have used the term *euangelion* for a book or writing, accepted as Scripture only ten of Paul's letters and an edited Gospel of Luke. In his argument with gnostic Christians, Irenaeus of Lyon (ca. 170–180) developed a principle called the *regula fidei* ("rule of faith"), based on varying lists of affirmations

---

13. The *Gospel of Thomas* is a gnostic work containing sayings of Jesus in gnostic clothing. Some scholars think it preceded the canonical Gospels, but the majority hold it to date from the early second century CE.

14. Joachim Jeremias, *The Unknown Sayings of Jesus*, trans. R. H. Fuller (London: SPCK, 1958).

drawn from the Scriptures themselves, that were upheld as parameters for the authenticity of scriptural writings. He was also one of the first to call Christian writings Scripture.[15]

One factor that contributed to the development of a fixed Christian canon was the Christian preference for the codex from at least 100 CE. The codex was bound like modern books as opposed to a scroll; this format made it possible to gather a large number of writings into a single book.[16] The letters of Paul were the first to be collected; 2 Peter 3:15–16 (ca. 140–150 CE) refers to them as Scripture.

Several gospels circulated in the second century in addition to the four that now stand

Image digitally reproduced with the permission of the Papyrology Collection, Graduate Library, University of Michigan.

P[46] is a third-century codex of the writings of Paul. The page shown here is from Hebrews, which was thought at the time to have been authored by Paul. Many scholars believe that the collected Pauline writings formed the nucleus around which the New Testament grew.

in the New Testament; examples include the *Protevangelium of James*, the *Gospel of Peter*, and the *Gospel of the Hebrews*. The divergences between the various gospels raised questions. By about 200 CE, the four Gospels and thirteen letters of Paul were widely accepted.[17] Eusebius (*Ecclesiastical History* 3.25.1–17), ca. 320–342, set out the first identifiable list of New Testament Scriptures, dividing them

---

15. Harry Y. Gamble, "Canon: New Testament," in *Anchor Bible Dictionary*, edited by David Noel Freedman et al. (Doubleday: New York and London, 1992), 1:852–61, at 855.

16. Unlike a scroll, one writes on both sides of a page of a codex, effectively doubling the amount of text carried by a given number of pages. Also, the codex format could contain a larger number of pages than a scroll without becoming unwieldy.

17. Harry Y. Gamble, "The Formation of the New Testament Canon," in *A History of Biblical Interpretation*, ed. Alan Hauser and Duane Watson (Grand Rapids: Eerdmans, 2003), 1:409–29, at 416.

into three categories: *recognized* as Scripture were four Gospels, fourteen Letters of Paul, 1 John, 1 Peter, and possibly Revelation; *disputed* were James, Jude, 2 Peter, 2 John, and 3 John; and *spurious* were *Acts of Paul, Shepherd of Hermas, Apocalypse of Peter, Barnabas, Didache,* and possibly Revelation. Different communities, however, continued to follow their own practices for some time: the Syrian community used a text that harmonized the four Gospels well into the fifth century CE. The first list that corresponds to the current canon of the New Testament is found in a text by Athanasius dated to 367 CE. This canon was affirmed at the Council of Hippo in 393.

The formation of the canon was no designed process, but the result of the interplay of contingent factors. However, certain criteria did play a role. The first was *apostolicity*—a writing had to be seen as either deriving from the era of the apostles or agreeing with what the early community took to be apostolic teaching. Another was *catholicity*—a writing had to be relevant to the church at large and not addressed only to a specific group. *Orthodoxy* required that a writing not contradict the "rule of faith." For example, bishop Serapion of Antioch initially allowed the *Gospel of Peter* to be read in church until he found its content to be contrary to the accepted faith.[18] Finally, a writing should be *traditional*, that is, in use in worship in most churches and from early times.

The formation of the various canons of the Bible reflects the values and concerns of various communities. Within both Judaism and Christianity, these canons developed over a significant period of time in both oral and written form. They came out of worshipping communities, and reflect those communities' experiences of certain texts as sacred. Although contemporary biblical scholars tend to study biblical texts as discrete literary productions, the fact that these texts are now preserved in various collections, each with its own focus and purpose, continues to affect how individual texts are interpreted.

---

18. *Ecclesiastical History* 6.12.3–6.

DISCUSSION QUESTIONS

1. As indicated in this chapter, many of the books of the Bible appear to have been subjected to multiple revisions and additions over an extended period of time. Should this pose a problem for believers, who regard these writings as "God's word"? Would an earlier version of a biblical text be "God's word" as well, or only the final revision?

2. While Christians and Jews both regard the Hebrew Bible as inspired Scripture, they often differ dramatically in their interpretations of the meaning of those Scriptures. Explain this phenomenon and offer examples. Along with the differences, are there also significant points of agreement between Jewish and Christian readings of these texts?

3. Discuss the criteria for acceptance of a given text as canonical. Given these criteria, would it be possible to add to the canon? Could new revelations be incorporated into the canon? If a previously unknown letter of Paul or collection of sayings of Jesus were discovered, should Christians accept it as canonical—assuming it could be proved to be authentic?

4. Describe the Septuagint and explain its significance for the differences that currently exist between the Hebrew Bible and the various forms of the Christian Old Testament.

5. By accepting certain writings as canonical, the Jewish and Christian communities assert their belief that they are, in some sense, "God's word." Given that these writings are also manifestly the work of human beings, is this belief inconsistent? Why or why not?

FOR FURTHER STUDY

Davies, Philip R. *Scribes and Schools: The Canonization of the Hebrew Scriptures*. Louisville: Westminster John Knox, 1998.

Gamble, Harry E. "The Formation of the New Testament Canon and Its Significance for the History of Biblical Interpretation." In *A History of Biblical Interpretation*, edited by Alan J. Hauser and Duane F. Watson, 1:409–29. Grand Rapids: Eerdmans, 2003.

McDonald, Lee Martin. *The Biblical Canon: Its Origin, Transmission, and Authority.* Updated and rev. 3rd ed. Peabody, MA: Hendrickson, 2006.

McDonald, Lee Martin, and James A. Sanders, eds. *The Canon Debate.* Peabody, MA: Hendrickson, 2002.

Sanders, James A. "Canon: Hebrew Bible." In *Anchor Bible Dictionary*, edited by David Noel Freedman et al., 1:837–52. Doubleday: New York and London, 1992.

Sundberg, A. C., Jr. " 'The Old Testament of the Early Church' Revisited," in *Festschrift in Honor of Charles Speel*, edited by T. J. Seinkewicz and J. E. Betts, 88–110. Monmouth, IL: Monmouth College Press, 1996.

Internet Resources

www.ntgateway.com/canon

A directory of internet resources related to the New Testament canon.

archive.org/details/BartEhrman-TheHistoryOfTheBibleTheMaking OfTheNewTestamentCanon

A series of audio recordings in which Bart D. Ehrman discusses the New Testament Canon.

www.bible-researcher.com/canon1.html

Article by Michael Marlowe on the Old and New Testament canons.

www.deadseascrolls.org.il/home

A library of images of fragments of the Dead Sea Scrolls.

2

Bible Translations

Stephen J. Binz, Corrine L. Carvalho, and Claudia Setzer

When one reads the Bible in translation, the first step in interpreting the Bible has already been done for the reader. To read a translation of the Bible is to take for granted the interpretations of other people, because a translation into any other language is always based on the interpretive decisions of the translators as to the meaning of the text in the original language.

Translation as Interpretation

Translating is the process of "carrying over" meaning from one linguistic culture into another. Because the process of translation is always also an interpretation, translators of the Bible must be experts in both the original language and the language of the translation. There is never a perfect, word-for-word correspondence between one language and another, especially between ancient languages like Hebrew and Greek and modern languages like English. The translator tries to communicate the meaning of words from an ancient culture in words of a very different culture, yet is always aware that the meaning of the original can never be fully captured.

There are two broad approaches to translating the Bible from its original languages into English, and the many translations of the Bible all fall into one or the other of these two categories. The first type of translation is called the formal equivalence method, or word-for-word translation. This type of translation aims at adhering as closely as possible to the form of the original writing. The translator tries to match word for word and phrase for phrase. Because these translations retain many of the subtleties and nuances of the original languages, they are generally better for serious study of the Bible. The New Revised Standard Version, the New American Bible (Revised Edition), and the Jewish Study Bible are just some of the translations that use the formal equivalence method.

The other type of translation is called the dynamic equivalence method, or meaning-for-meaning translation. This type of translation is less concerned with matching words than with matching the ideas and thoughts of the original text. The translator aims at identifying the meaning intended by the author and then expressing it as it would naturally be rendered in English. These translations, such as the Good News Bible and *The Message*, are sometimes intended for reflective and prayerful reading of the Bible.

There are two principle considerations when choosing a Bible in English.[1] First, the Bible must be a responsible translation. It should give the meaning of the original Hebrew and Greek texts as accurately as possible. Second, the Bible must convey that meaning in English that is clear and readable. For both of these reasons, a modern version of the Bible, translated in the past few decades, is best. Older translations, like the King James Version, are harder to understand, because they do not use modern English, and less accurate, because they do not draw upon the significant advances of more recent scholarship in the study of ancient languages.

Early Translations of the Bible

Because translation is always interpretation, the history of the Bible's translation within Christian contexts demonstrates the different ways the Bible functioned at various points in history and among various

---

1. There is actually a third consideration: the version must be based upon a "critical" text. That is, the Hebrew and Greek text that serves as the basis of the translation must be the product of textual-critical analysis, which studies and compares the variant readings found in surviving manuscripts of the Scriptures in the attempt to reconstruct as accurately as possible the original readings. Textual criticism was still in its infancy when the King James Version was translated, therefore that version (and its modern incarnation, the New King James) should be avoided for serious biblical study.

groups. In the early period of Christian history, there were various versions of the Bible. Christianity originated in the eastern part of the Roman Empire where Greek was the primary language, which is why the New Testament was written in Greek. These early believers also had available a Greek version of the Hebrew Scriptures, the Septuagint, which had been translated centuries earlier by Greek-speaking Jews. Where Greek was not the primary language, the Bible was translated into the language of the region. In Western Europe, where Latin held sway, there were many different Latin versions of the Bible until the Church commissioned Jerome to create an official version, called the Vulgate. This version became the only translation allowed in areas governed by the Roman Catholic Church until the Reformation.

Zev Radovan / www.biblelandpictures.com

The Septuagint, the most common ancient Greek translation of the Hebrew Bible, was the work of Greek-speaking Jews of Alexandria, in Egypt. This page from an early papyrus codex of the Septuagint is from Psalms. Psalm 23 ("The LORD is my shepherd, I shall not want") begins on line eight.

One of the debates that raged in the Church before the Reformation was whether the Bible ought to be translated into the languages that the common people spoke. The Roman Catholic Church prohibited these translations, but some biblical scholars defied the prohibition. John Wycliffe, for example, translated the Bible into English as early as the 1380s.

Martin Luther (1483–1546) and the other Protestant reformers championed the idea that everyone should be able to read the Bible. He supported the effort to translate the text into the vernacular and personally translated the Bible into German. In the Council of

Trent, the Roman Catholic Church reacted against this movement by upholding the Latin version as the authoritative version of the Bible, a position that remained in effect until 1943, with the papal document *Divino Afflante Spiritu*. The most influential English translation that came out of the Reformation was the King James Bible, also known as the Authorized Version, in 1611. Catholic English Bibles did exist before 1943, such as the Douay-Rheims (1582–1609), but these were translations of the Latin Vulgate.

Bible Translation in America

The Christian Bible has always played a prominent role in American culture. As a result there has been a vibrant tradition of various Bible translations. A number of early European settlers in America took seriously Jesus' injunction to "make disciples of all nations," beginning with native peoples. John Eliot learned Natick, the language of local tribes in the Massachusetts area, and translated the Bible in the mid-seventeenth century, creating *The Indian Bible*. Most efforts at converting the indigenous populations, however, used English versions of the Bible. As result, missionaries first attempted to teach native populations how to read English. William and Mary (1693) and Dartmouth College (1769) were founded to spread the Gospel to the natives as well as to educate young men for the ministry. By the nineteenth century, many religious groups founded colleges across the heartland, such as Knox, Grinnell, Oberlin, Notre Dame, Brigham Young, and Ohio Wesleyan, with the intent of promoting a religious education centering on biblical studies. Each group asserted its legitimacy on the American scene and optimism about the future by training young people in the group's own understanding of the biblical text. But they also contributed in harmful ways to the demise of native languages.

Engagement with the Bible was at the center of most American Christian spirituality. Many Americans, suspicious of institutions, gravitated toward more personal, free-form expressions of religious feeling. Two great revival movements stressed individual experience of the Spirit and independent interpretation. The First Great Awakening, in the 1730s and 1740s, is associated with George Whitefield and Jonathan Edwards. In a famous 1733 sermon Edwards speaks of the "spiritual and divine light" that is grounded in Scripture, but is "immediately imparted to the soul by God," giving authority to individual experience. In the Second Great Awakening, less than a hundred years later, Baptist and Methodist preachers traveled the country holding camp meetings and revivals. Some were women, like Helena Alter Davisson, a circuit rider in Indiana, and Phoebe Palmer, a founder of the Holiness Movement, which sought a second sanctification, or experience of the spirit. Pentecostalism emerged at the turn of the twentieth century, combining an emphasis on individual experience of the Spirit with a belief in the Bible as divine revelation.

Other religious groups around the same time also claimed their roots in Scripture, but sought a rationalist basis for religion and rejected ideas of sin and salvation that were prominent in the denominations that had sprung from John Calvin's theology. In a sermon, "Unitarian Christianity," in 1819, William Ellery Channing cited Scripture in support of the principles of Unitarianism, including a rejection of the Trinity and the Atonement doctrine. Unitarianism in America and its offshoot, Transcendentalism, thrived in nineteenth-century New England.

Which Bible were these groups reading? The dominance of Protestant groups in America meant that the most familiar translation was the King James Version of 1611. With the Second Great Awakening and the end of ties with Britain, however, Americans began to produce and distribute their own Bibles. The American Bible Society, founded in 1816, committed itself to distributing the Bible all over the world, sending out six million copies of the King James Version in its first thirty years. One initiative was to supply a New Testament to every Union soldier in the Civil War. The success of the society meant that copies of the King James were affordable and accessible, so even non-Protestants used it.

Because of the antiquated language of the King James Version, the Church of England produced the Revised Version in 1881 and 1885, adapting the language to the times. In America this became the American Standard Version, published in 1901. Many other translations followed, benefitting from the discovery of more ancient manuscripts, archaeological finds, and the emergence of text criticism. The Revised Standard Version appeared in 1946, updated as the New Revised Standard Version in 1989, while more conservative

Protestants produced a more literal translation as the New American Standard Version in 1971, updated in 1995.

A translation specifically intended for one's own religious group is an expression of identity and of one's claim on the text. Isaac Leeser (1806–1868), a Prussian Jew who came to America as a teenager and became a prominent figure in American Judaism, completed his translation of the entire Hebrew Bible into English in 1853, fulfilling a hope of many years, "to present to his fellow Israelites an English version, made by one of themselves." Based on the Masoretic Text, the authoritative Hebrew text, he was pleased to present "a version of the Bible that has not been made by the authority of the churches."

At the end of the nineteenth century, great waves of Eastern European Jews landed on American shores. The Jewish Publication Society took over a project to replace Leeser's translation with one done by committee in 1908, publishing the JPS Version in 1917. The motive for this project sprang from a sense that the American Jewish population was growing and English, "unless all signs fail, is to become the current speech of the majority of the children of Israel." A newer translation of the entire *Tanakh*, or Hebrew Bible, from the Masoretic Text, was published in 1985, known as the New Jewish Publication Society Version (NJPS).

Catholics too felt the need to assert their identity against the overwhelming influence of the King James Version. Frances Kenrick, later the archbishop of Baltimore, produced an English version of the Douay Bible based on the Latin Vulgate, appearing in sections in 1849 and 1860. The translation from the Vulgate, he says in his preface, is preferable to the Protestant version because it is "easy, smooth, and intelligible," while the latter is "rugged, constrained, and often obscure." After Vatican II, the bishops in the United States commissioned a new Catholic translation of the Bible, which they called *The New American Bible* (NAB) which was published in 1970. This was revised in 2010, to reflect Catholic liturgical use.

Translations continue to multiply, expressing the values and identity of groups and denominations. The Conservative Bible Project claims to offer translations free of "liberal bias," avoiding gender-neutral language and expressing free-market principles.[2]

2. See *http://conservapedia.com/Conservative_Bible_Project*.

Eugene H. Peterson, a biblical scholar and Presbyterian minister, offered a highly idiomatic translation in *The Message: The Bible in Contemporary Language*, to mixed reviews, becoming a best-seller in its category. Communities on the Sea Islands off the coast of South Carolina and Georgia, settled by emancipated slaves after the Civil War and preserving their own culture, now have the New Testament in their own language, Gullah. Young people have the New Century Version, in glossy magazines like *Revolve* for women or *Refuel* for men, complete with sidebars on negotiating high-school life.

Inclusive Language and Translation Principles

The fact that judgments are required of translators has become more obvious with the question of how to translate gendered terms into English. The issue is more apparent with Hebrew texts, because Biblical Hebrew has only two grammatical genders, masculine and feminine; there is no neuter in Hebrew. With respect to persons, in Hebrew, as well as Greek, feminine gender is used when referring to an individual who is female, a group of people who are all female, or a noun that is feminine (like "wisdom" or "city"). Masculine gender is used for persons who are male and for grammatically masculine nouns. Masculine gender is also used when either the gender of the person is not known or is not important, or when referring to a group of people of both genders. For example, when an ancient text refers to a group of people that includes both men and women, both Hebrew and Greek use only masculine nouns and pronouns.

Some masculine Hebrew and Greek words may have more than one meaning. For example, the word translated "man" may also mean "anyone." When translating biblical texts, translators must determine whether a given masculine noun or pronoun in the ancient text was meant to refer only to males or to anyone, regardless of gender. For example, Psalm 1:1 starts, "Blessed is the *'ish* (Hebrew for "man, person")." Should this be translated as "Blessed is the man," referring to males only, or should it be translated as "Blessed is the one," because it pertains equally to men and women? Either translation is grammatically correct; either translation requires a judgment by the translator. Sometimes the context clarifies the intended meaning, but not always.

Until recently, the divide between the ancient languages and modern English was not so stark. English formerly used "man" to refer to any person, regardless of gender, but recognition of the androcentric perspective of this usage has caused significant shifts in English. Most scholars and most educated public discourse no longer use "man" to refer to persons, people, or humanity in general. "Humanity" or "humankind" has replaced "mankind." This change in English usage has prompted a majority of biblical scholars, responding to modern sensitivities and the potential for misunderstanding if gender-specific language is used, to use gender-inclusive language in their translations when referring to both men and women.

The Bible is not just an ancient text. It is a text read and proclaimed in churches and synagogues around the world. The translation of terms meant to address a contemporary audience has to be part of the judgment of the translation. As a result, most translators today, when faced with a situation where the gender of the pronoun is unclear, prefer to translate it in a way that is inclusive of both men and women, since the Bible as sacred text addresses congregations of men and women. Even in places where one could argue that the original author might have had only men in mind, translators can still choose a gender-neutral term when the topic is one that today we know is pertinent for both genders. For example, while the psalmist might indeed be saying that "the man" who pursues wisdom is happy (since only men were educated), today when a psalm addresses a modern audience, it can be argued that "the one" is more appropriate, as men and women have equal access to education.

There is also an ongoing debate about the best way to translate pronouns referring to God in the Bible. In Hebrew and Greek, the pronouns for God are masculine, but the canon includes both male and female metaphors to describe God. Genesis 1:27 states that male and female (and here the Hebrew terms mean biological males and biological females) are both created in the image and likeness of God. Did the Israelites consider their God to be only male? While there are certainly more male metaphors than female ones in the Bible, female metaphors do occur. Due to the way the grammar

© Joe Stefanchik / KRT / Newscom

The presence of gender-specific language and cultural assumptions in the ancient texts pose problems for Bible translators, who must produce a translation that is both scholarly and appropriate for use in modern, mixed-gender worship settings.

works, if the ancient Hebrews did understand God as encompassing both male and female attributes, they would nonetheless have used only grammatically masculine nouns and pronouns to refer to God.

Translators vary regarding their treatment of pronouns for God. Some use masculine pronouns only when the language of a given text clearly depicts God as male (such as Ezek. 16, where God is a husband). Others retain the traditional male pronouns throughout the text, although usually without explanation for why they do so. Some Christian biblical scholars maintain that Jesus' references to God as "Father" require male pronouns for God, assuming that by "Father" Jesus meant a male and not what could also be translated as "parent."

Debates about inclusive language for both humans and God continue to this day. The United States bishops of the Catholic Church, in the revision of the *New American Bible*, wanted to restore traditional language throughout the text so that the people in the pews would recognize echoes with other prayers and teachings in the Catholic tradition. Consequently, the revision has less inclusive language than its predecessor. However, that translation was created specifically for liturgical use, rather than scholarly study. Translations that differ in regard to gendered language are helpful both for studying the text in its historical context and for understanding its influence on contemporary society.

The history of the translation of the Bible is part of the history of the interpretation of the text. Translations will always be revised, because they need to serve the changing communities that view the text as sacred. Translators must consider how the ancient words are best communicated to a modern audience and how a particular translation might be used.

DISCUSSION QUESTIONS

1. Describe the two main approaches to translating the Bible. Explain the advantages and disadvantages of each.

2. Explain the significance of the Septuagint, the Latin Vulgate, and the Protestant Reformation for translations of the Scriptures.

3. Describe the problem of androcentric language in the ancient texts, and the various ways that translators deal with it. What problems arise if androcentric language is allowed to stand in the text? Conversely, is it possible to go too far in the attempt to circumvent androcentric language?

4. How does the issue of androcentric language apply to terms for God? Is this problem different from the ancient texts' use of androcentric language for human beings? Would it be appropriate to translate the Lord's Prayer, "Our Parent . . ." or "Our Mother . . ."? Explain your position on these questions.

FOR FURTHER STUDY

Brown, Raymond E., et. al. "Texts and Versions." In *The New Jerome Biblical Commentary*, edited by R. E. Brown, J. A. Fitzmyer, and R. E. Murphy, 1083–1112. Englewood Cliffs, NJ: Prentice Hall, 1990.

Burke, David G., John F. Kutsko, and Philip H. Towner, eds. *The King James Version at 400: Assessing Its Genius as Bible Translation and Its Literary Influence.* Society of Biblical Literature Biblical Scholarship in North America 26. Atlanta: Society of Biblical Literature, 2013.

Ringe, Sharon H. "When Women Interpret the Bible." In *Women's Bible Commentary, Revised and Updated,* edited by Carol A. Newsom, Sharon H. Ringe, and Jacqueline E. Lapsley, 1–9. Louisville: Wesminster John Knox, 2012.

Setzer, Claudia, and David Shefferman. *The Bible and American Culture: A Sourcebook.* London and New York: Routledge, 2011.

3

Geography and Archaeology

Leslie J. Hoppe, OFM

The territory controlled by the ancient Israelite kingdoms of Israel and Judah was relatively small—about the size of New Jersey. From Dan to Beer-sheba (see 1 Sam. 3:20; 2 Sam. 3:10; 17:11; 24:2; 1 Kings 4:25), it is just 125 miles. From the Mediterranean Sea to the Jordan River (running through Jerusalem), it is about fifty miles. Because of its geographical location, this area had significance that transcended its size. It was the crossroads of the ancient Near East.

Geography of the Eastern Mediterranean Region

There were three geographical barriers to efficient east-west communications in the globe's eastern hemisphere: mountains, deserts, and seas. The Levant, the territory now controlled by Syria, Lebanon, Jordan, Israel, the Palestinian Authority, and Hamas, provided the only land passage that was relatively free of obstructions, making possible communication and trade between Egypt, Africa, and Arabia to the south, Anatolia to the north and Mesopotamia to the east. Travelers, merchants, soldiers, and refugees all met on this 125-mile long, fifty-mile wide corridor between the Mediterranean Sea and the Arabian Desert.[1]

---

1. See map 1, "The Table of Nations," and map 2, "The Tribal Territories," in the additional study aids section.

The Fertile Crescent is another name for the land mass where the east-west lines of communication meet in the Eastern Hemisphere. This sickle-shaped piece of land north of the Arabian Desert has water supplies sufficient to support agriculture that, in turn, enabled settlement in towns and villages. The Fertile Crescent is divided into two subsections. The eastern section is known as "Mesopotamia," a Greek name meaning "[the land] between the rivers." In the northern part of this region, the two rivers—the Tigris and the Euphrates—supplied water necessary for agriculture. The amount of rainfall allowed for settlements away from the rivers as well. The south was subject to spring flooding because the melting winter snows in the mountains ran off into its low-lying areas. At times, these floods were catastrophic and probably occasioned the composition of epics similar to the biblical flood story (Gen. 6–9). Here the kingdoms of Sumer, Assyria, and Babylon held sway from the fourth millennium BCE until the Greeks came in the fourth century BCE, followed by the Romans in the first century BCE.

The western part of the Fertile Crescent extends from the mountains of Lebanon in the north to the Red Sea in the south—a distance of five hundred miles. It is a geographically complex area. There are four topographical zones that run north-south in the region: the Coastal Plain along the Mediterranean Sea, the Western Highlands, the Rift Valley, and the Eastern Plateau. Besides these zones, an important depression, the Jezreel Valley, runs from northwest to southeast Israel, from the Carmel Range to the Rift Valley.

At the foot of Mount Hermon in the north, a major transverse fault causes the Rift Valley to drop suddenly as it begins its descent to the Red Sea. For most of that descent, the valley is below sea level. The Jordan River flows south from the Sea of Galilee in the center of the Rift Valley to the Dead Sea. The Coastal Plain widens, beginning just south of Mount Carmel, until it reaches Gaza along the shore of the Mediterranean Sea in the south. The Western Highlands descend in two steps (Upper and Lower Galilee) to the low-lying Jezreel Valley that connects the Rift Valley with the Mediterranean coast at Acco. South of the Jezreel Valley are the Central Highlands. Here the Israelite tribes emerged. Exploiting this region

© Shai Ginott/CORBIS

Terrace agriculture, which helps prevent soil erosion and water runoff, was popular throughout the biblical period in the Levant. The terraces shown here are found at Birkat Ram on Mount Hermon.

for agriculture required intense and constant labor. The hills had to be terraced both to provide a suitable place for the cultivation of grain and to control the runoff water. The Israelite tribes prospered there because most other peoples preferred to work the soil in the Coastal Plain or the foothills that did not pose the obstacles to agriculture found in the highlands.

Other important geographical subdivisions of the Levant include the area north of the territory of the kingdom of Israel. This region receives more than thirty inches of rain annually, making possible the grain production and lush pastures for which it was renowned. Tyre and Sidon, the principal cities along the Levant's northwestern coast, were prosperous ports and commercial centers. The southwestern coastal region did not have much agricultural potential or viable port facilities, but the Via Maris and other caravan routes crisscrossed through the area, and people lived off trade. The southern region received barely enough rain to support village agriculture. People living in these subdivisions of the Levant did not easily cooperate with one another, perhaps due to the geographical barriers separating them. People here had a strong regional consciousness and regarded outsiders with suspicion since there were continuing conflicts over the region's limited resources.

The Central Rift Valley, the Jezreel Valley, and several of the valleys along the Coastal Plain are covered by fertile alluvial soil, which can produce substantial crops when the supply of water is sufficient. The Plain of Sharon located in the center of the Coastal Plain, however, has a red, sandy soil that is not good for the grain, grapes, and olives that were staples in antiquity. The region was only marginally exploited for agriculture until modern times and remained a sandy marsh throughout the biblical period.

The soil in the highlands is formed from decomposing limestone, a hard sedimentary rock that turns into a rich, soft, red, and porous soil that sops up the winter rains and releases moisture during the dry summer months. Olive trees, in particular, thrive in this soil. Limestone also served as an excellent building material and was used extensively in antiquity for private dwellings and public, monumental structures. Above the limestone is a layer of chalk, and above this is sometimes another limestone layer.

While the soil in the western part of the Fertile Crescent is rich enough to support agriculture, the region does not have anything like the two great rivers (the Tigris and the Euphrates) of the eastern part. Most rivers in Israel flow only during the rainy season (November to March). The Jordan River, a perennial stream, is located in the Rift Valley, which rendered it useless for irrigation in antiquity because people were not able to move the water from the low elevation of the river to the land where it was needed, since the valley in which the river is located is narrow and deep. There are springs in the highlands, but they could not support intensive agriculture. The water for the soil and its crops had to come as rain, which was collected and stored in cisterns to be used during the dry season.

Weather Patterns

One can only speculate about the general weather patterns in antiquity. The data necessary to make definite conclusions are simply not available. It is probably a mistake to think that the climate in the

Levant has not changed appreciably since the biblical period. What follows is a description of the climate today; one must remember that there may have been some variations in antiquity.[2]

There are several features of the Levant's geographical setting that shape its weather patterns. First, it is close enough to the Sahara and Arabian deserts to feel intense heat in the summer, and to the Russian and Siberian Plains to experience their cold in the winter. Second, the Mediterranean Sea and the Arabian Desert are separated by only one hundred miles and the proximity of these two to the Levant has a distinct bearing on the region's climate. Third, weather patterns usually run west to east while the Central Highlands run north to south. The effect of this is to stall weather systems west of the mountains. The combination of these factors leads to the following: there are two seasons in most of the Levant. One is a dry season that generally runs from June 15 to September 15. The beginning and end of this season are quite regular. It almost never rains during this time. Before and after this dry season, there are transition periods of between four and six weeks. The other principal season is the wet season. Its beginning is not as predictable as that of the dry season.

Baal versus Yahweh

Having enough rain was a cause of great anxiety in ancient Israel. Many people relieved that anxiety through worshiping Baal, the Canaanite god of storms, who brought rain (see 1 Kings 17–18). Baal was the main rival of Yahweh, the ancestral deity of ancient Israel, for the loyalty of the people through most of the monarchic period.

---

2. Recent analysis of pollens from the Sea of Galilee's lake bed have found evidence of climate change in the thirteenth century BCE, which may explain the severe social and economic ferment of the period. See "Climate and the Late Bronze Collapse: New Evidence from the Southern Levant," *Tel Aviv: Journal of the Institute of Archaeology of Tel Aviv University* 40, no. 2 (October 2013): 149–75.

The rains do not fall evenly throughout the land. It rains more in the north than in the south and more in the west than in the east. The far north can receive as much as thirty inches of rain annually while Beer-sheba in the south receives about eight inches and is totally dry for five months (May–September). Jerusalem, in the center, receives about twenty-two inches of rain annually. Rainfall is always greater on the western side of the Central Highlands than on the eastern side, since the former is closer to the sea.

Livelihoods

The Levant was able to support farmers, shepherds, and merchants quite well. The shepherds led their flocks from one pasture to another by taking advantage of every hill and valley that had grass to feed their sheep. They could not stay in one place for long because the sheep would soon deplete the available resources. For shepherds, mobility was the key to survival. For farmers, by contrast, the key was stability, rain, and fertile soil. In difficult times, farmers sometimes converted their land holdings to flocks and herds. This broke their tie to a particular plot of land and allowed them to move to more fertile areas and to avoid oppressive taxation. The merchants required safe roads, enabling them to move from place to place without trouble. The farmers, shepherds, and merchants needed each other. For example, merchants depended on animals bred by shepherds and farmers. They also needed guides in unfamiliar areas. The shepherd provided animals to help the farmer with both the plowing and the threshing. The merchant facilitated exchange of goods among the people of the Levant.

Because of the Levant's geographical setting, adequate food production was a chancy affair in antiquity. The uncertain food supply was a source of great anxiety among the people of the region. They relieved this anxiety, in part, through religious practices. Because people believed that the Canaanite god Baal would provide the rain necessary to grow their crops, Canaanite religious practices were very attractive to the ancient Israelites (see 1 Kings 17–18). Attempts to control the international trade routes that passed through the Levant led to intense military confrontations among the nations in the region throughout the biblical period.

Biblical Archaeology

Archaeology is the study of the material remains of antiquity as opposed to its literary remains. Material remains include anything that displays or effects human activity, from microscopic pollens to monumental architecture. Archaeology uncovers these objects, identifies them, reconstructs them when possible and necessary, and then classifies them. Once these preliminary tasks have been completed, the more difficult ones begin: the artifacts are compared with examples from other regions, arranged in a chronological sequence, and related to previously known information.

The goal of archaeological projects is to reconstruct life in the ancient world, to profile the culture of the people who left these remains behind, and to help define the various types of human responses to different situations reflected in the archaeological record. Archaeology fills a void where literary sources are insufficient or nonexistent. The Bible is, after all, literature that comes from an elite group in ancient Israel. While the people who composed the books of the Bible may not all have been part of the social and economic upper class, they were people who had a keen sense of the values and beliefs of their ancestral religious tradition. But did they represent the way most Israelites believed and lived? Through the study of material remains, archaeology puts the Bible into a living context.

Biblical archaeology is a relatively new field of study. At the beginning of the twentieth century, a growing number of scholars believed that excavation would settle the question of the historical value of Old Testament narratives—especially regarding the settlement of the Israelite tribes in Canaan. Archaeology has shown that the emergence of the Israelites in Canaan was a complex affair, which the biblical narratives simplify. In the end, the high hopes of the first scholars who excavated in what is now the modern state of Israel and the Palestinian Authority were never realized. The first biblical archaeologists were confident that their new discipline would support the historical value of biblical narratives, but the excavation of sites like Jericho and Ai (see Josh. 6–9) has shown that these places were largely unoccupied in the Late Bronze Age (ca. thirteenth century BCE) when the Israelite tribes supposedly conquered them. As the methods of excavation and interpretation became more sophisticated, however, some archaeologists have virtually abandoned the goal of proving the Bible's historicity. They hold that the Torah and Former Prophets have a theological purpose and do not provide the kind of data necessary to reconstruct the history of ancient Israel. Some attempts at reconstructing that history are little more than paraphrases of the biblical text. A genuinely scientific account of ancient Israel's past needs to take into account the archaeological record as well as the available literary sources.

Most of the early archaeologists focused their attention almost entirely on sites related to ancient Israel's Scriptures. Few bothered with New Testament sites since the question of historicity was framed differently in relationship to the Christian Scriptures. No historian questions the existence of Jesus or Paul. Also, the historical period reflected in the New Testament was much shorter than that covered by the Old Testament and was illumined by a wealth of secular and religious literature. Finally, many scholars located the principal contribution of the New Testament in the area of theology, so it was thought that archaeology had little or nothing to contribute to illuminating the theological affirmations of the Christian Scriptures.

The rise of the sociological and anthropological approaches to biblical interpretation effected a dramatic change in the relationship between archaeology and the Christian Scriptures. It is clear that religious texts are bound to the societies that produced them. A prerequisite of informed biblical interpretation, then, is knowledge of those societies in which the biblical tradition took shape. Archaeology supplies the raw data necessary to profile the Jewish and Greco-Roman contexts in which the books of the New Testament emerged. Archaeology helps cultural anthropologists describe the people who wrote and first read the Christian Scriptures by defining the characteristics of the "Mediterranean person" in the first and early second centuries and all that this involved.[3]

Today the goal of archaeology is to recreate the world of the Bible using the material remains left by the people of that world. This assumes that the Bible is the product of real people, who lived at a real

---

3. Examples of the impact of archaeology on the study of the New Testament include Jonathan L. Reed, *Archaeology and the Galilean Jesus: A Re-examination of the Evidence.* (Harrisburg, PA: Trinity Press International, 2000) and John Dominic Crossan and Jonathan L. Reed, *Excavating Jesus: Beneath the Stones, behind the Texts* (San Francisco: HarperSanFrancisco, 2002).

time, had certain values, and functioned within political, economic, and social structures. It also assumes that the more we know about these people, the more we can know about the literature that they produced.

Science and Art

Archaeology is both a science and an art. A successful project requires a team of specialists: a surveyor, a stratigrapher, a ceramicist, a numismatist, a bone specialist, a botanist, an architect, a historian, a photographer, an artist, and a reconstruction specialist. More complex projects, such as those requiring underwater excavation, require additional expertise. Archaeology is the one science that systematically destroys a good part of its evidence. As excavation proceeds, each successive occupation layer is destroyed to reach the one below. To compensate for this, archaeologists have developed detailed and exact methods for excavation and the recording of finds. This allows the progress of the excavation to be reviewed by archaeologists who did not actually participate in the excavation project.

© AP Photo / Eyal Warshavsky

This archaeological team is excavating the remains of a two-thousand year old structure in Caesarea, on the coast of Israel. Archaeologists carefully map and record each layer before removing it in order to reach the next layer.

This aerial view shows Tell es-Sultan (ancient Jericho). Dame Kathleen Kenyon's work at this site in 1952–1958 pioneered many of the archaeological techniques that have since become standard.

© Todd Bolen / BiblePlaces.com

The method used in excavating biblical sites is usually some variation of the Wheeler-Kenyon method. Mortimer Wheeler developed the technique of stratigraphic excavation for use with sites from the classical period and Kathleen Kenyon adapted it for use on biblical sites. The basic approach is to peel off occupational layer by occupational layer, recovering artifacts and other evidence of human presence at the site. While the excavation needs to be done carefully, the recording of data requires even greater care. Those who study biblical texts all have the same basic data before them. Those who study the material remains of an ancient society have only one opportunity to see these remains in their context unless the progress of the excavation is duly and carefully recorded in such detail that it can be reconstructed from the final reports.

The excavation of a site is the easy part of any archaeological project. The difficult part, the interpretation of the artifacts uncovered in the process of excavation, is more akin to an art, requiring imagination and creativity from its practitioners. Without insightful interpretation, excavation cannot advance knowledge. Interpretation transforms a mass of data into a form that is accessible to the scholarly community. Pottery, coins, bones, seeds, artifacts (metal, stone, and wood), and structures must all be related in a coherent fashion. The interpretation of data is crucial in the archaeology of Israel because significant literary remains are so rarely found during excavations there. The goal of the interpretive process is to relate the site that has been excavated to other sites in the region, to understand the culture at the site, to reconstruct the diet, the work, the religion, the politics, the economy, the aesthetics, and the moral values of the people who lived at the site in antiquity.[4]

Before the development of archaeology as an academic discipline in the twentieth century, excavations were often little more than treasure-hunting expeditions that sought to uncover monumental buildings and find interesting and valuable artifacts for private collectors or museums. Biblical archaeology developed as an ancillary discipline to biblical studies especially to provide the data for reconstructing the history of ancient Israel. Today biblical archaeology is an independent field of study, a branch of Near Eastern archaeology with an agenda and a methodology independent of biblical studies. Its goal is to reconstruct the shape of ancient societies on the basis of the material remains left behind by the people of those societies. This involves much more than historical reconstruction. It includes every aspect of human endeavor, from the growing and preparation of food to the development of moral and religious values.

The early biblical archaeologists thought that their work would serve to establish the historical accuracy of Old Testament narratives—especially those dealing with the Exodus, the emergence of the Israelite tribes in Canaan, and the early monarchic period. This goal was not met. Archaeology has uncovered no evidence of a mass migration in the Sinai during the Late Bronze Age (1400–1250 BCE) when the escaped Hebrew slaves were thought to have made their

---

4. For examples of the reconstruction of the shape of an ancient society based on archaeology, see Avraham Faust, *The Archaeology of Israelite Society in Iron Age II* (Winona Lake, IN: Eisenbrauns, 2012) and William G. Dever, *The Lives of Ordinary People in Ancient Israel: Where Archaeology and the Bible Intersect.* (Grand Rapids: Eerdmans, 2012).

Biblical Archaeology or Syro-Palestinian Archaeology

Archaeologists who work in the Levant debate the appropriateness of calling their discipline "biblical archaeology" since archaeology has become a field of study in its own right. Some scholars prefer to call the discipline "Syro-Palestinian archaeology." This nomenclature has not really caught on. While people may continue to use the term "biblical archaeology," they now recognize its independence from biblical studies.

way through this area. Excavations of Jericho and Ai (see Josh. 6–8) suggest that these two sites were not occupied in the Late Bronze Age, at the time that the Bible claims they were attacked by invading Israelite tribes. Excavations in Jerusalem have not revealed the type of structures that one expects of the capital of a national state in the time of David. The concern for demonstrating the historicity of biblical narratives has, in part, spawned the production of archaeological frauds. By one estimate, 30 to 40 percent of the artifacts in the possession of the Israel Museum are fakes.[5] It is not surprising, then, that some archaeologists wish to break the close connection between biblical studies and archaeology.

Archeology makes a positive contribution to biblical studies by describing the world that produced the Bible. Archaeology provides to readers and interpreters of the Bible what journalists call "deep background"—that is, information that provides a context for a story. Being familiar with that deep background helps the interpreter to avoid making unwarranted conclusions about the text and helps the reader to read the Bible without reading "into" it. Still, some archaeologists suggest that archaeology break any connection with biblical

---

5. Ann Byle, "Update: Finds or Fakes?" *Biblical Archaeology Review* 30, no. 5 (Sept.–Oct., 2004): 52. See also Andrew G. Vaughn and Christopher A. Rollston, "The Antiquities Market, Sensationalized Data, and Modern Forgeries," *Near Eastern Archaeology* 68 no. 1/2 (Mar.–June 2004): 61–65.

studies and that the archaeological enterprise ought to be pursued as a humanistic enterprise simply to understand the world of antiquity. Of course, important components of that world were people's religious beliefs, practices, and values, which many people still consider normative for their lives today. It is very difficult to divorce archaeology in the Middle East from biblical studies.

Archaeology does, however, need to distance itself from contemporary political controversies. The interpretation of data from early excavations at Masada and Hazor reflect the nationalistic tendencies of the excavators more than a dispassionate interpretation of data. The destruction of the archaeological record as a result of renovations to structures on the Haram es-Sharif (the Temple Mount) in Jerusalem is inexcusable. Of course, archaeologists do not work in a vacuum. The Middle East is a cauldron of seething political and religious conflicts that can compromise the integrity of the archaeological enterprise. Archaeology should not be used to undergird any political or nationalistic agenda.

The growing sophistication of techniques employed by excavators and the genuinely scientific methods used to identify and interpret the results of excavation projects have transformed biblical archaeology. Those who study the biblical texts cannot afford to ignore the growing body of knowledge about the world of the Bible that archaeology has produced in the last hundred years. Archaeology demonstrates that the Bible is not a collection of timeless truths that have descended from the heavens, but is the principal artifact that discloses the beliefs of the ancient Israelites, early Jews, and early Christians. To understand the affirmations, negations, emphases, and patterns in the books that make up the Bible it is necessary to understand the world and culture of the people whose beliefs find expression in the Bible. Archaeology helps one understand those people and their culture. Biblical archaeology is one way that some people express their fascination with the origins of their religious tradition.

DISCUSSION QUESTIONS

1. In the ancient world, cities needed access to fresh water in order to survive. In the Fertile Crescent in general and the Levant

in particular, what sources of water were available and how did ancient peoples make use of these resources?

2. What are some things archaeologists can learn from archaeological excavations? What are some pitfalls they need to avoid?

3. What is the relationship between the Bible and archaeology? Why would some archaeologists want to avoid the term "biblical archaeology"?

FOR FURTHER STUDY

Benjamin, Don C. *Stone and Stories: An Introduction to Archaeology and the Bible.* Minneapolis: Fortress Press, 2010.

Davis, Thomas W. *Shifting Sands: The Rise and Fall of Biblical Archaeology.* New York: Oxford University Press, 2004.

Orni, Efraim, and Elisha Efrat. *Geography of Israel.* 4th rev. ed. Jerusalem: Israel Universities Press, 1980.

Internet Resources

www.bibleplaces.com
　　Photographs and descriptions of sites in Israel, Jordan, Egypt, Turkey, and Greece with emphasis on biblical archaeology, geography, and history.

www.virtualworldproject.com
　　Virtual tours of the ancient world with a primary focus on the Levant.

Methods of Biblical Interpretation

Corrine L. Carvalho

Many people assume that the Bible's meaning is clear. In American culture, the Bible is quoted, read, or appealed to so often that its meaning seems obvious. When the Bible is heard so frequently in modern English translations, it is easy to forget that these texts were written centuries ago by people whose language and culture were quite different from those of today. This lack of awareness has primarily three negative effects. First, it allows anachronistic attitudes to seep into contemporary interpretation, such as the assumption that all biblical texts presume that God is all knowing. Second, this ignorance of the cultural divide impedes a contemporary reader's ability to appreciate the complexity and nuances of this ancient literature. Third, contemporary readers can be confused by conflicting claims by various interpreters about what the text "means."

Since the Bible is not just an ancient text, like the Epic of Gilgamesh, but rather has some authoritative force for communities of faith, its meaning has been and continues to be consciously fleshed out. All readers have been trained to read through various social institutions such as school, home, church or synagogue, or the media. Sometimes these reading traditions are so internalized that they become invisible. For example, a reader from the United States who has not studied the ancient world is likely to assume that slavery in antiquity was basically the same as slavery in nineteenth-century America. In other cases one's community of interpretation is consciously invoked, as when a reader explores the meaning of a text within a particular religious tradition. For example, many Lutherans consciously read Paul's statement that

Christians are justified by faith in Christ (Gal. 2:16) through the lens of Luther's use of that text.

All interpretation contains elements of at least three voices. The text has a meaning within its own historical and cultural context (what is sometimes called the meaning "behind the text"); it has a meaning as a piece of literature, distinct from its historical context (the meaning "in the text"); and it remains meaningful to contemporary reading communities (the meaning "in front of the text"). Scholars use the term "hermeneutics" for various theories of how these different voices should relate to each other. Should the ancient voice, the meaning behind the text, be privileged, so that a particular faith community tries to replicate how the text's first readers would have understood it? What role should the literary artistry, the meaning in the text, play in determining how the text should be understood? Does the perspective of the contemporary audience, the meaning in front of the text, require that the ancient record be "translated" in order to be applicable today? Take a biblical law, such as the idea that all debts should be forgiven every fifty years (Lev. 25). Should Jews and Christians read this text as a command that is eternally binding for them? Is it appropriate to consider whether the "law" has only a literary or rhetorical function in the book of Leviticus (perhaps to illustrate God's mercy)? Or is it a model for thinking about how debt functions within a particular faith community? These are the kinds of questions involved in hermeneutics.

Even the most casual biblical reader is served by thinking about the ways that people interpret the text. Every reading is an interpretation; every statement that the text "means" something is an assertion either about its ancient meaning, the meaning of the words on the page, the meaning that the contemporary reader has made of it, or a combination of all three. Often conflicts about biblical interpretation stem from a lack of recognition of these various approaches.

Excavating a Text

Readers of the Bible sometimes assume that texts have a single meaning: the meaning intended by the original author. There is something attractive about the assumption. It is safe to assume that when ancient writers wrote these texts, they intended to

In this cylinder seal from northern Syria (ca. 800–600 BCE), the god Marduk battles Tiamat in a scene from the ancient Babylonian creation myth, *Enuma Elish*. Scholars have identified a number of similarities between this myth and Genesis 1.

communicate something to an audience (who were usually not readers, but more often hearers). Even if they intended their texts to have multiple meanings, they would have certainly seen some interpretations of their words as incorrect or beyond the scope of their intended meaning(s). Therefore, it is important to consider the meaning(s) that authors intended when they selected particular words and genres. This necessarily involves looking at the text within its historical context.

When scholars talk about the relationship between the Bible and history, they examine the historical evidence from antiquity. The massive archaeological discoveries in the twentieth century, in particular, have had a significant impact on the way scholars reconstruct Israel's history. For example, the discovery of creation texts in Mesopotamia with very similar accounts of a world-wide flood, such as is found in Genesis 6–9, has led scholars to recognize that Israel's creation stories reflected the accounts of creation found in other countries around them. Access to the texts of ancient Israel's neighbors, records of occupation and destruction, and religious artifacts have all created a much richer picture of the biblical world.

One of the most significant developments in biblical interpretation in the past fifty years has been the refinement of sociological approaches to the text. This method of biblical interpretation seeks to uncover how the texts reflect the interactions of different sociological groups in antiquity. The analysis of the social world behind the text has at least two aims. First, it provides a social description of how different groups interacted. For example, research on women's roles in some contemporary polygamous households has helped scholars understand the way the book of Genesis depicts the relationship between Sarah and Hagar. Second, the use of social theory can reconstruct gaps in the textual record. Although there are few texts that explicitly discuss the role of brides in the households of the husbands, scholars can use similarly structured societies to hypothesize that mothers-in-law continued the training of these daughters-in-law for their new roles as wives. Socio-cultural analysis has uncovered how ancient assumptions about social categories, such as the honor-shame dichotomy, the patron-client relationship, and the function of ancient prophets clarify biblical texts.

Biblical scholars are also concerned with the texts in their historical contexts: what is their compositional history, and how have they been preserved? Some biblical books repeat, almost verbatim, material found in other biblical books. Other books have material that was written over the expanse of centuries. Still others are collections of various discrete units of material. Each biblical book or scroll has its own compositional history. This has led to the development of distinct methods of biblical interpretation.

Source Criticism

In Old Testament studies, for example, the first five books of the Bible (called the Pentateuch or the Torah) have a number of inconsistencies, repetitions, and changes in style. These characteristics had long been noted, but beginning in the eighteenth century, scholars started to hypothesize that these features were the result of an editor splicing together material from two or more written sources. This theory has been so useful in analyzing the Pentateuch that it still holds sway today. Similarly, the near-verbatim repetition of material in the Synoptic Gospels (Matthew, Mark, and Luke) can best be understood as resulting from common written sources. This reconstruction of earlier written sources is called "source criticism."

Form Criticism

Although writing was important in the ancient world, the production of texts was very expensive. Therefore, most people would have had contact with the material preserved in the Bible through oral delivery such as a public reading, a priest summarizing teaching, or stories passed down within a community. Before the material was committed to writing, it was often handed down through oral tradition. This is especially obvious for material like the Psalms (words to music that was performed), the Prophets (oracles that were first spoken before an audience), Proverbs (maxims passed down within a community), and the sayings of Jesus. Scholars have uncovered the way biblical texts crystallize some of these oral traditions, through such things as formulaic wording and stock narrative motifs. This study of the oral stage of the material is called "form criticism."

Redaction Criticism

The conclusion that the biblical texts preserve a combination of earlier written and oral traditions leads to analysis of the texts' composition, the purposeful combination of these sources into a final text. Biblical scholars use the term "redaction" to describe this editing process. Redaction criticism focuses on the way a final editor or author has pulled together various strands of material to create the final text. This work is especially fruitful in the study of the Synoptic Gospels where it is clear that authors used and adapted earlier texts containing stories of Jesus.

Text Criticism

The Bible has been preserved in a number of manuscripts, but none of these extant texts are the original manuscripts. Significant differences exist between the readings preserved in these manuscripts. To give two examples: the Greek version of the book of Jeremiah has a different arrangement and some different material than the Hebrew version; the Greek arrangement leads to a slightly different focus on God's role in history than is found in the Hebrew arrangement. In the Gospel of Mark, different manuscripts preserve different endings to the book. Faced with such problems, scholars try to reconstruct how each variant reading developed, and attempt to ascertain which reading was original. This study of ancient text traditions is called "text criticism."

Other Methods of Biblical Criticism

While source, form, redaction, and text criticisms are the most common of the methods found under the rubric of historical criticism, they are not the only ones. For example, scholars compare biblical material with similar material found in either the ancient Near East or the Greco-Roman world. Tradition criticism traces how various complex traditions, such as the observation of Passover, or the significance of Zion, developed over time.

Historical questions open up the world assumed by the biblical authors. These approaches to the ancient texts hold significant sway in biblical interpretation because of the ways in which they explain biblical texts whose compositional features do not make sense to a contemporary audience or that reflect practices different from the modern world. Although a certain amount of technical training and expertise is needed to conduct historical research, even the casual reader of the Bible gains insight by learning about the results of historical-critical methods of interpretation.

Reading a Text: Literary Criticism, Narrative Criticism, and Other Approaches

Literary questions are essential in the understanding of any biblical text. The reader first must determine the genre of the text, since the genre impacts the way that a text is analyzed. In other words, it would be wrong to interpret a poem in the same way that one analyzes a genealogy. An epistle is not the same as a gospel.

Like historical criticism, literary criticism can take many forms, and the variety of literary genres in the Bible requires flexibility in the application of literary methods. While prose narrative might benefit from the application of narrative criticism that looks at plot and characterization, poetry can be better clarified through the lens of poetics, which focuses on metaphors, rhythm, and structure.

Some of these literary methods are expressly a-historical. For example, reader-response criticism focuses on how the reader creates meaning out of a text. Reader-response criticism does not assess the accuracy of an interpretation, as if a text has only a single meaning, nor does it put that reading in dialogue with an ancient reading. It simply focuses on how a contemporary reader makes sense of the text. It notes that, while readers may come to conclusions about what the text communicates concerning the past, the act of making meaning occurs through the act of reading.

Other literary methods engage broader theories of psychology and semiotics. Structuralism, which was popular in the 1970s, picks up Jungian ideas of a deep shared consciousness that allows texts to be meaningful across cultural and temporal divides. Structuralism looks at three levels on which texts are meaningful: the semantic level (what the words actually mean), the grammatical and social level (how the literary and cultural contexts limit meaning), and the deep structural level (how meaning transcends place and time). Today, post-structuralists have rejected a notion of a pure deep structure and instead point to the fact that claims about meaning always take place within various contexts that shape and determine that meaning.

Narrative criticism pays attention to all of the literary techniques of a text, such as plot, characterization, and imagery, in order to determine how texts communicate their meaning. Like most literary methods, it assumes that the final form of a biblical text is a coherent whole, no matter its history of production. Unlike reader-response criticism, however, this method is not necessarily a-historical. It takes into account the literary conventions of the ancient world. One way it does this is by interpreting a text from the perspective of the implied audience—that is, the audience that the text assumes.

More recently, biblical scholars have begun to explore the ideological and rhetorical elements of various biblical texts. There are several different methods of interpretation that fall under this category, but they all aim to uncover the sometimes hidden purposes behind the text's production. Rhetorical criticism examines how the language manipulates readers to focus on particular elements of a text or to assent to the text's assertions. Ideological criticism uses Marxist categories of class, coupled with race and gender, to show

how texts often advance the position of the elite. Both methods ask whose interests a given text serves.

Literary criticism also focuses on the polyvalence of biblical texts. Any piece of art can have multiple meanings; literary art is no exception. At its simplest level, awareness of the polyvalence of texts warns against assigning texts singular, flat meanings. At a more complex level, these competing meanings can result in undercutting the text's prevailing worldview. This latter approach is associated with deconstructionism. Deconstructionism seeks to uncover the ways that the dominant paradigm of the text, its central ideology, is often undermined within its own text. For example, the description of a contest between a true and a false prophet in 1 Kings 13 reveals some anxiety about the authenticity of people who claim to be prophets. A deconstructionist approach can also reveal the ways in which interpretations that result in claims of objectivity mask attempts to establish privilege for a particular group.

Many biblical scholars use elements from several literary methods in interpretive work. The ideology of the text, for example, cannot be understood apart from its wording or rhetoric. A rhetorical analysis depends on understanding how the specific wording creates the text's meanings. These analyses reveal how often the text has multiple meanings and how these texts and their interpretations can serve various interest groups.

Reading Communities

All readers belong to various reading communities. Education leads readers to have certain expectations of texts, to value some texts over others, to assess writing as "good" or "deficient." When it comes to the Bible, many people study it because they belong to a particular religious community for whom the Bible is sacred or authoritative. Often these communities communicate parameters within which biblical interpretation should take place. These parameters are often invisible to those who have been formed by them. For example, many Christians who have only heard the Bible in church assume that the whole Old Testament predicts the coming of Jesus. However, such parameters can become more visible and can be examined by engaging readings from a variety of perspectives. Biblical scholars interact with a variety of perspectives in order to reveal their own bias, or to engage aspects of the text they may have overlooked, or to employ a reading that might be more compatible with the ancient context. Even though the Bible is a sacred text to Jews and Christians, even these readers are not simply identified by their religious convictions. All people bring a complex mix of racial, gender, class, and other identities to their experience as readers. Although biblical study has historically been the work of educated Christian and Jewish males in particular, the democratization of education has led to a much more diverse community of biblical scholars. Advances in technology and communication have also led to a vibrant global community of biblical scholars. The impact that these various interpretations have had on the field is significant.

Gender and Biblical Interpretation

Women were among the first of the new voices to have an impact on biblical studies. In the United States, feminism first arose in the nineteenth century as women pushed for the right to vote. To help this effort, suffragists like Elizabeth Cady Stanton, in her *Women's Bible* (1895), addressed how sexist biblical interpretations contributed to women's lack of voting rights. But it was not until the 1970s, after women were increasingly admitted to graduate programs in biblical studies, that feminist biblical interpretation made a significant impact on the field. Today there are many types of feminist interpretations, but they can be grouped into three main categories: efforts to recover women's presence in and behind the Bible (for example, recognizing the presence of women among the addressees of Paul's letters); the use of ideological criticism to unmask the assumptions embedded in biblical texts (such as the ways in which the personification of Judah as an adulteress in Ezekiel 16 reveals male anxiety about women, according to some interpretations); and readings that resist or deconstruct the sexist assertions of the text (seen in some feminist attempts to view Vashti in Esther 1 as the true heroine of the story). Gendered reading of texts has also expanded to include readings that pay attention to the way masculinities are depicted. Others use queer theory, which looks at assumptions about gender that are imbedded in a text, often with the aim of dismantling some of those assumptions.

The Bible's Dangerous Readings

Christianity has had to come to terms with the ways in which traditional interpretations of the Bible have led to faith-based violence against non-Christians, especially following the Holocaust or Shoah. The Shoah forced Christians to recognize a long history of faith-based violence. Throughout Christian history, Jews living in European countries controlled by Christians often did not have the full protection of the law or were subject to violence to persons and property because Christians viewed them at best as rejecters of Christ and at worst as "Christ-killers" because of various New Testament texts. These texts include John 8; Acts 3:13–15; 1 Thessalonians 2:14–16; and especially Matthew 27:25, where the Evangelist has "the [Jewish] people as a whole" state, "His [Jesus'] blood be on us and on our children." European Christian encounters with Muslims were often violent, in the form of battles over land and property within Europe or through the Crusades. Although the biblical basis for this violence against Muslims is less explicit, the fact that texts like Deuteronomy 20:10–18 affirm the use of violence against Israel's enemies supported Christian assumptions that the use of violence against those who were religiously different was biblically warranted. These same texts fed into American Christians justifying their use of force against non-Christians. Whether it came in the form of the decimation of native populations under the umbrella of Manifest Destiny (the idea that God had given the North American continent to the people of the United States)[1] or through the harvesting of cheap slave labor from Africa justified by Christian slave-owners who thought that Noah had cursed Africans (Gen. 9:20–27), American Christians have to admit that they too have used the Bible to justify faith-based violence. Many biblical scholars, especially after World War II, have worked to promote readings that undercut claims that the Bible justifies such violence.

---

1. Some Christians justified destroying the religion of the indigenous people in North America by comparing them to the Canaanites in the book of Joshua. See Scott M. Langston, "North America," in *The Blackwell Companion to the Bible and Culture*, ed. John F. A. Sawyer, Blackwell Companions to Religion (Malden, MA: Blackwell, 2006), 198–216.

Liberation Theology

Liberation Theology also arose in the 1970s as a response to the racist and classist tendencies of some forms of Christian theology. It challenges the dominant European bias of much of Christian theology in part by engaging biblical texts that focus on God's care for the oppressed and marginalized, such as the liberation of Hebrew slaves in Egypt (Exodus) and Jesus' admonition to care for the "least" (Matt. 25:31-46). Liberation theologians read texts from the perspective of the poor and point out that the Bible's message of salvation for all people demands concrete action in the present. This liberationist approach has been especially prominent in communities oppressed on account of racial or ethnic identities. In addition to Latin American biblical scholars, practitioners of liberation theology include biblical scholars in Africa and Asia, along with Latino/Latina and African-American scholars in the United States. Many feminist interpreters also conduct their biblical interpretation under the umbrella of a liberation perspective.

Post-Colonialism

Some instances of liberation approaches to the text are part of a larger movement called post-colonialism. Modern colonialism involved not just the economic exploitation of colonized lands but also the creation of a ruling minority coming from outside an indigenous area, which then imposed its own cultural norms and values on the indigenous population. Following the two World Wars, colonized peoples increasingly questioned the cultural assumptions that they had adopted under colonizing regimes. Post-colonial interpretations point out the oppressive attitudes that are inherent in some biblical texts, and seek new ways of reading those texts that reveal the complex relationships between the powerful and the colonized. Many recent analyses of the prophetic texts that stemmed from the exile, such as Jeremiah and Ezekiel, seek to understand how these texts reflect the experience of displacement at the hands of the Babylonian Empire.

Cultural Criticism

Not all readings from the standpoint of racial or ethnic identity, also called contextual criticism, utilize liberation assumptions, however. Like feminist interpretation, contextual criticism can take many forms. Cultural criticism, for example, focuses on non-specialist appropriations of biblical texts by examining the "unofficial" or non-controllable vehicles for cultural expression, such as street art, popular music, paperback novels, television, and so on. By focusing on these non-scholarly vehicles of biblical interpretation, cultural criticism undercuts the authority of the elite. It is often used by these groups to show that interpretation of the Bible has been a vibrant part of communal expression, albeit in forms not usually studied by the academy.

© MissHibiscus / www.istockphoto.com

Popular, "unofficial" religious art can bring a thought-provoking, fresh perspective on familiar stories. In this folk-art nativity set, carved by an African artist, Jesus, Mary, Joseph, and the rest of the figures are clearly African.

Interpretation from Three Starting Points

Biblical scholars generally utilize a variety of interpretive methods. The meaning of the biblical text can never be exhausted. The various meanings of a text involve a conversation among those who produced the text, the actual reading of the text, and those who appropriate it in a modern setting.

Although the variety of biblical interpretations can be overwhelming, especially to a non-specialist, this vibrancy demonstrates the continued role that the Bible plays within various intersecting communities. An African-American teenager in Chicago might hear a sermon on the Gospel and the morality of today's world in the morning, and watch a television program on the historicity of the crossing of the Red Sea that evening. An upper-class woman in Minneapolis could participate in a Scripture-based retreat on one day, and then attend a feminist book club the next that focuses on the patriarchy of the Bible. A gay man in Haiti could pray the Psalms as part of his daily spiritual practices every evening, and write an article in the afternoon about how the Bible's sexual ideology was conditioned by its cultural assumptions. All readers of the Bible not only live within intersecting identities of race, gender, class, and religion, but they also read words on a page created by an ancient author that have meaning within the contemporary world. Various interpretations of the Bible arise out of the interaction of identities, texts, and history. The purpose of biblical interpretation is not to limit meaning to one universal norm, but rather to let the interactions among author, text, and reader create a conversation that is itself meaning-full.

DISCUSSION QUESTIONS

1. Pick a short biblical passage, like the story of Elijah and the widow (1 Kings 17:8–16) or Jesus and the woman from Syro-Phoenicia (Mark 7:24–30). List all the questions you might want to ask in order to understand the text fully. Then arrange the questions into 3 groups: historical questions about the text, literary questions, and questions about what it means for people today. Try to match some of those questions to the methods described here.

2. Reflect on the way your own life, upbringing, and current context affect the way you read a biblical text. What do you expect the Bible to contain, and why do you have those assumptions?

When you think about or interact with someone who comes from a different context, what expectations about the Bible would be the same as yours? What would be different?

FOR FURTHER STUDY

Anderson, Janice D., and Stephen D. Moore, eds. *Mark and Method: New Approaches in Biblical Studies.* Rev. ed. Minneapolis: Fortress, 2008.

Barton, John. *Reading the Old Testament: Method in Biblical Study.* Rev. ed. Louisville: Westminster John Knox, 1996.

Carter, Warren, and Amy-Jill Levine. *The New Testament: Methods and Meanings.* Nashville: Abingdon, 2013.

Carvalho, Corrine. *Primer on Biblical Methods.* Winona, MN: Anselm Academic, 2009.

Yee, Gale, ed. *Judges and Method: New Approaches in Biblical Studies.* Rev. ed. Minneapolis: Fortress, 2007.

Internet Resources

www.academic-bible.com

Provides free access to original language—Greek and Hebrew—editions of the Bible published by the German Bible Society.

5

The Bible in the United States

Claudia Setzer

Most presidents of the United States have taken their oath of office with their right hand on a Bible. Some, like Harry Truman and Barack Obama, have used two Bibles. Why does the president-elect place his hand on a religious object while pledging to uphold the Constitution of the United States, which prohibits government from promoting religion? Why, in a nation that prides itself on including people of all religions, or no religion, does the new president typically add to the oath "so help me God"?

The Paradox of the United States

The paradox of the United States springs from its dual heritage of republicanism and biblicism. The Founding Fathers, Jefferson, Adams, Washington, and others set up their government as an alternative to European models, where monarchies and state religions prevailed to devastating effect. The Founding Fathers carefully crafted a Constitution that requires no religious test to hold public office. The Bill of Rights leads with the First Amendment containing two clauses: the Establishment Clause, which rejects any state-sponsored religion, and the Free Expression Clause, which guarantees everyone the right to practice their religion. The individuals who created the Constitution were not irreligious, but concluded that societies work best when government stays out of religion. James Madison said that government protected every citizen's right to personal religion as much as to personal safety and property, and therefore could not favor any particular sect: "Rulers who wished to subvert the public liberty, may have found an established Clergy convenient auxiliaries. A just Government instituted to secure and perpetuate it needs them not. Such a Government will be best supported by protecting every Citizen in the enjoyment of his Religion with the same equal hand which protects his person and his property; by neither invading the equal rights of any Sect, nor suffering any Sect to invade those of another."[1]

Yet for more than a century before the revolution, many colonists had been immigrating to America for the purpose of establishing Christian societies. Scholar Frank Lambert calls these the Planting Fathers, both because many were farmers and because they planted new religiously-based societies in the New World. The Jamestown settlement had strategic and economic aims, but its charter from King James I of England invoked Providence and included among its goals the "propagating of Christian religion to such People, as yet live in Darkness and miserable ignorance of the true Knowledge and Worship of God." Puritan John Winthrop, while still on board the ship the *Arbella* bringing settlers to the Massachusetts Bay colony in 1630, gave a speech laced with biblical allusions and predicting, "We shall be as a city upon a hill" (Matt. 5:14, "A city built on a hill cannot be hid"). Connecticut's assembly adopted its "Fundamental Order," an early form of state constitution, based on the Scriptures as a model of "perfect rule for the direction and government of all men in all duties which they are to perform." William Penn founded the colony of Pennsylvania between 1681–1683 as a "holy experiment," which included tolerance of other religions and fair treatment for local Native Americans.

A century later, the Founding Fathers succeeded in separating governmental authority from personal religious belief and practice, but a congeniality to religion in public life remained. Thomas Jefferson, who affirmed to the Danbury Baptist Association "the wall of separation between church and state,"[2] nevertheless edited his own version of the New Testament, popularly called *The Jefferson Bible*. Showing himself a true Enlightenment rationalist, he removed all

---

1. James Madison, Section 8 of "Memorial and Remonstrance against Religious Assessments," 20 June, 1785, available at *http://press-pubs.uchicago.edu/founders/documents/amendI_religions43.html.*

2. *www.loc.gov/lcib/9806/danpre.html.*

references to the supernatural, including Jesus' miracles and Resurrection. John Adams, in the Treaty of Tripoli in 1797, reassured Muslim inhabitants of North Africa that "the Government of the United States of America is not, in any sense, founded on the Christian religion—as it has in itself no character of enmity against the laws, religion, or tranquility, of Mussulmen [Muslims]."[3] Yet he had written to his wife approvingly of the prayer and psalm recited before the meeting of the First Continental Congress in 1774, saying he "never heard a better prayer."[4] Both Jefferson and Adams no doubt imagined public religion as expressions of Protestant Christianity.

Balancing the two clauses of the First Amendment is not always easy, and their applications are constantly being tested. When Judge Roy Moore set up a granite monument of the Ten Commandments (Protestant version) in his courthouse in Alabama, it was removed

© Bob Daemmrich/Corbis

In 2005 the U. S. Supreme Court ruled that this display of the Ten Commandments at the Texas State Capitol Building in Austin did not violate the separation of church and state because it had historical as well as religious value.

---

3. *avalon.law.yale.edu/18th_century/bar1796t.asp.*

4. John Adams to Abigail Adams, 16 September 1774 (electronic edition), *Adams Family Papers: An Electronic Archive.* Massachusetts Historical Society: *www.masshist. org/digitaladams/.*

by court order in 2003 because it violated the Establishment clause. Yet a monument of the Ten Commandments remains on the grounds of the Texas state capitol building in Austin today without causing dissension. Cheerleaders at a public school who used Bible verses in their signs before football games in Fort Oglethorpe Georgia were ordered to stop in 2009, but the Fellowship of Christian Athletes remains a high school club. The borders between free expression of religion and government sponsorship of religion will continue to be tested.

Whose Bible?

Early settlers took seriously Jesus' injunction to "make disciples of all nations," beginning with native peoples. John Eliot learned Natick, the language of local tribes in the Massachusetts area, and translated the Bible in 1661, creating *The Indian Bible*. William and Mary (1693) and Dartmouth College (1769) were founded to spread the Gospel to the natives as well as to educate young men for the ministry. Many of today's private colleges and universities were founded in the nineteenth century by different denominations, each group asserting its legitimacy on the national scene by training young people in the group's own understanding of the biblical text.

Yet many Americans, suspicious of institutions, gravitated toward more personal, free-form expressions of religious feeling. Two great revival movements emerged, which stressed individual experience of the Spirit and independent interpretation. The First Great Awakening, in the 1730s and 1740s, is associated with George Whitefield and Jonathan Edwards. Edwards' famous 1733 sermon speaks of the "spiritual and divine light" that is grounded in Scripture, but is "immediately imparted to the soul by God." In the Second Great Awakening, less than a hundred years later, Baptist and Methodist preachers, men and women alike, traveled the country holding camp meetings and revivals. Pentecostalism emerged at the turn of the twentieth century, combining an emphasis on individual experience of the Spirit with a belief in the Bible as divine revelation.

Other religious groups around the same time also claimed their roots in Scripture, but sought a rationalist basis for religion, rejecting Calvinist ideas of sin and salvation. In a sermon, "Unitarian

Translations and Religious Identity

The religious diversity of the United States expresses itself in the many translations and editions of the Bible available. The well-known King James Version published in 1611 (also known as the Authorized Version), was the standard Protestant Bible and dominant version for much of the nation's history. Presented in more contemporary language, it was published as the Revised Version in Britain in 1885 and as the American Standard Version in 1901. In 1946 the Revised Standard Version came out, while a further revision produced the New Revised Standard Version in 1989. A more literalist version is the New American Standard Version published in 1995. These all remain popular, especially among Protestants. Many American Jews consult the newest translation of the Bible from the authoritative Hebrew text (called the Masoretic Text) in the New Jewish Publication Society translation from 1985. Catholics often look to the New American Bible Revised Edition, which came out in 2011, the culmination of work done since the publication of the New American Bible in 1970.[5]

Christianity," in 1819, William Ellery Channing cited Scripture as proof of the principles of Unitarianism, including a rejection of the Trinity and the atonement doctrine. Unitarianism and its offshoot, Transcendentalism, thrived in New England in the nineteenth century.

The Bible and Great National Debates

Bringing the Bible into controversies over social questions or asking "What would Jesus do?" is not new. Debaters of slavery, civil rights, women's rights, evolution, temperance, and labor have all tapped the wellspring of biblical ideas. These controversies were never solely

---

5. See chapter 2, "Bible Translations," for more on this subject.

about the Bible, but the Bible was used to legitimize positions. Often it has been invoked in support of both sides of an argument. The Constitution is the other authoritative document in the United States, and has been similarly invoked to support or oppose positions. In some cases, the Bible has favored the more progressive position, while at other times the Constitution has done so. The Bible also legitimated groups by providing an alternative model of reality. As the Israelites suffered under Pharaoh and Jesus suffered under the Romans, so too did suffering groups facing powerful opponents see themselves as favored by God and destined for victory.

Same-Sex Marriage

Rallies for and against same-sex marriage seem to assume a rudimentary knowledge of the Bible, if their signs are any clue. Opponents carry signs saying, "God made Adam and Eve, not Adam and Steve, Genesis 1:27," promoting an ideal of heterosexual marriage. Gay Rights rallies respond with signs like, "God Hates Shrimp," or "As Jesus Said about Gay People, '. . .'" The Gay Rights signs posit the impossibility of literal implementation of all biblical verses, and the silence of Jesus on sexual orientation.

Slavery

The United States' greatest social trauma, the Civil War, came about over the issue of slavery. The Bible was invoked by both supporters of slavery and abolitionists. Pro-slavery advocates seemed to have the Bible on their side. They noted the patriarchs who owned slaves (Gen. 15:3; 17; 20:14; 21:10; 32:22), the laws that assume slavery (Exod. 21; Lev. 25:44–46), Jesus' presumption of slavery (Matt. 6:24; Luke 12:42–47) and lack of condemnation of it, and Paul's apparent acceptance of it (e.g., Philem.; 1 Cor. 7:21). By means of a strange understanding of Genesis 9:20–28, they turned a curse against Canaan for his father Ham's sin into a permanent punishment of servitude for all of Canaan's descendants, assumed to be Africans. White supremacist theologians and ministers such as "Ariel," a pseudonym for Buckner Payne, A. Hoyle Lester, and Charles Carroll, promoted a bizarre theory of polygenesis, or multiple origins of the races, as late as the early twentieth century. They argued that Africans descended from the serpent, not from Adam and Eve,[6] and expressed horror at "miscegenation," or mixing of the races through intermarriage.

Abolitionists had to work differently with the words of the Bible. After a public debate spanned eighteen evenings at Lane Theological Seminary in Cincinnati in 1834, slavery was declared a sin and its immediate abolition was called for. Theodore Dwight Weld, one of the participants, refuted pro-slavery arguments in *The Bible against Slavery*.[7] He dismantled the curse of Canaan argument and argued that two of the Ten Commandments forbid slavery: "Thou shalt not steal" includes stealing another human being, and "Thou shalt not covet" means every person has a right to his own self and property. Others abolitionists, such as minister Albert Barnes, tried to undermine biblical examples of slavery by arguing that "slavery" means many things in Hebrew and Greek, including "service."[8] Although Jesus did not speak against slavery outright, some said, his humane teaching was a "seed growing secretly" (Mark 4:26–29) that would eventually bear fruit in slavery's demise.

African American slaves saw their own experience in the biblical stories, especially the Exodus. Slave owners brought white preachers to the plantations, and forbade teaching the slaves to read, perhaps fearing they would discover the Bible's tropes of liberation and God's rescue of the oppressed. Slaves sometimes held their own religious meetings in secret, and the narratives and songs of slavery are filled with biblical imagery. The biblical stories also provided a code to communicate plans of escape: "Steal Away to Jesus" could announce a secret meeting to take place, or "Wade in the Water" could recommend taking to the waterways to avoid slave-catchers nearby.

---

6. A. Hoyle Lester, *The Pre-Adamite, or Who Tempted Eve?* (Philadelphia: Lippincott, 1874), 20–46. For more on these writers, see Mason Stokes, "Someone's in the Garden with Eve: Race, Religion and the American Fall," *American Quarterly* 50, no. 4 (1998): 718–44.

7. *The Bible against Slavery: An Inquiry into the Patriarchal and Mosaic Systems on the Subject of Human Rights*, 4th ed., enlarged (New York: American Anti-Slavery Society, 1838), from Sabin Americana Digital Collection (Gale-Cengage Learning).

8. Albert Barnes, *An Inquiry into the Scriptural View of Slavery* (Philadelphia: Perkins and Purvis, 1846), passim.

Women's Rights

Abolitionist circles included many women who extended their quest for justice to women's rights. However, suffragists had mixed attitudes about the Bible. Some saw it as part of the problem, a series of proof-texts employed by men in power to keep women in subjection. Others saw the Bible as a liberating text that taught women's God-given equality and provided models of female leadership and piety. Others considered the Bible—and religion itself—to be largely irrelevant to the struggle.

Early feminists who looked to the Bible for support used the same methods as the abolitionists: scrutinizing meanings of particular words, seeking biblical models, elevating certain verses, arguing from Jesus' fundamental principles, and attributing Paul's remarks to his ancient context. The first extended argument for women's rights in the United States came from Sarah Grimké, an opponent of slavery from her youth and the sister-in-law of Theodore Dwight Weld. Her *Letters on the Equality of the Sexes*[9] to Mary Parker, the president of the Boston Female Anti-Slavery Society, were first published in newspapers in 1837. Grimké disposes of typical arguments for women's subordination from the Bible by concentrating on Genesis 1:26–27, the classic statement of human dignity in its male and female forms, and Galatians 3:28, Paul's programmatic rejection of gender (and other) differences for those baptized in Christ.

Identical arguments appear fifty years later in *Woman in the Pulpit*,[10] an extended case for women's ordination in the Methodist Church, written by Frances Willard, a powerful public leader and president of The Women's Christian Temperance Union. Willard goes beyond Grimké, however, in that she shows evidence of different voices in the text by lining up contradictory passages. Against Paul's statement that women should keep silent in the churches (1 Cor. 14:34), for example, she assembles passages from the Hebrew Bible and New Testament that show women praying, prophesying, and preaching. She speculates about tampering with the wording of texts in early manuscripts to minimize women's roles. In these exegetical

---

9. Elizabeth Ann Bartlett, ed., *Letters on the Equality of the Sexes and Other Essays* (New Haven: Yale University Press, 1988), Letter 1.31–34.

10. Frances Willard, *Woman in the Pulpit* (Boston: D. Lothrop, 1888), 27–32.

moves, she echoes the work of "higher" and "lower" criticisms, disciplines emerging from historical-critical scholarship, coming out of Europe and reported in the popular press. She notes how culture determines transmission when she cites a missionary she knows who, when preaching in China, removed Paul's references to women as fellow preachers, saying it would offend Chinese sensibilities.

African-American women, facing double discrimination over gender and race, generally viewed the Bible as their ally. Sojourner Truth cites the text in her famous "Ain't I a Woman" speech delivered to a women's rights convention in Akron,[11] by pointing out the foolishness of some literalist interpretations and saying that Eve's actions are no cause to deny women's rights: "I have heard the Bible and have learned that Eve caused man to sin. Well if woman upset the world, do give her a chance to set it right side up again." Jesus never turned women away, she notes, and he came into the world through God and a woman, with no help from any man. Virginia Broughton, the daughter of freed slaves, became a traveling preacher, organizing "Bible bands" for women to study the text daily. Anna Julia Cooper, the daughter of a slave mother, studied biblical languages at Oberlin College and earned a doctorate in history at the University of Paris (Sorbonne) in 1925. In her work, *A Voice from the South*,[12] she defends the cause of education for women of color as the key to advancement for the entire community. Like earlier feminists, she saw Christianity in its pure form as touting women's equality. She adopted the abolitionist idea of Jesus' teaching as a "seed growing secretly," which would eventually blossom into full rights for women.

Not all feminists gave the Bible such high marks. In *Woman, Church, and State*, Matilda Joslyn Gage indicts the Bible as the source of patriarchy in its depiction of a supreme God who is male and its promotion of bloodshed, destruction of enemies, and child sacrifice. It accepts polygamy, treats women as property, blames Eve for "the fall," and lays upon women a permanent curse that is enforced by

---

11. *The Anti-Slavery Bugle*, June 21, 1851, reprinted in Margaret Washington, ed., *The Narrative of Sojourner Truth* (New York: Random House, 1993).

12. Anna Julia Cooper, *A Voice from the South* (1892), electronic edition in *Documenting the American South*, http://docsouth.unc.edu.

© UIG via Getty Images

Shown above is a page from the manuscript of Elizabeth Cady Stanton's *The Woman's Bible*. The full commentary, authored by a number of female writers, frequently calls into question the biblical text's depiction of women.

church and state.[13] In her entry in *The Woman's Bible* (1898), she says one of its tendencies has been "degradation of the divinest half of humanity—woman. . . . In spite of some mystic or occult elements, we are investigating its influence upon woman under Judaism and Christianity, and pronounce it evil."[14]

Gage's virulence aside, *The Woman's Bible* is a complex and varied response to the Bible when compared to the work of earlier feminists. Edited by Elizabeth Cady Stanton, a pioneer of women's rights,

13. Matilda Joslyn Gage, *Woman, Church, and State* (Chicago: C. H. Kerr, 1893), 43–46, *openlibrary.org*.

14. *The Woman's Bible* (Mineola: Dover Publications, 2002 [1895–1898]), 2:208–9.

it considers passages featuring women, or pointedly excluding them, and appends comments. Showing features of nineteenth-century liberal Christianity, it is not a uniform document, and Stanton herself, the most prominent commentator, is not always consistent. *The Woman's Bible* is generally critical of the treatment of women in both the Old and New Testaments, although the bulk of it is devoted to the former. She notes, for example, that the permanent curse against Eve "is inserted in an unfriendly spirit to justify her degradation and subjection to man," yet her importance as mother of humanity is ignored.

Yet the commentary picks up on enlightened aspects of Scripture. The daughters of Zelophehad (Num. 27:1–11), for example, make their case for their right to inherit from their father. The Lord, speaking through Moses, agrees, and the daughters inherit. Cady Stanton muses that the New York legislature was not as reasonable when it came to the property of some prominent New York families.[15] The commentary lauds some of the women leaders of the Bible, like the judge Deborah or Paul's acquaintances, Priscilla and Phoebe. But it misses other opportunities, failing to note God's covenantal language to Hagar, and making little of Miriam's leadership. Jesus is assumed to be entirely egalitarian in his teaching, while Paul sometimes bears the blame for anti-woman prejudice in Christianity. Some of the commentators further shift the blame to Judaism, claiming it was Paul's "background" that is to blame, a position scholars today reject.

The real concern of this commentary is not the Bible itself, but its outsize effect on society: its use as justification for women's subordination by church and state. The authors did not blame only the Bible; they also indicted secular laws. As Cady Stanton says, neither their sons studying the law nor their sons studying the Bible rise from their studies with greater respect for women, but from these works "may have learned their first lessons of disrespect and contempt."[16]

Willard and Cady Stanton make reference to new methods of historical criticism that undermined ideas of biblical inerrancy (freedom from error) and unity. If the Bible was edited over time, using different documents, then human activity contributes significantly to

---

15. Ibid., 1.107–8.
16. Ibid., 1.76.

the finished product. Moreover, textual criticism demonstrated that no such thing as an original text is accessible. Those committed to the divine origin of the text mounted a defense. Two oil tycoons from California, the Stewart brothers, commissioned a set of twelve pamphlets called *The Fundamentals*, between 1910 and 1915. The pamphlets opposed "futile, rationalistic criticism" and affirmed belief in the Bible as "supernatural revelation, characterized by a clear internal structure." From this project the term "fundamentalist" was coined, although the actual ideas in the pamphlets are less strident than later fundamentalists, saying "let criticism have its rights," and "let purely literary questions about the Bible receive full and fair discussion." More liberal scholars reacted, writing their own sermons and pamphlets. Harry Emerson Fosdick gave a sermon, "Shall the Fundamentalists Win?" in 1922, which rallied "modernists," people who combined modern biblical criticism with their faith. He argued for "an intellectually hospitable, tolerant, liberty-loving church." The religious "right" and "left" of today are the heirs of the fundamentalist-modernist split.

Evolution

Fundamentalists and modernists predictably disagreed over the issue of evolution and its implication for understanding the Bible's account of creation. Although Darwin's *On the Origin of Species* (1859) and *The Descent of Man* (1871) stirred debate and some antagonism from clergy in England, by the time of his death in 1882 most in Europe had accepted his ideas. In the United States, people did not warm to evolutionary theory in the same way. Opposition to the teaching of evolution in the schools came to a head with the Scopes trial in Tennessee in 1925. The state had passed the Butler Act, which banned the teaching of evolution in favor of creationism, the belief that the biblical account of creation is literally true. A biology teacher named John Scopes tested the law by teaching evolution, triggering the famous trial. It became a national sensation, pitting the populist politician and fundamentalist William Jennings Bryan as prosecutor against the civil libertarian trial lawyer Clarence Darrow as counsel for the defense. The exchanges, publicized by H. L. Mencken, showed the differing attitudes toward the Bible as central to the debate. Darrow called Bryan as a witness to test the idea of biblical inerrancy.

Darrow submitted a guilty plea, which pushed the case toward federal appeal. Scopes' conviction was reversed two years later, but the Butler Act was not repealed until 1967.

Subsequent courts have repeatedly upheld the teaching of evolution and rejected creationism, or intelligent design, which says the "irreducible complexity" (biologist Michael Behe's term)[17] of the universe requires the existence of an intelligent designer. While Intelligent Design proponents shy away from talking about God as such, their theories clearly are congenial to creationism. A case in 2005 in Dover, Pennsylvania was brought as a suit by a group of parents who wanted a statement of intelligent design read alongside the teaching of evolution. The conservative Republican judge, rejecting their suit, ruled that teaching intelligent design violated

Darrow Interrogates Bryan at the Scopes Trial

Q. You claim that everything in the Bible should be literally interpreted?

A. I believe everything in the Bible should be accepted as it was given there: some of the Bible is given illustratively. For instance, "Ye are the salt of the earth." I would not insist that man was actually salt, or that he had flesh of salt, but it is used in the sense of salt as saving God's people.

Q. But when you read that Jonah swallowed the whale—or that the whale swallowed Jonah—excuse me please—how do you literally interpret that?

A. When I read that a big fish swallowed Jonah—it does not say whale . . . that is my recollection of it. A big fish, and I believe it, and I believe in a God who can make a whale and can make a man and make both what he pleases.

---

17. Michael J. Behe, "The Challenge of Irreducible Complexity," *Natural History* (April 2002): 74.

the Establishment Clause of the First Amendment, because it "is not science and cannot uncouple itself from its creationist, and thus religious antecedents."[18]

The Civil Rights Movement

During the Civil Rights movement in the mid-twentieth century the Bible was used seriously by only one side of the struggle. Preachers like Fanny Lou Hamer and Martin Luther King, Jr., effectively wove their story of struggle for equality with the biblical narratives of the Exodus and God's championing of the oppressed. Segregationists, who wanted to preserve white privilege, usually relied upon states' rights provisions in the Constitution. King frequently invoked the prophet Amos: "We will not be satisfied until justice rolls down like waters, and righteousness like a mighty stream" (paraphrasing Amos 5:24), meaning that God preferred social justice over empty ritual. King's last speech, the night before his assassination on April 4, 1968, eerily recalled Moses looking over the promised land before his death, knowing he would never enter it: "He's allowed me to go up to the mountain. And I've looked over. And I've seen the Promised Land. I may not get there with you. But I want you to know tonight that we, as a people, will get to the Promised Land."[19] In a speech at a mass meeting in Greenwood, Mississippi in 1963, Mrs. Hamer skillfully wove together the biblical story with the movement's own, saying, "You see, he [God] made it so plain for us. He sent a man in Mississippi with the same man that Moses had to go to Egypt, and tell him to go down in Mississippi and tell Ross Barnett [segregationist governor] to 'let my people go.'"[20] She treated as a basic truth Acts 17:26: God has "made of one blood all nations . . . for to dwell on the face of the earth" (KJV), meaning all humans are equal, regardless of race.

18. Kitzmiller v. Dover (2005), *ncse.com/files/pub/legal/kitzmiller/highlights/2005-12-20*.

19. Reprinted in *The Bible and American Culture*, ed. Claudia Setzer and David Shefferman (London: Routledge, 2011), 189.

20. Fannie Lou Hamer, Moses Moon Papers, Archives Center, National Museum of American History, Smithsonian Institution. Reprinted in *The Bible and American Culture*, 191.

The Bible and Popular Culture

For writers, musicians, and artists, the Bible provides a wealth of colorful images and narratives. Novels like *Moby Dick* or *Go Tell It on the Mountain* draw explicitly on biblical themes. Poets, including Emily Dickinson, Robert Lowell, and Samuel Menashe used biblical language and themes. Many films such, as *The Ten Commandments* or *Jesus of Nazareth*, re-tell the biblical narratives, while some, like *A Serious Man* or *Cool Hand Luke*, expand and interpret them in contemporary contexts. Pop, rock, and rap music is rife with biblical references, from Leonard Cohen's *Hallelujah* (1985) to Lauryn Hill's *Forgive Them Father*. Even video games assume biblical knowledge. The video game *Rock Band* includes Iron Maiden's *The Number of the Beast*, which includes citation of verses from Revelation, while the more recent *Binding of Isaac* video game (2011) parodies Genesis 22. Unlike the biblical story, this game features the mother as the one trying to kill Isaac. A more recent edition of the game, *The Wrath of the Lamb*, refers to the apocalyptic lamb in the book of Revelation.

Particular narratives, verses, and phrases from the Bible are common coin in American culture. A Pew survey[21] of Americans' religious knowledge in 2010 showed that most people living in the United States had some knowledge of the Bible. Most (63 percent) knew Genesis was the first book and knew about Moses (72 percent). White evangelicals and Mormons were the most knowledgeable, but atheists and agnostics also scored high. A politician writing a speech or a musician writing a song can expect biblical words to have a certain resonance to American ears, even if the hearer might not know why. When Ronald Reagan referred to the United States as "a shining city on a hill" in 1984, it carried some grandeur, even if most people could not recognize it as an allusion to John Winthrop's invocation of Matthew 5:14 aboard the *Arbella*. One cannot cite Shakespeare or Walt Whitman with the same expectation. We remain the inheritors of the Founding Fathers and the Planting Fathers, living in a republic imbued with biblical ideas.

---

21. "U.S. Religious Knowledge Survey," Pew Research Center Forum on Religion and Public Life Project, December 28, 2010, *www.pewforum.org*.

DISCUSSION QUESTIONS

1. In 1983, a joint resolution of the House and Senate called on President Reagan to proclaim 1983 "The Year of the Bible." Reagan signed it into law by Proclamation 5018. Had you been a member of the House or Senate, how would you have voted and why?
2. Many public high schools allow Bible study clubs to meet on school grounds. Under what circumstances can the Bible be read or studied in public schools? Do you think this should be changed?
3. Cite some examples of biblical phrases or ideas that appear in popular music and video games. What do you think is the effect of including these kinds of materials?
4. Look at inaugural speeches of past presidents (e.g., Lincoln's Second Inaugural, or Clinton's First Inaugural). Pick out the biblical lines or ideas. How and why are they used? What is the effect? Do these same presidents use biblical ideas in other speeches?

FOR FURTHER STUDY

Noll, Mark. *America's God: From Jonathan Edwards to Abraham Lincoln*. New York: Oxford University Press, 2005.

Prothero, Stephen. *American Jesus: How the Son of God Became a National Icon*. New York: Farrar, Straus, Giroux, 2004.

Setzer, Claudia, and David Shefferman. *The Bible and American Culture: A Sourcebook*. London and New York: Routledge, 2011.

Vowell, Sarah. *The Wordy Shipmates*. New York: Riverhead, 2008.

Internet Resources

www.sacred-text.com/wmn/wb/

The text of *The Woman's Bible*, edited by Elizabeth Cady Stanton.

6

The Bible and Art

Gale A. Yee

The interpretation of a biblical passage begins with a careful reading of the text. The interpretation of a work of art, similarly, begins with a careful "seeing" of the work: attention to detail, to elements that the artist emphasized or omitted. Contemplating a work of art that is based on a biblical text can enhance one's understanding of the text by drawing attention to the elements that the artist thought important or unimportant, the ways that the artist subtly shaped or even "corrected" the meaning of the text, and thus the theological significance that the author found in the text. The careful viewer of such a work of art is invited to enter into the artist's understanding of the text; by doing so, the viewer may be introduced to meanings that are new or unexpected. The viewer also must come to grips with the assumptions that he or she has brought to the text, which may differ significantly from the assumptions of the artist.

Close Reading/Close Seeing

The Bible is first and foremost written literature. Often, however, readers approach the text with a store of visual images already in hand. This is particularly true of familiar stories, such as the narratives of Adam and Eve, the Exodus, or of Jesus in the Gospels. Western culture has instilled in many readers a set of ingrained visual preconceptions about the stories. They believe that they already "know" the text in some way. They know that Eve was a beautiful Caucasian blond, who lured Adam into sin with an apple, because they see this image in countless paintings and even advertisements. They know that the creator God is an old, white, bearded male, because of Michelangelo's famous image in the Sistine Chapel of God going finger-to-finger with Adam. Moses looks like Charlton Heston in *The Ten Commandments*, and Jesus is a bearded white guy with long hair. These images are already present in the subconscious mind when readers encounter the Bible. By bracketing their culturally constructed visual preconceptions, interpreters make their first step in a critical examination of a biblical text by reading the text carefully and attending to what it actually says.

All methods of biblical interpretation (exegesis), such as historical criticism, literary criticism, or feminist criticism, involve close readings of the text, often in the original languages.[1] Close readings entail spending a lot of time with a text. One cannot simply skim a text to understand the historical situation that it describes or the author who wrote it. Nor can a single reading delve into the literary complexities of a text's narrative structure, characterization, point of view, imagery, or figures of speech. A single reading won't unmask, for example, the text's biased views toward women and gender relations. Reading closely helps contextualize the Bible in its historical ancient Near Eastern and Greco-Roman milieux, enabling readers to realize that the biblical characters lived in an ancient male-dominated society that hardly ever created visible images of God (aniconism), were not all white, and that often regarded women as seductive and inferior. Close reading entails much inter-disciplinary work in the task of interpretation, involving history, archaeology, languages, literary and critical theory, and the social sciences, just to name a few of those disciplines.

Visual exegesis examines how an artistic work interprets a particular text. A painting, for example, does not simply illustrate a biblical text. It visualizes a painter's interpretation of it. "The painter reads a text and translates his reading into a problem in representation, to which he offers a solution—the image."[2] The biblical author

---

1. See chapter 4, "Methods of Biblical Interpretation." Also consult Corrine Carvalho, *Primer on Biblical Methods* (Winona, MN: Anselm Academic, 2009).

2. Paolo Berdini, "Jacopo Bassano: A Case for Painting as Visual Exegesis," in *Interpreting Christian Art: Reflections on Christian Art*, ed. Heidi J. Hornik and Mikeal C. Parsons (Macon, GA: Mercer University Press, 2004), 169–86, at 170.

Aniconism

Aniconism is the prohibition of visual depictions of things, particulary images of God. Jews, for most of their history, have regarded the second commandment as a comprehensive ban on any images of God. Islamic art enlarges this tradition by banning the depiction of the human form. There have been exceptions to this prohibition, such as the Dura-Europos synagogue and some examples of East Asian Islamic art.

decides how to "tell" the story and this decision results in the text; the painter decides how to "show" the story, and this decision results in the painting.[3] Visual exegesis can be added to the biblical scholars' exegetical toolboxes, because it can help them see things about a text that they may have overlooked with other methods. Note the visual connotations in "see" and "overlooked" in the previous sentence. As with close readings of a text, close readings of a painting entail spending a lot of time with it. David Perkins laments those in a museum who stand in front of a picture, even one they like, for a mere half a minute before moving on to the next. Such persons often hastily dismiss a work without exploring what it has to offer. For Perkins, looking at pictures requires active participation, and, in the early stages, a certain amount of discipline, the same amount of discipline, I would add, required of an interpreter of a biblical text.[4] In fact, many of the methodologies of artistic analysis are similar to those of biblical analysis.[5] Close readings of a text and of a painting both take time to discover the various meanings they have to offer, historically, literarily, aesthetically, theologically, ideologically, and so forth.

---

3. J. Cheryl Exum, "Toward a Genuine Dialogue between the Bible and Art," in *Congress Volume Helsinki 2010*, ed. Martti Nissinen (Leiden and Boston: Brill, 2012), 473–503, at 474–75.

4. David N. Perkins, *The Intelligent Eye: Learning to Think by Looking at Art* (Santa Monica, CA: The J. Paul Getty Trust, 1994), 51–55.

5. Laurie Schneider Adams, *The Methodologies of Art: An Introduction* (Boulder, CO: Westview Press, 1996).

Sparking the Imagination/Making Us Ponder

It is not surprising that painters have plumbed the Bible as a source for their works. The Bible is filled with marvelous images as well as captivating narratives. Let us begin our exploration into the Bible and art by focusing on the familiar creation stories of Genesis 1–3. These chapters teem with images that spark the imagination. What are the visual elements in the story? What parts of the story create pictures in the imagination? What parts of the story does one "see" or "visualize"? What parts would *you* put into a picture? Perhaps it will be the chaotic seas and the darkness covering the face of the deep (1:2). Perhaps it will be the emergence of light out of the darkness (1:3–5). Perhaps it will be the earth bringing forth vegetation, lush plants of all kinds (1:11–12). Perhaps it will be the tree of life in the midst of the garden that God planted, or even the tree of the knowledge of good and evil (2:8–9). Perhaps it will be the first encounter between Adam and Eve (2:22–23). Perhaps it will be the moment when they are cast out of paradise with the cherubim and the revolving flaming sword preventing their return (3:23–24). What do you *see* as you read these chapters and how would you depict it in a painting yourself?

Scholars think that Genesis 1–3 was composed by two different authors that they call the "Yahwist" and the "Priestly" writers.[6] Even though images abound in these chapters, there are some aspects of the story that resist depiction, the foremost being the creator God. The earlier Yahwist creation story (Gen. 2–3) characteristically portrays God anthropomorphically, that is, like a human being. God seems to have hands, forming the first male from the ground, as well as a mouth and lungs to breathe life into him (2:7). God seems to have legs, because God walks around in the garden (3:8). Yet even here, viewers still do not obtain a sharp picture of what the divine being looks like. The later Priestly creation story (Gen. 1) avoids such anthropomorphism by having God simply speak creation into being: "And God said, 'Let there be X,' and there was X." The imagination becomes particularly mystified when encountering:

> So God created humankind in his image,
> In the image of God he created them.
> Male and female he created them. (1:27)

---

6. For more on the sources of the Pentateuch, see chapter 1, "The Formation of the Bible," and chapter 13, "Introduction to the Pentateuch."

What does the "image of God" look like? If humans are created in God's image, does that mean God has a body like humans? If so, what kind of body? Male or female? Or both? Moreover, for the artist, how does one represent "the image of God" pictorially?

Therefore, besides offering a profusion of images that spark our imaginations, the biblical text also gives us much to ponder. These ambiguities or absences in the text, the ones that defy description, present artists with a wealth of possibilities for interpretation. Recall the above quotation: "The painter reads a text and translates his reading into a problem in representation, to which he offers a solution—the image." Artists read Genesis 1–3 and translate the depiction of God into a visual problem to be pondered, to which they offer a solution—the image. Despite the usual prohibition of picturing God in Israelite religion, the history of art reveals that the predominant depiction of the creator God is as an ancient male.

Multiple Readings/Multiple Seeings

While historical criticism sought to determine the meaning of the biblical text as it was intended by the original authors, one of the major insights of the literary approaches to the Bible is the recognition of its polyvalent character. The biblical texts can have more than one meaning. Discovering what a text "means" involves the dynamic interplay among the author of the text, the text itself, and its reader.[7] For example, the ancient biblical writers were products of the social worlds in which they lived, and they were also involved in the production of that world through the production of the literary text. They were primarily elite literate males, who comprised a tiny specialized portion of the Israelite population. It was their particular religious perspectives and ideologies that became normative in the biblical texts. The texts that they proffered were their "readings" of the social worlds they inhabited, "readings" that described, legitimated, denounced, satirized, entertained, or exhorted those social worlds. Their readings were consumed or appropriated by other

---

7. Gale A. Yee, "The Author/Text/Reader and Power: Suggestions for a Critical Framework in Biblical Studies," in *Reading from this Place: Social Location and Biblical Interpretation*, ed. Fernando F. Segovia and Mary Ann Tolbert (Minneapolis: Fortress, 1995), 1:109–18.

readers, themselves products of their own social world. These later readers used these ancient texts in the production of their own "readings" of their particular world, in order to legitimate, satirize, entertain, and exhort that world.

Contributing to the polyvalence of the text is the impact of social location on the theory and practice of biblical interpretation. Such factors as gender, race or ethnicity, class status, sexual orientation, religious perspectives, political stances, and so on can influence how the biblical authors wrote the text and how its readers interpret it.[8] The question of meaning becomes more complex when one factors in the visual interpretation of a biblical story by the artist. Different factors of social location thus influence the author who wrote, the one who reads, the artist who paints, and the viewer who sees. These different layers of meaning at the level of the author, reader, painter, and viewer must be taken into account in trying to determine what the text means. This essay is principally concerned with the production of the visual "reading" of the biblical text and how the artists in their particular social location interpret artistically the stories they depict. Moreover, the viewers of the artistic work are also influenced by their own gender, race/ethnicity, class, sexual orientation, and so forth in interpreting its meaning. Each of these variables at the level of author, reader, painter, and viewer generate multiple meanings and multiple seeings of a visual piece.

To deal with these multiple meanings and multiple seeings, Cheryl Exum offers excellent questions for students to consider when assessing how a painter interprets a biblical story:

> To what features of the biblical text does a visual representation draw our attention? What aspects does it ignore or underplay? Does the artist respond to a perceived gap in the text or to questions unanswered by the text? Does the artist add something to the biblical text? Does she or he, for example, magnify something that is not very important in the biblical version? Does the visual representation illuminate

---

8. See the eighteen different categories students at New York Theological Seminary must complete in their self-inventory on factors that may influence their interpretation of the Bible; Norman K. Gottwald, "Framing Biblical Interpretation at New York Theological Seminary: A Student Self-Inventory on Biblical Hermeneutics," in Segovia and Tolbert, eds., *Reading from this Place*, 1:251–61.

dimensions of the biblical account in new and important ways, either positively or negatively? Is the artist's attitude to the subject the same as that of the biblical text? Does a painting attempt to represent the biblical story or reshape it to fit certain interests, or does it reuse its themes in order to oppose it? Whose point of view does the artist represent and how does this compare to the presentation of point of view in the biblical version? Does the artist involve the viewer in the painting? If so, how? Is the viewer invited to identify with a particular character or see a scene through a particular character's eyes? If so, does the artist identify the view with the same character the biblical writer encourages the reader to identify with? Does the painting alert us to something important that the biblical writer has left out or attempted to gloss over? Does the visualization enable or perhaps force us to "see" something we may have disregarded in the verbal narrative? Does it, by what it emphasizes or downplays, shed light on the biblical narrator's ideology? How are our assumptions about biblical characters influenced, or even shaped, by our encounters with their visual counterparts, and how does this affect the way we read their stories?[9]

We can now turn to some depictions of the story of Adam and Eve.

Genesis Frontispiece, Grandval Bible, Tours (ca. 840 CE)

Figure 1 is the frontispiece of the ninth-century Grandval Bible from Tours.[10] A frontispiece refers to the decorative visual opposite a book's title page. This particular one is a good example of early Christian Carolingian manuscript illumination.[11] It illustrates Genesis 2–3

---

9. J. Cheryl Exum, "Toward a Genuine Dialogue between the Bible and Art," in Matti Nissinen, ed., *Congress Volume Helsinki 2010*, 475–76.

10. A reproduction can be found in Dorothée Sölle, Joe H. Kirchberger, and Anne-Marie Schnieper-Müller, *Great Women of the Bible in Art and Literature* (Grand Rapids: Eerdmans, 1993), 13.

11. For a detailed study of this frontispiece, compared with others, see Herbert L. Kessler, "Hic Homo Formatur: The Genesis Frontispieces of the Carolingian Bible," *The Art Bulletin* 53, no. 2 (1971): 143–60.

Figure 1. In the Genesis Frontispiece of the Grandval Bible, Adam and Eve strongly resemble God, in whose "image" they were created.

rather than Genesis 1, and it seems to capture the major moments of these chapters in a four-band format, somewhat like a modern cartoon strip. Nevertheless, there are some noticeable interpretive choices this artist makes in the depictions. Before reading further, consider the general questions cited above, along with the following, which focus on these chapters: What aspects of Genesis 2–3 are depicted? Which are eliminated? Did the artist add anything to the story or change or modify it? How is God depicted? How are Adam and Eve depicted? Who are those middle two figures in the first band? How is the so-called "temptation scene" portrayed? Is this what you read in Genesis 3:6? How does the artist depict the expulsion from the garden? What does it look like outside the garden vis-à-vis inside it?

First of all, the artist is primarily concerned with the God/human relationship. He does not illustrate God planting a garden (2:8–9). The detailed description of the waters flowing out of Eden (2:10–14) seems to be reduced to the strip of blue across the first three bands. There is no naming of the animals by the man (2:19–20). God is pictured as a young, beardless, dark-haired male with a nimbus (halo). He is bending over Adam's already-formed body and is about to breathe the breath of life into him (2:7).[12] Skipping over the naming of animals, the artist depicts the excision of a rib from the sleeping Adam to create the woman. With out-stretched hand, God brings the woman to Adam, who points to her and exclaims, "This at last is bone of my bone and flesh of my flesh" (2:23). Note that God, Adam, and Eve all look alike. Their similarities can be found in other ancient artistic renditions to depict the notion that the human couple is created in the image of God.

At this point, the illumination departs from the biblical script. On the right side of band 2, God warns the couple not to eat from the tree of the knowledge of good and evil or risk death. However, this command was only given to the man in 2:16–17. Hence, the illumination "explains" visually how Eve would have known of this command in her encounter with the snake in 3:2. Although God points to a particular tree when he commands the couple not to eat of the tree, this tree is not the same one from which Eve picks on the left side of band 3. Do the flowers and early growth on the tree in band 2 perhaps mature into a tree with fruit in band 3, or is it a completely different tree? What do you think?

Genesis 3:6 clearly states that Adam was with Eve during her dialogue with the snake. Compare this scene with Figure 2 from the Codex Vigilanus of Madrid,[13] where both Adam and Eve are present

---

12. Ibid., 147–48.

13. A reproduction can be found in Sölle, Kirchberger, and Schnieper-Müller, *Great Women of the Bible in Art and Literature*, 17.

with the snake. Note also here that their genitals are already covered with fig leaves, a detail that occurs only after the man eats the fruit and "their eyes were opened" (3:7).

Figure 2. Artistic renderings of the temptation often emphasize Eve's guilt by depicting her alone with the serpent. This example, from the Codex Vigilanus, is more faithful to the biblical text; Adam is present, passively watching while Eve is tempted (cf. Gen. 3:6).

In the frontispiece Eve alone is conversing with the snake. She then materializes in a new scene where she offers Adam the fruit; the scene thus implies that she alone is guilty in listening to the snake and that she is responsible for her husband's fall. On the right side of band 3, God reappears again at the tree of the knowledge of good and evil from which he questions the couple with his pointed finger: "Who told you that you were naked? Have you eaten from the tree I told you not to eat?" Wittily, the illustration replicates the finger pointing with the man passing the blame on to the woman, and she, on to the snake. The snake is upright and so foreshadows God's curse that he will slither on his belly and eat dust as he goes (3:14). Visually, there is no naming of the woman as Eve, just as there is no naming of the animals, and God does not make garments for the couples (3:20–21). Moreover, Genesis 3:24 states that God drives the couple out from the garden, but here one of the angels evicts them.[14] Finally, the frontispiece depicts Adam and Eve's lives outside of the garden, a scene not present in Genesis 3. Eve presumably has just given birth to the oldest son, Cain, whom she is feeding. Adam is tilling the soil. The frontispiece expands pictorially on the results of God's prediction in 3:16–19, that Eve will bring forth children in pain, the ground will bring forth thorns and thistles, and Adam will till the earth by the sweat of his brow.

Miniature of Jean de Courcy, Seigneur de Bourgachard

We have just seen how a picture that seems to adhere closely to the biblical text exhibits some subtle adjustments to it upon close visual reading. The depiction of the Adam and Eve narrative in Figure 3 is the greatly enlarged miniature of Jean de Courcy, Seigneur de Bourgachard.[15] Go through the same questioning process as you did for the frontispiece before reading on.

---

14. The use of an angel may indicate the influence of a different artistic tradition. Kessler, *Hic Homo Formatur*, 151.

15. Reproduced in Sölle, Kirchberger, and Schnieper-Müller, *Great Women of the Bible in Art and Literature*, 11.

Figure 3. If the figure in the clouds is God, who is the figure below, speaking with Adam in this scene from the Miniature of Jean de Courcy, Seigneur de Bourgachard?

The illumination seems to depict a scene after the creation of the woman. God has just brought Eve to Adam, and they gently hold hands (Gen. 2:21–25). Adam and Eve are in a beautiful flowering garden filled with trees. Wild and domesticated animals peek from the trees on both sides of the painting. In the foreground, branches of the river flow out of Eden (2:10–14), continuing on the left in the distance at the base of the mountains. Sun, moon, and stars grace the sky above. Two peacocks are in the foreground at the bottom of the picture. Their depiction here may reflect the early belief that a pair of peacocks guarded the gates of Paradise, but they might have even deeper significance. Adam and Eve have more idealized white naked bodies than the more primitive looking ones depicted in the Grandval frontispiece and the Codex Vigilanus. Eve has the long flowing blond hair that will become her signature feature in the history of art. Her eyes are demurely cast down; she does not engage in the dialogue between the two males but remains passively silent.

The most puzzling feature of this illumination is that solemn, old, bearded male floating on the clouds above. Who is this figure, and if he is God, with whom is Adam speaking below? A clue to the identity of the figure above is the distinctive hat that he is wearing: a three-tiered papal tiara. The pope, from the Greek *pappas* "father," was and still is the bishop of Rome and the head of the Roman Catholic Church. Wearing the papal tiara signifies that the upper figure is most likely God the Father of the Trinity. His gesture is one of blessing upon the scene below. The nimbus surrounding the head of Adam's conversation partner indicates divinity, and if the individual above is God the Father, this figure is most likely the second person of the Trinity: Jesus. But Jesus does not appear in Genesis 2–3! How can one explain his presence here?

This painting engages in a type of medieval visual exegesis of the biblical text. The early and medieval church regarded the Bible as having four levels of meaning. The first is the *literal* sense, what the words simply say. The second is the *allegorical* sense—what the text meant at the literal level now means something else through the eyes of the Christian faith. For example, the sacrifice of Isaac (Gen. 22) prefigures Christ's death on the cross.[16] The crossing of the Red Sea anticipates the liberating waters of baptism (1 Pet. 3:21). The

---

16. See Robin M. Jensen, *The Substance of Things Seen: Art, Faith, and the Christian Community* (Grand Rapids: Eerdmans, 2004), 27–42, for an analysis of the levels of interpretation in visual depictions of Genesis 22.

tropological, or *moral* meaning reads a passage for lessons for upright conduct. The *anagogical* relates the passage to the eschatological end of time and the final judgment.

This illumination is an example of an *allegorical* visual exegesis that reads Genesis 2 from a Christian perspective. The pure white bodies emphasize the innocence of the first couple. Yes, they and their descendants will eventually sin, but Christ's presence at creation here foreshadows the time when he will redeem them through his death and Resurrection. The similarity of the red hair, beard, and facial features in both Jesus and Adam recall Romans 5:14, where Adam "is a type of the one who was to come." The painting seems to embody pictorially the theological insights of 1 Corinthians 15:47–49: "The first man was from the earth, a man of dust; the second man is from heaven. . . . Just as we have borne the image of the man of dust, we will also bear the image of the man of heaven." Having the God/man Jesus blessing the couple in Eden foretells his future coming to deliver humans from their sin and their resurrection into new life. This helps explain the presence of the peacocks, which for some early church writers were symbols of resurrection and immortality.[17]

Just as Adam is a prototype for Christ, Eve finds her counterpart in both written and visual traditions in the person of the Virgin Mary, who becomes the "new Eve."[18]

Book of Hours

Compare the Jean de Courcy miniature with Figure 4, whole page miniatures from a sixteenth-century book of hours from Rouen.[19]

The left page depicts the temptation story of Genesis 3. Note the similar body type for Eve in both visuals, as well as their long blond hair. This visual contains a common trope found in many

17. Diane Apostolos-Cappadona, *Encyclopedia of Women in Religious Art* (New York: Continuum, 1996), 289.

18. Robin M. Jensen, "The Fall and Rise of Adam and Eve in Early Christianity and Literature," in *Interpreting Christian Art: Reflections on Christian Art*, ed. Heidi J. Hornik and Mikeal C. Parsons (Macon, GA: Mercer University Press, 2004), 25–52, at 41–47.

19. To view online visit *http://bodley30.bodley.ox.ac.uk:8180/luna/servlet/detail/ ODLodl~1~1~43818~127960:Book-of-Hours--Use-of-Rouen-.*

Figure 4, panel 1. This illustration from a sixteenth-century book of hours makes a theological statement by juxtaposing Eve with the Virgin Mary; the artist suggests that the effects of Eve's disobedience (panel 1) are negated by Mary's submission to God's will (panel 2).

illustrations of Eve, namely the serpent with a woman's head. Often the serpent's head bears a striking resemblance to Eve herself, as it does here in the Book of Hours. This artistic convention underscores

Figure 4, panel 2.

sexist attitudes that regard both the snake and woman as the source
of male temptation and ultimately death. However, the placement of
the facing page on the right, illustrating the annunciation of Jesus'
birth to Mary, creates a visual of the new Eve that redeems the sin
of the first. Even though the serpent and Eve share blond hair and

similar facial features, the fact that Mary also has these same features reveals a theological interpretation that redeems Eve optically.

Conclusion

Paintings and other visuals depicting biblical scenes are not simply illustrations of the stories. They spark imagination and reflection by commenting on the texts and interpreting them, often expanding their original literal meanings to offer later theological insights. By viewing just the four pictures discussed here, it appears that the creator God is not always an old man with a white beard, that Eve was not always a blond, and that painters had no problem infusing Christian themes into the stories of the Old Testament. To achieve the most from both the textual and visual versions, one must spend time with both the text and the visual in close readings. Moreover, one must learn something about the literary and artistic history of the text and its painting. Every age leaves its gendered, ethnic, class-based, and cultural imprint in its visual interpretation of the biblical text. These paintings depict in culturally specific ways the human body, the divine self, and the attitudes regarding women of their era. The interaction between the text and the painting offer multiple readings and multiple seeings. Close readings of a text and of a painting both take time to discover the various meanings they have to offer, historically, literarily, aesthetically, theologically, ideologically, and so forth.

DISCUSSION QUESTIONS

1. How is interpretation of a biblical text similar to the interpretation of biblical art? How do they differ?
2. How might a work of biblical art offer insight into the artist's theological and sociological point of view?
3. In the depictions of the creation account from Genesis discussed above, what struck you as conventional? What was novel or unexpected? Has the analysis of these works changed your understanding of the creation account, and if so, how?

4. How is the interpretation of a biblical text affected when an artist depicts the characters as non-Caucasian—for example, as African, or Asian? What if the artist depicts God (or Jesus, or the Holy Spirit) as female?

FOR FURTHER STUDY

The following beautifully illustrated coffee-table books containing famous masterworks of the Bible offer a wealth of experiences for close readings of the visual text.

Bernard, Bruce. *The Bible and its Painters*. New York: Macmillan, 1983.

Calderhead, Christopher. *The Bible Portrayed in 200 Masterpieces of Painting*. Old Saybrook, CT: Konecky & Konecky, 2005.

———. *One Hundred Miracles*. New York: Welcome Books, 2004.

Frankel, Ellen. *The Illustrated Hebrew Bible: Seventy-Five Selected Stories*. New York: Abradale Press, 1999.

Haag, Herbert, Dorothée Sölle, Helen Schüngel-Straumann, Christoph Wetzel, Katharina Elliger, and Marianne Grohmann. *Great Couples of the Bible*. Minneapolis: Fortress, 2006.

Sölle, Dorothée, Joe H. Kirchberger, and Anne-Marie Schnieper-Müller. *Great Women of the Bible in Art and Literature*. Grand Rapids: Eerdmans, 1993.

Internet Resources

www.artbible.info/art/

A selection of biblical art from hundreds of artists.

www.textweek.com/art/art.htm

An art concordance with links to artwork indexed according to theme, biblical text, and lectionary date.

7

Jews, Christians, and Muslims: People of the Book

John Kaltner, Joel S. Kaminsky, and Younus Mirza

Jews and Christians are commonly referred to in the Qur'an as "People of the Book." Although they do not normally include themselves in that category, Muslims might also be identified in the same way since they share with their fellow monotheists the primary element associated with the People of the Book: a revealed scripture. The following essays present an overview of key aspects of the role their sacred texts play for followers of these three religious traditions. This treatment of the contents, use, and interpretation of their scriptures underscores some of the similarities and differences among the adherents of these faiths.

Scripture in Judaism

Joel S. Kaminsky

Contents

When Jews living in North America or the United Kingdom colloquially use the term "the Bible," they mean the Jewish Bible, containing only the books found in the Protestant Old Testament, and even then the Jewish order of books differs significantly from that found in Christian Bibles. One can best grasp these distinctions by unpacking the common acronym used to refer to the Jewish Bible: the Tanak. The three consonants in the term TaNaK stand for

Torah, a word meaning "instruction," "teaching," or "law" (Genesis–Deuteronomy); *Nevi'im*, the Hebrew word for "Prophets" (Joshua–2 Kings and Isaiah through Malachi); and *Kethuvim*, or the "Writings" (all the other books of the Jewish Bible). The most significant difference in the Christian order of the Old Testament is that the section containing the materials that run from Isaiah to Malachi occurs last in the Christian Old Testament. However, there are other major distinctions between the Christian Old Testament and the Jewish Tanak. To begin, one must reckon with the centrality of the first five books of the Jewish Bible, the Torah. The Torah is understood to contain God's direct revelation to his preeminent prophet, Moses. While the whole Hebrew Bible is viewed as sacred scripture, Judaism sees the Prophets and Writings as containing stories, prophecies, wisdom, and prayers of post-Mosaic Jews who sought to live their life according to the Torah of Moses. Note that these other two sections of the Tanak (the Prophets and Writings) begin with strong injunctions to meditate on the Torah day and night (see Joshua 1:7–8 and Psalm 1:2).

Yet this is not the whole story. Within Jewish tradition the Torah occupies such a central space that the term has come to take on two meanings. The first simply refers to the opening five books of the larger Jewish Bible, or Tanak. But in its more expansive meaning the term Torah can refer to any part, or all, of the vast trove of Jewish law and lore from antiquity to today. This dual usage is grounded in a larger rabbinic theory of the "dual Torah." The ancient rabbis, teachers of Jewish law and lore who lived during the first few centuries of the Common Era, believed that Moses actually received two Torahs from God on Mount Sinai. One Torah was considered to be *written* (the Pentateuch and in some sense the scriptures found within the whole Tanak), and the other was thought to be *oral* (the Oral Torah, the rabbinic traditions such as those found in the Mishnah and the Talmud, collections of post-biblical Jewish laws).

Use

The word "liturgy" refers to the rituals practiced and the readings used in religious settings. There is evidence found within the Tanak as well as within the New Testament that portions of the Jewish

Scriptures functioned liturgically in that they were read aloud in ancient communal religious gatherings, especially in the Temple and in synagogues. For instance, Deuteronomy 31:9–13 reports that every seven years "this Torah," likely referring to some form of the book of Deuteronomy, is to be read aloud to the whole community at the Festival of Booths (Hebrew, *Succot*). Luke 4:16–21 and Acts 15:21 imply that excerpts from the Torah and the Prophets were read on Sabbaths in synagogues. Further, it seems clear that Psalms were recited by individuals (e.g., Ps. 13) and many others were sung communally within the life of the temple in ancient times (e.g., Ps. 118, which features a call and response). However, the exact scope and regularity of the ancient liturgical use of the Torah and other parts of the Tanak remain unclear.

Once Jewish liturgical readings and prayers became standardized several hundred years ago, various pieces of the biblical text came to be used in the prayer service on a regular basis. These fall into several categories, including a cyclical pattern of communally reading through the whole Torah, a set of Prophetic extracts or lections paired with each Torah reading, the pairing of the five Megillot with five specific Jewish holidays (see below), and the incorporation of selections from the Torah, Psalms, and other biblical texts into the daily and weekly prayer book.

The most prominent use of the Jewish Scriptures is the tradition of reading through the entire five books of the Torah over the course of the Jewish ritual year. In this annual liturgical cycle, which in some Conservative and Reform synagogues occurs over three years, the Torah is divided into 54 portions, and each Torah portion, or *parashah*, is in turn paired with an excerpt from the prophetic books, called the *haftarah*. Because some of the standard weekly readings are displaced by Jewish holidays or the changing length of the Jewish lunar year, certain weeks may end up with double Torah portions. The reading cycle ends and begins each year at Simchat Torah ("rejoicing of the Torah"), which occurs each fall. Each weekly excerpt is named after a Hebrew word or phrase that occurs in the opening verse of each week's Torah portion. For example, the first is called *Bereshith*, the first word of Genesis, meaning "In the beginning." In addition, the five short *megillot,* or scrolls, are read on the following holidays: Song of Songs on Passover, Ruth on Shavuot, Lamentations on the

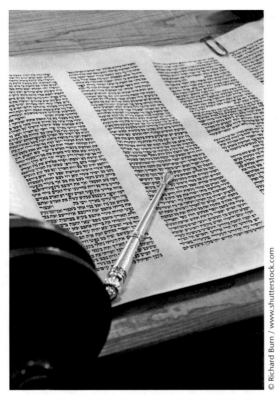

In keeping with ancient tradition, Torah scrolls intended for use in worship are meticulously hand-copied. The small silver implement seen above is a pointer, or *yad* ("hand"), which the reader uses to follow the text when reading the Torah.

ninth day of the month of Av, Qohelet (Ecclesiastes) on Succot, and Esther on Purim.

The liturgical practices surrounding the reading of the Torah reveal a number of widespread rabbinic theological assumptions about the meaning and significance of the Torah for Jews. For instance, a congregant is called to the Torah to recite a blessing both before and after each part of the lection is chanted. In particular, note the following phrase from the blessing one recites when a section of the lection is concluded: "Blessed is the Lord our God, King of the universe, who has given us a Torah of truth, and has planted everlasting life in our midst." A life that is dedicated to the practice of the Torah's commands and the study of the meaning of the Torah is seen as a key to obtaining immortality. The connection between Torah and immortality is yet further expanded in the rabbinic propensity to equate the notion of "Wisdom"—which the book of Proverbs describes as bestowing long life upon those who seek it—with Torah. Thus as the congregation returns the Torah scroll to the ark, words from Proverbs 3:17–18 are recited, which speak of Wisdom as "a tree of life for those that grasp her" (feminine pronouns are used for both Wisdom and Torah).

In addition to the regular weekly Torah readings, many of the daily and weekly prayers in Judaism are drawn from the Tanak. Most noticeably, many Psalms are included in the liturgy, and references drawn from the Exodus account, which describes how God redeemed the people of Israel and gave them the Torah, as well as famous passages like the Shema ("Hear, O Israel," Deut. 6:4) occur regularly. Further, the use of many ritual items like phylacteries—leather prayer boxes worn during weekday morning prayers—as well as *mezuzot*—miniature scrolls placed in metal or wood boxes that are mounted on door-frames in Jewish households and buildings—are derived from Deuteronomy 6:8–9.

Interpretation

Jewish tradition sees the Torah (both oral and written) as the blueprint for Jewish life. Much of the written Torah is filled with God's *mitzvot*, or commandments, concerning how one should live one's life, and in turn the rabbis spend a great deal of energy trying to apply these commands to ever new life situations. The ancient rabbis understood their own activities of interpreting and applying the Torah to new situations as simply making manifest aspects of the Oral Torah that Moses received at Sinai.

The Oral Torah was also seen as containing much of the backstory that helps one understand the often cryptic narratives found throughout the Tanak and enables one to unpack their meaning. This is done primarily through something called *midrash*, a verse-by-verse commentary that brings verses from across the Tanak to illuminate a given passage, and brings forth traditional rabbinic teachings about characters and events in the biblical text to expand upon and explain it. The ancient rabbis derived their interpretive insights from a very careful reading (some would say an *over*-reading) of the Hebrew. Often rabbinic interpretation is based upon unusual word usage, or even the numerical value of words, allowing the rabbis to fill in certain narrative gaps or explain oddities of the text. Thus in one rabbinic midrash we learn that the reason God appeared to Moses in a bush was to reveal to Moses the length of his lifespan, inasmuch as the Hebrew letters for the word "the bush" equal 120 and Moses lived to 120. But another midrash gives a theological explanation of the God's appearance in a bush: it teaches that no place in the world is devoid of God's presence, not even a lowly desert bush (*Exodus Rabbah* 2:5). Rabbinic interpretation also attributes significance to the juxtaposition of various passages, something that will be discussed in more detail toward the end of this essay; such an interpretive technique is echoed by recent narrative approaches to the Bible.

When one examines the ongoing Jewish tradition, which stretches over two thousand years, one quickly discovers that much of Jewish philosophical, mystical, legal, ethical, and theological thinking is preoccupied with attempting to understand and further elaborate upon the biblical text, especially the Torah; it continually finds innovative and ingenious ways for Scripture to speak to a new generation living in a different historical context. Furthermore, the vast post-biblical Jewish interpretive tradition regularly preserves not only differing but at times conflicting lines of interpretation. This carries on an ancient and venerable tradition that reaches back to the Bible itself.

In addition to deriving almost all of the 613 commandments that Rabbinic Judaism finds in the Written Torah and larger Tanak, there is a vast array of Jewish behavior and ethics derived indirectly from practices exhibited by characters (including God) within the Jewish Bible. For example, the rabbis derive a moral norm from the juxtaposition of the seemingly distinct stories found in Genesis 17 and 18. Male circumcision, a longstanding Jewish practice, is clearly authorized in Genesis 17, which describes how God commanded Abraham to have himself and all current and future males in his family circumcised. In the following story, which may have occurred well after the events in Genesis 17, God visits Abraham to announce the future birth of Isaac to Sarah. The rabbis assume that the textual proximity of these seemingly distinct stories is purposeful and teaches us that visiting the sick is so important that even God visited Abraham as he was recovering from his circumcision. Similarly, the rabbis stress the importance of clothing the naked and burying the dead by noting that the first act God does for Adam and Eve as a couple is to clothe them (Gen. 3:21), and the last act he does for Moses at the close of Deuteronomy is to bury him. Thus the Jewish Scriptures are not simply an ancient collection of texts that describe Jewish origins, but rather they are the continuing focal point of contemporary Jewish practice as well as the touchstone of ongoing theological reflection.

Scripture in Christianity

John Kaltner

Contents

Among the religions of the People of the Book, Christianity is unique in that its adherents do not agree on the writings that constitute its sacred Scripture. Although all Christians agree with regard to the books that constitute the New Testament, different groups disagree significantly with regard to the Old Testament. This disagreement relates to both the content of the writings and the order in which they appear. The result is several different canons, or sets of authoritative texts, which are similar but not identical. In the West, there are two dominant canons: the one used by Protestant communities, and the one used by Roman Catholics.[1] The Catholic Church views as canonical certain books—which they term the "deuterocanonical writings"—that the Protestant churches reject because they are not found in the Bible of Judaism.[2] The additional writings are, however, present in the ancient Greek translation of the Old Testament known as the Septuagint, which has played a prominent role

---

1. The Greek Orthodox canon differs slightly from the Roman Catholic canon. To compare, see the chart "Canons of Scripture" in the additional study aids section.

2. Protestants refer to the deuterocanonical writings as the Apocrypha.

in both Roman Catholic and Orthodox Christianity. Consequently, when reference is made to the "Christian Bible," the first issue that must be addressed is whose Bible is being discussed. The Protestant Old Testament is identical to the Tanak of Judaism as far as its contents are concerned, but there are certain differences in the grouping and order of the books. Unlike the tri-partite structure of the Tanak, the Protestant canon has four parts: Law, History, Wisdom, and Prophecy. The Roman Catholic and Orthodox canons adopt the same four-part structure, but with some differences. Included among the Historical Books are Tobit, Judith, and 1–2 Maccabees, while the two additions to the Poetic Books are Wisdom of Solomon and Sirach, which sometimes goes by the name Ecclesiasticus. In the Prophetic Books, Baruch is inserted after Lamentations. Another significant difference is that additions to the books of Esther and Daniel are included in the Catholic and Orthodox canons because these extra sections are found in the Septuagint. Some scholars have suggested that these additions to Esther and Daniel could be Greek translations of Hebrew or Aramaic original texts that are no longer available to us. Finally, the following works are considered to be canonical by some Orthodox churches even though they are not found in the Bibles of Catholicism or other Orthodox communities: 1–2 Esdras, The Prayer of Manasseh, Psalm 151, and 3–4 Maccabees. It would therefore be more accurate to state that there are three, not two, Christian canons.

Even though Protestant Christianity does not deem these deuterocanonical books to be canonical, some Protestant Bibles include them in a separate section titled "Apocrypha" (from a Greek word meaning "hidden") between the Old and New Testaments. The distinct character of each of the biblical canons can be seen in the fact that Jewish, Protestant, Roman Catholic and Orthodox canons all agree only on the order and contents of the first section of the Hebrew Bible/Old Testament, known as the Pentateuch or Torah.

Use

Because of differences within the many denominations, it is difficult to discuss Christian practices regarding use of the Bible without engaging in overgeneralization. Nonetheless, similarities among the various groups suggest that certain ways of behavior and customs regarding Scripture are typical of the experiences of a majority of Christians.

The Bible plays a central role in Christian worship and devotion, both personal and communal. Biblical passages are sometimes quoted or alluded to within liturgical contexts. For example, in many churches priests and ministers, when celebrating Communion, utter the words spoken by Jesus at the Last Supper as recorded in the Gospels and in 1 Corinthians ("This is my body . . . ," Matt. 26:26–29; Mark 14:22–25; Luke 22:19–20; 1 Cor. 11:23–26). Similarly, the Our Father or Lord's Prayer is commonly recited by congregations during community worship (Matt. 6:9-15; cf. Luke 11:2–4). Other biblical allusions found in the liturgies of some Christian denominations include prayers that contain the phrases "Holy, holy, holy, Lord God of hosts" (cf. Isa. 6:3), "Lord, I am not worthy that you should come under my roof" or variants thereof (cf. Matt. 8:8), and "Lamb of God who takes away the sin of the world" (John 1:29).

In canonical order, the first books of the New Testament are the four Gospels, which tell of Jesus' life, death, and Resurrection. The epistles of Paul, however, are older, and were the first Christian writings to be regarded as sacred Scripture (see 2 Peter 3:15–16).

Related to this is the Bible's role in the sermons preached in Christian worship services. Similar to Jewish practice that is mentioned in the New Testament (Acts 13:15, 27; 15:21) and is associated with Jesus himself (Luke 4:15–21), biblical passages have been read and commented upon in churches since the earliest centuries of Christianity. These sermons typically draw on biblical themes to explore their relevance for later audiences. In modern times many denominations use the same lectionary (from the Latin *lectio*, "reading"), a book that contains the scriptural passages that are to be read on a given day or occasion. Such resources were a part of Christian worship as early as the fifth century. The current Revised Common Lectionary that was released in 1994 is based on the *Ordo Lectionum Missae* ("Order of the Readings for Mass") of the Roman Catholic Church.

The Revised Common Lectionary is used in a growing number of primarily English-speaking churches. It has been accepted by both the United States and Canadian Conferences of Catholic Bishops, and it is the official lectionary of the Lutheran, Episcopal, Presbyterian, Methodist, Disciples of Christ, United Church of Christ, and American Baptist denominations, among others. In addition, it is used in many churches in the United Kingdom, Australia, and the Philippines. The Revised Common Lectionary is arranged on a three-year cycle of Sunday readings that includes portions of every biblical book (as well as some apocryphal writings), and it contains the four readings that are to be read each week: a selection from the Old Testament, a portion of the book of Psalms, a New Testament non-Gospel passage, and a Gospel reading. The lectionary also contains the readings to be proclaimed on Easter, Christmas, and other important feast days, as well as those to be used for special occasions like baptisms, weddings, and funerals.

The Bible is also frequently read for devotional purposes, in both informal and more structured settings. Many Christians read the Bible privately on a regular basis, and resources such as one-year study Bibles help them work their way through the text. Bible study groups are common gatherings in many churches, and they bring individuals together to read and reflect upon Scripture to develop and sustain their spiritual lives. A more formal example of Christian prayer centered on the Bible can be seen in the Liturgy of the Hours, also known as the Divine Office, which is composed of a set of prayers and biblical readings, especially Psalms, that are to be recited throughout the day and that vary in form and number depending on one's denomination. While it is most closely associated with the monastic life and the clergy, the Liturgy of the Hours is not limited to those groups. Forms of the Divine Office are found primarily in the Roman Catholic, Orthodox, Lutheran, and Anglican Churches.

Interpretation

Throughout history Christians have interpreted the Bible in many different ways, and there is no single universally accepted method of studying the text. The roots of the interpretive process can be seen in the earliest sources that have come down to us. The New Testament engages in interpretation of Jewish Scriptures through frequent quotations and allusions. This is usually done for christological purposes, in order to support or illustrate a given author's view of Jesus and the significance of his life. An example is seen in the prophetic fulfillment citations that are a prominent feature of Matthew's Gospel. More than any other Gospel writer, Matthew frequently comments upon events in Jesus' life by using a variation of the formula "All this took place to fulfill what had been spoken by the Lord through the prophet" and then citing a prophetic passage from the Old Testament (e.g., Matt. 1:22; 2:15, 17; 12:17–21; 21:4–5).

The frequency of such citations and allusions to the Jewish Scriptures in the New Testament indicates that the early followers of Jesus sometimes combed such sources for passages that would bolster their claims about him, and thereby interpreted the earlier writings through a christological lens. Two other ways of reading texts that were especially popular in the early centuries of Christianity were typology and allegory. In these interpretive techniques, events and figures in the Old Testament were seen as symbolizing Jesus or aspects of Christian faith. An example is seen in Romans 5:14, where Paul presents Adam as a precursor of Jesus.

Academic study of the Bible by Christians (and Jews) began to develop in the eighteenth century. In keeping with the Enlightenment thought current at the time, the new approach stressed the authority of the individual over and against that of institutions like the church. This new approach, which came to be known as the historical-critical method, took shape primarily within the context of Protestant Christianity. One of the rallying cries of the Reformation was *sola scriptura* ("Scripture alone"), and the denominations that emerged from the movement were more open to embracing new ways of reading the Bible than the Roman Catholic Church was. Protestant interpretation privileges Scripture as the primary source of Christian theology and practice, and from its inception it has tended to question the role of extra-scriptural sources like ecumenical councils, church teaching, and much of the accumulated earlier interpretation like that produced by the church fathers.

The way Scripture is interpreted is a distinguishing feature that separates the Protestant and Roman Catholic churches. The latter community emphasizes church tradition as the perspective from which the biblical text is to be read, and the Roman Church has issued many statements on how the Bible should be interpreted. In descending order of importance, the three main forms of Catholic teaching are (1) conciliar documents issued by an ecumenical council; (2) papal documents which are occasionally revised by later papal writings; and (3) curial documents published by a department or office within the Vatican. Within the first category, Vatican II's *Dogmatic Constitution on Divine Revelation* marked an important shift in Catholic teaching. Promulgated in 1965 with the Latin title *Dei Verbum*, the document reiterated the long-held tenet that both Scripture and Church tradition are divinely revealed. At the same time it also endorsed historical-critical study of the Bible, thereby allowing Roman Catholics to use the same methods available to Protestants and others. This shift was anticipated in *Divino Afflante Spiritu*, a document of the second type issued by Pius XII in 1943 that allowed Catholics to make use of modern methods of biblical study that had been previously forbidden.

In general, biblical interpretation within the Orthodox Church has more in common with that found in the Roman Catholic Church. The Orthodox make less use of the historical-critical method than do the other branches of Christianity, and the important role of tradition aligns them more closely with Catholics. For example, both groups often cite and draw upon the exegetical works of the church fathers that are commonly known as the patristic writings. Among the chief characteristics of biblical interpretation within the Orthodox Church are the following: (1) a belief in the authority, primacy, and unity of Scripture; (2) a sense of the interconnection between Scripture and church tradition, especially the teachings and interpretations of the church fathers; (3) a preference for the spiritual interpretation of biblical texts; and (4) a view of Jesus Christ as the interpretive lens for understanding the entire Bible.

Scripture in Islam

Younus Mirza

Contents

The Qur'an, the sacred text in Islam, consists of 114 chapters, which are largely arranged by length from longest to shortest. Each chapter has a name based on a word, person, sound, or theme found in the chapter. It is also common to identify each chapter with a number. The earliest revelations, which were given to Muhammad, are preserved at the end of the Qur'an, and they are usually the chapters that Muslims memorize and recite in their daily prayers. Each chapter is divided into verses (*āyāt*, literally "signs"). The longest chapter has 286 verses (chapter 2, titled *al-Baqara*), while the shortest has only three (108, *al-Kawthar*). The entire Qur'an contains around 6,300 verses and is approximately the size of the New Testament.

Qur'anic verses are identified as either Meccan or Medinan, depending on the city in which the Prophet Muhammad (570–632) was living when they were revealed to him. The revelations represent the different stages of the Muslim community, with Mecca being associated with the initial stage of proselytization, while Medina is the city where the community gained political power. Thus the Meccan verses tend to focus more on the theological and spiritual elements of the faith, and the Medinan ones stress the legal and social dimensions of the community. Nevertheless, there is a great deal of overlap between the Meccan and Medinan verses, and many chapters contain verses from both locations.

The Qur'an is unlike the Bible's narrative prose sections in that it is structured in rhymed prose. For the most part, the Qur'an does not rely on narrative but rather sound and poetic imagery. The Prophet Muhammad and his Companions would recite portions of the Qur'an in liturgical services as well as to potential converts. After the Prophet's death, the Companions began the process of writing down and canonizing the Scripture.

The Qur'an is further marked by different readings (*qirā'āt*) of the text. These readings represent the dialects of the various Arab tribes, and they give subtle differences in meaning. For instance, in the opening chapter (*al-Fātiḥa*), a verse that speaks of God as the "master (*mālik*) of the Day of Judgment" can also be read as "king (*malik*) of the Day of Judgment." The sciences of the Qur'an (see below) also record various non-canonical verses (*shādh*) that were recited by early Companions of the Prophet but are not supported by the canonical text.

The word "Qur'an" means "recitation" or "reading," which highlights the oral nature of the text. Islamic tradition maintains that the Qur'an was revealed in Arabic, allowing the Arabs to fathom its message (12:2). While many translations of the Qur'an are available, especially in the modern period, these translations are considered only as interpretations. The original Arabic continues to be understood as "the Qur'an," and many Muslims try to learn Arabic to better appreciate its contents.

The Qur'an sees itself as a continuation of previous divine books from the Torah to the New Testament (*Injīl*). This is one of the reasons why the Qur'an speaks of itself as a "book" (*kitāb*), even though it was originally a series of oral revelations. The notion of "book" also expresses the unified message of the Qur'an's contents.

The Qur'an's central message is to reform and revive aspects of earlier monotheism and set the parameters for a righteous community. The Qur'an calls for absolute monotheism, in which God is distinct from His creation (42:11). The text describes God as living, all-powerful, omniscient, yet all-merciful and kind. God does not rest, tire, or sleep (2:255). He possesses the entire universe, and everything is subject to His control and will (67:1). If all the trees were pens and the oceans ink, they would not be able to encompass God's words, for God is all-mighty and wise (31:27).

Thus the Qur'an condemns the idea of associating (*shirk*) God's distinct nature with other beings since it distracts from his exclusive position. As a consequence, the Qur'an distances itself from the notion of Jesus being divine or the "Son of God." Rather, Jesus is repeatedly mentioned as the "son of Mary" and hence a human being and righteous prophet. For instance, in one eschatological verse God asks Jesus if he had ever called on people to worship him and Jesus responds, "May You be exalted! I would never say what I had no right to say—if I had said any such thing You would have known it. You know all that is within me, though I do not know what is within You. You alone have full knowledge of things unseen." The qur'anic Jesus adds that he only preached to his people the message to "worship God, my Lord and your Lord" (5:116). Jesus is therefore similar to Muhammad, who was commanded to say, "I am only a human being, like you, to whom it has been revealed that your God is One. Anyone who fears to meet his Lord should do good deeds and give no one a share of worship due to his Lord" (18:190). God sent human Prophets from Adam to Muhammad, including Jesus, to call humanity to worship only Him.

Another predominant aspect of the Qur'an is its emphasis on the Day of Judgment and the hereafter. The Qur'an stresses individual accountability where humans will have to testify for their faith and actions (39:7). The Qur'an therefore spends a considerable amount of time convincing humanity that judgment will occur and that resurrection at the end of time is possible. The Qur'an, for instance, explains that God created humans from a mere drop of sperm that became a blood clot and finally human beings, both male and female. The Qur'an then asks, "Does He who can do this not have the power to bring the dead back to life?" (75:40). Just as God has the capability to create humans from a mere sperm, He has the power to resurrect them.

Those who are judged worthy will be rewarded with paradise, and those who are not will be punished with hellfire. The Qur'an describes paradise as a place of eternal bliss, filled with gardens, rivers, and virtuous company. Hell, in contrast, is a place of painful punishment, full of fire, torture, and evil companionship. While the people in heaven praise and thank God for the reward of paradise, the inhabitants of hell are remorseful over their evil actions and are dejected over their final abode. The graphic descriptions of heaven and hell are meant to inspire belief and righteousness while warning of the consequences of disbelief and corruption. As the Qur'an asks, "Should we treat those who submit to Us as We treat those who do evil?" (68:35). Those who submit to God will be rewarded with paradise, while those who engage in evil will be recompensed with hellfire.

Use

The Qur'an is regularly used in Muslim religious life and practice. Muslims are required to recite the opening chapter (*al-Fātiḥa*) in their daily prayers, as well as some other additional verses of their choice. Certain chapters in the Qur'an are recommended to be recited in weekly Friday prayers, such as the chapter titled "The Congregation" (62, *al-Jum'a*), which legislates Friday prayer. In Ramadan, the holy month of fasting, many Muslims try to recite the entire Qur'an or attend supererogatory prayers (*tarāwīḥ*) where the prayer leader (*Imām*) attempts to recite the entire text over the course of the month. In these communal settings, the prayer leader recites the Qur'an orally while the followers listen to the recitation. The Imam is usually a trained specialist in qur'anic recitation who has either memorized the entire Qur'an or large portions of it. In these individual and communal settings, the Qur'an continues to be read in its original Arabic, highlighting the enormous importance of the language in Islamic liturgy.

Outside of Ramadan, Muslims may also attempt to read parts or the entire Qur'an while reflecting on its meanings and trying to implement its teachings. The idea of reading the entire Qur'an (*khatm*) was the practice of the early community, and there are different scholarly opinions on how long it should take, ranging from one week to a year. Traditionally, the Qur'an is read on special occasions such as marriages, events celebrating the birth of a child (*'aqīqa*), and funerals. While there are no specific religious texts prescribing the recitation of the Qur'an at these functions, Muslims often read the Qur'an in these ceremonies to obtain its wisdom and blessing.

The Qur'an is further used extensively in Islamic art and architecture. Islam developed the concept of aniconism whereby depictions of human figures were shunned to avoid the community falling into polytheism (*shirk*). As a result, calligraphy became a very

In Islamic understanding, only the original Arabic text is truly the Qur'an; a translation is merely an interpretation. This manuscript copy exhibits the decorative geometric patterns and calligraphy that are hallmarks of Islamic art.

important aspect of Islamic art, with the Qur'an being beautifully displayed in manuscripts, ceramics, palaces, and mosques.

Interpretation

The qur'anic codex is remarkably similar across Islam's various sects and schools of thought. While they may recite the Qur'an differently, Muslims generally read from the same qur'anic text. The theological differences among the various groups appear less in the Qur'an itself than in the rich tradition of qur'anic commentary (*tafsīr*). Similar to Jewish midrash, the *tafsīr* literature presents a line-by-line explanation of the Qur'an that elucidates the scripture's message and explains difficult passages. Qur'anic exegetes vary in how they interpret the Qur'an, with some emphasizing Arabic language and linguistics, and others traditions associated with the Prophet and the early community. In essence, *tafsīr* represents the believers' attempt to understand the divine word and reflect on how it continues to be relevant through time and place.

Various Islamic movements employ *tafsīr* to justify their creeds and political aspirations. For instance, the two largest sects within Islam, the Sunnis and Shi'is, use *tafsīr* to promote their contrasting doctrines. Shi'is contend the Qur'an supports the succession of the Prophet Muhammad's cousin and son-in-law 'Ali after Muhammad's death, and they point to verses such as "Obey God and obey the messenger and those in authority among you"(4:59) to justify this idea. Shi'i exegetes interpret "those in authority among you" as referring to 'Ali, his sons Hasan and Husayn, and the subsequent Shi'i spiritual leaders (Imams). Sunni exegetes, in contrast, have interpreted the same verse as referring to the first and second caliphs, Abu Bakr and 'Umar, and the rulers selected by the larger Muslim community.

Tafsīr also incorporates non-canonical verses and uses them to provide possible explanations of the text. For instance, verse 5:89 gives one of the expiations for breaking an oath as fasting "three days." Some non-canonical readings add the word "consecutively" (*mutatābi'āt*) to the verse, requiring the believer to fast "three days consecutively" rather than at different times.

In modern times, qur'anic commentaries have taken a more thematic approach by focusing on contemporary issues such as the role of women or interfaith relations. These qur'anic works analyze a group of verses dealing with a specific issue and then summarize the scripture's view regarding the topic.

Another genre to develop in Islamic history was that of the sciences of the Qur'an (*'ulūm al-Qur'ān*). The sciences of the Qur'an literature summarizes the various qur'anic disciplines, such as its language, structure, and compilation. Islamic seminaries incorporate science of the Qur'an manuals into their curriculums to help students better understand the Qur'an's history and its ancillary disciplines.

DISCUSSION QUESTIONS

1. What are some of the most striking similarities regarding the ways that Jews, Christians, and Muslims use and interpret their sacred texts? What impact might these similarities have on relations among members of the three faiths?

2. What are some of the most striking differences regarding the ways that Jews, Christians, and Muslims use and interpret their sacred texts? What impact might these differences have on relations among members of the three faiths?

FOR FURTHER STUDY

Brettler, Marc Zvi. *How to Read the Jewish Bible.* New York: Oxford University Press, 2007.

Cragg, Kenneth. *A Certain Sympathy of Scriptures: Biblical and Qur'anic.* Brighton, UK: Sussex Academic Press, 2004.

Ipgrave, Michael, ed. *Scriptures in Dialogue: Christians and Muslims Studying the Bible and the Qur'an Together.* London: Church House Publishing, 2004.

Kaltner, John. *Introducing the Qur'an: For Today's Reader.* Minneapolis: Fortress, 2011.

Lodahl, Michael. *Claiming Abraham: Reading the Bible and the Qur'an Side by Side.* Grand Rapids: Brazos Press, 2010.

Mattson, Ingrid. *The Story of the Qur'an: Its History and Place in Muslim Life.* 2nd ed. Malden, MA: Wiley-Blackwell, 2103.

Sommer, Benjamin D. *Jewish Concepts of Scripture: A Comparative Introduction.* New York: NYU Press, 2012.

Zetterholm, Karin Hender. *Jewish Interpretation of the Bible: Ancient and Contemporary.* Minneapolis: Fortress Press, 2012.

8

Theological Reading of the Bible

Patricia K. Tull

Becoming acquainted with the Bible may be compared to approaching a new city. The closer one comes, the more complex the detail. From a plane window, even Manhattan's tallest buildings appear tiny. The island seems self-contained, skyscrapers delimiting Central Park's green rectangle, themselves bounded by the blue Hudson and Harlem Rivers and the East River estuary. From the sky all appears unified, quiet, settled. But on the ground, up close, complexities appear: construction sites, traffic jams, boarded buildings, people in business attire passing people in ragged garments on every sidewalk. Sounds overlap: buses, horns, jackhammers, music, voices. Paradoxes appear: the city is both new and old, both cosmopolitan and insular, both wildly wealthy and grindingly poor. It is possible to examine ever more closely: sidewalk cracks, weeds, roots, nematodes, molecules. But one sees best on a human scale.

Similarly, the more carefully one reads the Bible, the more complex and paradoxical it appears. Standing back to survey the whole landscape yields general understanding: Scripture appears bounded by its two covers, delimited by its table of contents. Examining a passage verse by verse yields a multitude of complex minutiae. Interpretation is usually managed, however, on the scale of a passage ten to twenty verses long, connected with other nearby or similar passages.

Readers find complexity in Scripture's landscape, whose many layers and landmarks were developed by countless writers, most of whose names and lives are forgotten. Complexity imbues the project of reading an ancient book that was not written for the contemporary world at all, and of ferreting out understandings relevant to ever-shifting cultural milieus. For persons of faith, hearing divine communication through words that are not only ancient but human involves both theological and interpretive complexity.

Many Christians believe they ought to know the Bible better, but find the prospect intimidating. They may respect Scripture's authority, and may read it carefully, hoping for clear direction. Yet they face obstacles informational (what is this strange ritual?), ethical (why divine violence?), cosmological (must one believe in demons?), and literary (why these genealogies?). Even familiar Gospel narratives raise moral and existential questions some hesitate to ask. Dashed hopes for easy enlightenment may only discourage more.

Readers perceive correctly that understanding Scripture is difficult. Like a foreign language—which it is, both literally and figuratively—Scripture can never be fully mastered. At the same time, Scripture can reward even beginning readers who learn the basics about its origins, settings, contexts, and contents, and it can continue to yield discovery for a lifetime. Indeed, the questions Scripture raises and the ethical dilemmas it provokes are as much a part of the enterprise of theological reading as is the wisdom it provides.

Reading Scripture is aided by knowledge of historical and sociological backgrounds underlying its various parts. A reliable study Bible can provide preliminary information. To delve deeper, it is helpful to learn major events, names, and concepts assumed by biblical writers, assisted by histories, commentaries, and Bible dictionaries.

But it is not enough to fill in the background behind the Bible. Imaginative empathy for the perspectives of ancient writers can deepen understanding. Setting aside, at least to some extent, expectations about how the Bible ought to speak, readers may approach it as one would approach a person one would like to know better—with interest and curiosity.

Scripture's Own Practices

Scripture's own rhetorical methods and areas of concern can guide readers. The Bible is built on narrative, as is evident from the first three words of Genesis, "In the beginning," and from the Bible's various conclusions—for Jews the end of 2 Chronicles, "Let him go up!" and for Christians the end of Revelation, "Come, Lord Jesus." It begins with God as the fountainhead of time. Yet it is more ray than segment, geometrically speaking, since it does not conclude with some past event, but rather points forward toward sequels unfolding beyond its own limits. Throughout, Scripture proceeds as literature, by dramatic unfolding, by metaphorical speech used to represent God and human life in the presence of God, and by an evolving panoply of expressions that draw from, augment, and even overturn previous expressions found within its own pages.

Much may be learned from Scripture about ancient geography, history, technology, sociology, and politics. The Bible, however, does not train attention on diversions readers might find entertaining, such as what angels look like or how many of them can dance on the head of a pin, nor even on how Moses parted the waters (see Exod. 14:21–29) or how Jesus walked on them (see Mark 6:45–52), nor on what finally became of the Ark of the Covenant or the Apostle Paul. Nor does it attend to other questions that occupy moderns, such as how exactly the universe originated, when precisely the world will end, or how, in the meantime, to gain happiness by becoming wealthy or even by assembling a comprehensive, systematic theology. Rather, Scripture tells complex stories of humans bound in relationship to God and to the created world, including other humans. It offers responses to perennial problems such as injustice, violence, natural disaster, disappointment, sickness, and bereavement. It explores the contours of family, work, service, and faith. It seeks to build fortitude, hope, and trust in the good intentions of the Creator. It offers case studies of self-seeking to be avoided, and templates of lovingkindness to emulate. The Bible is not systematic. Rather it is situational, pastoral, and relational.

Scripture's great themes unfold in dramatic loops and swerves. Central to these are, in the Hebrew Bible, exile and return, danger and rescue, enslavement and freedom, chaos and order, despair and unexpected deliverance. The New Testament follows this dramatic trajectory, telling of crucifixion and resurrection, suffering and redemption, persecution and vindication, apocalyptic battle and new creation. Throughout, the Bible displays strong preference not for endless cycles of either harm or good, but for reversal, threats that often, though not always, dissolve into renewed well-being for humans and creation.

Theological Authority

The Bible may be read for a variety of reasons—such as to find historical information, aesthetic enjoyment, or cultural understanding. Christians and Jews read Scripture because they view it as carrying theological authority not only for ancient communities, but for themselves as contemporary believers. They read the Bible for insight into who God is, who human beings are, and how humans are meant to live in the created world, how they are challenged to serve God. As biblical scholar Phyllis Bird says, Scripture "lays demands on its hearers—for the ordering of community, family, and individual life—but it also provides the means to fulfill those demands."[1]

Paul writes an epistle in this ninth-century manuscript illumination from the Monastery of St. Gallen. Christians believe that the writings of the Apostle Paul are sacred Scripture, which raises a theological question: In what sense can a human author's words also be "God's word"?

---

1. Phyllis Bird, "The Authority of the Bible," in *The New Interpreter's Bible*, ed. Leander E. Keck et al. (Nashville: Abingdon, 1994), 1:40.

The vast majority of believers would assert that Scripture, though inspired, is also the product of human authors, with all that that implies. Moreover, these human authors were shaped by cultural and historical contexts far removed from the modern world. Consequently, it is reasonable to ask why contemporary believers view the Bible as authoritative at all. Why not simply attend to the most recent wisdom of theologians and spiritual leaders, just as one would normally consult up-to-date medical or scientific knowledge rather than ancient Greek texts?

The biblical texts themselves offer precedents for receiving the words of human beings as a message from God, and ancient words as authoritative for later readers. Exodus 20 and Deuteronomy 5 narrate God's proclaiming the Ten Commandments in a voice heard by all, and God's own finger recording these words on two stone tablets.[2] Both stories say, however, that the frightened Israelites wanted to keep their distance, and insisted that Moses mediate God's will to them from that time on. Moses' speeches in Deuteronomy also collapse time, characterizing words from the past as being directed toward later peoples. Moses tells the generation born in the wilderness years after the giving of the commandments that they themselves had been present at the holy mountain to receive God's words. In the same sentence he instructs them to pass these words to their own children (Deut. 4:9–10). Thus he telescopes both past and future, rendering these mediated commandments transgenerational, if not timeless.

The history of biblical illustration also gives precedent for receiving human words as a message from God. Most biblical texts, taken at face value, contain little to suggest that they were written to be read as authoritative words—or even to be read at all—by generations far in the future. Many passages began as folk tales, romances, spiritual or even secular poetry, pragmatic proverbs, verbal rebuke, or encouragement for particular people, family genealogies, memoirs, or letters to specific communities. The idea of Scripture as theological authority evolved over time, as writings that were valued by succeeding generations continued to be copied, compiled, preserved, and revered.

---

2. Bird, "Authority of the Bible," 39. The two accounts appear to disagree on the intelligibility of God's voice to the people. Exodus 20:18–19 implies the people did not hear a voice, but only thunder and trumpet blasts, but Deut. 4:12 says they heard words.

Throughout this development, cultural shifts and lost information rendered some of these ancient writings increasingly difficult to understand. Even before the first century CE, the Jewish Scriptures seemed filled with cryptic messages in need of decoding. Members of the Qumran community, for instance, compiled commentaries on the prophets in which they creatively applied the ancient words directly, line by line, to their own events and leaders. According to the commentary on Habakkuk found at Qumran (1Q pHab), for instance, the ancient prophet was referring directly to struggles unfolding between the community's leader—called the Teacher of Righteousness—and his enemy, the Wicked Priest. The Qumran sectarians seem to have taken for granted that Scripture speaks to them about matters close to home. To what extent they thought the ancient prophets specifically or exclusively foretold their circumstances is not clear.

The Gospel of Matthew similarly quotes from or alludes to at least ten passages from throughout the Old Testament in the nativity story alone, applying them directly to Jesus' birth in a manner that defies modern standards of exegesis. For instance, Matthew 2:15 cites Hosea 11:1 as a reference to Jesus, though in its original context it self-evidently refers to the nation of Israel. Extracting these resources from Scripture's vast mines, Matthew claims that these various ancient words are fulfilled in Jesus' story. The Apostle Paul likewise redeploys Scripture to meet contemporary needs. For instance, he quotes Deuteronomy 25:4, "You shall not muzzle an ox while it is treading out the grain," a stricture against frustrating the animal's need for nourishment while working. He introduces this passage to clinch his argument for his own compensation, saying, "Is it for oxen that God is concerned? Or does he not speak entirely for our sake?" (1 Cor. 9:9–10). First Peter 1:10–12, the New Testament's most assertive claim of this nature, announces boldly, perhaps even brashly, that the ancient prophets did not comprehend their own words, since these were meant not for their own times but for the far future.[3]

---

3. Fred C. Craddock observes, "It is one thing to say an Old Testament writer addressed his own generation in ways that spoke anew to Christians later, and quite another to say the writer spoke over the heads of his contemporaries to address persons in a far distant future. These words from 1 Peter push the modern reader to think through this most vital issue because it is not purely academic; Jewish-Christians relationships are implied and imbedded here, as well as how one reads both testaments" (*First and Second Peter and Jude*, WBC 53 [Louisville: Westminster John Knox, 1995], 26–27).

Early mainstream Judaism also found ways to assimilate and contemporize the biblical message. For instance, the rabbinic writers of the *Babylonian Talmud* inherited a book of Psalms that ascribes to King David numerous psalms that clearly referred to events centuries after his death, a problem rational interpreters, ancient or modern, would wish to resolve. Psalm 137, which begins, "By the rivers of Babylon," records the anguish of sixth-century BCE exiles following Jerusalem's destruction. How could David have written it? One Rabbi Yehuda solved the puzzle boldly: David could obviously foresee the future, not only the Babylonian destruction of the First Temple, but also the Roman destruction of the Second Temple in 70 CE, since by "Edomites" (v. 7), David meant "Romans."[4]

In short, early Christians and Jews alike held that the ancient Scriptures reliably transmitted divine messages to their generation—messages in a bottle, so to speak, to be teased out by creative interpretation.[5]

Biblical interpretation today struggles with these ancient assumptions. Protestant fundamentalists tend to agree with the first conviction, upholding scriptural consistency, accuracy, divine origin, and applicability. But they tend to deny that interpretation is necessary, because they believe that Scripture speaks clearly and literally to people today.

Christian non-fundamentalists reverse these emphases. Mainstream interpreters increasingly acknowledge Scripture's polyphony, that is, its multiple and sometimes competing testimonies concerning not only theology but even events. Kings and Chronicles narrate the same events differently. Two flood narratives intertwine in Genesis 6–8, offering discrepant details. Even the four Gospels tell distinct stories impossible to harmonize fully.

Mainstream Christian interpreters also recognize the role of human writers in Scripture's origin and development, finding God's word directed toward themselves not literally on the pages of an inerrant text, but in the witness of the Holy Spirit speaking through Scripture, the interaction of text and reader, or the contemporary

---

4. *Babylonian Talmud*, *Gittin* 57b, quoted in James Kugel, *In Potiphar's House: The Interpretive Life of Biblical Texts* (San Francisco: HarperSanFrancisco, 1990), 174–75.

5. James Kugel, *How to Read the Bible: A Guide to Scripture, Then and Now* (New York: Free Press, 2007), 14–16.

preaching of the word. Thus they differ with both ancient assumptions and modern fundamentalist claims concerning Scripture's consistency and divine origins. On the other hand, mainstream Christian interpreters agree with the ancients that the Bible requires interpretation. They tend to use more disciplined interpretive methods, and allow that while Scripture speaks to people today, it also spoke to people in times past, and will not be exhausted before the next generation comes along. Still, modern readers recognize that interpretation is as much art as science, and outcomes are affected by readers' as well as by writers' settings.

A Dialogical Approach

Some modern readers, troubled by the Bible's competing testimonies, feel compelled to downplay or even to deny the divergences. Yet if those who canonized Scripture preferred to retain two distinct creation narratives and four distinct Resurrection accounts, for example, modern readers may find positive value in recognizing the variations and appreciating what each offers. Genesis 1 places humans in close relationship to the land animals who appear immediately prior to them, whereas Genesis 2 emphasizes human dependence on the soil out of which human beings were formed. Mark emphasizes the terror the messenger inspired at the tomb, while the other three Gospels elaborate stories of unbelief, recognition, and revelation.

Diversity of not only fact but theological viewpoint likewise fills the Bible, even on central matters such as the nature of deity, the inclusion of outsiders, and the meaning of suffering and evil. The book of Proverbs, for instance, claims that human virtue is reliably rewarded in this life, but Job's story refutes such a view and teases out injustices that Proverbs ignores. Failure to negotiate divergences between Proverbs and Job would force readers to diminish these differences or to discount one viewpoint or the other. But placing Proverbs and Job side by side awakens fuller appreciation of both the gains and the limits of human effort, and of the magnitude of sin, suffering, and hope in human experience.

Just as two eyes can see stereoscopically, and two ears can better pinpoint sources of sound, recognizing variety in the viewpoints contributing to Scripture opens a perspective on its rich depth. Such complexity may not have been intended by any one writer, but

The naming of the animals, shown here in the Aberdeen Bestiary (twelfth century), occurs in only one of the two Genesis creation accounts. The Bible does not attempt to reconcile the two accounts; instead, it places them side by side, in dialogue with each other.

believers find it authorized by the tradition that retained multiple accounts side by side, impeding all attempts to place ultimate trust in any "tamed" truth—that is, in anything less than the Almighty "I AM WHO I AM" (Exod. 3:14). James Sanders attributes the Bible's durability, in fact, to its "essential diversity, its inherent refusal to absolutize any single stance as the only place where one might live under the sovereignty of God."[6]

6. James A. Sanders, *Torah and Canon* (Eugene, OR: Wipf & Stock, 1999; orig. pub. 1972), 116.

The dialogical spaces opened within Scripture invite readers to consider how to negotiate the distance between Scripture and themselves. Not only do biblical passages themselves differ, but modern readers find some texts more appealing than others. Christians can neither dismiss nor accept the Bible *in toto*. Many Christian readers try to bypass this problem by revering the New Testament, with its "God of love," while dismissing the Old Testament, with its "God of wrath."[7] But closer reading reveals, first, that both Testaments are shot through with speech that delights as well as speech that appalls, and second, that what appears promising and what appears problematic can be indivisibly intertwined.

Taking cues from the Bible's own inner dialogues, readers can regard interpretation as an engaged conversation between biblical writers in their own ancient settings and contemporary readers in theirs. Both ends of this conversation are fruitfully robust. Readers are not helped by passivity, checking their brains at Scripture's doorway, nor by approaching Scripture as if it were a dead specimen to be analyzed. Instead of practicing either passive submission to a domineering Scripture or disinterested dissection of an inert text, readers can interact with Scripture and its writers in what Martin Buber called an "I-Thou" relationship.

Buber viewed dialogue as the primary means of human knowing. Invoking Buber, Michael Signer adds, "The Bible is, in Hebrew, *Miqra*, 'that which calls out or exclaims.' It can be understood only by the reader who is to become a partner in the dialogue, one who expects the text to be as relevant today as it was to previous generations."[8] In such a relationship, readers proceed with awareness of their own subjectivity and autonomy, and with awareness of the subjectivity and autonomy, in their own times and places, of scriptural writers. Readers discover truths in relationship—in the dialogue the biblical writers and canonizers already created by placing so many different voices side by side, and in the dialogue they carry on with biblical writers. Reading Scripture with empathetic

---

7. In an extreme form, this is the heresy of Marcionism, named after a second-century bishop who rejected the Old Testament and claimed that the God who inspired it was not the same as the God whom Jesus called his Father.

8. Michael A. Signer, "How the Bible Has Been Interpreted in Jewish Tradition," in Keck et al., eds., *The New Interpreter's Bible*, 1:80.

attention to thoughts generously shared, readers learn better who these ancient people were, what they cared about, what befell them and how they evaluated it, what they aspired to, and how they understood themselves to have experienced God. Readers find insight not only by considering key figures, but also by recreating the perspectives and imagining the experience of writers. Exploring the world through their eyes, and then returning to themselves with the insight gained thereby, persons of faith may see their own spiritual journeys more clearly.

Finding the Middle Distance

To engage in such dialogue is to stand at a middle distance from Scripture, not imagining that one can fully identify with its writers, nor that one can handily reject their views. Peter Gomes emphasizes the importance of taking the Bible seriously enough to read it carefully. Not to read it at all, or to set it aside when reading becomes challenging, is to fail to honor what it offers. But to attempt to read it too literally and prescriptively, bracketing out or ignoring the writers' literary skill, subtlety, cultural setting, writing practices, and theological and ethical assumptions, likewise constitutes a failure to take it on its own terms. Gomes warns persons of faith against three temptations, here treated as two:[9]

"Worship of the Bible, making it the object of veneration and giving it the glory due to God," and "worship of the text, in which the letter is given an inappropriate superiority over the spirit," both make idols of Scripture and its words. As Bird points out, the Bible "points beyond itself to God, whose purposes and nature are never fully or finally expressed in historical communications."[10]

"Worship of the [present] culture, in which the Bible is forced to conform to the norms of the prevailing culture," makes an idol of the present generation. When one's personal norms dominate one's thinking, and don't allow Scripture to interrogate them, one might as well not read at all.

---

9. Peter Gomes, *The Good Book: Reading the Bible with Mind and Heart* (New York: HarperCollins, 1996), 36.

10. Bird, "Authority of the Bible," 63.

These temptations amount to making one cultural setting and its assumptions normative, measuring the other with a foreign yardstick.

Modern people are fundamentally unable to adopt ancient cultural norms to the abandonment of their own. People are products of their culture, immersed in an ethos as ubiquitous as the air they breathe. If they cannot become natives by visiting another country—no matter how long they stay—much less can they adopt as their own an ancient culture that no modern person can visit for even a moment. At most they can only imagine they are doing so, while retaining their own unexamined assumptions. One might as well wear a flannel bathrobe and call it shepherd's clothing as imagine that one has sufficient cultural knowledge to adopt the Bible's norms.

Yet despite these limitations, empathetic readers may find unexpected insight, just as travelers to foreign lands can return with keener insight about their own cultural assumptions. North Americans may take consumerism for granted until visiting a place that is less economically driven. Many people may not recognize their own prejudices until they meet people who do not share them, or who have different, surprising prejudices. Similarly, glimpsing Scripture's norms often opens questions about one's own. Sometimes, acknowledging the differences, readers may prefer to retain their own values, and may wish to "talk back" to scriptural claims. At other times they may find themselves challenged to "listen in," and to try on something else.

Talking Back

An example of the first scenario, a valid preference for wisdom in contemporary culture, may be found in reactions to the Bible's treatment of women—or often, its lack of treatment. Patriarchal assumptions, accompanied by failure to perceive women's skills and to honor their gifts, are widespread in both testaments of the Bible. The world is rarely seen through women's eyes. Seldom does one witness two women conversing, and almost never, for instance, a mother and daughter. Disobedient Israel, deserving of degrading punishment, is compared to a cheating wife, but not to a cheating husband. The few points where women are portrayed more positively do not overcome scriptural patriarchy so much as underscore its dominance. Biblical

© Catacomb of Via Latina, Rome, Italy / The Bridgeman Art Library

This fresco from the catacombs of Rome illustrates a scene from John 4 in which Jesus converses with a Samaritan woman—shocking his disciples. Most biblical texts reinforce the patriarchal assumptions of ancient society, but some, like this one, undermine them.

attitudes toward women inspire questions about the assumptions of both the biblical writers and Christian interpreters. Parallel issues arise when one encounters many scriptural writers' views of slavery, and of human and divine violence.

Readers must first examine whether, in each case, their problem is with the ancient text itself or with its traditional interpretation. Genesis 3, for instance, does not fault Eve more than Adam, nor does it call her evil, manipulative, gullible, or greedy. But subsequent interpretation, beginning even in biblical times, found it convenient to blame Eve (see, for instance, Sir. 25:24). From a modern perspective, today's reader may find elements in the story that earlier readers could not see.

But sometimes it becomes impossible to assent to a biblical passage's message. Reclaiming the text by ignoring or interpreting away its scandal may be tempting. But the more honest decision to grant

Scripture freedom to differ fundamentally from the modern reader, and to grant oneself the latitude to differ with ancient writers, can enrich contemporary theological thinking. Given the Bible's multiplicity, it is often the Bible itself that inspires objections to particular texts. Problematic scriptural claims challenge readers to explore why they are disturbed. Have these texts been employed in support of injustices? Are there parallel situations today? While many people may be tempted to reject or ignore biblical passages that promote patriarchy or violence, there is value in working through a text's troubling features.[11]

Listening In

Examples of the second scenario, of scriptural challenges to the contemporary status quo that may edify, are prevalent as well. For instance, wide gaps have evolved between biblical and contemporary understandings of economy and ecology. The law of the Jubilee Year, with its underlying assumptions that all land belongs to God and that large-scale economic redistribution refreshes community health, challenges modern views of land ownership (see Lev. 25). Other Sinai laws concerning responsibility to society's vulnerable people underscore the insight that the natural resources humans enjoy are entrusted for stewardship, not bestowed as largesses. Jesus' sayings about the impossibility of serving both God and wealth (Matt. 6:24) dispute the gospel of economic growth, and his admonition to "consider the lilies" (Matt. 6:28–29), trusting God's provision for daily needs, calls the widespread practice of hoarding into question. One cannot take such passages seriously without examining their distance from economic assumptions common today.

Less widely recognized are the distinct understandings Scripture offers regarding the place of humans in creation. Especially in the past few centuries, as human power to exploit the earth's resources has multiplied, readers have zeroed in on three verses—Genesis 1:26–28—as if they were the sum total of the Bible's teaching about

---

11. An especially helpful treatment of such issues may be found in Julia M. O'Brien, *Challenging Prophetic Metaphor: Theology and Ideology in the Prophets* (Louisville: Westminster John Knox, 2008).

the natural world. An incomplete reading of this passage has led people throughout the ages to assume that God had given people license to dominate and exploit, mine and discard, use up and pollute every resource in the natural world. And indeed, Western readers have at times interpreted the idea that humans are made in the image of God as suggesting not simply that all people possess equal worth in God's eyes, but that human beings—though created of the same elements as the rest of God's creatures—are somehow more like God than like other creatures, vice-regents surrounded by subjects. The very next verse, however, demonstrates that human beings are on the same footing as God's other creatures by asserting that God gives the world's food not to human beings alone but to all animals. Similarly, God commands all creatures to be fruitful and multiply, and throughout the creation account God repeatedly expresses delight in all created things.

A distorted reading of Genesis 1:26–28 ignores not only 90 percent of Genesis 1 but the rest of Scripture overall, which views humans as creatures subject to the wild forces of nature, and which is populated by a host of other creatures in whom God delights, whose interests and needs God favors. Scriptural writers' closeness to nature, to agriculture, and to the dangers of the wild embued them with operating assumptions very different from those of the present day, assumptions from which the modern reader may benefit.

In short, for people of faith, ancient Scripture "always seems to have the remarkable ability to become the locus of people's deepest inner fumblings and mumblings: those words suddenly contain so much . . . they become the theater of the soul."[12] Modern readers enter this theater through examining Scripture both critically and empathically, grappling with its complexity, antiquity, and foreign sensibilities, with its own visions of the holy, and with modern disagreements over interpretive practices. Persons of faith are rewarded by finding ancient companions in the shared vocation of serving God.

---

12. Kugel, *How to Read the Bible*, 688.

DISCUSSION QUESTIONS

1. How is reading Scripture similar to reading a foreign language?
2. As discussed above, there are some passages in Scripture in which the biblical author interprets earlier Scriptures and applies them to his own day. What do these examples contribute to the question of how to read the Bible today?
3. Readers often feel that the diversity of positions found in the various parts of Scripture constitutes a problem, but the author suggests such diversity has positive value. Do you agree? Explain.
4. What is meant by having a "dialogue" with Scripture? How does this approach contribute to the reader's understanding?
5. What does the author mean by "talking back" to Scripture? What does the author mean by "listening in"?

FOR FURTHER STUDY

Bird, Phyllis. "The Authority of the Bible," in *The New Interpreter's Bible*, edited by Leander E. Keck et al., 1:33–64. Nashville: Abingdon, 1994.

Gomes, Peter. *The Good Book: Reading the Bible with Mind and Heart.* New York: HarperCollins, 1996.

Kugel, James. *How to Read the Bible: A Guide to Scripture, Then and Now.* New York: Free Press, 2007.

O'Brien, Julia M. *Challenging Prophetic Metaphor: Theology and Ideology in the Prophets.* Louisville: Westminster John Knox, 2008.

Part 2

The Old Testament

9

The Social World of Ancient Israel

John J. Ahn and Corrine L. Carvalho

The social worlds that lie behind the Jewish Scriptures varied greatly over the long history of ancient Israel. These documents testify to different social formations, such as the transition from a tribal system to a monarchy. Often the texts also reflect the social contexts of their elite authors, especially in the periods during and following the exile (587 BCE). As a result, even texts that describe the glories of the monarchy often do so through the lens of the collapse of that society.

The social structures of this ancient world can be divided into at least five different, although interconnected, systems: pastoral nomads, tribal patriarchy, monarchy, forced migration, and colonization. The Israelites tend to attach the first three to specific periods of their history, while the last two better describe the social worlds of the biblical authors.

Pastoral Nomads in Genesis

The depiction of the generations from Abraham to Jacob suggests that Israel went through what sociologists call a pastoral nomadic stage. Pastoral nomads own little land themselves, following their herds to various open pastures, but their livelihood depends on commerce with cities and other settled areas. Their economic role in the larger society is based on products associated with sheep and goats (dairy products, wool, and occasionally meat). These groups are based on a tightly interdependent household structure led by a male who both governs and protects the group.

In this Egyptian mural from about 1890 BCE, the colorfully clothed figures represent Semitic traders. According to the biblical account, the ancient Israelites believed that their ancestors had been semi-nomads like the traders depicted here.

For many decades of biblical studies, scholars were split on whether the earliest Israelites were nomadic or settled. Then anthropological studies of nomadism noted that certain ancient groups of people exhibited different types of nomadism, with varying relationships to settled cities and agriculturists.[1] Such groups traditionally were more settled during the agricultural cycle, but when the cycle ended they would move about from place to place with their herds. The Genesis accounts seem to be describing people who followed this pattern. When the season was not ripe for farming, they practiced nomadic pastoralism, venturing from location to location.

The Israelites associated this social structure with their distant past, the period of Abraham and his offspring. In part, these stories contributed to the Israelites' consistent depiction of themselves as a group that originated in some land outside of Israel (for Abraham, Ur of the Chaldeans or Mesopotamia). The description of their life

---

1. See, e.g., M. Rowton, "Enclosed Nomadism," *Journal of the Economic and Social History of the Orient*, 17, no. 1 (March 1974): 1–30.

probably reflects the authors' own experience of nomadic groups more accurately than the lifestyle of their distant ancestors. That experience probably shaped the recording of various oral stories, which were attached to specific places, rituals, and traditions. In these biblical stories, the groups were named after an important ancestor. They worshiped a clan-like god, sometimes associated with household gods (Gen. 31:19), at portable sanctuaries that they carried with them. Remnants of this pastoral period persisted in the tribal system that formed the basis of Israelite society even after there was a settled monarchy.

Tribes of Israel

The Israelite texts traditionally list twelve tribes or kinship groups that descended from Jacob, which populated the settled areas of Israel. The biblical traditions connect these tribes with the basic social structure of the pastoral nomads. An Israelite tribe is a family or kinship group that traces its origins to a male ancestor from whom the group takes its name. The tribal leader is usually (but not always) an elite male, who is able to make decisions for the group (and is thus called a "judge"), and also to defend the tribe.

The similarities between tribal and pastoral nomadic societies mask significant differences, however. Most significantly, the tribes of Israel were settled, meaning that their economic base was agriculture. Tribes owned land, and that land was distributed among the males who were enlisted in that tribe's genealogy. As a settled group, they were also able to develop more complex products dependent on a class of skilled workers. Their family groups were no longer so tightly bound to each other, and therefore were both larger and more fluid, better equipped to adapt to outsiders.

In addition, as economic production increased, cities could develop. The Israelites, like their neighbors, viewed cities as the height of social development. Walled cities offered protection from invaders, provided a center for commerce and business, and served as religious centers for outlying areas. They were generally administrative centers, not centers of mass population like modern cities. Tribal leaders mustered their own troops in times of crisis, hired local priests to run their sanctuaries, and supported local judicial decisions through courts of elders.

The household formed the basis for tribal organization. This household structure was relatively stable throughout Israel's history. Households of landowners were not nuclear families. They were run by the eldest male of the household (meaning that they were patriarchal in structure). The family unit centered on the house of the father (Gen. 24:38) for security, status, and identity—although references to the house of the mother also occasionally occur (Gen. 24:28; Ruth 1:8; Song 3:4; 8:2). The father, as the male patriarch, controlled internal household codes and external communication. Both internal and external behavior either brought honor or shame to the household unit. A family's ability to function within the larger tribal system depended on their maintenance of a status of honor.

Households included multiple generations of the offspring of this head of the household. Because ancient Israel always allowed for polygamy, the households often included both high status wives (wives whose fathers were landowners), as well as lower status wives. The latter are sometimes called "concubines," but it is more accurate to speak of wives who were not from landowning families. Marriage within the clan or tribe was preferred. Since the family was the basic economic unit in the tribal system, children's obligations toward parents were emphasized throughout life and into the parents' old age (Exod. 20:12; 21:15, 17). There also appears to be an interest in keeping land in the family. In Numbers 36:1–12, for example, Zelophehad's daughters are able to inherit their father's land in the absence of sons, so as to preserve the paternal lineage.

The household also typically included slaves and servants of various types. The Israelite laws reflect at least two types of slaves: debt slaves, who could include other Israelites (see for instance, Exod. 21:2–11 and Deut. 15:7–17), and permanent slaves (Deut. 20:13-14), who were usually foreigners. The household could also include skilled laborers who were permanently attached to a particular family or patriarch. A household, then, functioned as a small agri-business.

The Israelite tribal systems were hierarchical. People at the bottom could be socially ostracized, economically destitute, and physically vulnerable. The Israelite texts called for care of these groups, which included women not protected by a landowning male (a word translated as "widows"), children and men also not protected by a landowner ("orphans"), and anyone else not found in the genealogies of landowners ("resident aliens" or foreigners; see, e.g., Deut. 24:17). Even with these exhortations, however, the reality was that they were dependent on the kindness of the elite.

With landed settlement, allegiances among households became common, as a way of defending land-holdings and strengthening the community. But it was often difficult for the various families, clans, and tribes to unite. The biblical texts attest that the full tribes did not readily take on the responsibility of supporting each other, especially militarily (see, e.g., Judg. 5:17). It seems that a major threat from a common enemy was required to compel the twelve tribes of Israel to unite. The tribes would also come together for religious gatherings to seek blessing for warfare and ask for the protection of women, children, land, and goods. This social construct is called "amphictyony," and was first identified among the Greek city-states.[2]

The Monarchy

Very little literature has survived from the period of the tribal system of Judges. Most likely, very little literature was produced during that period, partly because there was not a sufficient economic base to support a scribal class (or other classes of skilled specialists). Eventually pressures from outside of Israel forced the tribes to band together under the rule of a king. The development of a monarchy marks a significant shift in Israel's social structure. Although the royal dynasty was itself a household, that household subordinated all of Israel's other institutions so that they now served the interests of the monarchic state. The advantage for Israel was that the system provided unity and a mechanism for much quicker responses to crises, but the disadvantage was that it undercut clan allegiances and siphoned off economic resources, placing more people at the margins than had been the case under the tribal system.

Under the monarchy, households, clans, and tribes continued to exist, but they had less self-direction and much less control of their own economic products. The monarchy led to a taxation system to

2. Martin Noth, *Das System der zwölf Stämme Israels*, Beiträge zur Wissenschaft vom Alten und Neuen Testament 4 (Stuttgart: Kohlhammer, 1930; reprint Darmstadt: Wissenschaft Buchgesellschaft, 1966).

support a national army, a royal bureaucracy, and a state religion. This taxation sometimes became exorbitant, leading families to abandon their ancestral land (Mic. 2:1–2). The monarchic system disrupted local governance by setting up national courts, undercutting the authority of local elders. While the army's ostensible function was to defend the nation as a whole, it also enabled a king to defend his own rule in the case of revolution.

For the biblical texts, the most important effect of the monarchy, however, was the creation of a national religious center in Judah, the Temple of Jerusalem. The surviving texts generally celebrate this creation of a national shrine. This may be due in part to the fact that these texts were written by scribes, and temples were centers for scribal activity. Some texts, however, hint at the social disruption that resulted from this centralization. The national Temple was in the hands of one particular priestly clan chosen by the king. This decision led to the demotion of priests from other clans or families, further concentrating political power in the hands of just a few families.

A number of Israelite texts attest to injustices during the monarchies of Israel and Judah. Criticism arose from various sources, but the Israelite tradition highlights the role of prophets in both supporting the state (e.g., Isaiah) and critiquing it (e.g., Micah). From a sociological perspective, then, it is not surprising that texts stemming from or reflecting on this period often feature the roles of prophets.

Cross-cultural comparative studies on mediums, seers, witches, sorcerers, shamans, diviners, mystics, and intermediaries have provided new insights on the study of ancient Israel's categories of "prophet" (Deut. 18:15), "man of God" (1 Kings 17:18), "company of prophets" (literally, "sons of prophets"; 2 Kings 2:3), and "seer" (1 Sam. 9:11). A prophet's message was heard as the moral and ethical compass of its time. Prophets were investigative reporters and editorial commentators that brought hidden social injustice and religious abuse to the front page. Moses was the exemplary prophet (Deut. 34:10–12). Others, like Moses, would rise up and teach the people to follow God's rules and regulations. "Central prophets," like Isaiah and Ezekiel, who supported the monarchy and Temple, had influence on international, national, and state affairs. In contrast, "peripheral prophets," such as Micah, spoke of regional and city-town matters. A prophetic speech, sometimes called an "oracle," often began with a stereotypical phrase (e.g., "Thus says the LORD") that set out the prophet's claim that the message came directly from the divine realm. Because of this divine element, the prophets were able to speak against the abuses of the monarchy. As bearers of charisma and heralds with divine oracles, prophets were accepted as messengers from God.

Exile and Forced Migration

The period of the exile to Babylon (597–538 BCE) had a profound impact upon the people of Judah. Scholarly discussion of the exile has tended to focus unhelpfully on the destruction of the Temple (587 BCE) and its rebuilding (515 BCE). The exile is less about the Temple than about the people who experienced a series of three forced migrations.

In 597, king, scribes, military, prophets, skilled workers, and other upper classes and skilled classes, totaling about 10,000 people,

© Israel Museum, Jerusalem, Israel / The Bridgeman Art Library

In this bas-relief from Ninevah, Judean captives are forced into exile following the siege of Lachish in 701 BCE. Over the next century and a half, many thousands of Judeans would follow them into exile in Mesopotamia.

were forced to migrate from Judea and were resettled in Babylon. A majority of the Judean people remained in Judea. Ten years later, after King Zedekiah revolted against Babylon, King Nebuchadnezzar sent an army to Judah. All the houses in Jerusalem were burned down, along with the Temple, thereby destroying the Judean economy. An additional group of about seven thousand people who survived the fighting were displaced and resettled to Babylon. Five years later (582), the Babylonians came a third time and took an additional thousand Judeans to Babylon. The most painful part of these migrations was the social collapse of an entire generation. On top of the deaths that resulted from the successive wars, those who survived faced a variety of horrors, including rape, mutilation, and torture. This horror is epitomized in the story of King Zedekiah, who was forced to witness the execution of his sons before his own eyes were put out (2 Kings 25:7).

The exile destroyed every social structure of the monarchic state. The monarchy and Temple were destroyed. Households were stripped of land. The exile of the elite left lower classes who depended on them without any economic support. Slaves had no home; lower-class wives and their children were left bereft of any source of income. The Judean elites were replaced by foreign-appointed governors whose main interest was supporting the economic well-being of Babylon. The most that the poor could hope for was to grow food for their invader's army. These effects were felt most acutely around Jerusalem.

The Babylonians used repeated forced migrations to supply labor for rebuilding their own war-torn cities, like Nippur. The biblical records of these events are better understood by applying the results of modern sociological theories of forced migration to these texts. There are three types of forced migration: one that is the result of explicit policy decisions by a government, one that is the result of external conditions, and one that does not involve a geographical relocation. It is perhaps easiest to start with this last category.

"Derivative forced migration" or "static migration" results from geopolitical causes and shifts that change national borders.[3] For

---

3. John J. Ahn, *Exile as Forced Migrations: A Sociological, Literary, and Theological Approach on the Displacement and Resettlement of the Southern Kingdom of Judah*, Beihefte zur Zeitschrift für die alttestamentliche Wissenschaft 417 (Berlin: De Gruyter, 2011), esp. 40–47.

example, after World War I, thirteen new states were created between the territories of Finland to Greece, and from Germany to the Soviet Union. Since the Neo-Babylonians expanded and included Judah into their re-mapped empire when Jehoiachin peacefully relinquished his throne in 597, derivative forced migration best describes the displacement in 597, as Judah had ceased to exist as an independent nation. Derivative forced migration also describes the Judeans that remained in the land of Judah after 587 and 582, experiencing an exile-less exile.

"Purposive forced migration," where populations are purposefully removed from their homeland, has a variety of motivations. They can be profit-driven (Uganda 1972), race-related (Germany 1920, South Africa 1948, Darfur 2005), religiously motivated (Spain 1492, Northern Ireland 1960, Greece and Turkey 1923), or revenge-centered (Tutsi and Hutus of Rwanda-Burundi 1962, Sudan 2005), to name a few. The Babylonians practiced purposive forced migration of Judean elites to Babylon in 587 and 582 for a variety of reasons: for international security, to punish Zedekiah's rebellion, and to sustain regional economic growth in Babylon through the resultant forced labor.

"Responsive forced migration" is a voluntary migration, in contrast to the other two, which are involuntary forced migrations. In response to forces of political or natural oppressions of tyranny, warfare, or domestic or climate-related change, people choose to migrate. An example would be the 582 group of Judeans, including Jeremiah, who voluntarily crossed the border into Egypt (Jer. 42:1–43:7) in fear of Babylonian revenge for the assassination of their appointed governor.

These three types of migration lead to at least three new social groups: exiles (former elites), internally displaced persons (poorer populations), and refugees. Most of the biblical texts reflect the experience of the exiles. The Neo-Babylonian government used these displaced and resettled persons, including the royal family, bureaucrats, scribes, priests, military personnel, artisans, and smiths, for the development of its arable land and dilapidated infrastructure. Maintaining the irrigation canals for agricultural production would have been the start for such rehabilitation of the infrastructure. Ethnic enclaves were formed around these irrigation projects in urban areas like Nippur or in other arable, rural areas, a fact attested in the archaeological record.

Internally displaced persons are those who are displaced from their home but who have not crossed a recognized border. After the exile, some Judeans could no longer live in their ancestral homes, especially in and around Jerusalem. The Judeans of 587 and 582 experienced armed conflict, violence, and human-made disaster (Deut. 28:48–57). The Babylonians forced the labor class in Judea or the "people of the land" out of their homes. This led to a displaced population remaining in the land. Even those who were able to maintain their original landholdings experienced a significant social disruption with the loss of monarchy and temple.

Refugees are people who voluntarily cross a border, fleeing for their lives. These people are pushed from their social, cultural, and economic moorings due to potential or imminent threats to their physical safety, security, dignity, liberty, and property. This results in a loss of national citizenship and disruption to social relationships, such as kinship ties, neighborhood networks, and individual and collective identity. The story of the murder of Gedalaiah, the Babylonian-appointed governor of Judea, demonstrates that the fate of those internally displaced in Judea was intertwined with the fugitives who, against Jeremiah's warning (Jer. 42:19), fled to Egypt (Jer. 41:16).

Giving identity to these last two groups is a difficult and important undertaking. Zechariah 8:19 lists four fast days commemorating the catastrophe of Jerusalem: the start of the siege (the tenth month: Jer. 52:4), the breaching of Jerusalem's wall (the fourth month: Jer. 52:6–7), the destruction of Jerusalem (the fifth month: Jer. 52:12–13), and the assassination of Gedaliah (the seventh month: Jer. 41:1–2). The Babylonians used the surviving population, which the texts call "the poorest people of the land," for the production of wine and other crops (2 Kings 25:12; Jer. 52:16). The timing of the assassination of Gedaliah suggests that its purpose was to disrupt Judah's production of summer fruit, wine, balm, and other goods that flowed into Babylon (2 Kings 25:25).

The effects of forced migrations on all three of these groups (exiles, refugees, and internally displaced persons) are seen most clearly, however, in texts coming from subsequent generations. While the three waves of deportations in 597, 587, and 582 were all the experiences of what is called first generation migrants, those who were taken to Babylon as teenagers or younger (the "1.5 generation") would have had a completely different experience from that of their parents. In addition, those who were born in Babylon, the second generation, also had a very different experience from either the first or 1.5 generations. The same can be said about the third and fourth generations. Their experiences were less bitter, and their identity was more hybrid, the result of an unconscious merging of both Israelite and non-Israelite culture. Some of those generational shifts can be seen in the following chart:

Generation	Group	Select Social Issues
First Generation	Adults who became exiles, refugees, and internally displaced persons	• Loss of social status and honor • Trauma • Loss of social identity and experience of forced labor (exiles) • Displacement (exiles and refugees)
1.5 Generation	Teenagers or younger at time of disaster	• Tensions over assimilation • New social and economic context
Second Generation	First genera-tion born to 1.5 generation	• Assimilation to dominant culture, in part through education • Economic and social disparities leading to marginalization within communities
Third Generation	Born to second generation (Per-sians allow pop-ulations to return to their ancestral homes)	• Uncertainty as to which land is their "home" • Internal debates over which group (exiles or people of the land) is the "true" Israel • Uncertainty about whether to return to Judea (exiles and refugees)

Colonization

The fall of Jerusalem marked another transition in Israel's history. After that date, Judea remained a colony of a succession of foreign empires (Persia, Greece, and Rome), with one brief period of self-governance following the Maccabean Revolt, which began in 167 BCE. The cultural effects of colonization are found throughout the biblical records. Post-colonial studies note that one of the results of colonization is the hybrid identity that is created among those colonized. While indigenous populations try to maintain their native identities, complex economic and social factors lead to the acceptance of many of the cultural norms of the colonizers.

In Judea, this assimilation is seen across the various social groups, even though their experiences varied. For example, the descendants of the exiles, who came from the upper and skilled classes, assimilated to mainstream Babylonian culture (probably through education), while maintaining some degree of their own ethnic and religious identity. Simply put, these groups "made it" in Babylon. However, there remained in Judea an underclass, who continued to be exploited by both the Babylonians and the returning exiles, who were the former elites of Judea.

These tensions are found throughout the biblical record. For example, Isaiah 40–55, written at the end of Babylonian colonization, contains poems urging the second and third generation of the exiles to return to Jerusalem. The rhetoric of these poems suggests that a sizable number from this group had no desire to return to a place that they no longer viewed as "home." Texts written around the beginning of Persian rule, such as Isaiah 56:3 and Nehemiah 10:30, express concern about "foreigners" living among them; these foreigners probably included Jews whose parents had intermarried with the ruling ethnic group. The narratives in Daniel 1–6, written under Greek colonization, depict a young generation of men working successfully under foreign rule who nevertheless take risks to maintain elements of their Jewish identity.

Under the colonial systems, Jews were able to live as a distinct group in or near their former ancestral land. The Persians allowed them to have a certain amount of political autonomy and considerable religious freedom, as long as they recognized the Persians as their overlords and accepted the empire's heavy taxes. The Temple at Jerusalem was rebuilt with Persian support and remained a major social vehicle for Judean identity throughout this "Second Temple period." Tolerance of Jewish practices continued through most of the period of Greek control (332–167 BCE), although within the Jewish community tensions mounted over how much assimilation to Greek customs was acceptable. This mounting tension exploded when Antiochus Epiphanes attempted to suppress traditional Jewish religious practices, touching off the Maccabean Revolt.

Political structures varied throughout the long history of colonization in Judea (after 538 BCE), but most of the local leaders were native Jews appointed by the foreign government. This led to tensions within the native population, since those who succeeded in this system were those who cooperated with the colonizers. As a general rule, those who cooperated most with the foreign overlords were also the ones who were most willing to assimilate to their overlords' culture. In response, groups who opposed foreign rule often stressed Jewish practices, such as circumcision and dietary restrictions, that marked them as different from the colonizers.

The context of exile and colonization can be traced throughout biblical literature in both overt and subtle ways. For example, the narrative framework for Israel's re-telling of its history, whether that is found in Genesis or in the stories of Israel's move toward a monarchy, can be read through the lens of generational consciousness. It shapes the way Israel tells its own story, such as the four-generational framework (Abraham, Isaac, Jacob, and Joseph) found in the book of Genesis. It is also found in the stories of Israel's conquest and settlement in the land. For example, after the death of first generation Israelites, including Moses, in the wilderness (Num. 1–27), the second generation of Israelites (Num. 28–42) find themselves under Joshua, a transitional leader. It should be noted that Joshua is not depicted as second generation since he was not born in the wilderness. Moreover, if he was indeed a first generation, he would have died in the wilderness with the first generation. In fact, Joshua is a transitional figure, reflecting the status of a 1.5 generation. The elders who are born in the wilderness are considered the second generation. The third generation is the period of the judges who ruled the tribes in the first stage of settlement, with the fourth generation being the kings, which in turn initiates a new generational history. The later Israelite authors and redactors highlighted these multigenerational depictions, reflecting their own multigenerational experience of exile and displacement.

These biblical authors brought their experiences of displacement and trauma to the biblical record at every point. The legal texts in the Pentateuch, ostensibly given to Moses before there was even a nation of Israel, reflect the concerns of the exiles, that Israelite identity should be maintained even outside of the land. The preservation of the prophetic texts provided both an outlet for the collective memory of the traumas they endured, as well as a rationale for the disasters that had befallen them. In this way, the prophetic texts offered hope because they affirmed the power and character of the God that they worshipped. The contrast in the historical accounts in Samuel–Kings and Chronicles demonstrates how two distinct groups used stories of the monarchic period to address issues arising in their contexts of exile and colonization, Kings by focusing on the failures of the people during the monarchy, and Chronicles by depicting the community as a pious group united by worship of God, rather than a nation seeking political independence.

The various social contexts that Israel and Judah experienced have left deep marks throughout the literature that has been preserved in the Jewish Scriptures. This includes traces of early stages of Israel's history, such as tribalism, preserved through oral and written records. These remnants of earlier stages, though, are found in texts reflecting later social contexts, especially the experiences of exile and colonization. Such social elements as concern over honor and shame, the value of kinship ties under a patriarchal structure, and the idealization of a monarchic politico-religious system gave later generations hope and identity.

DISCUSSION QUESTIONS

1. Describe the main elements of the five different social structures found throughout Israel's history.

2. Describe the transition from a tribal social structure to monarchy. What did Israel gain by this change? What did Israel lose?

3. In what ways did exile and colonization affect economics, leadership, and religion?
4. If Judea had never been subjected to colonization and its elite citizens driven into exile, how might the Hebrew Bible be different today? Are there themes that are present now that would be downplayed or eliminated, or vice versa?
5. Read Deuteronomy 28; how do the details of the curses reflect a later context of exile and colonization?

FOR FURTHER STUDY

Ahn, John. "Diaspora Studies," in *The Oxford Encyclopedia of Biblical Interpretation*, edited by Steven McKenzie, 217–25. New York: Oxford University Press, 2013.

Ahn, John. *Exile as Forced Migrations: A Sociological, Literary, and Theological Approach on the Displacement and Resettlement of the South Kingdom of Judah*. Beihefte zur Zeitschrift für die Alttestamentliche Wissenschaft 417. Berlin and New York: De Gruyter, 2011.

Ahn, John, and J. Middlemas, eds. *By the Irrigation Canals of Babylon: Approaches to the Study of the Exile*. Library of Hebrew Bible. Old Testament Studies 526. New York: T & T Clark, 2012.

Carter, Charles, and Carol Meyers, eds. *Community, Identity, and Ideology: Social Science Approaches to the Hebrew Bible*. Winona Lake, IN: Eisenbrauns, 1996.

Clements, Ronald E., ed. *The World of Ancient Israel: Sociological, Anthropological, and Political Perspectives*. New York: Cambridge University Press, 1989.

Esler, Philip Francis, ed. *Ancient Israel: The Old Testament in Its Social Context*. Minneapolis: Fortress Press, 2006.

Internet Resources

www.mapsofwar.com/ind/imperial-history.html
An animated map depicting the history of colonization of Israel.

10

Religion of Ancient Israel

John L. McLaughlin

The Hebrew Bible (Old Testament)[1] represents a collection of traditions spanning the full range of ancient Israel's history. These traditions received their final form, however, at the end of this period (ca. fifth–second centuries BCE). Scholars believe that much of the traditional material was reshaped and rewritten in this later period, to reflect better the needs and perspective of the religious community at that time. Consequently, the reader cannot simply assume that the current biblical text accurately depicts the religious practices of, say, David or Abraham. It is possible, however, to recover some early aspects of Israelite religion through a close, careful reading of the biblical literature, supplemented at points by information from extra-biblical texts and evidence from archaeological excavations. The following brief introduction to this vast topic focuses on a few central aspects of Israelite religion, noting along the way some earlier elements that were discarded by the time of the Second Temple period (ca. 538 BCE–70 CE).

Yahweh

Israelite religion is centered on the worship of their God, Yahweh. The word Yahweh is actually the verb *hwh* ("to be") in a masculine,

---

1. For Protestants, the Old Testament contains only the books found in the Hebrew Bible. Catholics and Orthodox accept these books as well, but also accept certain deuterocanonical (or apocryphal) books. See chapter 11, "Old Testament Apocrypha and Pseudepigrapha," and the chart "Canons of Scripture" in the additional study aids section.

third-person singular, causative form. One might translate it, "He causes to be," or, "He creates," or perhaps, "He gives life." As such, Yahweh may be a descriptive title rather than an actual name. Ancient believers increasingly ascribed sacredness to this word and eventually they stopped pronouncing it, saying instead *adonai* ("my Lord") whenever they encountered Yahweh as they read Scripture. The Hebrew text was originally written without vowels:[2] "Yahweh" appeared as "YHWH" in the text. Around 750 CE, Jewish scholars introduced a system of "vowel points," signs added above and below the consonantal text to represent the vowels. By that time, it was established practice to read *adonai* whenever one encountered YHWH in the biblical text, so these scholars added to the word YHWH the vowels for the word they would actually pronounce there: adonai. Christians, translating the Hebrew text into English during the Middle Ages, were unaware that the vowel points around the word "YHWH" actually belonged to a different word entirely, and simply read what they saw, resulting in "Jehovah." This is the equivalent of putting the vowel from cat into the consonants from dog; the resulting "dag" is no more a real word than Jehovah. Most modern English Bibles respect the traditional Jewish reluctance to pronounce the name Yahweh, and instead use the word LORD, with all letters capitalized to indicate that this is the divine name and not the common noun for "lord."

The origins of the worship of Yahweh are obscure. According to Exodus 3 (and another version in Exodus 6), the name was first revealed to Moses at the burning bush at Mount Sinai (Mount Horeb). According to these accounts, Yahweh explains that, although the Israelites do not yet know him by that name, he is the same God that the Israelites' ancestors had worshipped: "The God of your father, the God of Abraham, the God of Isaac, and the God of Jacob" (Exod. 3:6; Exod. 6:3, however, identifies him as *El Shaddai*, usually translated "God Almighty"). Moses asks for God's name in order to convince the people that he was indeed sent by their god. But if the Israelite slaves in Egypt already knew their god as either "the God of your father" or "God Almighty," providing this new name would

2. In ancient Hebrew, some of the consonants could double as vowels, but the writing system was very incomplete.

have proved nothing to them. Therefore, the account preserves hints that not only the name Yahweh, but also the god bearing that name, was new to the Israelites.

In fact, Yahweh may have been a Midianite god. According to the text, Moses was tending the flock of his father-in-law, Jethro, "the priest of Midian" (Exod. 3:1), when he encountered the burning bush on Mount Sinai/Horeb. Moreover, Mount Sinai/Horeb is called "the mountain of God" (3:1) *before* Moses spoke with God there, suggesting that it was already a sacred site within his father-in-law's territory. In addition, after the Israelites escaped from Egypt and arrived at Mount Sinai they offered sacrifices to Yahweh. However, the ritual gathering was not presided over by Aaron, the high priest of Israel, but rather by Jethro, "the priest of Midian," who said, "Now I know that Yahweh is greater than all gods" (Exod. 18:11). This implies that Jethro already knew Yahweh, but had now come to a greater understanding of him. In effect, the text of Exodus as it currently stands asserts that Yahweh was the traditional God of the Israelites' ancestors, but the text also appears to preserve elements of an earlier tradition in which Yahweh first became known to the Israelites at the time of the Exodus.

The God of Justice

Yahweh's liberation of slaves from Egypt revealed his fundamental characteristic, namely his frequent intervention on behalf of the weakest members of a society. The importance of this idea is reflected in the fact that it recurs in different parts of the Hebrew Bible, as summarized at the end of this section. In the ancient world, people thought their nations reflected the divine realm. Each nation had a pantheon of gods with a chief god who ruled over subordinate deities, including the servant gods at the bottom of the divine hierarchy. Similarly, most human societies had a king at the top of the social structure, followed by his family and royal bureaucracy, and so on down to the slaves. Since this hierarchical structure reflected the way things were in heaven, it was seen as the will of the gods, and so it was useless to fight it. Acceptance of social inequality was especially marked in Egypt, where pharaoh was not just appointed by the gods, but was considered the incarnation of Ra, the chief god of Egypt. But in the biblical account, Yahweh opposed such a hierarchical system with its inherent oppression of those in the bottom tier of society. Yahweh did not just reverse the positions, putting the slaves in charge, but instead rejected a society in which the rich and powerful could mistreat the poor and powerless. He led the Israelites out of Egypt (the Exodus) to Mount Sinai/Horeb, where he gave them laws that established the Covenant not just with him but also with each other.

The Torah

Scholars recognize not only that the laws in Exodus, Leviticus, Numbers, and Deuteronomy stem from various periods in Israel's history, but also that the importance of individual laws varied over time and place. For instance, laws that reinforced ethnic and religious identity, such as those dealing with circumcision, their external appearance (for example, clothing or hair style and length), and diet, would have been more important in the daily life of Israelites deported by the Assyrians or the Babylonians than the laws concerning sacrifices in what was, for them, the distant Jerusalem Temple. But by depicting all biblical laws as originating at Mount Sinai, the biblical editors link Israelite religion in all its stages to the Exodus and the Covenant.

The Pentateuchal laws can be grouped into two main types. One type consists of the "religious" laws that establish the formal aspects of ancient Israelite religion, the ritual expression of the Israelites' dedication to Yahweh. Such legislation mandates various types of sacrifices and religious festivals. But the Hebrew Bible also contains numerous "social" laws that create a framework for the peoples' social relationships. By combining these two types of laws within the same books, the biblical editors indicated that the Israelites' relationship with God was intricately connected with their relationships with each other: one could not be in a proper relationship with Yahweh without being in a proper relationship with other people. This complementarity can been seen in the Ten Commandments: the first few laws, prohibiting idols and establishing the Sabbath, deal with interactions with God, but the majority, outlawing mistreatment of one's parents, lying, theft, adultery, and especially coveting, deal with interactions among human beings.

Those basic elements of human relationships are developed in greater detail by the Pentateuch's social laws, which are characterized by the obligation to treat others with respect and dignity, especially the vulnerable members of Israelite society. Exhortations to remember "the orphan, the widow and the stranger in your land" are repeated regularly in the legal and prophetic material (see, for instance, Deut. 27:19 and Jer. 7:6). Israelite society was patriarchal, with male relatives expected to protect women and children. But an orphan no longer had a father and a widow had left her father's home only to have her husband die, so both were deprived of their male protector. Meanwhile, the "stranger in your land" was not an Israelite, so she or he had no Israelite relatives to ensure proper treatment. The repeated admonitions to remember these three groups shift the obligation to protect them from a specific individual, no longer present, to the entire community. Since they do not have an immediate male relative to ensure they are treated fairly, everyone must do so.

Many of the social laws are reinforced by Yahweh's reminder, "I brought you out of Egypt, that land of slavery," and the admonition, "Remember that you were slaves in Egypt." These exhortations call upon the people to act like Yahweh did when he freed them from slavery: they too must intervene for the weakest members of their society. Moreover, these admonitions call for the establishment of a community that would be the opposite of their former existence of oppression and exploitation. Thus the laws reject slavery (Deut. 23:15–16; 24:7), prohibit charging interest on a loan (Deut. 23:19), and even prohibit keeping a poor person's cloak as collateral overnight because that individual needs the cloak as a blanket (Deut. 24:12–13). This latter law appears next to a prohibition against entering a person's home to take an item as collateral (Deut. 24:10–11), which creates the amusing scenario of a lender waiting outside to collect it each morning and returning it at night.

Other regulations address the very structure of society. The first of these is the Sabbath Year (Deut. 15:1–18). Every seven years (hence the Sabbath Year), all debts were to be forgiven and all persons who had sold themselves into debt-slavery, a form of indentured servitude for a specified period of time, were to be set free, even if the agreed-upon time had not been completed. Lenders were exhorted to be generous to their brothers and sisters seeking to borrow close to the

© Erich Lessing / Art Resource, NY

In this ostracon from Yavneh Yam (ca. 630–609 BCE), a worker lodges a complaint against his employer for taking his garment in pledge and refusing to return it. Throughout the ancient Near East, ostraca (broken bits of potsherd) were used to record short documents like this.

Sabbath Year (15:9–11) and to provide for those set free (15:13–14). The section concludes by linking Israel's treatment of others with Yahweh's treatment of them: "Remember that you were a slave in the land of Egypt, and the LORD your God redeemed you; for this reason I lay this command upon you today" (Deut. 15:15).

The Sabbath Year was supplemented by the Jubilee Year (Lev. 25:8–55). Every fifty years, in addition to cancelling monetary debts and indentured servitude, the people were to return all land to the original owners or their descendants. Every Israelite family was given a portion of land to grow food, raise flocks, and otherwise ensure life's necessities. However, sometimes people were forced to sell their ancestral property in order to pay debts. The Jubilee Year ensured that they were not landless forever and also ensured that no one became too powerful by amassing huge amounts of land in perpetuity. Once again, God's speech ties this legislation to the deliverance of the Israelites from bondage in the Exodus: "For to me the people of Israel are servants; they are my servants whom I brought out from the land of Egypt" (Lev. 25:55).

The Prophets

Unfortunately, people did not always put into practice these ideals of justice, especially for the weakest members of society. The problem of social injustice became acute after the establishment of the monarchy, with its accompanying bureaucracy. As the king and upper classes gained more and more power, they exploited and oppressed the poor. But the rise of kings and their elite supporters was paralleled by the appearance of prophets in Israel to remind the powerful of their covenant obligations. Nathan rebuked David for his adultery with Bathsheba and murder of her husband Uriah (2 Sam. 12), and Elijah chastised Ahab and Jezebel for executing Naboth on false charges in order to steal his ancestral vineyard (1 Kings 21). Amos condemned the rich for excessive banqueting while ignoring "the ruin" of the poor (Amos 6:1–7). Isaiah denounced those who bought up land to create large estates, evicting the former owners (Isa. 5:8); he also condemned those who made laws that oppressed the poor and needy, particularly "widows" and "orphans" (Isa. 10:1–2). Micah rebuked those who confiscated land (Mic. 2:1–2); he compared the rulers, who should have enforced justice, to cannibals who skin people and cook them in caldrons (Mic. 3:1–3). All the prophets linked their insistence on justice to the Exodus, God's liberation of their ancestors from slavery.

The Writings

The concern for justice in the Hebrew Bible is not limited to the prophets. Nehemiah, upon becoming governor of Judah, cancelled debts and oversaw the return of land and repayment of interest that had been charged (see especially Neh. 5). The wisdom literature frequently denounces economic exploitation through false scales and weights (e.g., Prov. 16:11; 20:23) and exhorts those in power to defend the needy (Prov. 31:8–9). The Psalms persistently intercede for the weak, the helpless, and the oppressed, condemn those who attack them (e.g., Ps. 10:8–10), and pray that the king may rule with God's righteousness and justice (e.g., Ps. 72:1–2).

Concern for social justice was not unique to ancient Israel. The legal and religious literature of Egypt and Mesopotamia also advocate protection of the poor, the orphan, and the widow. In a text from Ugarit (a northern Syrian kingdom of the fourteenth–twelfth century BCE), a prince justifies deposing his father because he failed to protect the orphan and the widow. The distinctive feature of the Hebrew Bible is its concern to link social justice to their God's intervention on their behalf, in the Exodus.

Ritual Practices in Israel

In ancient Israel, most communal worship was conducted at local sanctuaries located on hilltops called "high places." Although they were mostly open-air sites, perhaps with a tent shrine, they were laid out much the same as the Temple in Jerusalem. The Jerusalem

© Todd Bolen / www.bibleplaces.com

Although Deuteronomy 12 insists there can be only one legitimate sanctuary, ancient Israelites worshiped Yahweh at a number of sites in addition to Solomon's Temple in Jerusalem, including this small, iron-age temple in Arad. Its floor plan is similar to that of the Jerusalem Temple.

Temple's layout was similar to temples excavated in surrounding countries, such as a neo-Hittite temple at Tell Taynit in Turkey and the Baal Temple at Ugarit, as well as an Israelite one at Arad. The Jerusalem Temple consisted of a porch or vestibule through which one entered the main room, at the other end of which was a smaller cube-shaped room popularly known as the "Holy of Holies." Normally only priests entered the Temple building, and only the high priest could enter the Holy of Holies, once a year on Yom Kippur (see below). Most worshippers remained in the outer courtyards, where sacrifices were offered on an elevated altar.

King Josiah (641–609 BCE) tried to centralize cultic worship in Jerusalem alone, and the high places were denounced as pagan deviations from the true Israelite religion. Previously, however, they were considered legitimate places of worship, as seen in Samuel's sacrifices in a number of locations (see, for example, 1 Sam. 7:9 [Mizpah]; 11:15 [Gilgal]; 16:1–6 [Bethlehem]) and Elijah's offering on Mt. Carmel (1 Kings 18). After the Babylonians destroyed the temple in 587 BCE, such non-sacrificial forms of worship as prayer and reflection on Scripture grew in importance. Even after the Jerusalem Temple was rebuilt in 515 BCE, those living at a distance were unable to participate regularly in the Temple sacrifices, leading to the development of the synagogue as a center for Jewish religious life. Nonetheless, Jewish temples did exist in Egypt during the post-exilic period, at Elephantine (sixth century BCE) and Leontopolis (ca. 154 BCE).

Offerings

As mentioned earlier, some laws deal with the ritual expression of Israel's relationship to Yahweh through sacrifices offered at sanctuaries (eventually only at the Jerusalem Temple). The early chapters of Leviticus (1–7) regulate a variety of sacrifices serving a variety of functions. Each regulation specifies the nature of the offering (for example, an unblemished animal, whether male or female, types of grain, or unleavened bread) and how the sacrifice was to be conducted.

The Burnt Offering (Lev. 1; 6:9–13) gets its name from the burning of the entire animal as an offering to Yahweh. Since none of the sacrifice was consumed by the worshippers, it expressed total dedication to God. It could be offered as part of the daily worship on behalf of the whole community or by an individual as an act of atonement.

Grain Offerings (Lev. 2; 6:14–18) were given from the fruit of one's labor in the fields, and therefore symbolized the offering of oneself as a gift to the deity. The entire offering would initially be placed on the altar in dedication, but only a portion of it was actually burnt. The rest was given to the priests as food for them and for their families.

Peace Offerings (Lev. 3; 7:11–36) involved animal sacrifice, but like the grain offerings only a portion was burnt as an offering to God. The rest was returned to the one making the offering, to share with whomever she or he chose. It was offered in thanksgiving to Yahweh for some action on his part, in fulfillment of a vow, or simply as an act of praise and worship. It was commonly offered alongside the whole burnt offering, with the two together signifying a meal shared by the human worshiper and God.

Purification Offerings (Lev. 4:1–5:13; 6:24–30) cleansed impurity that affected the sanctuary when someone violated a divine prohibition. For such sins committed by priests or the entire community the priest sprinkled the blood of a sacrificed animal seven times before the curtain separating the Holy of Holies, then daubed some on the horns of the incense altar inside the temple and poured the rest outside, at the base of the altar used for burnt offerings. For sins by a ruler or an ordinary person, the blood was daubed on the horns of the altar for burnt offerings and the rest poured at its base. The different regulations indicate that sins by a priest or the whole community had a greater polluting effect than those of lay individuals, requiring that the blood be used inside the temple itself.

The Reparation or Guilt Offering (Lev. 5:14–6:7; 7:1–10) compensated for both intentional and unintentional wrongdoing. As such, one could sacrifice an animal for this purpose or donate a comparable amount of money. In the case of defrauding a person, the worshiper also had to repay the full amount plus 20 percent.

Israelite religion included a number of holy days. The most frequent was the Sabbath, celebrated every seven days. On the Sabbath, the people were to cease all work. Exodus 20:11 links the Sabbath to God resting on the seventh day of creation (Gen. 2:2) but in

Deuteronomy 5:15 the Sabbath rest commemorates God bringing the Israelites out of slavery in Egypt, where they had no rest. Either way, a weekly pause from labor distinguished the Israelites from their neighbors, who had no such practice. In addition to this weekly observance, the feast of the New Moon marked the beginning of each month as a day of celebration with specific sacrifices, but little else is said about it.

Festivals

Three annual festivals originated in the agricultural cycle but were also associated with the Exodus experience. The Feast of Unleavened Bread occurred during the spring barley harvest, at which time old yeast was thrown out and new yeast developed. This festival was also called Passover, recalling the night when the destroying angel "passed over" (i.e., spared) the Israelites in Egypt who had marked their houses with the blood of a sacrificed lamb. The Feast of Weeks (also called Shavuot [Hebrew] or Pentecost [Greek]) was observed fifty days later in conjunction with the wheat harvest, and also celebrated the establishment of the Covenant at Mount Sinai. The Feast of Booths (also known as Succot or Tabernacles) marked the fall harvest of fruit, olives, grapes, and late grains. During this harvest the workers camped in the fields overnight to maximize the time spent harvesting, and their tents recalled the forty years dwelling in tents in the wilderness.

Two other annual feasts followed shortly after. Rosh Hashanah (the New Year) was an occasion to be reconciled with God and neighbors. Leviticus 23:24 dates this feast to the fall, but in Exodus 23:16 and 34:22 the year begins in the spring; the difference may distinguish between agricultural and cultic cycles, or may reflect a shift from the pre-exilic (Exodus) and exilic (Leviticus) practice. Yom Kippur (The Day of Atonement) was observed ten days after Rosh Hashanah (Lev. 16:1-28). The high priest slaughtered a goat and sprinkled its blood inside the Holy of Holies in order to purify this innermost part of the temple. He then laid his hands on a second goat (a "scapegoat"), acknowledged the nation's sins, and then drove the goat, and by extension the nation's sins, into the wilderness.

Diet

Another element of ancient Israelite religion was dietary restrictions, known today as kashrut or kosher laws. Various land, sea, and air creatures were forbidden as food, most famously shellfish and pork (see Lev. 11 and Deut. 14). Scholars have proposed various explanations for these prohibitions, including hygiene (pigs or shellfish sometimes cause food poisoning), avoiding animals popular elsewhere (as pigs were among the Philistines), or rejection of animals inconsistent with the pattern of God's creation: fish *swim* in the water, birds *fly* in the air, and animals *graze* on the land (see Gen. 1). But none of these explanations apply consistently to all the dietary restrictions, nor are they mentioned in the biblical text. Instead, Leviticus 11:44–45 links these taboos to a requirement that the Israelites be holy as God is holy, because he brought them out of Egypt (cf. Deut. 14:2, 21). Thus their distinctive food habits distinguished them from their neighbors as a daily reminder of their special relationship with Yahweh and the reason for it. While diet distinguished the Israelites throughout their history, dietary practices took on extra significance as a means of maintaining identity for Israelites deported to the Assyrian and Babylonian Empires.

The Bible is mostly silent about religious practices within the family homes, but some observations are possible. Archaeological excavations reveal that many Israelite homes included shrines dedicated to Yahweh or other deities. Numerous small female figurines have been found throughout Judah, including in Jerusalem itself; many scholars think they are fertility symbols, and maybe even the image of a goddess. Archaeologists have also uncovered incense altars in some homes, indicating that ritual worship occurred away from the larger sanctuaries as well.

© Erich Lessing / Art Resource, NY

Female figurines like the ones shown here have been found in the excavation of many ancient Israelite houses. While their exact significance is disputed, they point to some form of religious observance in private homes.

Family-centered religious practices focused on ensuring the family members' fertility and divine protection from harm. Such so-called "popular" religion is often contrasted with what was presumed to be the "orthodox" religion outlined above, but this is a false distinction. Family religion was an integral part of ancient Israelite religion. It had its own very specific concerns that were not included in the biblical material dealing with the larger community's practices.

The Development of Israelite Monotheism

Another important element in ancient Israelite religion is monotheism, the belief that only one god exists. Casual readers of the Bible often attribute Israelite monotheism to Moses, if not hundreds of years earlier to Abraham, but close attention to some biblical texts indicates otherwise. To begin with, the First Commandment's order not to worship other gods (Exod. 20:3) presupposes that other gods do exist. This is consistent with ancient beliefs that each country had its own pantheon of gods and a chief deity ruling that nation. Thus, in Judges 11:24, Jephthah acknowledges that the god Chemosh gave the Ammonites their land. According to 2 Kings 3:27, the King of Moab sacrificed his son in order to get his god to intervene against an Israelite siege; the result was that "great wrath" came upon the Israelite army and they were routed. Deuteronomy 4:19 even asserts that Yahweh gave the "hosts of heaven" to the other nations to worship.

Biblical texts not only acknowledge that other gods existed among the nations, they also indicate that the Israelites worshiped deities in addition to Yahweh. Writing from a later theological viewpoint, most texts condemn such worship as apostasy, but some indications remain that at an early stage many Israelites accepted the worship of other deities as an acceptable part of Israelite religion. This can be demonstrated easily in the case of Asherah, the wife of El, the chief god of the Canaanite pantheon. The Hebrew Bible contains almost forty references to Israelites using cultic objects bearing her name (usually translated as "sacred poles"), even putting one in the Jerusalem Temple (see Deut. 16:21; 2 Kings 21:7).

Eighth-century BCE inscriptions from Kuntillet Ajrud in the northern Sinai and Khirbet el-Qom in Judah refer to "Yahweh and his *asherah*," the latter being one of these cultic objects. In a few instances the term refers to the goddess herself (see Judg. 3:7; 1 Kings 15:13; 18:19; 2 Kings 21:7; 23:4). Even some devout followers of Yahweh did not oppose her. For instance, Elijah destroyed the prophets of Baal after his victory over them on Mt. Carmel, but spared the four hundred prophets of Asherah (1 Kings 18:19–40). Shortly thereafter, Jehu led a coup against Jezebel and her son and purged Samaria of Baal worship, but when his son came to the throne "the [Asherah] *remained* in Samaria" (2 Kings 13:6; emphasis added), which means it was there during Jehu's reign. Only four verses in all the pre-exilic prophetic books oppose Asherah, and many scholars think they were added by later editors.[3] In short, prior to the Babylonian exile, even the most "orthodox" Israelites considered Asherah worship an acceptable part of Yahwistic religion.

© Zev Radovan / www.biblelandpictures.com

This inscription from Kuntillet Ajrud in southern Israel refers to "Yahweh and his Asherah," possibly meaning Yahweh's divine consort. The figures may be intended to represent Yahweh and Asherah.

---

3. Isaiah 17:8, 27:9; Jer. 17:2; and Mic. 5:14.

Over the centuries the Israelites moved from polytheism to monotheism. The first stage of this process was the opposition to Baal by prophets like Elijah and Hosea. Once people accepted that Baal was incompatible with dedication to Yahweh, it was much easier to exclude additional deities. Shortly before the Babylonians conquered Jerusalem in 587 BCE, the Deuteronomistic History, as well as prophets like Jeremiah and Ezekiel, promoted "monolatry" or "henotheism," the view that the Israelites should only worship Yahweh but without denying the existence of other gods. During the Babylonian exile, Second Isaiah made the leap to the earliest explicit statement of monotheism in the Hebrew Bible: "I am the LORD [i.e., Yahweh], and there is no other; besides me there is no God" (Isa. 45:5; see also 44:6, 8; 45:8, 18, 21–22).

In conclusion, ancient Israelite religion was rooted in traditions about the God Yahweh liberating a group of slaves from oppression in Egypt. In response, a good relationship with Yahweh was considered inseparable from a good relationship with others, which is reflected in the mixture of cultic and social laws in the Pentateuch. The ancient Israelites also initially worshipped other gods (polytheism), but with time they began to reject certain gods, eventually moving through a stage in which other gods were acknowledged but only Yahweh was worshipped (monolatry or henotheism) and culminating in monotheism, the belief that Yahweh was the only true God.

DISCUSSION QUESTIONS

1. How does the development of ancient Israelite belief into monotheism affect the interpretation of biblical texts that condemn the worship of other gods? What are the implications of this development for reconstructing the Israelites' understanding of how God dealt with them?

2. What was the importance of the Exodus in the ethical demands of ancient Israelite religion?

3. What are some of the theories that seek to explain the rationale behind the classification of certain foods as "clean" and certain others as "unclean." What explanation seems most plausible to you, and why?

4. Describe the rituals that were practiced at the Jerusalem Temple in ancient Israel. What was the purpose of these rites?
5. Where did ancient Israelites worship besides the Jerusalem Temple? Describe these forms of worship.

FOR FURTHER STUDY

Albertz, Rainer. *A History of Israelite Religion in the Old Testament Period.* Translated by John Bowden. Old Testament Library. Louisville: Westminster John Knox, 1994.

Dearman, J. Andrew. *Religion and Culture in Ancient Israel.* Peabody, MA: Hendrickson, 1992.

Hess, Richard S. *Israelite Religions: An Archaeological and Biblical Survey.* Grand Rapids: Baker Academic; Nottingham: Apollos, 2007.

Lemaire, André. *The Birth of Monotheism: The Rise and Disappearance of Yahwism.* Washington, DC: Biblical Archaeology Society, 2007.

Miller, Patrick D., Jr. *The Religion of Ancient Israel.* Library of Ancient Israel. Louisville: Westminster John Knox, 2000.

Smith, Mark S. *The Origins of Biblical Monotheism: Israel's Polytheistic Background and the Ugaritic Texts.* Oxford and New York: Oxford University Press, 2001.

11

Old Testament Apocrypha and Pseudepigrapha

John C. Endres, SJ

A number of the literary works produced by ancient Jewish and Christian communities have, for various reasons, not been universally accepted as inspired Scripture. Some of these works—the Apocrypha—are accepted as "deuterocanonical" by some, but not all, Christian groups. Others—pseudepigraphical Old Testament works and apocryphal early Christian writings—have been rejected. This chapter offers a brief introduction to Old Testament Apocrypha and Pseudepigrapha.

Apocrypha (Deuterocanonical Scriptures)

During the Second Temple era (approximately 538 BCE to 132 CE), various Jewish groups authored an enormous amount of literature that was not included in the Hebrew Bible. The Septuagint (abbreviated LXX) includes a number of writings not found in the Hebrew Bible, but which were widely accepted in the early Christian church. Saint Jerome held doubts about these additional books, which he termed *Apocrypha*, but he agreed to translate them into Latin for the Vulgate Bible. Saint Augustine instead favored the wider canon of the LXX, and the Vulgate translation, with the Apocrypha, continued to be the biblical text in use by the Catholic Church until the time of the Reformation. The Catholic Church terms these additional books *deuterocanonical*, meaning "second canon" (i.e., in addition to the books of the Hebrew Bible). Martin Luther reverted to

Jerome's objections and terminology by rejecting the apocryphal books, but he did allow them to be included in his Bible—in a special section between the books of Malachi and Matthew. At the Council of Trent (1546), the Catholic Church officially accepted as inspired and canonical seven of these books from the Vulgate: 1–2 Maccabees, Judith, Tobit, Baruch (with the Letter of Jeremiah), Wisdom of Solomon, and Sirach, plus the expansions of Esther and Daniel found in the LXX and Vulgate.[1] As a result, these Deuterocanonical Books appear in Catholic Bibles, interspersed with historical, poetical, and prophetic books. Protestant Bibles, beginning with early Luther Bibles, either exclude these books completely or relegate them to a special section, between the Old Testament (Malachi) and the New Testament (Matthew). Sometimes this added section also includes other apocryphal works (Prayer of Manasseh, 3 Ezra, 4 Ezra, and 3 Maccabees). A related term for such books, "intertestamental," seemingly refers to the period in which they were written, the approximately four centuries between Malachi and Matthew, but the term may have originated in reference to the physical (spatial) location of these books in Protestant Bibles, sandwiched between the Old and New Testaments.

In this handbook, Tobit, Judith, and 1 and 2 Maccabees are discussed with the historical books, and Wisdom of Solomon and Sirach are discussed in the wisdom section. This essay comments only on the five remaining apocryphal texts (Baruch, Prayer of Manasseh, Psalm 151, and 3 and 4 Maccabees) and the Pseudepigrapha.

Pseudepigrapha

A much larger collection of extra-biblical Jewish texts, however, stands alongside the Hebrew Bible and the Apocrypha/Deuterocanonicals, often described as *Pseudepigrapha*. Some use the term *pseudepigraphical* to refer to texts that have been falsely ascribed to an ancient author whose name would have commanded respect and lent authority to the particular text. Such texts, even when they fail to attain canonical status, witness to the lively religious imagination of people

---

1. See also chapter 1, "The Formation of the Bible," and the chart "Canons of Scripture" in the additional study aids section.

schooled in the Scriptures of the Old Testament. These writings often present more details about the great biblical figures in Genesis. They often answer questions that ordinary folk might have asked about such biblical figures. Some questions also emerged in the Aramaic Targums (Jewish translations of the Bible into Aramaic), while others prompted religious imaginations to compose new texts that interpreted the biblical stories for people in a new context or different historical era. Most of these texts are preserved in Greek, Latin, or Slavonic, and date from the second century BCE to the first century CE. The term *Pseudepigrapha* does not refer to a fixed collection of texts, so it is not possible to give an exact list of them.

Biblical Characters Revisited

This essay thus focuses on the way the Jewish religious imagination questioned, reflected on, re-told, and interpreted important biblical characters in Apocrypha and Pseudepigrapha. This approach differs from the historical approach of many scholars (where the books are considered in their presumed historical context)[2] or from the literary approach (in which these books are grouped with those of similar literary type or genre, such as testaments, narratives, histories, or apocalypses).[3] This approach aligns more closely with the study of exegetical traditions (linked to biblical texts).[4]

Two comprehensive works, *Jubilees* and Pseudo-Philo's *Biblical Antiquities*, refer to or "retell" a great amount of the Old Testament and mention many "biblical persons" known from those Scriptures.[5]

---

2. Cf. George W. E. Nickelsburg, *Jewish Literature between the Bible and the Mishnah*, 2nd ed. (Minneapolis: Fortress Press, 2005).

3. Cf. Michael E. Stone, ed., *Jewish Writings of the Second Temple Period: Apocrypha, Pseudepigrapha, Qumran Sectarian Writings, Philo, Josephus* (Van Gorcum: Assen; Philadelphia: Fortress, 1984); also Robert A. Kraft and George W. E. Nickelsburg, *Early Judaism and its Modern Interpreters* (Philadelphia: Fortress; Atlanta: Scholars Press, 1986).

4. Cf. James L. Kugel, *Traditions of the Bible: A Guide to the Bible as It Was at the Start of the Common Era* (Cambridge, MA: Harvard University Press, 1998).

5. There are three collections of these works widely available in English translation: R. H. Charles, *The Apocrypha and Pseudepigrapha of the Old Testament* (Oxford: Clarendon, 1903); J. H. Charlesworth, ed., *The Old Testament Pseudepigrapha*, 2 vols. (Garden City, NY: Doubleday, 1983 and 1985); and H. F. D. Sparks, *The Apocryphal Old Testament* (Oxford: Clarendon, 1984).

Jubilees

Written in Hebrew, *Jubilees* survives partially in Latin and Hebrew, and wholly in Ethiopic. It narrates a revelation of the Angel of Presence to Moses involving the "events" and laws of the Torah, from the creation to the Exodus, including much material not found in the Bible. Its narratives feature many biblical characters—like Adam and Eve, Enoch, Noah, Abraham, Rebekah, Jacob, Joseph, and Moses—with more positive attention to women than is found in the Bible. This book reflects a great desire to understand better all the stories and issues raised by a reading of Genesis 1 to Exodus 12.

Biblical Antiquities

Pseudo-Philo's *Biblical Antiquities* was written in Hebrew but is preserved fully only in a Latin text. It narrates the biblical history from Adam to the death of Saul, with numerous interpretive touches and a significant focus on women in the story.

Individual biblical characters (Adam and Eve, Enoch, Noah, Abraham, Rebekah, Jacob, Dinah, Joseph, Moses, Baruch, Job, David, Solomon, Manasseh, and the Maccabees) are the focus of a number of apocryphal and pseudepigraphical works.

Adam and Eve

Adam and Eve feature in the *Life of Adam and Eve*, a Latin text that may be based on a Greek work known as the *Apocalypse of Moses*. It explores issues such as the sin of Eve and Adam, their death, burial, and resurrection on the last day, and also the character Satan.

Enoch

Enoch receives little attention in the Bible. He appears in a genealogy (Gen. 4:17–18) and his life is summarized in Genesis 5:21–24, which states cryptically that he "walked with God" and "God took him." Since Genesis does not mention his death, the brief notice spawned a great deal of interest and speculation, and some Jewish thinkers concluded that he was located in heavenly circles, in the company of

Although fragments of the original Hebrew text of *Enoch* have been found, the complete text survives only in Ethiopic translation, as in this manuscript. The Ethiopic Church alone accepts *Enoch* as canonical, although the author of Jude quotes it as sacred Scripture (Jude 5, 14–15).

the angels. So much material attaches to his name (three "books" of Enoch) that he can be considered the most important biblical character in this era. *First Enoch* is composed of five distinct booklets; it stands out as the most unusual and important of the pseudepigraphical books. Written in Aramaic, the whole book is preserved only in Ethiopic and includes: the Book of the Watchers (chs. 1–36, also preserved in Greek); the Parables of Enoch (chs. 37–71); the Book of the Luminaries or the Astronomical Book (chs. 72–82); the Book of Dreams (chs. 83–90, which includes the Animal Apocalypse, chs. 85–90); and the Epistle of Enoch (chs. 91–105). Enoch emerges as a type of prophetic-apocalyptic figure, delivering words and teachings of great significance; ultimately he appears as a kind of savior figure.

Additional Enoch traditions appear in later texts: *2 Enoch* (Slavonic) and *3 Enoch* (*Hebrew Apocalypse of Enoch*, also known as the *Book of Hekhalot*). *Jubilees* also treats Enoch (*Jub.* 4:16–26). In this text Enoch demonstrates great cultural learning, and is removed from his family and taken to the Garden of Eden.

Noah

Noah appears in several works that elaborate on the narratives in Genesis. The *Genesis Apocryphon*, an Aramaic text found at Qumran, narrates his birth and his blameless life. *Jubilees* also interprets his role, connecting him with the covenant, the calendar, and the feast of Shavuot. Finally, several references to a lost document about Noah led some scholars to postulate a lost *Apocalypse of Noah*.

Abraham

Abraham's portrayal in Genesis is expanded in the *Testament of Abraham*, where God gives him an opportunity to compose a testament before his death. More surprising is a drama in which Death and Michael the archangel struggle with him, but the book ends without the writing of a testament. This Testament survives in two recensions: one in Greek, and the other a Slavonic *Apocalypse of Abraham*, where Abraham perceives the idols of his father's house, and then takes a heavenly journey described in seven visions, including a view of the sins of human beings on the earth. Abraham in *Jubilees* also gives three Testaments (chs. 20, 21, and 22).

Rebekah

Rebekah does not have a text associated with her name, but she is a major character in *Jubilees*, where she preserves the covenant by orchestrating the lives of her sons Jacob and Esau, and especially by blessing Jacob (ch. 25) and giving a last testament (ch. 35).

Jacob

Jacob plays an important role in *Jubilees* 19–45, where he appears as the central covenant mediator for Judaism. One of the most important pseudepigraphical texts is the *Testaments of the Twelve Patriarchs*, featuring the sons of Jacob and his wives and concubines. Drawing from the scene in Genesis 49 where Jacob at his deathbed gathers his sons around him and predicts future events for them and their descendants, these testaments offer a distinct literary document for each son. Each text recalls an incident in the life of a patriarch where a particular ethical virtue was highlighted; then the patriarch exhorts his offspring to emulate that ethical stance. Some examples are Reuben, concerning thoughts; Simeon, concerning envy; Levi, concerning priesthood and arrogance; Joseph concerning self-control when tempted by the wife of Potiphar, and fraternal love for his brothers who had wronged him. These texts warn people against common human failings: lust, anger, envy, deceit, hatred, love of money. The present text clearly contains Christian terminology and notions, sparking a continuing debate about its Jewish or Christian origins.

Dinah

Dinah, daughter of Jacob and Leah, was raped by Shechem, son of Hamor (in Gen. 34). This vivid narrative sparked much interest for Jewish writers of the era. In *Jubilees* 30 the violent reaction of her brothers Simeon and Levi (killing the men of Shechem) was justified as an act opposing intermarriage with non-Jews. Other texts reflecting this incident include *Testament of Levi* (chs. 2–7), *Aramaic Levi Document* (chs. 1–2, 6), Judith (ch. 9), *Pseudo Philo* (ch. 8), and Josephus, *Jewish Antiquities* (1.337–41).

Joseph

Joseph, son of Jacob, was included in the *Testaments of the Twelve Patriarchs*, and also in *Jubilees* (chs. 39–46). Joseph's story also inspired another Hellenistic work, *Joseph and Aseneth*. Expanding on Genesis 41:45, this romance narrates the conversion of the daughter of Potiphera, required for her to marry Joseph. This Jewish work was preserved only by Christians, where its popularity may be due to its focus on conversion and a scene somewhat reminiscent of the Eucharist.

Moses

Moses figures prominently in two pseudepigraphs and one history. *Jubilees* opens at Mount Sinai, where Moses receives from the Angel of Presence a revelation involving the law and testimony, which he is to pass on to Israel. Here many laws related to stories of the patriarchs and matriarchs actually derive from later Mosaic laws. In the *Testament of Moses*, the leader addresses his final words to Joshua with predictions about the future life of his people. Preserved in only one Latin manuscript, the text focusing Moses' prayer for divine compassion reflects a crisis situation. The *Exagōgē* (leading out) section of *Ezekiel the Tragedian* offers numerous interpretive details about Moses and the Exodus.

Isaiah

Texts connected to prophetic figures also abound. Isaiah is featured in the *Martyrdom of Isaiah*, a Jewish work forming the first section of the Christian text, *Ascension of Isaiah*. The prophet is about to be put to death by agents of the evil King Manasseh; this story of martyrdom resembles similar scenes in 2 Maccabees 6–7.

Baruch

Baruch, the scribe of Jeremiah, appears in the deuterocanonical book of Baruch; the *Letter of Jeremiah* forms the last chapter of this deuterocanonical book. *2 Baruch*, or the *Syriac Apocalypse of Baruch*, was probably a Hebrew text but is now extant only in Syriac. It portrays Baruch in an account of the sixth-century BCE fall of Jerusalem, where he utters laments and questions about God's justice. It holds out some hope for the future, while reflecting theologically on Rome's destruction of Jerusalem (cf. also *4 Ezra* [=2 Esdras]).

The Sibyl, an Extra-Biblical Prophetess

The *Sibylline Oracles* presents itself as a text given by the Sibyl, an aging Greek prophetess whose oracles usually interpret historical-political situations. This collection of twelve books in Greek includes both

The *Sibylline Oracles*, ostensibly the predictions of a Delphic prophetess, was probably authored by Alexandrian Jews and expanded by Christians over several centuries. The work left its mark on Christian art; a number of sybils appear along with prophets in the ceiling of the Sistine Chapel.

Christian and Jewish texts. In the late Middle Ages these female prophetic figures held prominence in Christian art and spirituality. The Sistine Chapel intersperses Sibyls and prophets of the Old Testament; the *Dies Irae*, a Latin sequence used in Requiem Masses, mentions the Sybil along with David. In Book 3, this Sibyl identifies herself as daughter-in-law of Noah (*Sib. Or.* 3.827).

Job

Job, a wisdom figure in the Bible, stars in the *Testament of Job*, a Greek text that obviously depends on the LXX version of Job. In this testament, the narrative section (with Satan as adversary) stands out more than the ethical advice, which focuses on patient endurance. Job undergoes conversion and demonstrates great knowledge of heavenly realities; at its conclusion, his soul is taken to heaven in a chariot.

David

David appears in *Psalm 151*, found in the LXX and also in Hebrew at Qumran (Psalms Scroll from Cave 11). It recounts God's choice of David and his conquest of Goliath in 1 Samuel 16–17. Because it appears in the LXX, it comprises part of the Apocrypha.

Solomon

Attribution to Solomon added authority to OT texts connected with wisdom, such as Proverbs and Ecclesiastes. Inspired by Psalm 72, the *Psalms of Solomon*, also found in the LXX, offers eighteen poems attributed to him and oriented to the situation of Pompey's conquest of Jerusalem in 63 BCE. Psalm 17 of this collection features a Messiah figure and suggests a sensibility about suffering from oppression. The *Odes of Solomon* is a collection of forty-two odes attributed to Solomon. Preserved in Syriac, Greek, and Coptic, it has affinities with the Qumran *Hodayoth* (Thanksgiving Songs), and also with the Gospel of John; they likely were composed by a Jew in the early second century CE.

Manasseh

Manasseh was considered the most wicked king of Judah by the Deuteronomistic Historian (2 Kings 21), but the Chronicler relates that he repented and was rehabilitated (2 Chron. 33). The Latin *Prayer of Manasseh*, from Christian sources, could easily be imagined as the prayer mentioned in 2 Chronicles 33:18–19. Its heart-felt sense of penitence and trust in God's compassion continue to attract worshipers. Found in medieval Vulgate manuscripts, it was included as part of the Apocrypha by Luther and the King James Version.

Figures of the Maccabean Revolt

The Maccabees figured prominently in two deuterocanonical books, *1* and *2 Maccabees*, part of the Catholic and Orthodox canon. *Third Maccabees*, which is actually about Jews living in Egypt, offers assurance that God protects his people, especially at critical points of suffering. Memorable scenes include the saving of the Jews in a stadium from elephants intended to kill them, but who became inebriated and unable to carry out their task. A Greek historical romance, it appears in the LXX, in the Orthodox canon, and in Luther's Apocrypha, but not in the Vulgate.

Fourth Maccabees argues that reason can dominate over the force of one's passions. Another text from Alexandria, it develops its point by retelling martyrdom scenes known from 2 Maccabees 6–7. The notion of expiatory suffering, justifying the noble deaths narrated in those chapters, is well developed. It appears in an appendix to the Greek Orthodox Bible.

Although other examples could be adduced, this collection amply demonstrates how the Apocrypha and especially the Pseudepigrapha basically derive from fascination with texts considered sacred among Jews, and which derive from the Bible. Testaments and apocalypses, retold narratives, prophetic poems and psalms, all witness to the ongoing power of the Scriptures. Readers and hearers of these texts—individuals and communities—cannot help but wonder how these stories and persons might impact and inspire their own lives if they allow their religious imagination greater scope.

DISCUSSION QUESTIONS

1. Most of the writings discussed in this chapter were ultimately rejected from the Jewish canon and the canons of most Christian groups. Does their rejection appear reasonable? Why, or why not?

2. Would the development of Jewish or Christian beliefs have been significantly different if more of these texts had been accepted as canonical? Explain your answer.

3. In keeping with the male-dominated culture of the time, most of the major characters in this literature are male, but a number of female characters also feature prominently, including Eve, Rebekah, Dinah, Asenath, and the Sybil. Why do you suppose the authors of the Apocrypha and Pseudepigrapha found the stories of these five women to be so interesting?

4. As discussed, the figure of Enoch receives scant attention in the Bible but is arguably the favorite character in this literature. What was there in the Enoch story that so attracted the interest of authors in this period?

FOR FURTHER STUDY

Charlesworth, J. H., ed. *The Old Testament Pseudepigrapha*. 2 vols. Garden City, NY: Doubleday & Company, 1983 and 1985.

Nickelsburg, George W. E. *Jewish Literature between the Bible and the Mishnah*. 2nd ed. Minneapolis: Fortress Press, 2005.

12

Jewish Biblical Interpretation

Amy-Jill Levine

According to Ben Bag-Bag, a rabbinic contemporary of Jesus, Israel's Scripture is both ground of and guide to life: "Turn it and turn it again, for everything is in it; contemplate it and grow grey and old over it, and stir not from it, because you can have no better rule than it" (*Mishnah Avot* 5.22). This statement presents several initial details necessary for understanding Jewish biblical interpretation.

First, Scripture study is the responsibility of all the people of Israel. To make the text accessible, especially given high illiteracy rates in antiquity, Jews read the text aloud to the congregation (see Luke 4:16; Acts 15:21). In the Second Temple period, congregations offered Aramaic paraphrases (called *targumim*, meaning "translations") in the land of Israel and points east, where Aramaic had replaced Hebrew as the language of most Jews. Today, in synagogues across the globe, Scripture is chanted out loud in Hebrew while congregants have copies of the vernacular.

All Jews can and should participate in Torah study, including women (although like that of Christian women, Jewish women's formal participation in scriptural interpretation was rare before the late twentieth century). According to legend, Beruriah, the daughter of the martyred Rabbi Haninah ben Teradyon (early second century CE) and the wife of Rabbi Meir, daily studied three hundred legal matters (*Babylonian Talmud Pesahim* 62b), offered authoritative legal rulings (*Tosefta Bava Qamma* 4.9), and gave profound pastoral counseling (*Midrash Proverbs*).

Second, the text speaks to each reader; its manifold richness cannot be restricted to one interpretation. The Psalmist wrote, "Once

God has spoken; twice have I heard this" (Ps. 62:11a). However, the Hebrew can also be translated: "One thing God has spoken; two things I have heard." This idea of multiple meanings receives development in rabbinic commentary. Quoting Jeremiah 23:29, which describes the divine word as "like a hammer that breaks a rock in pieces," the *Babylonian Talmud* (*Sanhedrin* 34a) states that one verse of Scripture offers multiple teachings. According to another rabbinic commentary, *Numbers Rabbah* 13.15–16, the Torah has seventy faces (Hebrew: *shiv'im panim la-Torah*).

The traditional form of Jewish study is to debate texts with a fellow student. Much like United States Supreme Court records, rabbinical texts preserve debates and record minority opinions (*mahloket*). As *Mishnah Avot* 5.17 states, "Every dispute that is for the sake of

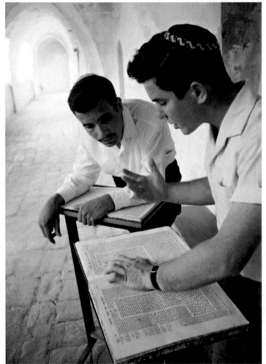

In traditional Jewish practice, students of Torah work together, in pairs. Jewish biblical interpretation is a conversation with many partners, past and present.

heaven will endure." *Babylonian Talmud Eruvin* 13b concurs: sages may disagree, but "the statements of both are the words of the living God."

This approach is consistent with Judaism's nonhierarchical structure: Jews have no single authority such as a pope or a bishop. Just as certain interpreters have major influence in Christian thought (e.g., Augustine, Aquinas), so within Judaism certain interpreters have recognized authority (e.g., Rashi [1040–1105], Maimonides [1135–1204]), but disagreement with their teaching exists. Hasidic movements have leaders who determine interpretation, but these leaders have authority only over their specific group. Modern Jewish movements (Reform, Reconstructionist, Renewal, Conservative, Orthodox, etc.) have different approaches and cite different authorities to interpret Scripture, and individual Jews may and do disagree with their rabbi's interpretation.

Appreciation for multiple readings is connected to the self-definition of the Jewish community. Judaism is not simply a religion (i.e., a movement one enters because of a particular faith or belief), although there are "Jews by choice," that is, people who convert to Judaism. Jews are also a "people" with a common ancestry (from Abraham and Sarah) and a homeland (Israel). From the second century CE, Jews have recognized any child of a Jewish mother as a Jew; more liberal branches of Judaism today recognize as Jewish the child of either a Jewish mother or father, provided the child is raised as a Jew.

This sense of peoplehood more easily allows for multiple readings and internal disagreement: readers may disagree, but still be in the fold. In religions where membership is determined by "belief," multiple readings may be discouraged, since incorrect belief (i.e., heresy) removes the reader from the community.

Third, Judaism has a history of biblical interpretation, as the sources cited above portend. When informed Jews study Scripture, they engage in dialogue and debate with other interpreters over two millennia.

The Scriptures of Synagogue and Church[1]

The Bible of Judaism today is the "Masoretic Text," twenty-four Hebrew books standardized sometime between the ninth and eleventh centuries CE. Because written Hebrew originally consisted only of consonants (compare short-hand, or text-messaging), the Masoretes (the name is derived from a Hebrew term connoting the handing down of tradition) added vowels. Also controlling accuracy is the *Masorah*, a medieval commentary providing details on vocalization, variant readings, brief explanatory annotations, the counting of letters and words, and other details to ensure the standardization of copies. In antiquity, although the text was not fully standardized, the deep connections between the biblical materials found among the Dead Sea Scrolls and the medieval version suggest that the text has remained relatively secure for two millennia.

Translation

New Testament writers did not generally follow the Hebrew Scriptures that became the Masoretic Text; they based their writings on Greek translations (e.g., the Septuagint) developed by Jewish communities outside the land of Israel. The differences in the texts inevitably created different interpretations.

Isaiah 7:14 provides the most famous example of this translation difference. The Hebrew describes a "young woman" (*'almah*) who is pregnant; she is thus presumably not a virgin (cf. the NABRE, "The young woman, pregnant and about to bear a son," and the NRSV "The young woman is with child and shall bear a son"). Her pregnancy serves as a sign to King Uzziah that his political problems will abate (7:16). The Septuagint translates *'almah* as *parthenos* (cf. the Parthenon, the temple of the virgin Athena). *Parthenos* need not mean "virgin," as the Septuagint of Genesis 34:3 indicates by calling Dinah a *parthenos* after her relations with Shechem. Matthew 1:23

---

1. Additional discussion related to the history of various canons can be found in chapter 1, "The Formation of the Bible"; see also the chart "Canons of Scripture" in the additional study aids section. For discussion of issues related to translation, see especially chapter 2, "Bible Translations." For discussion related to Christianity, Judaism, and Scripture, see chapter 20, "The Christian Bible and the Jews," and chapter 16, "Introduction to the Prophetic Books."

reads Isaiah 7:14, in Greek, as referring to a "virgin" and finds this prediction fulfilled in Jesus' miraculous conception.

Understandings of Isaiah 7:14 separated Jewish and Christian interpreters as early as the second century. The church father Justin Martyr (*Dialogue with Trypho* 67, ca. 160) records the Jewish view that the text refers to a "young woman" rather than a "virgin," and that "the whole prophecy refers to King Hezekiah." Justin responds, "Your teachers . . . have altogether taken away many Scriptures from the [Greek] translation." That is, Jews changed the text. The charge is illegitimate, as the Dead Sea Scrolls demonstrate.

Punctuation

Early biblical manuscripts not only lack vowels, they also lack punctuation; from this lack, again the Jewish tradition finds opportunity for multiple interpretations. Isaiah 40:3–4 offers an excellent example of how new punctuation can change meaning. Speaking to Jewish exiles in Babylon, Isaiah announces the good news that they will return home: "In the wilderness prepare the way of the Lord, make straight in the desert a highway for our God." The placement of the punctuation is determined by the context: Isaiah is telling the people to build a highway in the desert to facilitate their return to the land of Israel.

Removed from its original literary and historical context, the text can read, "The voice of one crying out in the wilderness: 'Prepare the way of the Lord, make his paths straight,'" which is how it is quoted in the Gospel of Mark (1:3). It is also one possible interpretation of the abbreviated quotation of this passage (the "voice" is not mentioned) in the Dead Sea Scrolls (1QS [the *Community Rule* from Cave 1] 8:14–16). Mark's readers may well have taken the "Lord" in the quotation as a reference to Jesus and the term "way" as an allusion to the "Way," the self-designation of Jesus' earliest followers (see Acts 9:2).

Canonical Order

The terms by which Jews and Christians identify their Scriptures also highlight differences. The church's "Old Testament" necessarily portends a "New Testament." For Jews, the text is called *Miqra*

(Hebrew, "that which is read, reading") and, more commonly, the "Tanak," an acronymn for Torah [the Pentateuch], *Nevi'im* [Prophets], and *Kethuvim* [Writings]. The Jewish Bible is thus a complete text, not "Part 1" of a larger revelation.

Complicating the identification of the Bibles of synagogue and church is the list of contents in the Christian "Old Testament." For Catholic and Orthodox readers, the "Old Testament" includes the deuterocanonical texts (Judith, the additions to Daniel and Esther, 1 and 2 Maccabees, Sirach [Ecclesiasticus], etc.) written by Jews before the time of Jesus and preserved in Greek. Many Protestants reject these texts as "Old Testament Apocrypha." Anglicans and some Lutherans, although they would not consider these books to be "deuterocanonical" in the same way that Catholics and Orthodox do, permit these works to be read in liturgical context and as such deem them worthy of respect. Jewish tradition displays knowledge of these texts, but the books are not in the Jewish canon. Further complicating biblical identification is the question of which original texts are believed to be inspired: whereas Protestant and Catholic readers share with the Jewish community the Hebrew version of Israel's Scriptures, the Orthodox churches proclaim not the Hebrew but the Greek version (the Septuagint).

Canonical order creates a second distinction. Christian canons place the book of Ruth between Judges and 1 Samuel; in Jewish canons, Ruth appears in the *Kethuvim*, the Writings. More telling of the distinction between synagogue and church is the placement of the prophetic books. The Old Testament ends with Malachi's prediction of Elijah's return: "Lo, I will send you the prophet Elijah before the great and terrible day of the Lord comes. He will turn the hearts of parents to their children and the hearts of children to their parents, so that I will not come and strike the land with a curse" (Mal. 4:5–6; 3:23–24 in the Hebrew text). The Gospels associate John the Baptist with Elijah (Mark 1:2–4), and read the prophets as predicting Jesus' advent. For the church, the Old Testament, beginning with sin in Eden and ending with Malachi's eschatological prophecy, anticipates the New Testament, wherein sin is redressed and prophecy fulfilled.

Judaism tells a different story. Tucking the prophets (*Nevi'im*) in the middle of the canon, the Tanak ends with the *Kethuvim*. This order is ancient: Josephus knows the "five books of Moses," "the

Prophets" and "remaining . . . books" (*Against Apion* 1.39–41; cf. Luke 24:32, 44). The *Kethuvim* concludes in 2 Chronicles 36:23 with Cyrus of Persia's edict to the Jews in Babylon: "The Lord God of Heaven has given me all the kingdoms of the earth, and has charged me with building Him a House in Jerusalem, which is in Judah. Any one of you of all His people, the Lord his God be with him and let him go up" (JPS). A few medieval Hebrew manuscripts end not with Chronicles but with Ezra-Nehemiah. The same message prevails in both cases, since Nehemiah's final verse, "Remember me, O my God, for good" (13:31b) echoes "God" (*elohim*) and "good" (*tov*) from Genesis 1. Both Jewish canonical orders thus do not point forward to new teachings or a new canon; instead, they encourage readers to return home both literally and textually, to look again, to turn it and turn it.

Hermeneutical Lenses

Scriptural Emphases

Judaism emphasizes the Pentateuch or Torah (Hebrew, "instruction"). Some congregations read the entire Pentateuch, divided into fifty-four *parashiyyot* (Hebrew, "divisions"; singular: *parshah*), annually; others follow a trienniel cycle. Each *parshah* has an accompanying reading (*haftarah*, Hebrew for "conclusion, departing") from the *Nevi'im* (Prophets) or *Kethuvim* (Writings). Thus texts interpret one another. Christian lectionaries (readings from the Old Testament, Psalms, Gospels, and Epistles) create different principal intertexts and thus different interpretive emphases. Further, Christian lectionaries draw primarily from the Prophets rather than the Pentateuch. Consequently, many laws that define Jewish identity are not proclaimed in Christian worship; nor do Christians hear, liturgically, the frequent promises of the land. In turn, passages the New Testament associates with Jesus, such as Isaiah 61:1 (see Luke 4:18), do not appear in the Jewish liturgical readings.

Liturgy yields another difference in scriptural emphasis. Most Jewish holidays have assigned readings (as the Gospel Passion Narratives are read during Holy Week): on Purim, the book of Esther is read; on Shavuot (Hebrew, "weeks"; compare the Christian "Pentecost"), to celebrate both the spring harvest and the giving of the Torah, the book of Ruth is read; on the ninth of the month of

Av (early August), the date on which both Temples were destroyed, Lamentations is read (some Jewish communities also read Job). Only a few passages from these books are scattered in Christian lectionaries. Consequently, Jewish biblical familiarity differs from Christian biblical familiarity.

Two more differences between Christian and Jewish understanding arise in the form by which Scripture is presented. In synagogues, the Torah is chanted in Hebrew from a hand-written scroll. In most churches the text is read in the vernacular, from a book.

Theological and Anthropological Presuppositions

Jews and Christians, broadly speaking, read through different theological and anthropological positions. For example, the church traditionally finds in Genesis 1:26, "Then God said, 'Let us make humankind in our image,'" an indication of the Trinity, for "In the beginning was the Word" (John 1:1). Judaism proffers several understandings: God takes council with the angels to model the practice of the greater consulting with the lesser (*Genesis Rabbah* 8.3–4); God tests readers, who might fall into the heresy of polytheism (*Genesis Rabbah* 8.8); the plural signals divine majesty, and so on. Likely the original meaning reflected the ancient Near Eastern notion of the heavenly court (cf. 1 Kings 22:19–22; Ps. 29:1–2; 82; Isa. 6:8; etc.).

The story of Adam and Eve (who disappear from the Tanak after Gen. 5) also receives distinct interpretations. For traditional Judaism, the disobedience of the first couple neither alienates humanity from God nor creates the sinful urge. Rather, Judaism views humanity as having both a good inclination (*yetzer ha-tov*) and an evil inclination (*yetzer ha-ra'*); human beings are thus capable of moral choice. One can curb the evil inclination by following Torah (*Babylonian Talmud Kiddushin* 30b).

Attention to Adam and Eve developed in early Hellenistic Judaism (see Sir. 25:24), a development found also in Romans 5:12–20 (cf. 5:19, "For just as by the one man's disobedience the many were made sinners, so by the one man's obedience the many will be made righteous"), and 1 Timothy 2:12–15 appeals to Eve's sin to restrict women's roles. Augustine claimed that "the deliberate sin of the first man is the cause of original sin" (*Marriage and Concupiscence* 2.26.43), an idea alien to Jewish thought.

A third major place where Jewish and Christian understandings part concerns the identification of Isaiah's Suffering
Servant. For the church, the Servant is Jesus, "wounded for our
transgressions . . . upon him was the punishment that made us
whole. . . . Like a lamb that is led to the slaughter" (Isa. 53:5, 7; cf.
Acts 8:30–35; also John 19:34, 37; Rev. 1:7). Jewish tradition principally understands the Servant as the people Israel, wounded in
exile, whose return to Zion demonstrates divine power and providence. The debate over the Servant's identification appears as early
as Origen's *Against Celsus* 1.55 (248 CE): "In a discussion with some
whom the Jews regard as learned I used these prophecies. At this the
Jew said that these prophecies referred to the whole people as though
of a single individual, since they were scattered in the dispersion and
smitten, that as a result of the scattering of the Jews among the other
nations many might become proselytes."

Given Judaism's affirmation of multiple readings, additional
interpretations of the Servant appear. The *Babylonian Talmud Sotah*
14a connects Isaiah 53:12 to Moses, and the *Jerusalem Talmud Sheqa-
lim* connects Isaiah 53:4 to Rabbi Akiba. The *Babylonian Talmud
Sanhedrin* 98b queries: "The Messiah—what is his name? . . . The
rabbis say, The Leper Scholar, as it is said, 'surely he has borne our
griefs and carried our sorrows: yet we did esteem him a man with
leprosy, smitten of God and afflicted'" (*Targum Jonathan* on Isa. 42:1;
52:13 says something similar).

Halakah: "Oral Law" or "Oral Torah"

The Torah does not come with an instruction manual for following each commandment (traditionally numbered at 613), and
therefore Jewish communities always have had to determine the
correct path. Such interpretation is called *halakah*, from the Hebrew
"to walk." For example, Exodus 31:14 forbids "work" on the Sabbath
(also 31:15; Deut. 5:15; Neh. 13:22; Isa. 56:6; Jer. 17:22–27), but
what constitutes work? *Mishnah Shabbat* 7.2 delineates thirty-nine
labors forbidden on the Sabbath. There are also codicils, for example,
cutting is forbidden but circumcision is not; laws must be overridden
to save a life.

Such interpretation, initially transmitted orally, became known
as the Oral Torah; Gospel references to the "tradition of the elders"

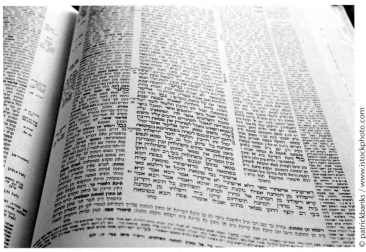

A page from the Talmud graphically conveys the character of the study of Torah; layer upon layer is added to the commentary. The text in the center is the Mishnah, the oldest layer of the Oral Torah.

(Matt. 15:2; Mark 7:3–4) are likely connected to this practice. Around 200 CE these interpretations were codified in the *Mishnah* (Hebrew: "instruction, repetition"), a compendium of Jewish law and lore. Interpretation continued in the *Tosefta* (Aramaic: "additional [material]" or "supplement"; completed ca. 250). Then commentaries on the Mishnah developed: the *Yerushalmi* (*Jerusalem Talmud*, completed ca. 400) and the *Bavli* (*Babylonian Talmud*, completed ca. 600). The *Bavli* is the principal authoritative text for contemporary Judaism. Printings of the Talmud display the text of the *Mishnah* surrounded by Talmudic commentary (known as *gemara*, Aramaic for "study"), surrounded by other commentaries; the text visually suggests that if the pages could be larger, ever-new readings would appear. Halakhic discussion continues to this day.

Rabbinic thought ascribes equal value and antiquity to both Written and Oral Torahs. *Mishnah Avot* 1.1 records, "Moses received the Torah from Sinai and transmitted it to Joshua. Joshua transmitted it to the Elders, the Elders to the Prophets, and the Prophets to the Men of the Great Assembly." Subsequent verses bring the tradition to the date of the Mishnah.

Knowledge of the Oral Torah provides important correctives to the view that Jewish teaching is restricted to the Tanak. For example, Matthew 5:38–39 mentions the teaching of "an eye for an eye and a tooth for a tooth" (Exod. 21:23–24; Lev. 24:19–20; Deut. 19:21). Like Jesus, Jewish interpretation resists a retributive approach. The rabbis (*Mishnah Bava Qamma* 8.1; *Babylonian Talmud Bava Qamma* 84a) observe that the commandment cannot literally be fulfilled for no two eyes or limbs are equal. Therefore, they conclude, in the case of injury, the responsible party pays for damages, pain, medical expenses, loss of work due to injury, and anguish or embarrassment.

Aggadah: Jewish Storytelling or Midrash

Complementing halakah is *aggadah* (Aramaic: "tales" or "narratives"; compare the Hebrew *haggadah* ["narrative, tale"], the book read in Jewish homes at the Passover meal). Aggadic materials convey moral lessons and practical advice, but they are not legally binding. The principal form of *aggadah* is *midrash* (Hebrew: "to seek" or "to ask").

Some midrashic materials provide additional information about biblical figures such as Abraham and Moses (*Genesis Rabbah*; *Exodus Rabbah*), just as early Christian writings recounted stories about Jesus and Mary's childhood (*Infancy Gospel of Thomas*; *Protevangelium of James*). Such accounts are more common in Jewish, Catholic, and Orthodox settings than in Protestant thought, given Protestant emphasis on *sola scriptura* (Latin for "Scripture alone").

Early Jewish interpreters believed that every word of the text had purpose—there were no superfluous terms, or even superfluous letters. For example, Genesis 22:2 reads in the NRSV, "He said, 'Take your son, your only son Isaac, whom you love, and go to the land of Moriah, and offer him there as a burnt offering on one of the mountains that I shall show you.'" The Hebrew literally states, "Take your son, your only [son], [the son] whom you love, Isaac. . . ." Jewish commentators queried the descriptions and order—son, only son, loved son, Isaac—and found a dialogue. "Take your son," says God; "I have two sons," replies Abraham, "Ishmael and Isaac." God specifies, "Your only son." Abraham parries, "I have only one son with Sarah, and only one son with Hagar." God further specifies, "The one whom you love." Given that Abraham had just banished Ishmael and his mother, his response is poignant: "I love them both." Only then does God state, "Isaac" (from Rashi, following *Babylonian Talmud Sanhedrin* 89b).

Midrash can also convey profound moral views. Commenting on Israel's Exodus from Egyptian slavery, the *Babylonian Talmud Megillah* 10b states that the angels wanted to sing songs of joy, but God responded, "The creations of My hands are drowning in the sea, and you are singing songs?!" God was referring to the Egyptians.

Reading Strategies

Rabbinic readers resist idiosyncratic interpretations that dismiss plain meanings, rely on special knowledge gained through revelation, or rest on the exclusive authority of an individual. This emphasis on the communal and logical versus the individual and inspired is epitomized by the famous account of the "oven of Akhni" (*Babylonian Talmud Bava Metzi'a* 59b). Although one rabbi makes his case that the oven is kosher on the basis of miracles, ranging from a river flowing backwards to a voice from heaven (a "*bat qol*," cf. the divine voice in Gospel accounts of Jesus' baptism and transfiguration), his case is defeated. The sages resist mystically inspired, individual readings, citing Deuteronomy 30:12 ("It [i.e., the Torah] is not in the heavens"). The responsibility for interpreting Scripture rests with the community and not with personal charisma.

The various strategies for interpretation include:

A. *Middot* (Hebrew for "measurements, norms") comprise sets of hermeneutical rules, from the seven ascribed to Rabbi Hillel, an older contemporary of Jesus, to the thirteen associated with the early second-century CE Rabbi Ishmael, to the thirty-two ascribed to the late second-century Rabbi Eliezer ben Jose the Galilean. Of the various techniques, the following two are the most well known, and are found in the New Testament.

Qal vahomer, or "from the lesser to the greater" (an *a fortiori* or *a minori ad maius* argument), known also in classical and Christian contexts, argues that if a minor premise is accepted, then "how much more so" (the standard formulation) is something major acceptable (see, e.g., Matt. 12:11–12).

Gematria, a Hebrew term likely derived from the Greek *geo-metria* (i.e., "geometry"), assigns numerical values to Hebrew letters (Aleph=1, Beth=2, and so on), and then compares the value of the word or phrase to another word or phrase with the same value. Gematria explains Revelation 13:18: the Hebrew letters spelling "Nero Caesar" add to 666.

B. *Pardes* (Hebrew for "orchard"; "paradise" is a cognate term) is an acronym for four reading strategies presented in the *Zohar*. This thirteenth-century Spanish text, traditionally ascribed to the second-century CE Rabbi Simeon Bar-Yohai, provides instruction in *Kabbalah* (Hebrew, "tradition, that which is received"; simplistically described as "Jewish mysticism"). P stands for *peshat*, the plain or "literal" meaning. R is for *remez* ("hint"); this approach seeks allegorical or symbolic interpretations. D is for *darash*, "inquire" or "seek"; it looks for the metaphorical meaning. S is for *sod*, "mystery" or "secret"; here interpretation derives from inspiration. These readings possibly both informed and were informed by Christian hermeneutics. From the patristic era, the church recognized multiple approaches: literal/historical, allegorical, moral (tropological), and anagogical (metaphysical/eschatological/symbolic/mystical/inspired).

C. *Allegory*, in which a textual reference has a corollary in the external world, is in Jewish interpretation principally associated with Philo of Alexandria (ca. 20 BCE–50 CE), whose works were preserved by the church (see Eusebius, *Ecclesiastical History* 2.17; Jerome, *On Illustrious Men* 11). For example, Philo describes circumcision as symbolizing "the excision of the pleasures which delude the mind" (*On the Special Laws* 1.9). Allegories appear in the New Testament (for example, Paul's allegory of Sarah and Hagar in Gal. 4) and remained popular in Christian exegesis. Generally, Jewish thought valued the plain meaning (*peshat*) and resisted complete allegory.

D. *Pesher* (Hebrew: "interpretation") is associated primarily with the Dead Sea Scrolls. *Pesher* finds in biblical texts meanings accessible only to select readers. For example, 1QpHab (*Pesher Habakkuk* from Qumran Cave 1) 7.1–5 comments on Habakkuk 2:1 and following verses, "God commanded Habakkuk to write the things that were coming on the last generation, but the fulfillment of the epoch He did not make known to him. And as for the words, that a person may read it swiftly; their interpretation (*pesher*) concerns the Teacher of Righteousness, to whom God made known all the mysteries of the words of His servant the prophets."

This approach, which lifts the texts from their historical and narrative context and finds contemporary applications, resembles the Gospels' fulfillment citations, for example Matthew's reading (1:23) of Isaiah 7:14. *Pesher*-type readings sometimes appear in later books of the Tanak—Daniel (9:2, 24) interprets Jeremiah's prophecy (Jer. 25:11–12; 29:10) of a seventy-year exile as referring to the author's own circumstances—but eventually *pesher* interpretation, associated with revelatory rather than logical or intertextual argument, substantially drops out of Jewish exegetical practice.

E. *Typology* suggests that anterior texts present a type or a first draft of something found in the present or that something on earth has its real existence in heavenly spheres. In the New Testament, the approach is notable in the Epistle to the Hebrews. This type of interpretation also lacks much purchase in Jewish sources, in part because it limits textual meaning (once the prophecy is "fulfilled" or "completed," it has done its job and thus is no longer relevant) and in part because it requires specialized or inspired interpretation.

Modern and Post-Modern Approaches

Jewish biblical interpreters, like Christian ones, come from and speak to various communities, from the ultra-Orthodox to the secular. Feminist, Queer, Liberationist, Ecological, Diasporic, and other readings that emphasize the author's subject position appear in Jewish interpretation, as they do in Christian and secular contexts. Jewish and non-Jewish interpreters familiar with earlier Jewish commentary draw on rabbinic/midrashic interpretation, with its attention to multiple meanings, plays on words, and intertextual conversations, to enhance literary-critical approaches and to find ever-new ethical teachings.

The term "Israel" traditionally means "one who wrestles with God" (see Gen. 32:29), and one way Jews engage in this wrestling, or striving, is to wrestle with the text. This wrestling is manifest in the previously noted rabbinic refusal to accept "an eye for an eye" literally, in the midrash concerning God's mourning over the deaths of the

Egyptian soldiers, and in the dialogue imagined between Abraham and God in which Abraham tries to resist the command to sacrifice his son. When the biblical text could be understood as promoting a morally problematic action, Jewish tradition insists on such wrestling. Thus the text, in Jewish reading, is more than a document of history, more than a repository of great literature, and more than a revelation of the divine. It is a book that prompts moral questions even as it promotes moral responses. Turning it and turning it, the Jewish community engages past interpretations, asks new questions, and finds new meaning.

DISCUSSION QUESTIONS

1. If a text can have multiple interpretations, how does one distinguish between stronger and weaker readings? Consider a particular method of interpretation: does that method take into account historical context? literary context? linguistic analysis? how the text has been understood over time by the communities that hold it sacred? Are there other controls over interpretation?

2. Unless they are also believers in Jesus (i.e., messianic Jews), Jews do not find Jesus present in the Scriptures of Israel. They do not regard Jesus as having fulfilled messianic predictions since there is yet to be peace on earth or an end to disease, poverty, exile, and death. Christian readers, on the other hand, often see Jesus predicted and even present in the pages of Genesis, Isaiah, or the Psalms. What do these different interpretations say about the interpretive methods traditionally employed by Jews? by Christians?

3. Jewish interpretation of Scripture is primarily concerned with the way one lives one's life in accord with divine will. With that goal in mind, how does one determine which biblical instructions are to be taken literally and which metaphorically? What teachings are to hold for all times, places, and peoples, and what teachings should be seen as specific to their own immediate historical contexts?

4. The term "Israel" is frequently understood to mean "one who wrestles with God"—which includes wrestling with the biblical

text. Are there texts that you find problematic? Is it possible to address passages that appear to promote war, sexism, homophobia, ethnocentrism, or religious exclusivism without simply rejecting the biblical text?

5. Marcion, a second-century Christian teacher, proclaimed that the God of the Old Testament was distinct from the God of the New Testament: the former was an inept, jealous god of wrath whereas the God Jesus proclaimed was a benevolent god of love. Although the Christian church rejected this view (known as "Marcionism") and condemned it as heresy, many misconceptions about the Jewish Scriptures persist—for example, that the God of the Tanak is a God of wrath, and that Jews worshiped (and worship) this God out of fear or through a sense of needing to earn divine love ("works righteousness"). Where do such misconceptions originate? How might one correct these misunderstandings?

FOR FURTHER STUDY

Berlin, Adele, and Marc Zvi Brettler, eds. *The Jewish Study Bible.* New York: Oxford University Press, 2004.

Brettler, Marc Zvi. *How to Read the Jewish Bible.* New York: Oxford University Press, 2007.

Levine, Amy-Jill, and Marc Zvi Brettler, eds. *The Jewish Annotated New Testament.* New York: Oxford University Press, 2011.

Sommer, Benjamin D. *Jewish Concepts of Scripture: A Comparative Introduction.* New York: New York University Press, 2012.

Zetterholm, Karin Hedner. *Jewish Interpretation of the Bible: Ancient and Contemporary.* Minneapolis: Fortress Press, 2012.

Internet Resources

The following websites provide articles and resources on Judaism and Jewish life:

www.myjewishlearning.com
www.jewfaq.org/index.shtml
www.jewishvirtuallibrary.org/jsource/judaism.html

13

Introduction to the Pentateuch

Carol J. Dempsey, OP

"In the beginning when God created the heavens and the earth" (Gen. 1:1) are the opening words of the Bible and the initial words of the Bible's first main division, the Pentateuch. The Pentateuch begins the dramatic story of God's relationship with all of creation, and specifically with the human community. In general, the Pentateuch, also known as the Torah, is a body of literature that contains a wide variety of literary forms, especially laws. As a work of literature, the Pentateuch begins with a story about creation (Gen. 1) and ends with Moses on Mount Nebo (Deut. 34), viewing the land that has been divinely promised to the Israelite people.

Although the Pentateuch reads, at times, like a history book, the contents are not meant to be an accurate historical account of what took place. Rather, the writers and later editors of the Pentateuch were often more interested in describing and explaining why something happened instead of recording actual details of events.

The Pentateuch also proposes a theological agenda that always needs to be considered in the context of ongoing critical theological reflection. The Pentateuch ought not to be treated as a scientific document, especially with regard to the creation account, nor should the Pentateuch be viewed as a textbook. The Pentateuchal stories reflect the ancient people's experience of the sacred, which, like other biblical stories, are historically, culturally, and theologically conditioned. The beauty of the Pentateuch is its ability not only to inspire but also to transform the lives of readers down through the ages.

Title and Books of the Pentateuch

The title "Pentateuch" is from the Greek, *pentateuchos*, meaning "five scrolls." The title is not attested before the second century CE, and it is used primarily by Christians. In the Jewish tradition, the Pentateuch is known as the Torah—meaning "instruction" or "law"—and is considered the most important division of the Tanak. The Pentateuch consists of five separate books, each with its own integrity. Derived from Greek and Latin, the names of the five books are Genesis (Hebrew: "In the Beginning"), Exodus (Hebrew: "And These Are the Names"), Leviticus (Hebrew: "The Law of the Priests"), Numbers (Hebrew: "In the Wilderness"), and Deuteronomy (Hebrew: "These are the Words"). In the compositional and redactional processes, the books were woven together so as to present one continuous story. Within the Jewish canon, these five books are regarded as having even greater authority than the Prophets and the Writings, the other two divisions of the Jewish canon.

Genesis

Genesis, the first book, can be divided into two segments: chapters 1–11, primeval history, and chapters 12–50, ancestral history. The book opens with the story of creation (chs. 1–2), which begins on a cosmic scale with the creation of the universe and the earth and all it contains (1:1–2:4a), followed by a more detailed description of the creation of plants, animals, and human beings from an anthropocentric perspective (2:4b–25). Clearly, the garden is the locus of activity, with human beings having a prominent role to play in the story (2:7–8, 15–25).

The story of creation is followed by a series of narratives describing the transgressions of humankind (chs. 3–11) and God's response to such transgressions. The narratives in Genesis 12–50 fall into three cycles of stories: the Abrahamic Cycle (11:27–25:18), the Isaac and Jacob Cycles (25:19–36:43), and the Joseph Cycle (chs. 37–50). Each of these three cycles depicts the great patriarchs and matriarchs of Israel, namely, Abraham, Sarah, Isaac, Rebekah, Jacob, Rachel, Leah, Zilpah, and Bildad, as well as their children and other women and men like Hagar, Laban, Dinah, Tamar, Potiphar, and many more characters in the struggle of daily life lived under divine promise (e.g., ch. 15) and, at times, divine judgment (e.g., 19:1–29). Genesis closes with Jacob's family reunited in Egypt, the place where Jacob and Joseph eventually die (49:33; 50:22–26).

Exodus

Egypt is the initial setting for Exodus, the second book of the Pentateuch. This book describes the oppression and suffering of the Israelites under the control of a despotic pharaoh who, unlike the benevolent pharaoh of Joseph's day (Gen. 47:1–12), feels threatened by the Israelites and oppresses them with forced labor (Exod. 1:8–22). Their suffering becomes the impetus for the raising up of Moses (3:1–12) who, under divine compunction, leads the people out of bondage (chs. 14–15) and through the wilderness (chs. 16–40) en route to the promised land. The climax of the Exodus story occurs when the Israelites reach Mount Sinai. There they receive a mutual covenant between their God and themselves (19:1–25) that includes God's law (chs. 20–24; 34). The Israelites have now become a "people" and not just a "family" as they were in Genesis. The latter part of Exodus focuses on instructions for building the tabernacle and its completion, culminating in the "tabernacling" of the deity. This focus on the tabernacle marks them as a people bound by worship of their God.

Leviticus

Leviticus, the third and shortest book of the Pentateuch, continues thematically the story of Exodus. Leviticus opens with how one should make sacrifices and offerings following the completion of the tabernacle. This book includes many regulations dealing with sacrifices and offerings (e.g., chs. 1–7), edible and forbidden food (ch. 11), the priesthood (chs. 8–9, 21), obligations of holiness (e.g., chs. 19–20), and feasts (e.g., ch. 23). Its main theme is Israel's call to holiness (20:26). The Israelites are exhorted to be holy, but ultimately God is the one who consecrates them (21:8; 22:9, 32). Leviticus 19 focuses on holy living. Furthermore, the command to love in 19:18 becomes the climax of all the preceding commandments. This command to love includes not only one's neighbor but also one's self.

Numbers

The fourth book is Numbers, which opens with the numbering of the Israelite tribes and their organization as a people on the march (chs. 1–2). This book describes the wanderings of the people in the wilderness for forty years. The lengthy delay before entering the promised land of Canaan was the result of the people's rebellion against their God and their leader Moses (14:13–45). During these wanderings, the Israelites had a variety of experiences, some positive, some painful (e.g., 21:1–9; 31). In the wilderness, God appoints Joshua to be Moses' successor (Num. 27:12–23; cf. Exod. 33:11). The book recounts the fate of the old Israelite generation who were eyewitnesses to the Exodus event out of Egypt. The beginning of the first generation begins in Exodus 1:5 (cf. Gen. 46:8–27). The end of the first generation, along with signs of hope in the midst of death, occurs in Numbers 21–25. Numbers 26–36 records the rise of a new generation on the edge of the promised land. The book concludes with a series of laws and instructions that assume an imminent conquest of Canaan.

Deuteronomy

The last book of the Pentateuch is Deuteronomy, which is Greek for "second law." The text is almost entirely Moses' final instructional address to the Israelites (chs. 5–26), which includes an entire code of laws (chs. 12–26). The setting is the plains of Moab, located on the east side of the River Jordan. The book also describes a covenant confirmation to be performed after the occupation of the land at Shechem (ch. 27) and a series of blessings and curses (ch. 28). This covenant at Moab corresponds to the primary one made at Horeb (chs. 29–30). The book closes with the death of Moses in Moab, right after Moses sees the land promised to the Israelites (34:1–8). Joshua, having been introduced in Exodus as Moses' assistant (Exod. 33:11) and then as Moses' successor (Num. 27:12–23), assumes his role as leader of the Israelites (Deut. 34:9), which sets the stage for texts that follow the Pentateuch. The Pentateuch ends with the Israelites still outside of the promised land.

Authorship of the Pentateuch

The study of the authorship of the Pentateuch has a long history.[1] Prior to the Enlightenment in the eighteenth century, Jewish and Christian scholars affirmed Mosaic authorship of the Pentateuch. The medieval Jewish writer Ibn Ezra (ca. 1092–1167), however, began to notice that the Pentateuch contained material that appeared to contradict the concept of Mosaic authorship. Only within the last few centuries has a thorough challenge to Mosaic authorship been launched. Baruch Spinoza (1632–1677) and Richard Simon (1638–1712) noted that the five books were full of repetitions and contradictions and seemed to lack a single author. Jean Astruc (1684–1766) proposed that multiple sources were used; however, he still thought that Moses was the one who combined the sources. Johann Gottfried Eichhorn (1744–1803), following Astruc, pointed to further stylistic distinctions between the two sources (or "strands") in Genesis that he identified as the Yahwist (J) and the Elohist (E). Karl David Ilgen made a further refinement to the theory. He identified two distinct E sources and one of J, thus arguing for three sources.

Soon various hypotheses emerged with respect to the formation of the Pentateuch. Alexander Geddes (1737–1802) proposed the Fragmentary Hypothesis. He argued that the books of Genesis to Joshua had been composed during the reign of Solomon from fragmentary sources. Heinrich Ewald (1803–1875) suggested the Supplementary Hypothesis, whereby a single core document E was supplemented by J and strands from the book of Deuteronomy. W. M. L. de Wette (1780–1849) suggested that the composition of Deuteronomy should be linked to the religious reforms undertaken by King Josiah around 621 BCE. Julius Wellhausen (1844–1918) proposed the Documentary Hypothesis. According to this hypothesis, the Pentateuch is the product of four separate written documents, J,

---

1. For further discussion on the history of the Pentateuch and pentateuchal studies, see T. Desmond Alexander, *From Paradise to the Promised Land: An Introduction to the Pentateuch* (Grand Rapids: Baker Academic, 2012); Joel S. Baden, *The Composition of the Pentateuch: Renewing the Documentary Hypothesis* (New Haven: Yale University Press, 2012); Diana Vikander Edelman, et.al., *Opening the Books of Moses* (Bristol, CT: Equinox Press, 2012); T. Desmond Alexander and David W. Baker, *Dictionary of the Old Testament: Pentateuch* (Downers Grove, IL: InterVarsity Press, 2003); Joseph Blenkinsopp, *The Pentateuch: An Introduction to the First Five Books of the Bible*, Anchor Bible Reference Library (New York: Doubleday, 1992).

E, D, P, otherwise known as the Yahwist (ca. 950 BCE), Elohist (ca. 850 BCE), Deuteronomic (ca. 600 BCE), and Priestly writers (ca. 500 BCE). These dates are all hypothetical.[2]

Wellhausen's hypothesis continues to be one of the leading theories of Pentateuchal composition, but many scholars today are more inclined to suggest that JEDP were originally four traditions that were passed down orally and eventually written down. Since Wellhausen, others have made significant contributions to the question of the Pentateuch's formation, including Hermann Gunkel (1862–1932) and Gerhard von Rad (1901–1971). Gunkel pioneered studies in the oral traditions that lay behind the source documents. He raised the possibility that traditions contained in J, E, D, P might have been composed some time prior to their inclusion in these sources. Von Rad proposed that existing cultic traditions had been gathered and edited by the Yahwist. He dated the Yahwist's activity a century earlier.

By the last quarter of the twentieth century a number of scholars began to reexamine the process by which the Pentateuch was composed. Rolf Rendtorff (1925—) denied the existence of J and E as self-contained documents. He also argued that the Yahwist never existed. John Van Seters (1935—) questioned the existence of E, redefined the nature of the Yahwist, and argued that J was a figure of the exilic period. Jacob Milgrom (1923–2010) was sympathetic to the idea of various sources but challenged Wellhausen's dating of them. He proposed that P predates D. Norman Whybray (1923–1997) rejected the criteria by which the different source documents are distinguished. He favored placing the composition of the Pentateuch in the exilic or post-exilic period.

Thus biblical scholarship is deeply divided on how the Pentateuch was composed, and the dates of compositions differ by several hundred years. Although the nature of the sources and their respective dates of composition remain much in doubt, scholars continue to work with the Documentary Hypothesis and its many modifications. The end of the twentieth century saw less of a concern for authorship and more interest in the theological message of the received form of the canon (canonical criticism) as well as an interest in the literary artistry of the Pentateuch, at least among American biblical scholars.

---

2. See the chart on the Documentary Hypothesis in chapter 1, "The Formation of the Bible."

Literary Fabric of the Pentateuch

The Pentateuch has a rich literary fabric. Within the body of the Pentateuch as a whole about twenty-five doublets exist, resulting in many contradictions. For example, Genesis 1 and 2 contain two different versions of the creation account. The first version (1:1–2:4a) is typically classified as the Priestly version; the second version (2:4b–25) is traditionally labeled the Yahwist version. Other examples of doublets include the genealogy of Adam (4:17–26 and 5:1–28, 30–32); the flood story, in which different versions are woven together; the genealogy from Shem (10:21–31 and 11:10–26); and the Abraham and Sarah wife-sister scenario (12:10–20 and ch. 20). Several historical places and sites are called by two different names, including Horeb/Sinai (Exod. 3:1 and 19:1–6, 16–25) and Hebron/ Mamre (Gen. 13:18 and 18:1).

© Daniel Blatt

This mountain, where Moses is supposed to have received the Torah from God, is called both Sinai and Horeb in the Bible. Duplicate place names like these suggest that the biblical texts combine traditions that previously circulated separately.

The Pentateuch, broadly divided into law and narrative, is composed of prose and poetry that expresses both narrative continuity and diversity. These five books contain a variety of literary forms such as genealogies (e.g., Gen. 25:12–18; 36); etiologies (e.g., Gen. 47:13–26); rituals (e.g., Deut. 26:1–11); blessings, such as Moses' final blessing on Israel (Deut. 33); myths, such as the story about the sons of the gods[3] (Gen. 6:1–4); call narratives, especially with respect to Abraham (Gen. 12) and Moses (Exod. 3); poetic songs (Exod. 15); and sagas, which are long narratives with episodic structures developed around stereotyped themes, ideas, or objects, as in the case of the family narratives about Abraham (Gen. 12:1–25:10) and Moses (Exod. 2–6).

Themes within the Pentateuch

One prominent theme in the Pentatuech is creation (Gen. 1–2). Everything that has been created is not only good (1:4, 10, 12, 18, 21, 25) but very good (1:31). Promise is another important theme. Various narratives describe promises made and promises fulfilled. Noah receives a divine promise that never again will the earth be destroyed by a flood (9:11). Abraham and his descendants are promised a land (12:1), which comes to fulfillment in the book of Joshua; they are also promised progeny (12:2).

Covenant, another theme, appears in the promise that God makes with Noah (Gen. 9:1–17). God also makes covenants with Abraham (Gen. 15, 17) and, by extension, his descendants, Isaac and Jacob. God makes a covenant with Moses and the Israelites, which becomes known as the Sinai Covenant (Exod. 19:4–6). For Israel, covenant means a sharing in blessing and righteousness, and Israel's responsibility is to act justly and rightly, to be in "right relationship"

---

3. Although the NRSV (and many other translations) render this phrase "the sons of God," a growing number of scholars are suggesting that "the sons of the gods" is more accurate. In Hebrew the word for "God" is *'elohim*, which is a plural noun form and thus can also be translated as "gods." In Genesis 6:2 and 6:4, *'elohim* has a definite article, so one may translate the phrase "the sons of the gods." In the context of Genesis 6:1–4, this appears to be the more appropriate translation since the passage concerns the quest for immortality and refers to the Nephilim and the mythic warriors of old, i.e., Hercules, Odysseus, etc.

with God, with one another, and with all of creation. The Pentateuch contains covenants that are irrevocable, irreversible, and unconditional with respect to the God of Israel's love for the people. Besides divine covenants, the Israelites also make covenants with other individuals, as in the case of Abraham and Abimelech (Gen. 21:22–34).

Much of the material from Exodus to Deuteronomy concerns law. Two forms that the laws take are apodictic and casuistic. An apodictic law gives a simple command or prohibition—for example, "You shall not murder" (Exod. 20:13). A casuistic law indicates how to deal with a specific situation, if and when it happens to arise— for example, "When a slaveowner strikes a . . . slave . . ." (Exod. 21:20–21; cf. Exod. 21:22–25, 26–27; Lev. 5:1–6). Within the Pentateuch, many laws are set down to preserve the "common good" among the Israelites (e.g., Exod. 21:12–36). Other laws are of a social and religious nature (e.g., Exod. 22:16–31). The Pentateuch also gives expression to an ancient Near Eastern law called *lex talionis*, sometimes called "an eye for an eye and a tooth for a tooth" (e.g., Exod. 21:23–25). This law was meant to be humane and was designed to prevent the escalation of violence. For example, if someone stole another's property, the thief could not be put to death in punishment; only if someone took the life of another could the offender's life be required. The law also assured equal treatment among all classes of people. For example, the crime of murdering a slave or poor person was just as grave as the murder of a rich person or king.

The Concept of Law

For Israel, the concept of law was inseparable from the idea of election and covenant. Law, election, and covenant rested on God's initiative and God's great love for the people. Covenant stressed the gift of God's intimate relationship with Israel, a relationship that required fidelity to God's law. The law was meant to be God's gracious instruction throughout Israel's life; thus the law was never burdensome. Those who taught the law included priests, prophets, sages, and parents.

Many of the laws found throughout the Pentateuch are grouped in law codes: the Covenant Code (Exod. 20:22–23:19), the Holiness Code (Lev. 17–26), the Priestly Code (various passages throughout the Torah), the Ritual Decalogue (Exod. 34:13–26), and the Decalogue (Exod. 20:2–17), otherwise known as the Ten Commandments. The Decalogue is the most famous of all law codes and is reiterated in Deuteronomy 5:6–21. Its first part calls the Israelites to be in right relationship with their God (Exod. 20:2–7); the second part calls the people to embrace Sabbath rest and to remember that this day is holy to their God (Exod. 20:8–11); the third part calls the Israelites to be in right relationship with one another and with the natural world (Exod. 20:12–17).

The Pentateuch provides a rich understanding of the law, which for the Israelite people is more than a set of rules and regulations. Torah is also instruction: it teaches a way of life that emphasizes an ethical vision of love for God, for one another as one's self, and for all creation. The law expresses a preferential option for those who are the most vulnerable within the society, namely, the poor, widows, orphans (the fatherless), and resident aliens or sojourners (Deut. 14:28–29; 24:17, 19–21). In terms of judgment, however, all people are to be treated with justice without partiality being shown to the poor or deference given to the great (Lev. 19:15). Israel is called to obey the law so that the people can live on the land securely (Lev. 25:18–19).

Salvation, or redemption, is another theme. The Pentateuch features a wide variety of stories and poems that celebrate Israel's God at work throughout history and through people, saving the Israelites from whatever is causing them to suffer, including famine (Gen. 41:25–36; 47:1–6; Num. 11:1–9, 31–35), physical oppression (Exod. 1; 3:1–10; Deut. 26:5–9), and transgression (Gen. 9:1–17). Israel's story of deliverance from slavery in Egypt begins with the bold acts of two midwives, Shiphrah and Puah (Exod. 1:15–22), continues with the selfless act of a Levite woman (Moses' mother) who lets go of her baby son to protect him from slaughter by the Egyptians (Exod. 1:22–2:4), and reaches its high point when an Egyptian woman—the daughter of pharaoh—rescues the Hebrew baby boy who is set in a papyrus basket and placed in the Nile River. Pharaoh's daughter takes the baby as her own son and names him

"Moses" (Exod. 2:5–10). The Egyptian pharaoh had sent out an edict ordering the massacre of all boys born to Hebrew women; pharaoh's daughter defies this edict. Through Moses, the Israelites are freed from Egyptian bondage (Exod. 3:1–15). Even as they approach the land that has been promised to them, the Pentateuch features Israel's God helping the people to defeat their enemies (Deut. 2:26–3:22).

Other themes include forgiveness and reconciliation, as exemplified in the story of Joseph and his brothers (Gen. 42:1–47:26), and deception and trickery, as related in the stories about Isaac, Esau, and Rebekah (Gen. 27), Joseph and Potiphar's wife (Gen. 39), and Tamar and Judah (Gen. 38). One final theme is dreams. Several characters within the Pentateuch have dreams or are able to interpret dreams, all of which advances the plot and narrative action of various stories. Joseph's dreams will have a dramatic effect on his life and the lives of his entire family (Gen. 37:1–11). Joseph's ability to interpret pharaoh's dreams will secure him a position in pharaoh's household (Gen. 41). Jacob's dream gives direction to his life and brings him consolation (Gen. 28:10–22).

Theologies of the Pentateuch

Many different theologies are present within the Pentateuch's five books. From Genesis, and specifically Genesis 1–2, emerges a theology of creation. These chapters describe how an ordered universe came forth from chaos and how each aspect of creation functions not only independently but also interdependently (e.g., Gen. 1:28–30). Everything in creation is good; nothing is evil and nothing is to be feared (Gen. 1:31). All of creation has intrinsic goodness by virtue of its existence and not because of its utilitarian purpose or worth (Gen. 1:10, 18, 21, 25). The Priestly writer makes clear that God's spoken word is efficacious. When God speaks, something happens (Gen. 1:1–2:4a).

Within the creation story is also a theology of blessing extended to both the animals (Gen. 1:22) and human beings (Gen. 1:28). In the ancient world, blessing was a sign of affirmation that brought with it the gift of fertility (Gen. 1:22, 28). Human beings are said to be created in God's image, according to God's likeness, which implies that they will have a share in the tasks of blessing, of participating

Edward Hicks' "Peaceable Kingdom" paintings convey the harmony between human beings and the natural world that is described in the biblical creation accounts.

fully in creation, and being good governors of and within creation (cf. Ps. 104). With respect to creation, human beings are to exercise dominion, which means to care for all of creation—to "cultivate" and "care for" the garden (Gen. 2:15). The Priestly version (Gen. 1:1–2:4a) and the Yahwist version (Gen. 2:4b–25) offer a portrait of human beings that is complementary. Although sexual differentiation exists between the male and the female, both human beings are depicted as having intrinsic equality: "Male and female he created them" (Gen. 1:27); "This at last is bone of my bones and flesh of my flesh" (Gen. 2:23). Finally, both the first human being and the animals share a common origin: they both come from the ground (Gen. 2:7, 19).

Together, the Priestly and Yahwist versions of creation show that the relationship between human beings and the natural world, specifically the animals, is a harmonious order based on the Creator's justice and righteousness, which flows from the Creator's care for all creation. Furthermore, nowhere in Genesis 1–2 is there any evidence of bloodshed or violence. Human beings and predators do not kill animals for food; all are sustained by a vegetarian diet (Gen. 1:29–30). Thus both the Priestly and the Yahwist versions speak of relationships that exist among all aspects of creation. Only later, after violence has entered into the world, do animals become food for humans (Gen. 9:1–3).

In the book of Exodus, the Exodus experience becomes the heart of Israel's understanding of God and the foundation for Israel's faith. The Exodus experience as described by the biblical writer serves a fourfold theological function: It (1) reveals who God is (Exod. 3:6; 14–15); (2) establishes a mutual, intimate relationship between God and the Israelites (6:7–8; 29:45–46); (3) illustrates and recalls to mind God's divine power, sovereignty, compassion, and love (6:6; 7:5); and (4) celebrates God as a liberator who makes and keeps promises, who not only hears the cry of the oppressed (2:24) and observes their misery (3:7) but also does something about it (chs. 3–15).

The way that liberation takes place for the Israelites, however, calls for ongoing theological reflection. For example, the Israelites' initial liberation occurs through a series of divine wonders (3:20), otherwise known as plagues (see 7:14–10:29; 12:29–32), the worst of which is the tenth, the death of the Egyptians' firstborn children. The accounts of the plagues are highly imaginative, and their relationship to any natural or historic events is doubtful. Within the context of the biblical account, the plagues become a means to liberation for the Israelites, since they are directed against their Egyptian oppressors. For the Egyptians, however, the plagues are heartbreaking and violent. As it stands, the Exodus text seems to legitimize the use of violence to counteract injustice—a position that can be questioned on theological, ethical, and practical grounds.

Two of the theologies that emerge from the book of Deuteronomy are a theology of retribution and a theology of love. Deuteronomy 28 outlines a series of blessings for those who keep God's covenant (Deut. 28:1–14) and a series of curses for those who break it (Deut. 28:15–68). This Deuteronomic theology of retribution becomes part of the fabric of the later books of the Bible. It is countered by the Deuteronomic theology of love, which reminds the Israelites that they are a chosen people, chosen out of love (Deut. 7:7–11) and called to love their God (Deut. 6:1–9) and to love their neighbors as themselves (Deut. 10:19; cf. Lev. 19:18). For Israel, the essence of the law is love of God, love of self, and love of neighbor (Deut. 10:12–22). To this end, they are to "circumcise" their hearts (Deut. 10:16; cf. 30:6; Jer. 4:4) so that they can be a people of love. The book of Deuteronomy, as well as the Pentateuch as a whole, also makes clear that Israel's God is "God of gods and Lord of lords" (Deut. 10:17). Israel's God is sovereign.

Other theological themes of the Pentateuch include: (1) remembering (e.g., Gen. 8:1; 9:14–16; Exod. 32:13; Lev. 26:42; Num. 15:39–40; Deut. 5:15; 8:18; 9:7, 27); (2) worship, expressed in exhortations to honor God (Exod. 33:10) and warnings not to serve other gods (Deut. 8:19; 11:16; 30:17); and (3) the call to holiness. The Israelites are to be holy because their God is holy (Lev. 20:26). Finally, the Pentateuch presents a myriad of images of God, including creator (e.g., Gen 1:1), liberator (Exod. 14:30), lawgiver (Exod. 19:5–6), and judge (Num. 16:5–7).

In sum, the Pentateuch is a collection of five books whose authorship remains unknown but whose content continues to be a source of inspiration and challenge for people today.

DISCUSSION QUESTIONS

1. What are some points of connection among the five books of the Pentateuch?

2. Early sources tell of how the Buddha, as a young man, observed the struggles of farm laborers, their toiling beasts, and the countless insects, snakes, and frogs being overturned by their plows. He was moved by this experience to seek an answer for such suffering. How does the Buddha's experience relate to the opening chapters of Genesis? How does it relate to the opening chapters of Exodus?

3. Consider examples of suffering population groups seeking liberation in the world today; are there points of similarity between their story and the concept of liberation presented in the book of Exodus? Are there fundamental differences?

4. What are the major themes of the Pentateuch? Are these themes relevant to life today?

5. What was the Israelites' understanding of law? How is that similar to your understanding of law? How is it different?

FOR FURTHER STUDY

Alexander, T. Desmond. *From Paradise to the Promised Land: An Introduction to the Pentateuch.* Grand Rapids: Baker Academic, 2012.

Alexander, T. Desmond, and David W. Baker, eds. *Dictionary of the Old Testament: Pentateuch.* Downers Grove, IL: InterVarsity Press, 2003.

Eskenazi, Tamara Cohn, ed., and Andrea L. Weiss, assoc. ed. *The Torah: A Woman's Commentary.* New York: Women of Reform Judaism, Federation of Temple Sisterhood: URJ Press, 2008.

Fretheim, Terence E. *The Pentateuch.* Nashville: Abingdon, 1996.

Kaminsky, Joel S., and Joel N. Lohr. *The Torah: A Beginner's Guide.* Oxford: Oneworld Publications, 2011.

Laffey, Alice L. *The Pentateuch: A Liberation-Critical Reading.* Minneapolis: Fortress, 1998.

Introduction to the Historical Books

Leslie J. Hoppe, OFM

The books of the Bible originally were copied and transmitted on parchment strips sewn together to form scrolls. The Romans developed the book format (the "codex"), which replaced the scroll by the seventh century CE. The rabbis, however, held that the book format was not acceptable for public reading so Jews continued to use scrolls in worship. But as the book format became more popular, the order in which the individual books of the Scriptures were to be arranged became an issue. It is inconvenient to have more than one book in a single scroll, but the codex can contain multiple books, which raises a question: in what order should the books be arranged?

The Arrangement of the Books of the Bible

The rabbis divided the books of the Hebrew Bible into three general categories: the Torah, the Prophets, and the Writings. The Prophets were subdivided into two subcategories: the Former Prophets (Joshua, Judges, Samuel, and Kings), which contain historical narratives, and the Latter Prophets (Isaiah, Jeremiah, Ezekiel, and the Twelve, i.e., the "minor" prophets), which are collections of prophetic oracles. The third division, the Writings, included all the books that did not fit into the previous two categories. When the books of the Hebrew Scriptures were transmitted in book format, the order of the books reflected this arrangement.

Beginning in the third century BCE, Jews living in Egypt began translating the Hebrew Scriptures into Greek because their facility with Hebrew had diminished. The most common form of this Greek translation was known as the Septuagint. The first Christians adopted the Septuagint as their Bible. When the Septuagint was arranged in book format, two significant differences between it and the rabbinic Bible became obvious. First, the books in the Septuagint were arranged differently from those in the rabbinic Bible, and second, there were several books in the Septuagint that did not appear in the rabbinic Bible.

The Septuagint arranges the books by two criteria: chronology and literary type. This leads to a four-part division of Law, History, Wisdom, and Prophecy. In addition, it contains extra books not found in the Hebrew Bible. These additional books are called the *Apocrypha*, i.e., "hidden" books. Protestants in general accept only the books found in the Hebrew Bible as canonical, though the arrangement of books of the Old Testament in Bibles used by Protestants follows that of the Septuagint rather than that of the Hebrew Bible. The Catholic and Orthodox churches accept several books of the Apocrypha as canonical, referring to them as *deuterocanonical* books. The books of the Old Testament in Catholic and Orthodox Bibles follow the order of the Septuagint.[1]

The Historical Books

This introduction deals with the second division of the collection of canonical books in Christian Bibles, i.e., the "historical books." The early Christian theologians used the term "historical books" to refer to the books from Genesis to Esther, but over time this term became restricted to the books from Joshua to 2 Maccabees for Catholic and Orthodox churches and Joshua to Esther for Protestants. It is important to realize that these books are not histories in the contemporary sense of the word; rather, they are narratives, stories. Some are about individuals, for example, Esther and Tobit, while others are about the people of Israel and Judah. At least three are most probably

---

1. See also chapter 1, "The Formation of the Bible," and the chart "Canons of Scripture" in the additional study aids section.

works of fiction (Tobit, Judith, Esther), while others, such as the books of Kings, do contain information that historians have used to reconstruct the history of Israel. Still it is essential that readers today recognize that these books are intended to convey religious ideas rather than to provide historical information. They convey theology in story form, similar to the parables of Jesus in the New Testament.

Jewish	Protestant	Roman Catholic	Orthodox
Former Prophets	Historical Books	Historical Books	Historical Books
Joshua Judges 1 and 2 Samuel 1 and 2 Kings	Joshua Judges Ruth 1 and 2 Samuel 1 and 2 Kings	Joshua Judges Ruth 1 and 2 Samuel 1 and 2 Kings	Joshua Judges Ruth 1–4 Kingdoms (the same as 1 and 2 Samuel and 1 and 2 Kings)
	1 and 2 Chronicles Ezra Nehemiah	1 and 2 Chronicles Ezra Nehemiah	1 and 2 Chronicles 1 Esdras 2 Esdras (same as Ezra and Nehemiah)
	Esther (short version)	Tobit Judith Esther (long version) 1 and 2 Maccabees	Judith Tobit Esther (long version) 1, 2, and 3 Maccabees (4 Maccabees as an appendix, if included)

Joshua–2 Kings

Among the "historical books" are two multi-volume collections: the Deuteronomistic History of Israel and the Chronicler's History. The former includes the books of Joshua, Judges, 1–2 Samuel, and 1–2 Kings. The rabbis grouped these books together, calling them the Former Prophets. Jewish tradition held that these books were written under prophetic inspiration by Joshua, Samuel, and Jeremiah. Like most books of the Bible, the books of the Deuteronomistic History are anonymous. They tell the story of the people of Israel in their land from the time they entered it under the leadership of Joshua until the time of the exile of Judah under the Babylonians. Biblical scholars use the term "Deuteronomistic" to describe these books because they believe that they stem from the Deuteronomist—that is, the same sources or authors responsible for the book of Deuteronomy. The Deuteronomistic History interprets the course of the kingdoms of Israel and Judah from the perspective of the principles of the book of Deuteronomy, which at one time probably served to introduce these books. Foremost among these principles is that obedience to the Torah brings God's blessings upon Israel while disobedience brings divine judgment. Another important principle is that the only legitimate place to offer sacrificial worship is the Temple of Jerusalem.

In the Deuteronomistic History, Israel's story is told not to provide information but motivation. Its purpose is to convince its readers that the people of Israel can have a future only if they choose the way of obedience. The story of Israel in its land illustrates the consequences of choosing the path of disobedience and infidelity, and ought to persuade readers to be absolutely faithful to God alone and to live by the commandments in the Torah.

While there is general agreement about the basic religious thought of the Deuteronomistic History, there is no agreement about its date, authorship, and composition. It is clear that sources were used in the composition of this work—for example, the stories of the individual judges in the book of Judges, the stories about the rise of David to kingship (1 Sam. 16–2, Sam. 5), the stories about the succession to David's throne (2 Sam. 9–20; 1 Kings 1–2), and the stories about Elijah and Elisha (1 Kings 17–2 Kings 8). Some of these sources, which have not survived to the present, are cited in the biblical text, including "the Book of Jashar" (Josh. 10:13), "the Book of the Annals of the Kings of Israel" (1 Kings 14:19), and "the Book of the Annals of the Kings of Judah" (1 Kings 14:29). But was the Deuteronomistic

History finally the work of a single author or were there multiple authors with an editor putting the books together as we now have them? Proposed dates for its composition range from the seventh to the fourth centuries BCE. It is most likely that the books received their final form sometime after the fall of Jerusalem (587 BCE) and that they were intended to explain the reasons for the fall of the two Israelite kingdoms[2] and the end of the Davidic dynasty, the destruction of the Jerusalem Temple and the scattering of its priesthood, and the exile of the leadership classes of Judah to Babylon.

The Deuteronomistic History is a literary and theological masterpiece. Its engrossing stories about ancient Israel's heroes and villains, its kings and prophets, and some ordinary folk are vehicles for persuading readers that obedience to the written, authoritative law found in the Book of Deuteronomy is the way to restore their nation's relationship with God and secure a future in the land promised to their ancestors. The central importance that the Book of Deuteronomy came to have in Judaism is a testament to the achievement of the unnamed author of the Deuteronomistic History.

Ruth

The Septuagint ordering of books places Ruth immediately after Judges since Ruth's story is set in the time of the judges (Ruth 1:1). The date of composition is debated. The book has its own value and charm, but its placement in Christian Bibles interrupts the flow of the Deuteronomistic History. The rabbis placed Ruth in the third division of their canon, the Writings. Like Tobit, Esther, and Judith, the work focuses on the story of an individual, the surprising tale of the great-grandmother of David, a poor Moabite widow who ends up in Judah because she refuses to abandon her mother-in-law. Ruth is unique for its focus on two destitute women, and it reveals some of the struggles and threats such women endured in the ancient world. While God is not an active character in the story, the text implies that Yahweh rewards Ruth's devotion to Naomi, her acceptance of Naomi's God as her own, and her willingness to take action to achieve some kind of security for the two of them.

---

2. See Map 3, "The Kingdom Years," in the additional study aids section.

1–2 Chronicles

Following the books that comprise the Deuteronomistic History in the Christian Old Testament comes another multi-volume "history": the Chronicler's History. At one time, scholars assumed that this history included 1–2 Chronicles, Ezra, and Nehemiah, but that view is no longer widely held. The Chronicler's history begins with nine chapters that are almost exclusively taken up with genealogies, beginning with Adam (1 Chron. 1:1) and concluding with the family of Saul (1 Chron. 9:35–44). The Chronicler's story of Israel ends with the decree of Cyrus the Persian, urging the exiles from Judah to return to Jerusalem and rebuild the Temple (2 Chron. 36:22–23). One function of the genealogies is to assure the returnees that they stand in continuity with the ancestors of all Israel. From the Chronicler's perspective, this continuity gives legitimacy to the restoration.

The Chronicler's narratives begin with the death of Saul and the consequent accession of David (1 Chron. 10:1–11:3), who is the central figure in 1 Chronicles. While the Deuteronomistic Historian does not hesitate to give a prominent place to the description of David's flaws (e.g., his adultery with Bathsheba and the murder of her husband in 2 Sam. 11), the Chronicler totally ignores these and describes David as almost exclusively concerned with preparing for the building of the Temple, arranging the duties of the priests and Levites who will serve there, and instructing the Temple's musicians and other personnel. The Chronicler's portrait of David reveals the author's belief in the centrality of worship in Jerusalem's Temple for the life of all Israel. While the Deuteronomist underscores the importance of obedience to the Torah, the Chronicler points to David as an example of someone who is devoted entirely to the worship of Israel's ancestral deity. The Chronicler's portrait of Solomon likewise omits details that may detract from the image of a monarch almost totally consumed with the proper worship of God in the Temple of Jerusalem. For example, the Chronicler's history passes over Solomon's descent into idolatry (1 Kings 11).

The Chronicler's story of the two Israelite kingdoms is colored by significance attached to the Temple of Jerusalem. For example, in 2 Chronicles 13, the speech of Abijah makes it clear that the principal offense of the kings of Israel was their failure to recognize Jerusalem as the only legitimate setting for Israel's worship. The Chronicler is clearly calling the Samaritans, who lived in the territory of the former kingdom of Israel, to recognize the exclusive claims on the Temple of Jerusalem. For the Chronicler, the future of all Israel depends on its commitment to the worship of its God in the only place where legitimate worship may be offered: the Temple of Jerusalem. The rabbinic arrangement of the books of the Hebrew Scriptures underscores this. The Hebrew Bible ends with the decree of Cyrus (2 Chron. 36:22–23), which calls the exiles to return to Jerusalem and rebuild the Temple.

Ezra–Nehemiah

Another form of the decree of Cyrus appears at the beginning of Ezra (1:1–4), providing continuity between the books of Chronicles and Ezra and Nehemiah. It is likely that Ezra and Nehemiah were composed as sequels to Chronicles as they describe the progress of the restoration following the return of the exiles, who were encouraged by Cyrus to return to Jerusalem. According to Ezra and Nehemiah, Judah's restoration resulted from implementing the policies of Persian kings, Cyrus and Artaxerxes,

Ezra 1–6 describes the rebuilding of the Jerusalem Temple in accordance with Cyrus' decree. In Ezra 7 the focus shifts to the restoration of Jewish life through obedience to the Torah. The Persians allowed subject peoples to have a measure of autonomy by upholding local, traditional laws as long as these did not undermine Persian rule. The narratives from Ezra 7 to the end of Nehemiah describe how the imposition of Mosaic law affected the Jewish community in Jerusalem, which was to be rebuilt and repopulated in accord with the wishes of the Persian king, Artaxerxes.

A special feature of both Ezra and Nehemiah is their insistence on separation from non-Jews. Ezra ends with the requirement that Jewish men abandon their foreign wives and any children from their marriages with these women (Ezra 10:6–44). Nehemiah builds a wall around Jerusalem, a visible sign of the separation of Jews from all Gentiles (Neh. 6:1–19; 12:27–43; 13:1–3). Despite the efforts of Ezra and Nehemiah, the restoration is far from satisfactory since Judah was simply a sub-province of the Persian Empire. The books of Ezra and Nehemiah do not hint at how or when the restoration will be complete. These books simply describe the beginning of the restoration: the rebuilding of the Temple, the reestablishment and repopulation of Jerusalem, and the people's commitment to the Torah.

Tobit

From narratives about the people of Israel as a whole, the focus of the next books in some Christian canons is on individuals who face formidable personal struggles. In the Catholic canon, Nehemiah is followed by the story of Tobit. Tobit is not among the books of the Hebrew Scriptures. Still, some Jews of antiquity valued it—several copies of Tobit were found among the Dead Sea Scrolls. Eastern Churches generally include Tobit in the canon of the Old Testament. Catholics include Tobit among the deuterocanonical books while Protestants place it with the Apocrypha.

The title character is a Galilean who finds himself living as an exile in Nineveh, the capital of the neo-Assyrian Empire. He tries to lead a good life, but he meets misfortune when he is accidently blinded. His story is interwoven with that of a certain Sarah who lives in Media, an Iranian kingdom. She married seven times, with each of her husbands dying during their wedding night, slain by a demon. Tobit's son Tobiah is the bridge connecting the two stories. In the course of finding a cure for his father, he meets and marries Sarah. With the help of the angel Raphael, he is able to survive his wedding night with Sarah and affect the cure of his father's blindness. As a coda to the story, Tobiah lives long enough to hear of Nineveh's fall, for which he thanks God.

The book of Tobit is among the most skillfully crafted stories in the Bible. It has several motifs similar to ancient Near Eastern folktales. It is set in Assyria, where Tobit and his family were taken as exiles following the fall of the kingdom of Israel in the eighth century, though the book was likely composed in the third or early second century BCE. Its message is directed to all Jews living outside their ancestral homeland, encouraging them to remain faithful to the values and practices of their ancestral faith even among peoples that do not share these values. Doing so may be difficult, but they can count on God's support in their struggles to remain faithful. The underlying theological idea is similar to that of Deuteronomy: in the

Important characters in the book of Tobit include the angel Raphael and the demon Asmodeus, who was probably envisioned as a being similar to the Assyrian demon shown here. Belief in angels and demons developed significantly in the Second Temple period.

end God will bless those who are faithful. While Tobit is numbered among the "historical" books of the Old Testament, its purpose is not to provide historical data, but to affirm traditional Israelite morality, especially the values connected with family life and charity toward those in need.

Judith

The book of Tobit, which depicts Jews living in exile in Assyria, displays an openness to Gentiles (Tob. 13:11; 14:6–7). The book of Judith, which follows Tobit in the Catholic and Orthodox canons, views Gentiles as threats to Judah's existence. The threat comes in the person of Nebuchadnezzar, who sends his army under Holofernes to punish those nations that did not support his war against Arphaxad, the king of the Medes. Holofernes enjoys success in his campaigns until he comes to the village of Bethulia in Judah. Judith's decisive actions lead to the assassination of Holofernes and the route of his army.

On the surface, the story of Judith reads like a historical account, but there are so many historical and geographical errors in the text that those who first heard or read the book no doubt recognized the story for what it really was: an entertaining and engrossing tale of a great Israelite victory against the longest odds, a victory that was possible because of the initiative taken by a woman. The story is not about any actual battle. It is rather a thinly veiled critique of the community's male leadership, whose failures are magnified by the intervention of a woman who accomplished what they could not. This is the supreme irony of a book that is full of ironies.

The book purports to relate events that took place shortly after the return from exile (Jth. 4:3), but it was probably composed some time after the Maccabees defeated the forces of the Seleucid Empire (165 BCE). Indeed, the book presents Judith as a female counterpart of the Maccabees, defeating the enemies of Judah when that seemed all but impossible. One of the goals of Holofernes' expedition was to "destroy all the gods of the land" so that people would then worship Nebuchadnezzar alone (3:8). The worship of the king as a god places this story squarely in the Greek period. The Seleucid king Antiochus IV (who ruled 175–164 BCE) thought of himself as Zeus manifest.

Despite its Deuteronomic flavoring, there is no evidence that the Jews of Palestine ever considered Judith canonical. No fragments of the Aramaic or Hebrew versions of Judith were found at Qumran. Christians were divided on the question of canonicity. Jerome was skeptical, though Augustine accepted the book as inspired. Protestant Christians include Judith among the Apocrypha while Catholics number it among the Deuterocanonical Books.

Esther

Both Judith and Esther are tales featuring beautiful Jewish women whose courageous exploits save their people from impending disaster.

The book of Judith mentions God frequently. It portrays Judith as living a life of fasting and prayer, and it alludes to characteristic Jewish beliefs and practices. In contrast, the Hebrew version of Esther never mentions God or any Jewish religious practices or institutions. And yet the book of Esther found its way into the rabbinic Bible while the book of Judith did not.

Like Judith, the book of Esther sees Gentiles as potential threats to the existence of the Jewish people. The setting is the Persian court, where the king chooses Esther as his queen after his first wife displeases him. Esther's uncle Mordecai, a high official in the Persian court, discovers a plot against the king and saves the king from assassination. The king is understandably very grateful. This arouses the jealously of Haman, another court official, who decides to eliminate his rival Mordecai and all Jews residing in Persia. Mordecai learns of Haman's plot and enlists Esther in a plan to turn the king against Haman. Mordecai's plan is successful and the Jews of Persia are safe. Mordecai orders the Jews to celebrate their deliverance during the two-day festival of Purim (Esther 9:23).

The acceptance of the Hebrew version of Esther was not without controversy. As late as the fourth century CE, there were rabbis who did not include Esther among the books they considered sacred. The Greek version of Esther has an extra 107 verses that give the book a religious flavor. The additions make the deliverance of the Jews the result of prayer to God, who controls the fate of Israel. Even so, Christians too had questions about the book's canonical character, with the Eastern churches generally rejecting the book and the Western church accepting it. Today Protestant churches accept the shorter (Hebrew) version of the book and place the additional verses among the Apocrypha, while Catholic and Orthodox Bibles view the longer Greek version as the sacred text.

1–2 Maccabees

These two historical books found in Catholic and Orthodox canons refocus attention on the Jewish community in Palestine. First Maccabees covers a seventy year period (175–104 BCE) that witnessed the improbable rise of an obscure priestly family to political and religious leadership of the Jewish community. The story of the Maccabees begins with a notice of Alexander the Great's death (323 BCE) and the events in Palestine following the accession of Antiochus IV as ruler of the Seleucid Kingdom (175 BCE). Antiochus' anti-Jewish laws prompted a priest named Mattathias and his sons to take up armed resistance. Their success led to their receiving the sobriquet of *Maccabee*, that is, "Hammer." Following the death of Mattathias, each of his sons in succession assumed the leadership of the Jewish community. At first their leadership was primarily military in nature but eventually it came to include the religious and political spheres as well (1 Macc. 14:25–49). One purpose of 1 Maccabees is to support the sons of Mattathias in the role they came to play in the Jewish community of Palestine.

Second Maccabees does not continue the story of the family of Mattathias. Rather, it offers another version of that story focusing on the purification of the Temple, which was necessary because of its desecration by Antiochus IV. The book claims to be an abridgement of a five-volume work of a certain Jason of Cyrene (2 Macc. 2:23) and covers events from 180 to 161 BCE. Second Maccabees is less interested in crediting the leadership of the Maccabees, instead pointing to God's powerful intervention as the source of the victories that led to the rededication of the Temple (see, e.g., 2 Macc. 11:1–13).

Neither 1 nor 2 Maccabees is part of the Hebrew Scriptures. They came into the Christian canon of the Old Testament through their inclusion in the Septuagint. The church's first theologians considered these two books as authoritative, but Luther, followed by Protestant churches, included them among the Apocrypha. The Septuagint also contains 3 and 4 Maccabees, which are considered canonical by the Greek Orthodox Church.

The Value of the Historical Books

At one time, modern histories of ancient Israel were little more than paraphrases of the biblical narratives. Today that is no longer the case, largely because of archaeological excavations in the Holy Land. Excavation of places such as Jericho, Ai, and Jerusalem has shown that the biblical stories of the Israelite tribes' settlement and the reigns of David and Solomon do not reflect the realities of the historical periods in which these stories are set. Also, most of the historical books place a heavy emphasis on the divine causation of events. For example, the fall of the kingdom of Israel is blamed on Israel's sins and failure to heed the message of the prophets (2 Kings 17). The expansionist policies of the aggressively militaristic neo-Assyrian Empire are largely ignored. The biblical histories are quite selective in what is reported. For example, Omri was among the greatest kings of Israel, yet the Deuteronomist basically dismisses him, summing up his reign in a mere six verses (1 Kings 16:23–28). In the Deuteronomist's view, Omri's achievements are not worth mentioning, since he was guilty of the sin of Jeroboam. The Chronicler ignores Omri almost completely, mentioning him only in passing (2 Chron. 22:2).

King Omri of Israel receives little notice in the biblical text, but his significance is attested by extra-biblical sources. The "Mesha Stele," above (ca. 840 BCE), celebrates Moab's victory over an Israelite king who is identified only as a descendant of Omri, founder of the Israelite dynasty.

© RMN-Grand Palais / Art Resource, NY

At the same time, one cannot dismiss the historical books as without merit as resources for the modern historian of Israel, but readers need to recognize that the goal of each of these histories was to make it clear that Israel had a future, despite its infidelity to its God. The authors affirm that judgment is not their God's last word to their community, Israel's infidelity notwithstanding. These affirmations transcend the judgments that historians usually make, but they represent the fundamental beliefs of those unnamed writers who penned the historical books.

DISCUSSION QUESTIONS

1. The Books of Joshua and Judges assert that ancient Israel acquired the land that was to be the setting for its subsequent history by means of violence, driving out its previous inhabitants at the behest of God—posing ethical problems for persons who view this account as sacred Scripture. Is the problem any easier when one recognizes that the text does not record actual historical events?

2. The books of Ruth, Esther, and Judith each present a woman as the principal character of a story. What does this say about the role and status of women in ancient Israel?

3. The portrait of David in the Chronicler is markedly different from the portrait of David in the Deuteronomistic History. How can these differences be explained?

4. The military conflicts described in the books of Maccabees are one result of the conflict between Jewish and Greek cultures. What was at the heart of that conflict?

5. The books of Ezra (ch. 9) and Nehemiah (ch. 13:23–31) express adamant opposition to the marriage of Jews with Gentiles. What was the reason for their opposition to mixed marriages?

FOR FURTHER STUDY

Halpern, Baruch. *The First Historians: The Hebrew Bible and History.* San Francisco: Harper & Row, 1988.

Nelson, Richard D. *The Historical Books.* Nashville: Abingdon, 1998.

Provan, Iain. "The Historical Books of the Old Testament." In the *Cambridge Companion to Biblical Interpretation*, edited by John Barton, 199–211. Cambridge: Cambridge University Press, 1998.

Sternberg, Meir. *The Poetics of the Biblical Narrative.* Bloomington, IN: Indiana University Press, 1985.

Van Seters, John. *In Search of History.* New Haven: Yale, 1983.

15

Introduction to the Wisdom Literature and the Psalms

William P. Brown

What is wisdom? Survey ancient philosophers and modern psychologists, and you will find no consensus except for one shared conviction: whatever it is, wisdom is more than knowledge, more than "know-how." It involves making sound judgments and doing the right thing. Wisdom grapples with questions of justice and fairness. Most fundamentally, wisdom is about making sense of life in all its complexity and acting accordingly. Wisdom acknowledges both the limitations and the possibilities of human existence. It identifies what is most important in the art of living. Mediating between the traditions of the past and the novelty of experience, wisdom is ever ongoing and open-ended.

The so-called wisdom literature of the Bible presents a powerful testimony to wisdom's open, dynamic nature. The corpus includes a remarkable variety of books: Proverbs, Job, and Ecclesiastes in the Hebrew Bible, as well as Ecclesiasticus (or Sirach) and the Wisdom of Solomon in the deuterocanonical or apocryphal works. (The book of Psalms, which features a number of "wisdom psalms," will also be included in this introduction.) All these books are irreducibly distinct yet very much interrelated. If the wisdom corpus were a choir, both harmony and dissonance would resound at almost every chord.

According to rabbinic tradition, Solomon wrote the Song of Songs in his youth, Proverbs in his prime, and Ecclesiastes in his old age.[1] Historical naiveté aside, the rabbis recognized wisdom's

---

1. *Song of Songs Rabbah* 1.6.17.H.

ever-evolving nature by setting wisdom within the context of the ever-forming, ever-changing self. As if to match the literary diversity of this corpus, biblical wisdom reflects a variety of sources and contexts. Certain aphorisms in Proverbs have their origin in a rural, agricultural context, others in urban centers and the royal court. More extensive instructions seem to have their home in an educational context, although we have no explicit evidence of formal schooling until the time of Sirach (180 BCE). Some of the sages behind the instructions were evidently well versed in other languages, including Egyptian, and they adapted wisdom from neighboring cultures. As a whole, the wisdom literature offers a smorgasbord of insight and instruction.

The wisdom corpus occupies a distinctive niche within the Hebrew canon. Proverbs, Job, and Ecclesiastes make no explicit mention of the paradigmatic events of ancient Israel's history, such as the Exodus or the giving of the Law at Sinai/Horeb. This changes significantly, however, with the later Greek books of Sirach and the Wisdom of Solomon. On the face of it, Hebrew wisdom holds only modest interest in Israel's worship life, in contrast to the Psalms. Corporate history and cultic hymnody are not wisdom's domains. More sweeping, there is nothing explicitly said about God in the Hebrew wisdom corpus that could be considered uniquely Israelite, Jewish, or Christian. Israel's sages, moreover, had no qualms about incorporating the wisdom of other cultures. Wisdom's universal appeal, in short, constitutes its canonical distinctiveness.

Biblical wisdom has been, and continues to be, studied from a variety of approaches, from form-critical to feminist, from sociological to theological, in part because it is such an elusive yet distinctly accommodating body of literature. The literature is both humanistic and theological in its focus on both the individual and creation. For the biblical sages, the whole world was their classroom. Shaping the human will was their goal. The sages recognized that moral conduct was informed by the world's order and that the world's order, in turn, was sustained by right conduct.

Proverbs

The book of Proverbs is a collection of collections of instructions and, yes, proverbs. Most of the book of Proverbs contains short sayings, with its bookends consisting of more extensive instructional material ("lectures" and "interludes"). Whereas the book itself is attributed to Solomon (1:1), the titles or superscriptions of the various sections indicate a more diverse origin. Agur (30:1) is an otherwise unknown sage, perhaps a non-Israelite. So also is Lemuel (31:1). Moreover, Proverbs 22:17–24:22 ("Words of the Wise") is dependent upon a corpus of Egyptian wisdom, *Instruction of Amenemope*. The wisdom reflected in Proverbs is eclectic in content and international in origin. Nevertheless, it was only natural to attribute the book as a whole to Solomon, who is remembered as the quintessentially wise king (see 1 Kings 3; 4:29–34; 10:1–13), despite his many wives and religious failings (1 Kings 11:1–13).

The book of Proverbs begins with a statement of purpose, a prologue featuring a veritable collage of values and virtues: shrewdness, prudence, discretion, skill, instruction, insight, and wisdom (1:1–7). While certain virtues ensure the successful completion of goals, others are distinctly moral in orientation, including "righteousness, justice, and equity" (v. 3). Together they commend a sense of fairness and right relation in community and with God, and contribute an ethical dimension to the mix. Following this verse, the introduction

Proverbs 22:17–24:22 borrows extensively from the much older Egyptian work, *Instruction of Amenemope*, shown above. The wisdom tradition was shared across many ancient Near Eastern cultures.

highlights the importance of inculcating these values for the young (v. 4). It is no surprise that much of the material that follows the prologue is cast as a father's address to his son (see 1:8; 2:1; 3:1, 11; 4:1; 5:1, 7; 6:1; 7:1). Wisdom begins in the home, with children learning from their parents. But wisdom is not just for the young: "Let the wise also hear and gain in learning, and the discerning acquire skill" (1:5). Proverbs is for the young and old alike. Even the wisest have something to gain from (re)reading the book.

The last verse in the prologue provides the religious framework for the introduction. Sometimes called the "motto" of Proverbs, 1:7 situates wisdom in the context of holy reverence: "The fear of the LORD is the beginning of knowledge" (see also Prov. 9:10; Ps. 111:10). Such godly "fear" is not meant to paralyze or cause shivers down the spine. Quite the contrary, it is meant to move one forward toward gaining wisdom from God. "The fear of the LORD is the beginning" of a journey, of one's growth in wisdom. This kind of "fear" is humility mixed with awe over the God who creates, works wonders, and imparts wisdom (see 3:5–7). Call it "fear seeking understanding" (à la St. Anselm). The "motto" of 1:7 ensures that wisdom is nothing without reverence of God, that wisdom is more gift than possession, and it is priceless (see 3:13–18).

The book of Proverbs features various speakers, all vying for the reader's attention: parent, peer, and Wisdom herself. The personified figure of Wisdom appears in chapters 1, 8, and 9. That Wisdom is personified as female is no accident. Her deliberate gendering has led interpreters to conclude that the book of Proverbs as a whole was written primarily for a young male audience. Wisdom serves to both cajole and woo her audience to accept her teachings. Her profile is matched by another female figure described in chapter 7: the "loose woman" (cf. 2:16; 5:3), better translated as the "strange (or foreign) woman." She represents folly, and the reader (addressed as "son") is repeatedly warned against her. Both Wisdom and the strange woman share public space (1:20–22; 7:12) and issue similar invitations (9:4, 16), but their messages could not be more different. Wisdom stresses marital fidelity and joy, honor, prosperity, and life. The strange woman offers illicit sex, broken relationships, disgrace, and death. The feminine polarity that runs throughout the book is a product of patriarchal convention; it is Proverbs' version of

© Mark Gallery, London, UK / The Bridgeman Art Library

Lady Wisdom sits enthroned in this seventeenth-century Russian icon. In several wisdom texts Lady Wisdom is depicted as both a divine attribute and as a personal agent of God in the creation and ordering of the cosmos (see Prov. 8).

the "Madonna and the whore." The polarity also reflects the social tensions between foreigners and natives living in ancient Palestine during the Persian period, a time of tumultuous restoration beginning in the late sixth century and extending until the late fourth century BCE.

A central text, Proverbs 8:22–31 establishes Wisdom's preeminent place in creation. Indeed, her account is not so much about creation as about the one who describes it. The poem is her grand soliloquy with a distinctly rhetorical purpose: Wisdom lifts her voice to persuade the reader of her inestimable worth and authority. Moreover, at the end of her testimony Wisdom depicts herself as a child frolicking with God and the world (vv. 30–31). (The NRSV translates v. 30 "I was beside him, like a *master worker*," but see the footnote for the alternative reading, "little child." The Hebrew is unclear.) By claiming an intimate, lively association with both the creator and creation, Wisdom aims to capture the imagination and, in so doing, claim once and for all the reader's allegiance to the God of wisdom. In Proverbs, Wisdom has a voice.

Job

Not so in Job; wisdom becomes much more elusive. Associated with the theme of suffering, the book of Job has inspired artists, poets, psychologists, playwrights, and even political analysts. Readers over the centuries have marveled over its profound and subversive character. Literarily, the book of Job is a potent mix of prose and poetry, polyphonic in both style and message. Existentially, Job's story questions conventional views of how the world works. Dripping with irony, Job excels in the art of subversion.

It is best to think of Job as a thought experiment rather than as a historical narrative. Given its penchant for raising questions and subverting texts and traditions, Job has been called the one book of the Bible that is against the Bible. In the face of rigidified forms of conventional, biblical norms, the book of Job effectively hits the "reset" button on religious piety, and it does so in the end by reaching back to the world of beginnings, back to creation itself, as well as by venturing forward beyond the boundaries of human culture, Israelite or otherwise.

As a thought experiment, the book of Job revels in "What if?" questions about human integrity, divine intention, and the nature of the universe, all converging on the character of Job. What if the paragon of righteousness were to fall into unimaginable ruin? What if piety were more than a matter of reward and blessing? What if righteousness invited vulnerability? What if God were no protector of the righteous? What if the world were not to operate morally? What would be the shape of human integrity in such a world? What would it mean to "fear God" in a world devoid of retribution and filled with the possibility of disaster?

The book of Job is mostly talk: talk between Job and his three friends, Eliphaz, Bildad, and Zophar (chs. 3–14, 15–21, and 22–27), an unexpected interloper, Elihu (chs. 32–37), and, of course, God, whose presence is also dominated by discourse, a "whirlwind" of words (chs. 38–41). Throughout these dialogues and speeches, the human speakers attempt to make sense of Job's predicament. They fail, Job included. Indeed, the wisdom poem in chapter 28 delivers a judgment on all that has been said thus far: wisdom cannot be found; it remains ever beyond human reach. Instead, the "fear of the Lord" (28:28, echoing Job 1:1 and Prov. 1:7) is all that matters.

God's appearance in the "whirlwind" marks the climax of the book, but it does not resolve the issue of suffering as posed by Job. Indeed, God's "answers" are themselves full of questions that challenge Job and put him in his place within the greater cosmos. God presses Job on his limited knowledge of the world, from the heights and depths of creation to the denizens that populate the wilderness, both land and sea. God opens Job's eyes to an utterly mysterious and wondrous view of the world. And Job's response is equally mystifying: is he penitent or not? (There are various ways to translate the all-important crux of 42:6.) In any case, it is clear Job has a change of heart and finds resolution in the end, however that is to be explained.

Matching the prosaic style of the prologue (chs. 1–2), the epilogue (42:7–17) concludes the story. On the surface, it seems like simply a recapitulation of the beginning. Job gets restored to his lofty and wealthy position as patriarch of a new family. But things have changed, irrevocably so: Job, rather than his friends, is vindicated by God for having spoken "what is right" (42:7). Job gratefully receives restorative help from family and community (v. 11). He treats his children differently, as evident when he gives his daughters a share of the inheritance, an act unprecedented in biblical law (v. 15). Even at its prosaic conclusion, Job's story is full of ironic twists and surprising outcomes. In its final form, Job generates searching questions and challenging reflections about life in a world that does not operate retributively or simplistically. The book is a searing testimony to the limitations of human wisdom.

Ecclesiastes

The same goes for Ecclesiastes (Greek translation of *Qoheleth*), a book replete with contradictions, paradoxes, and ambiguities. Attributed to Solomon, Ecclesiastes is the Bible's most enigmatic book. Yet for all its interpretive challenges, the book has an uncanny ability to speak to a wide range of readers across generations. Such is its genius.

The main character of the book calls himself Qoheleth (NRSV: "the Teacher"), but his historical identity remains shrouded in mystery. His allegedly royal pedigree (1:1, 12) fades largely after the first two chapters. His name, or better self-title, means something like "assembler." Like an auditor, the sage takes an inventory of life by collecting the "data" of experience, both individual (his own) and collective (tradition). And like a teacher, an "assembler" of students, Qoheleth candidly shares the results of his work.

Qoheleth aims to investigate everything by means of wisdom, through observation and scrutiny, in order to discover God's purposes in the world. Some regard Qoheleth as the Bible's only empiricist. But for all his efforts, this quintessential sage fails to find what he desires. Wisdom, he discovers, is beyond him. Enjoyment and toil yield no lasting gain. The world and all that goes on, cosmically and culturally, indicates no direction, let alone any progress. "The same fate befalls" everyone, the fool and the wise, human and animal alike (2:14; 3:19).

Qoheleth's "royal" experiment has failed. Unlike Job, Qoheleth is not privy to divine revelation. His verdict on all that he has seen and studied is "vanity" or futility (1:2; 12:8), the book's single-word thesis. The word itself (Hebrew: *hevel*) conjures the image of vapor, something ephemeral and insubstantial. But in view of life's frailty and futility, Qoheleth does not counsel despair but instead commends joy, seven times: 2:24–26; 3:12–13, 22; 5:18–20; 8:15; 9:7–9; 11:7–10. Through his failure to find all-encompassing Wisdom, the elder sage nevertheless comes to new understandings: the value of a "non-profit" existence, the redemptive import of enjoyment, a life of simplicity, the danger of extreme righteousness (7:16), God's inscrutability, the tenuousness of life, and the pervasiveness of chance. Perhaps his most profound insight is, "A living dog is better than a dead lion" (9:4). In Qoheleth's hands, wisdom is minimized to only relative worth, but worth it still has.

Sirach (Ecclesiasticus)

Sirach and the Wisdom of Solomon are not included in the Jewish and Protestant canons. They are, however, found in the Septuagint, as well as in the Old Latin and Vulgate translations. Known as "Ecclesiasticus" ("the Church's book") in the Vulgate, Sirach was written by one Jesus son of ("ben") Eleazar son of ("ben") Sirach (50:27) sometime before 180 BCE. The "Prologue" of the book, written by Ben Sirach's grandson, states that Ben Sirach's work is for those who "wished to gain learning and are disposed to live according to the law." He describes his grandfather as a deft reader of Scripture. This is confirmed from the contents of the book itself. Sirach draws not simply from past wisdom traditions but across the entire range of biblical tradition, which the grandson refers to as "the Law . . . , the Prophecies, and the rest of the books." This marks a significant development regarding wisdom's scope, which now bears a distinctly "canonical" breadth largely lacking in earlier wisdom literature.

Within the wisdom tradition, Sirach draws most heavily from Proverbs. As in Proverbs 8, Wisdom according to Sirach is fully personified and divinely originated (1:1–4, 9–10). Most significant, Wisdom comes to be identified with the Law, perhaps best explicated in chapter 24, the centerpiece of the book. Wisdom's origins are indisputably divine, and her scope is nothing short of cosmic and international (24:5–6), and yet Jerusalem becomes Wisdom's home. There on Zion she "took root in an honored people" (v. 12). Like a towering tree, Wisdom grew, her splendor compared to the exotic aromatics used in the Temple (vv. 13–17). Ben Sirach's greatest innovation lies in identifying Wisdom with the Law of Moses. In the final outcome, Wisdom is Torah, "the book of the covenant of the Most High God" (24:23–34). With her new identity, Wisdom begins to be integrated into the larger story of ancient Israel's journey of faith. But that is only the beginning.

Wisdom of Solomon

This Greek book finds an even more prominent place for wisdom within Israel's story of faith. The Wisdom of Solomon represents a highpoint of Greek influence on Jewish faith. One distinctive feature is the book's belief in immortality, presented as the solution to the problem of human evil. Of particular interest is Wisdom's expanding profile. As with Sirach, the anonymous author, taking on the voice of Solomon, draws heavily from Proverbs 8 by profiling Wisdom in full personified splendor. Wisdom (*sophia*) is "radiant" and eager to make herself known to all who seek her (6:12–14). Wisdom is cast as Solomon's greatest love and desire, surpassing that of health and beauty, wealth and power (7:8–10). Through Wisdom, the character of Solomon receives vast knowledge, including "the structure of the world and the activity of the elements," astronomical and meteorological phenomena, zoology, and botany ("the virtues of roots"), as well as esoteric knowledge (7:17–22; cf. 1 Kings 4:33). In Wisdom, science and mystery co-exist quite happily.

Solomon describes Wisdom as his "bride," even though she co-habits "with God" (8:2–3, 9). Through Wisdom, Solomon will gain immortality and ensure a lasting legacy among his people (v. 13). Wisdom, ultimately, is the gift of God. In his prayer, Solomon acknowledges both his own frailty and Wisdom's power and intimacy with God: Wisdom "sits by [God's] throne" (9:4); Wisdom "knows [God's] works" (v. 9); Wisdom saves (v. 18).

Indeed, Wisdom has a long track record of salvation. Chapter 10 details this as part of the biblical story of faith: it was Wisdom who protected Adam (10:1–2), saved the earth (and Noah) from the flood (v. 4), preserved Abraham (v. 5), rescued Lot (v. 6), rescued Jacob (vv. 9–12), and delivered Joseph (vv. 13–14). Most dramatically, Wisdom rescued the Israelite slaves in Egypt (vv. 15–21). She inspired Moses to act, guided the slaves out of bondage to the Red Sea, "led them through deep waters," and "drowned their enemies" (vv. 18–19). Wisdom, it turns out, was God's agent of salvation all along.

In these latest books, Wisdom's scope expands to the point of embracing God's word ("Law") and God's saving agency in the world. In them, Wisdom becomes the face of divine providence. Here, she reaches her apotheosis, the height of her transcendent power by making her home squarely within Israel's most sacred traditions. Such is wisdom's trajectory, from experiential knowledge to salvific agency, from wisdom to Wisdom.

Psalms

Although the book of Psalms is not considered part of the wisdom corpus—it is, after all, attributed to David rather than Solomon—there are suggestive connections. For one, Psalm 1, which introduces the Psalter, profiles the righteous and the wicked. Both have their respective "ways": the way of the righteous is protected by God, whereas that of the wicked will "perish." Indeed, righteousness and the figure of the righteous individual appear throughout the Psalms. "The Lord tests the righteous and the wicked" (11:5). The "entrance psalms" stipulate the qualities of those worthy of entering the Temple, qualities of righteousness (15:2–5; 24:3–5). In Psalm 34, the righteous in particular are saved by God: "When the righteous cry for help, the Lord hears, and rescues them from all their troubles" (v. 17). The profile of the righteous in Psalms, distinct from Proverbs, fully acknowledges the reality of suffering: "Many are the afflictions of the righteous, but the Lord rescues them from them all" (v. 19). With the exception of Job, the "righteous" in the wisdom literature fare much better.

Various psalms, including Psalm 34, are considered "wisdom psalms," although the exact number remains a matter of debate. Those most often identified as such include Psalms 32, 37, 78, and 111–112. Each one adopts a distinctly didactic tone that distinguishes them from most other psalms, which address God. We can broadly categorize the various kinds of biblical literature in terms of who is addressing whom: (1) human beings addressing God, (2) God addressing human beings, and (3) human beings addressing human beings. Whereas the wisdom corpus falls primarily under the third category (with the exception of Job 38–41), the Psalms, remarkably, cover all three categories, but with a predominant emphasis on the first.

The Psalms consist primarily of human words directed to God in various ways. Although not limited to them, the Psalter features three main genres: complaint, praise, and thanksgiving (in both individual and communal forms). They share in common the conviction that God responds to human speech. In complaint, the most frequently attested genre in the Psalter, God is cast in the role of witness and deliverer. God's attention is directed to the speaker's grievance regarding illness, persecution, slander, or some other form of social injustice or physical debilitation. God is called upon to bear witness and to act on behalf of the speaker. In thanksgiving, the speaker acknowledges God for having resolved the speaker's complaint. In praise, God is given credit for who God is: creator, sustainer, and redeemer, merciful and abounding in steadfast love (*hesed*).

Whereas the wisdom literature contains a trove of instructional material spanning centuries of ethical and theological reflection, the Psalter provides a treasure of Israel's liturgical life, whether in centralized worship in the Temple or in more informal, small-scale cultic occasions. As the Psalms have their home primarily in worship, wisdom operates at the home, the royal court, the marketplace, and in educational settings. Yet there is one thing they share in common: a vision of life that is lived individually and communally. It is no accident that the first word of the Psalter is "happy" (*'ashre*), a designation that serves to commend the kind of person who seeks what is good and righteous, including God (e.g., Pss. 2:12; 34:8; 41:1; 106:3; 119:1–2). From Psalms 1:1 to 146:5, commendations are made that would lead one to imagine the Psalter as a manual of "happiness," or better, a hymnbook for wholeness (although "hymnbook" is not the only thing the Psalter is). Something comparable could be said of the wisdom literature, particularly Proverbs. "Happy are those who keep [wisdom's] ways" (Prov. 8:32; cf. 14:21; 16:20; 20:7; 29:18). Wisdom commends a life of integrity that embodies "righteousness, justice, and equity" (1:3). Each corpus thus shares a vision of life as it should be lived.

Finally, one could also claim a "genetic" connection between the wisdom corpus and the Psalter, whose respective origins later tradition would trace back to ancient Israel's first two kings: the flawed and penitent warrior David and the wise but troubled king Solomon. Psalms and wisdom are tied, ultimately, by their shared, painful struggle toward living life in God's presence.

DISCUSSION QUESTIONS

1. Which wisdom book do you find most appealing? Which do you find least appealing? Explain your preferences.

2. What constitutes wisdom in terms of the biblical tradition? What is meant by wisdom in the popular usage of the term? How are the two similar? How do they differ?

3. How does the wisdom corpus of the Hebrew Bible (Proverbs, Job, and Ecclesiastes) differ from that of the Hellenistic wisdom books (Sirach and the Wisdom of Solomon)?

4. Some have argued that the book of Job does not belong in the wisdom corpus. Do you agree? What makes Job stand out as unique, and what does it share in common with the other wisdom books?

5. If Job and Qoheleth were sitting together in a bar over a beer (see Eccl. 2:24), what do you imagine them saying to each other? Would one be critical of the other, or would they agree?

6. What would be lacking theologically if the wisdom books had not been included in the biblical canon?

FOR FURTHER STUDY

Brown, William P. *Psalms*. Interpreting Biblical Texts. Nashville: Abingdon, 2010.

———. *Wisdom's Wonder: Character, Creation, and Crisis in the Bible's Wisdom Literature*. Grand Rapids: Eerdmans, 2014.

Creach, Jerome F. D. *The Destiny of the Righteous in the Psalms*. St. Louis: Chalice Press, 2008.

Davis, Ellen F. *Proverbs, Ecclesiastes, and the Song of Songs*. Westminster Bible Companion. Louisville: Westminster John Knox, 2000.

Fox, Michael V. *A Time to Tear Down and a Time to Build Up: A Rereading of Ecclesiastes*. Grand Rapids: Eerdmans, 1999.

Janzen, J. Gerald. *At the Scent of Water: The Ground of Hope in the Book of Job*. Grand Rapids: Eerdmans, 2009.

McCann, J. Clinton, Jr. *A Theological Introduction to the Book of Psalms: The Psalms as Torah*. Nashville: Abingdon, 1993.

Murphy, Roland. *The Tree of Life: An Exploration of Biblical Wisdom Literature*. 3rd ed. Grand Rapids: Eerdmans, 2002.

Yoder, Christine Roy. *Proverbs*. Abingdon Old Testament Commentaries. Nashville: Abingdon, 2009.

16

Introduction to
the Prophetic Books

Marvin A. Sweeney

The Latter Prophets of the Tanak—the Hebrew Bible—include the prophetic books of Isaiah, Jeremiah, Ezekiel, and the Book of the Twelve Prophets (Hosea, Joel, Amos, Obadiah, Jonah, Micah, Nahum, Habakkuk, Zephaniah, Haggai, Zechariah, Malachi).[1] The Old Testament, the Christian form of the Hebrew Bible, includes the Prophets as the final section of the Old Testament immediately prior to the New Testament, but this section differs from the Latter Prophets in that it includes not only the three major prophets (Isaiah, Jeremiah, and Ezekiel), plus the twelve Minor Prophets as individual books, but also a few other texts that are traditionally linked to the prophets, such as the books of Daniel and Lamentations.

The Latter Prophets of the Tanak and the Prophets of the Old Testament express the respective theological outlooks of Jewish and Christian forms of the Bible. In the Tanak, the Latter Prophets portray the exile of Israel as a disruption of the ideals of the Torah and anticipate the restoration of those ideals in the Writings. In the Old Testament, the Prophets portray the exile and restoration in anticipation of the New Testament. Prophets in the ancient world acted as spokespersons for their respective gods. Prophets attempted to interpret the major historical, economic, and religious events of their day, identified the divine will in relation to those events, and called

---

1. See the time line in the additional study aids section. The prophets are represented in a bar near the bottom of the timeline.

upon their contemporaries to follow the prophets' understanding of the divine will.

All four books of the Latter Prophets appear together under the general rubric of prophets, but each book has a distinctive outlook based in part on the social identity of each prophet: royal counsellor, Levitical priest, Zadokite priest, and so forth. Taken together, the books of the Latter Prophets present their respective understandings concerning the significance of the fall of Jerusalem and the projected restoration of Jerusalem and the Temple.

Isaiah

Isaiah generally appears first in the order of the Latter Prophets, and it functions as the most prominent dialogue partner for the other prophetic books. Modern critical scholarship identifies historical layers within the book, which results in reading Isaiah as a three-part composition. Isaiah 1–39 portrays the eighth-century prophet, Isaiah ben Amoz, also known as Isaiah of Jerusalem or First Isaiah. This prophet argued that the Assyrian invasions of Israel and Judah constituted divine judgment because of the failure to adhere to YHWH,[2] but he also posited restoration under an ideal Davidic monarch in Jerusalem once the judgment was complete. Isaiah 40–55 presents the work of an anonymous prophet of the exile known as Deutero-Isaiah or Second Isaiah, who announced that the divine judgment of the Babylonian exile was over and that the time for Israel to return to Jerusalem was at hand. Isaiah 56–66 presents the work of anonymous prophets from the early postexilic or Persian period, identified collectively as Trito-Isaiah or Third Isaiah, who discussed various aspects of the restoration of Jerusalem, Judah, and the Jerusalem Temple. Although this model is largely correct, an exclusively historical reading of Isaiah impedes a full grasp of its literary and theological coherence.

A synchronic literary reading of Isaiah points to several fundamental concerns. The book presents itself entirely as the vision of

---

2. Many Jewish scholars write the divine name in this form, reflecting the Jewish tradition that the divine name is never uttered. See chapter 10, "Religion of Ancient Israel," for discussion of renderings of the divine name.

the eighth-century prophet, Isaiah ben Amoz. Isaiah's vision therefore extends forward for some four centuries, from his own period during the times of the Assyrian invasions of Israel and Judah through the Babylonian exile and the early Persian period. Overall, it contends that both the destruction of Israel and Judah by, respectively, the Assyrians and Babylonians and the restoration of Jerusalem under Persian rule are acts of YHWH that reveal YHWH's sovereignty over all creation. The famous swords into plowshares passage near the beginning of the book in Isaiah 2:2–4 signals that the Gentile nations will come to Jerusalem (Zion) to learn divine Torah. Ultimately, the book of Isaiah envisions a future of world peace, in which the Jerusalem Temple stands as the holy center of Israel and the nations.

There are several very remarkable dimensions to Isaiah's depiction of this ideal scenario. For one, the book is especially concerned with the issue of righteous Davidic kingship. Indeed, many have pointed to the ideological grounding of First, Second, and Third Isaiah in the royal Zion traditions of the house of David. A diachronic or historical reading of the book points to each prophet's respective viewpoint. Isaiah ben Amoz, the royal counselor, holds that YHWH will defend Jerusalem, the site of YHWH's Temple, and the house of David forever (see Isa. 36–39; cf. 2 Sam. 7). He looks forward to an ideal, righteous Davidic king, perhaps Hezekiah. Deutero-Isaiah contends that the Persian King Cyrus is YHWH's anointed monarch as the Davidic covenant is applied collectively to all Israel. Trito-Isaiah contends that YHWH is the true king, whose Temple in Jerusalem serves as royal throne and footstool in a new heaven and earth. At this level, the three major historical portions of the book are in debate with each other, as each asserts its own respective view of ideal kingship for Israel. But when read synchronically, the three positions combine into one so that the book of Isaiah ultimately calls for Judah to submit to Persian rule as an expression of YHWH's ultimate sovereignty in the newly restored world of creation.

Jeremiah

Although Isaiah's perspective agrees with Ezra-Nehemiah, which portrays the reestablishment of a Temple-based Jewish community in Jerusalem under Persian rule as the fulfillment of the great prophet's vision, Isaiah's prophetic colleagues are not so accommodating. The prophet Jeremiah is a major case in point. The book of Jeremiah presents him as a prophet like Moses (cf. Deut. 18:15) who also functions as a priest (cf. Lev. 10:11). He lived during the final years of the kingdom of Judah, and he saw the ultimate decline and destruction of Judah as the Babylonians destroyed the city and the Temple and carried the people off to exile. In general, modern historical scholarship contends that Jeremiah calls the Temple into question as a source for national security, sharply criticizes the house of David, and focuses especially on impending judgment against Jerusalem for a failure to observe divine instruction while saying relatively little about the restoration of Jerusalem.

As interpreters consider the synchronic literary dimensions of the book, additional issues come to light. One is intertextuality, particularly with regard to Jeremiah's relationship with the book of Isaiah. Indeed, Jeremiah appears to cite or to allude to many passages from the book of Isaiah. An example is the prophet's portrayal in Jeremiah 5–6 of YHWH's plans to bring a far-off nation to punish Judah, which draws heavily on similar statements in Isaiah 5. Although Jeremiah appears to agree with his senior colleague Isaiah about YHWH's intention to bring punishment, he disagrees on its ultimate timing and its target. Isaiah announced judgment against northern Israel and against Jerusalem and Judah, but he never claimed that Jerusalem would be destroyed.

Jeremiah's Temple sermon in Jeremiah 7 presents a striking critique of the contention that the presence of the Jerusalem Temple would guarantee the security of the city. At his trial for sedition in Jeremiah 26, Jeremiah in true priestly fashion maintains that security is achieved only insofar as the people abide by divine Torah. Without adherence to YHWH's Torah, the Jerusalem Temple will be lost just as Shiloh was lost centuries before. Jeremiah's differences with Isaiah are also evident in his confrontation with the prophet Hananiah in Jeremiah 27–28. When Jerusalem falls under Babylonian rule, Hananiah contends that YHWH will act to deliver the city within two years, a position consistent with that of Isaiah a century earlier. Jeremiah, by contrast, wears a yoke around his neck to symbolize his message that Jerusalem must submit to Babylon in keeping with the will of YHWH. During the ensuing confrontation, Hananiah breaks

Jeremiah's yoke, but Jeremiah returns with an iron yoke to reiterate his message. Hananiah's death ultimately identifies him as a false prophet, and Jeremiah's message is confirmed by subsequent events. Hananiah's position is in fact that of Isaiah: YHWH will defend the city. The identification of Hananiah as a false prophet generally obscures an important point to be drawn from this confrontation: Jeremiah considers Hananiah's—and therefore Isaiah's—message of security for the city of Jerusalem to be false prophecy. In Jeremiah's view, Jerusalem would face war, destruction, and seventy years of exile prior to restoration. Jeremiah 30–31 employs the image of the weeping Rachel to portray Israel's return to Jerusalem, but it does so in the context of a new covenant in which Torah is inscribed on the hearts of the people. Whereas the book of Isaiah maintains the continuity of YHWH's covenant with David/Jerusalem/Israel as the basis for its portrayal of Jerusalem's restoration, the book of Jeremiah posits a change in covenant that will ultimately result in the restoration of the city and its people. Interpreters might note that Jeremiah's vision of the future, in contrast to the full form of the book of Isaiah, envisions the restoration of a righteous Davidic monarch.

Ezekiel

Ezekiel belonged to the primary line of priests that served at the altar of the Jerusalem Temple since the time of Solomon: he was a Zadokite. His education, practices, and use of Temple-based imagery, such as the use of imagery from the Holy of Holies of the Jerusalem Temple to describe the throne chariot of YHWH and the sacrificial destruction of Jerusalem in Ezekiel 1–11, point to this role.

A synchronic reading of the book enables readers to gain an understanding of its full theological significance. The vision of the new Temple in Ezekiel 40–48 clearly stands as the culmination of the book; it expresses Ezekiel's understanding of divine purpose in which YHWH first abandons the Temple so that it and the city might be purged of its impurity and then returns to it so that the new Temple might stand as the holy center of creation. Ezekiel portrays the destruction of Jerusalem much like the offering of the scapegoat at the Temple on Yom Kippur (see Lev. 16): the men dressed in white linen act as priests in carrying out the sacrificial ritual by marking and recording those to be burnt and by setting the fire much as one ignites the sacrifice on the altar. Those who are left unmarked are killed in the destruction of the city, while those who are marked are sent out to the wilderness of exile. Ezekiel is a Zadokite priest, and he employs the imagery and conceptual categories for purification and holiness that are characteristic of the Zadokite priesthood.

Ezekiel shares some characteristics with his prophetic colleagues. He shares with Isaiah a theological foundation in the Zion tradition, although he focuses on YHWH's sanctification of Zion as the permanent site for the Temple in contrast to Isaiah's interest in the House of David. He sees some diminishment of the role of the Davidic monarch, but he differs from the book of Isaiah in that he does not dismiss the Davidic king in favor of a foreign monarch; instead, he clearly places the king under the authority of the Temple and its priesthood. Ezekiel likewise shares some concerns with Jeremiah. Like Jeremiah, he refutes the proverb, "the parents have eaten sour grapes, and the children's teeth are set on edge" (Ezek. 18:1–4; cf. Jer. 31:27–30), insisting instead that people suffer, not for the sins of their parents, but for their own wrongdoing.

But Ezekiel's debate is not primarily with his prophetic colleagues; rather, it is with the priestly tradition in which he has been trained. For example, his discussion of individual moral responsibility in Ezekiel 18 draws extensively on the Holiness Code of Leviticus 17–26 to portray the actions of the righteous and the wicked in similar terms, such as the worship of idols, the slaughter and eating of meat, sexual activity, justice to the poor. But he differs markedly from the Torah by stating that individuals alone are responsible for their actions, whereas the Torah indicates that YHWH may punish later generations for the wrongdoing of their ancestors. His description of the restored Temple, its sacred precincts, and its altar differs greatly from the requirements of the Torah in many details. He deliberately eats impure food to illustrate his life as an exile in a land that is not holy (Ezek. 4:9–15). His depiction of YHWH's throne chariot (1:4–28) draws in part on the imagery of the ark in the Holy of Holies in the Temple (see, e.g., Kings 8:1–13), but it also draws upon motifs from the depiction of Mesopotamian gods,

This Phoenician coin (fourth-century BCE) shows a divine figure riding a flying chariot (cf. Ezek. 1). The inscription identifies the deity as "YHW"—that is, Yahweh.

such as Assur, who flies in a throne chariot at the head of his armies.

Ezekiel employs traditions found in the Torah, but his differences suggest that he is in dialog with them, insofar as he reinterprets them to meet the needs of a very new situation. He is a Zadokite priest, raised for holy service in the Jerusalem Temple, but he finds himself deprived of that Temple in a foreign land that can hardly be described as holy by Temple standards. And yet he strives to act as a priest in very different conditions to sanctify that land by demonstrating the reality of the divine presence even in Babylonia. In this respect, he demonstrates that YHWH is indeed sovereign of all creation.

Daniel

The book of Daniel is a pseudepigraph. There was no Babylonian period prophet named Daniel. Rather, the biblical figure of Daniel was based on a Canaanite sage named Dan El, who was known in the Ugaritic Aqhat epic as a wise figure who was able to save the life of his dead son, Aqhat. Ezekiel cites him as one of three figures, including Noah and Job, who is able to save the lives of others (Ezek. 14:14).

Daniel is not a book of prophecy. Most scholars identify it as an apocalypse. Daniel is included in the Christian canon of the Prophets because, by the Hellenistic period, when Daniel was written, the definition of prophecy had begun to shift so that prediction was increasingly seen as prophecy's essential characteristic. In the monarchic and Persian periods, when the biblical prophets were writing, prophecy was a means to discern divine purpose in the contemporary world; predictions of judgment and restoration portrayed likely outcomes based upon human behavior and divine intent, but were not themselves the focus of the prophet's message.

Like other examples of the apocalyptic genre, such as *1 Enoch*, *2 Baruch*, *4 Ezra*, and the New Testament book of Revelation, the book of Daniel is designed to disclose divine purpose for the future. Although it portrays Daniel and his companions in the Babylonian exile, it is clearly written to support the Hasmonean (Maccabean) revolt against the Syrian Seleucid Empire during the years 167–164 BCE. It makes major mistakes in the presentation of history; for example, Belshazzar was not the son of Nebuchadnezzar, he was never king of Babylon, and there was no figure known as Darius the Mede. The monstrous figure in Nebuchadnezzar's dream is an example of a Hellenistic colossus figure; such figures were not constructed in the Babylonian period. Indeed, Daniel's final vision begins with an accurate portrayal of the conflict between the Ptolemaic rulers of Egypt and the Seleucid rulers of Syria in the Hellenistic period up to the point of the Jewish revolt against the Seleucids in 167–164 BCE (Dan. 10:1–11:39). The final section, however, offers an imaginative view of the defeat of "the king of the north" that never actually came to pass (Dan. 11:40–12:13). With its portrayal of the resurrection of the dead, the book is designed to convince Jews to join the Hasmonean revolt based on the expectation that YHWH will grant victory to the Jews and restore their supporters to life if they are killed in battle against the Seleucids. Jewish tradition places Daniel in the third section of the Tanak, the Writings, where it appears prior to Ezra and Nehemiah, which likewise speak of the restoration of the Temple.

The book encourages Jewish identity and portrays the Seleucid monarch, Antiochus IV Epiphanes (reigned 176–163 BCE), as an unjust oppressor who must be overthrown. The court tales of Daniel 1–6 make this agenda clear. In Daniel 1, Daniel and his companions are Jewish exiles put to work in the Babylonian administration. They are given Babylonian names and assigned rations, but they request to eat only vegetarian food so as not to violate the Jewish dietary laws by eating non-kosher food. YHWH protects them, and they thrive by maintaining their Jewish identities and practices. In Daniel 2, Nebuchadnezzar asks Daniel to interpret a dream based on the image of a colossus made of different elements. Daniel informs the king that the image refers to the downfall of the future kingdoms that would oppress Israel, including Babylon, Persia, the Medes, and the Hellenistic kingdoms culminating in Antiochus IV.

Daniel 3 portrays YHWH's protection of Daniel's friends, Shadrach, Meshach, and Abednego, who are thrown into a fiery furnace when they refuse to worship Babylonian gods. Daniel 4 portrays Nebuchadnezzar's madness, demonstrating YHWH's control over him. The narrative plays on Antiochus' claims to be *Epiphanēs*, Greek for "Manifest God," when he ordered worship of himself as a god in the Jerusalem Temple; in fact, many Hellenistic wags of the time referred to him as Antiochus *Epimanēs*, "Antiochus the Mad!"

Daniel 5 portrays Belshazzar's banquet, in which he brings out the captured holy Temple vessels so that his guests could drink from them. But a divine hand writes on the wall in Aramaic, *mene, mene, tekel, upharsin*, which means, your days have been numbered (*mene*); you have been weighed (*tekel*) and found wanting, and your kingdom

The story of Daniel in the lion's den, depicted in this fifth-century Tunisian mosaic, illustrates God's power to protect those who are faithful. The book was written at the time of the Hasmonean revolt, when Antiochus IV was pressuring the Jews to abandon their religious traditions.

will be divided (*pharsin*) and given to the Medes and Persians. Daniel 6 portrays YHWH's protection of Daniel in the lion's den, when Daniel is sentenced to death for continuing to worship YHWH against the king's order.

The second half of the book (chapters 7–12) presents a sequence of visions of YHWH's plans to overthrow the oppressor. The sequence begins in Daniel 7 with the throne vision, much like that of Isaiah 6 and Ezekiel 1, in which YHWH appears as the Ancient One and passes judgment against a series of kingdoms culminating in the Seleucids who oppress Israel. Daniel 8 portrays YHWH's plans for the future beyond the Babylonian period, specifically the conflict between the Persians and Medes on the one hand and the Greeks led by Alexander the Great on the other, represented in the vision by a ram and a goat. Daniel 9 interprets Jeremiah's prophecy that the Babylonian exile would last for seventy years (Jer. 25:11–12; 29:10–14) as a prediction of the time when YHWH would bring to an end the Seleucid oppression of Judah (Dan. 9:24–27). And finally, Daniel 10–12 presents Daniel's last vision, using language from Ezekiel (Ezek. 1–3) to portray the defeat of "the king of the north"— the Seleucid Empire led by Antiochus IV—and the restoration of Jerusalem and the Temple as the holy center of Judaism. In sum, the experience of the Babylonian exile in Daniel becomes a paradigm for interpreting divine intent in relation to later oppression.

The Twelve Minor Prophets

Although Christian Bibles treat the Twelve Prophets as twelve discrete prophetic books, the Jewish Bible treats the Twelve as a single book with twelve components. The issue is complicated by the Septuagint form of the book, which employs its own distinctive hermeneutical perspective by presenting the Twelve Prophets in a very different sequence from that of the Masoretic Text. The following will focus on the sequence of the Masoretic text of the Jewish Bible, which is the sequence employed in most English translations of the Christian Bible.

The Masoretic Text sequence indicates a deliberate concern with Jerusalem and its relationship to YHWH and the nations of the world. The Book of the Twelve has intertextual relationships with a wide variety of texts from the Bible, particularly the book of Isaiah, which facilitate consideration of the role of Jerusalem and its relationship with the nations in YHWH's plans for the future world.

Hosea

Hosea, a northern prophet from the late eighth century, addresses the potential disruption in the relationship between Israel and YHWH, but envisions resolution when Israel returns to YHWH and the house of David in Jerusalem. Hosea employs his own marriage to Gomer bat Diblaim, whom he accuses of harlotry, to symbolize Israel as the bride of YHWH who has abandoned her husband to seek other lovers. A close reading of the book indicates that Hosea objects to Israel's relationship with Assyria during the reign of Jeroboam ben Joash, which called for Israel to trade with its ancient enemy Egypt. Hosea consequently calls for the overthrow of the Jehu dynasty so that Israel might realign with Aram, where its ancestors originated, and thereby restore its relationship with YHWH (Hos. 1:4–5 and 12:10–12).

Joel

Joel, likely a fourth-century prophet, employs motifs from the natural world, including locust plagues and images of grain, to focus on YHWH's defense of Jerusalem from the nations. Ultimately, Joel looks to the day of YHWH as the time when YHWH will defend Jerusalem from the nations that threaten it.

Amos

Amos was a mid-eighth-century prophet who points to the restoration of Jerusalem and Davidic rule following YHWH's punishment of Israel and the nations. As a Judean farmer and sheep broker, Amos was compelled to bring his produce to the northern Israelite sanctuary at Beth El insofar as Judah was a vassal of Israel during the reigns of Jeroboam ben Joash of Israel and Uzziah ben Amaziah of Judah. Although the reason for such heavy taxation was Israel's need to pay tribute to its own ally, Assyria, Judeans like Amos were left with little on which to survive. In Amos' view, YHWH would overthrow Jeroboam ben Joash and restore the rule of the house of David as in the days of Solomon (Amos 1:2 and 9:9–12).

Obadiah

Obadiah focuses on YHWH's judgment against Edom as a representative of the nations and its submission to Israel at Zion on the day of YHWH. Although traditionalists sometimes identify Obadiah with Elijah's ninth-century associate (1 Kings 18:1–16), his references to Edom's role in the destruction of Jerusalem point to a setting during the Babylonian exile.

Jonah

Jonah tempers Obadiah's scenario of judgment by raising the question of YHWH's mercy to a repentant Nineveh. Jonah ben Amittai is mentioned as a prophet from the time of Jeroboam ben Joash of Israel in 2 Kings 14:25, but the book appears to be a Second

© Cameraphoto Arte, Venice / Art Resource, NY

The book of Jonah has a number of whimsical touches—such as Jonah being swallowed by a great fish, as in this fourth-century mosaic. Nevertheless, the book makes a serious point about God's concern for the well-being of all people, Jews and Gentiles alike.

Temple period literary work that reflects on the notions of divine mercy and judgment. The book raises a question: why should Jonah accept YHWH's forgiveness of Nineveh, the capital of Assyria, when Assyria will ultimately destroy his homeland?

Micah

Micah, a late eighth-century prophet from Judah's western border with Philistia, portrays the rise of a new Davidic monarch in Jerusalem who inaugurates a period of world peace after punishing the nations for their assaults upon Israel. But Micah was a war refugee who was forced to flee to Jerusalem when the Assyrians invaded Judah and devastated his homeland during Hezekiah's revolt against Assyria. He raised questions about how decisions made by the kings in Samaria and Jerusalem ultimately have consequences for the entire land.

Nahum

Nahum was a late seventh-century Jerusalem prophet who celebrates the downfall of the oppressive Assyrian empire. The Assyrian empire had destroyed northern Israel and sent much of its surviving population into foreign exile, never to return. Nineveh was the major enemy of Israel and Judah in ancient times. Assyria's enemies greeted its downfall with feelings analogous to the rejoicing of the allies in World War II over the downfall of Nazi Germany and Imperial Japan.

Habakkuk

Habakkuk raised questions concerning divine justice when the Babylonians threatened Judah during the reign of Jehoiakim ben Josiah in 605 BCE. Habakkuk asked YHWH why he permitted the wicked Babylonians to oppress Judah. YHWH's reply indicates that he will bring about Babylon's downfall.

Zephaniah

Zephaniah was a late seventh-century Jerusalemite prophet who spoke in support of King Josiah ben Amon's program of national restoration and religious reform. Zephaniah's portrayals of divine judgment against the wicked were designed to convince his audience to support Josiah's reforms.

Haggai

Haggai was a late sixth-century Jerusalemite prophet who called upon the returned people of Jerusalem to rebuild the Temple at the time of the restoration of Jerusalem in the early Persian period. He was a royalist who envisioned the rise of a new Davidic monarch as a result of the restoration of the Temple.

Zechariah

Zechariah was a late sixth-century colleague of Haggai who predicted that the nations would acknowledge YHWH at the Jerusalem Temple following a period of world-wide war. Zechariah was a Zadokite priest whose eight visions point to the significance of the rebuilding of the Temple in Jerusalem. Although many take his final vision in (6:1–15) as pointing to the restoration of a new Davidic king, the present text posits that Joshua ben Jehozadak, the high priest, would emerge as the new ruler who would wear the crown and sit on the throne with a priest by his side. Zechariah 9–14, often viewed as a later proto-apocalyptic segment of the book, contains two prophetic pronouncements that envision the return of a righteous Davidic king to Jerusalem and the ultimate defeat of the nations, who would then acknowledge YHWH at the Jerusalem Temple.

Malachi

Malachi recaps the initial concerns of Hosea by calling for the observance of divine Torah, thereby rejecting calls for a divorce or disruption of the relationship between Israel and YHWH. His work is generally ascribed to the early Persian period following the completion of the Temple. He calls for support of the Temple and its priesthood.

Each of the Prophets addresses the problems of exile and restoration in his own way. Isaiah envisions a restored Jerusalem/Israel that will serve as a source for divine Torah and be ruled by a foreign

252 ● ANSELM COMPANION TO THE BIBLE

monarch in the context of YHWH's recognition throughout the world. Jeremiah envisions the restoration of Israel to Jerusalem and the restoration of righteous Davidic rule based on divine Torah following the punishment of the nation. Ezekiel envisions the purification of Jerusalem and the world at large as the process by which a new Temple will be built at the center of Israel and all creation. The Book of the Twelve anticipates a period of world conflict in which the nations will recognize YHWH at the Jerusalem Temple after their defeat by YHWH's Davidic monarch. Indeed, each takes up the problem of Israel's exile as articulated in the Former Prophets by envisioning a restoration of Jerusalem/Israel at the center of a new creation. Each engages in debate, both with the tradition and with their prophetic colleagues, concerning the character of the future restoration.

DISCUSSION QUESTIONS

1. What was prophecy in ancient Israel and Judah? How is prophecy different from merely predicting future events?

2. Who are the three major prophets? Give examples of the main theme(s) of each.

3. Give an example of a prophet who embraces a theology supporting the Davidic monarchy and the Jerusalem Temple. Give an example of a prophet who is critical of the monarchy or the Temple.

4. Why do Christian Bibles include the book of Daniel among the prophets? How does modern biblical scholarship understand the genre of Daniel?

FOR FURTHER STUDY

Blenkinsopp, Joseph. *A History of Prophecy in Israel*. Louisville: Westminster John Knox, 1996.

Petersen, David L. *The Prophetic Literature: An Introduction*. Louisville: Westminster John Knox, 2002.

Sweeney, Marvin A. *Form and Intertextuality in Prophetic and Apocalyptic Literature*. FAT 45. Tübingen: Mohr Siebeck, 2005.

Sweeney, Marvin A. *The Prophetic Literature*. IBT. Nashville: Abingdon, 2005.

Part 3

The New Testament

17

The Social and Historical Context of the Greco-Roman World

Eric Stewart

The texts that comprise the New Testament were composed in what is called the Greco-Roman world. "Greco-Roman" refers to the period from the Greek city-states, particularly of Athens (sixth–fourth century BCE), the rise and conquests of Alexander the Great, the Hellenistic kingdoms that arose in the wake of Alexander's death, and the rise of the Romans as the dominant power throughout the Mediterranean world, finally ending with the fall of Rome in the early fifth century CE. Though each of these periods is significant for understanding biblical texts, the New Testament texts were composed in their entirety during the period of Roman rule over the eastern Mediterranean lands in which these texts were written. Properly, then, the period of the development of the New Testament texts is the Roman world, but the term "Greco-Roman" is still apt for a number of reasons. The Romans conquered the Hellenistic kingdoms, but they did not destroy their Greek cultural legacy. Greek was, throughout the Roman period, the most common administrative language in the eastern parts of the Roman Empire, including Greece, Asia Minor, and the land of Israel. All of the New Testament texts were composed in Greek under Roman rule.

The Romans conquered Judea by 63 BCE. At first the area was ruled largely through client kings, local elites who pledged loyalty to Rome and promised to keep public disorder in check, but eventually the Romans ruled Judea through a series of procurators. The most well-known of these for the study of the New Testament, of course, is Pontius Pilate, who held this post from 26 to 36 CE. Roman rule of the land of Israel lasted until well after the empire became Christian. One of the major events that shaped the lives of many Judeans, including many followers of Jesus, was the Jewish-Roman war that lasted from 66 to 73. During this war, the rebuilt Temple (the "Second Temple") in Jerusalem was destroyed by the Romans.

Though the civilizations of the Greek, Hellenistic, and Roman periods differed from one another in many ways, and Israelite culture differed from each, all of these agrarian Mediterranean cultures also shared broad similarities. These features include collectivism, honor, patronage, and kinship structures.

Collectivism

First-century Judea and the surrounding societies were collectivist cultures. Collectivism is the idea that one's identity derives largely from one's place within a social grouping. Individualism, the primary way of conceiving the self in modern North America, largely developed during and after the period of the Enlightenment (seventeenth and eighteenth centuries CE). Individualism stresses that people are integrated wholes themselves, independent of others for their identity. Collectivism, on the other hand, identifies people by their key social relationships. "In collectivistic cultures people are interdependent within their in-groups (family, tribe, nation, etc.), give priority to the goals of their in-groups, shape their behavior primarily on the basis of in-group norms, and behave in a communal way."[1]

The biblical genealogies serve to indicate family, clan, and tribe membership (Gen. 46:8–27; Josh. 15:20–62; Matt. 1:1–16; Luke 3:23–38). Children are known as sons and daughters of their parents (chiefly their fathers in ancient Mediterranean societies). Child-rearing in collectivist cultures emphasizes conformity to in-group norms (Sir. 30:1–6). Children are expected to be obedient and do nothing to dishonor their families. In patriarchal, collective cultures, the father has complete authority over the son (Gal. 4:1)

---

1. Harry C. Triandis, "Individualism-Collectivism and Personality," *Journal of Personality* 69 (2001): 907–924, at 909.

In the Greco-Roman world, children were trained to assume the roles assigned to them by their family connections and status within society. Elite males held positions of dominance; in general, only sons of elite families—like the students in this fourth-century relief—received a formal education.

and obedience is expected (Luke 15:29; Eph. 6:1; Col. 3:20). Even the God of Israel is known to the Israelites by a collective designation—the God of Abraham, Isaac, and Jacob (Mark 12:26; Acts 7:32). In this way, this God is designated as the God associated with ancestors of the Israelites, cementing Yahweh's place as the deity to be honored by the Israelites.

In most cultures of the biblical period, mobility was limited, though more common in Hellenistic and Roman times. Such societies are often collectivist in outlook. Collectivists frequently are known by the place of their origin or residence. Jesus of Nazareth, Mary of Magdala, and Paul of Tarsus are a few of many biblical examples of people being associated with a particular place.

Collectivists take their social cues from the group, and they put the needs and welfare of the group ahead of individual interests. In agricultural societies, in which the subsistence of the group is continually challenged due to droughts, storms, illness, warfare, and other calamities, members of extended family groups tend to focus on the preservation of the group, sometimes at the expense of the welfare of the individual. Situations in which the survival of the group is at stake generally increase the emphasis on group needs. In the absence of forced population shifts or severe hardship, families live in the same place, farming the same land, often for generations.

As a rule, people in collectivist cultures highly value their in-groups, but they often "report negative attitudes toward their out-groups."[2] In the New Testament, out-groups are frequently the focus of derision, whether for ethnic reasons (John 4:9; Gal. 2:15; Titus 1:12) or for ideological reasons (1 Cor. 5:1, 11; Rev. 2:6, 15). Second Corinthians 6:14–18 warns the followers of Jesus not to "be mismatched with unbelievers," an effort to prevent intermarriages with persons not belonging to the in-group.

Honor

Perhaps the most significant of the broad similarities among Mediterranean cultures is the notion of honor. Greek, Roman, and all of the ancient Near Eastern cultures were honor cultures. Such cultures deal with honor similarly, though what is viewed as honorable might differ from culture to culture. Honor is a person's claim to status within a community or society, plus the social acknowledgement of that claim. A person might claim to be the "best" or the "most" something, but without public recognition of that claim, it is merely seen as arrogance or conceit. Honor can be earned or achieved through various means. Though both men and women pursued honor and attempted to preserve their in-groups honor ratings, honor worked somewhat differently for men and for women.

Warfare offered a major way of winning honor. Achilles is remembered for being the finest of the Greek warriors. Many of the Roman emperors won their place through sustained success in battle. The Israelite tradition is also filled with heroes known for their exploits on the battlefield: Joshua, David, Judas Maccabaeus. That the New Testament lacks such examples is due both to Roman rule and Jesus' admonition against violence (Matt. 5:38–41). The reality of Roman imperial power meant that the earliest followers of Jesus, like their compatriots, could not have hoped to overthrow Roman rule by military confrontation. The author of Revelation, however, recognizes heavenly beings for their accomplishments in battle (Rev. 12:7–12; 19:11–16).

---

2. Triandis, "Individualism-Collectivism and Personality," 914.

Other ways of achieving honor included success in education, poetry, athletics, and many other endeavors. Honor could also be given to someone by a more powerful person or figure. Jesus is granted honor at his baptism by being identified as God's Son (Mark 1:9–11; 2 Pet. 1:17). Paul is granted honor by God, receiving God's grace and being designated an apostle (Gal. 1:1, 15). Jesus informs his disciples that he will grant them the honor of sitting on twelve thrones of judgment (Matt. 19:28). More honorable people could also grant honor to their inferiors (Luke 14:7–11). Within the New Testament, enduring suffering makes one honorable (2 Tim. 2:12; Heb. 10:36; 11:29–38).

God's honor was of paramount importance to the Israelites. Israel's praise of God publicly recognized God's honor status. Concern for God's honor can be seen throughout the New Testament (John 5:23; Rom. 14:6; 1 Tim. 1:17; 6:16; 1 Pet. 2:12). The desire to honor Yahweh motivates passages that mock idols (Isa. 44:18–20; Wis. 15:7–17), and it is also the logic behind the commandment, "You shall have no other gods before me" (Exod. 20:3; cf. Matt. 4:10; Mark 12:28–32). Paul, building on this tradition, suggests that other divine beings who are honored are not divine at all, but rather they are demons; honoring them is not an option for persons who would be faithful to Jesus (1 Cor. 10:20–22). In heaven God is always honored (Rev. 4:8–11).

In ancient Mediterranean societies, it was expected that only men would participate in public life, including politics, work outside the home, and warfare. The realm of domestic life, of maintaining and operating the household, pertained to women. These realms frequently overlapped because various parts of homes were open to the public, particularly in the Roman world.[3] Many studies of honor cultures have focused on the public world of men; comparatively few have explored the notion of honor among women. Those few suggest that women had their own honor codes. Among women, "honesty, confidence, friendship, and industriousness" were honorable values.[4] The protection of the sexual exclusivity of women was an important part of the honor code in ancient Mediterranean societies. Failure

---

3. Carolyn Osiek and David L. Balch, *Families in the New Testament World: Households and House Churches* (Louisville: Westminster John Knox, 1997), 24–35.

4. Ibid., 40.

to protect the sexual reputations of the females of a family made it harder to arrange marriages for the women of the family with other honorable families. The household codes of the New Testament, though they should be read as representing the interests of the authors of the texts in which they occur rather than as descriptive of actual cases of the behavior of women, show special concern for male control of women's behavior (Eph. 5:22–24 ; Col. 3:18; 1 Tm. 3:11).

Patronage and Other Patterns of Exchange

Ancient Mediterranean societies were agrarian. When compared to horticultural societies, agrarian societies were advanced in technology and production, advanced in military technology, controlled more expansive empires with much larger territories, had larger populations, regular warfare, (generally) monarchical governments, pre-industrial cities, limited literacy, political religion, and marked social inequality.[5] Increased harnessing of animal power, the development of better and stronger metal instruments, especially iron plows, and the development of the wheel characterized agrarian societies. These developments made possible more sophisticated weaponry—which also meant that a given individual was no longer capable of producing weapons of the same quality and sophistication as another individual with greater means. These technological advancements, together with an increase in warfare and the increased size of the territory of empires, increased the social distance between those at the top of the social order and those further down. This social distance contributed to a marked increase in social inequality.

The social structure of agrarian societies might be best imagined as a pyramid.[6] Those at the top of the social structure, the ruler and the elites, comprised a small percentage of the population. In the Roman Empire, for example, estimates are that less than 2 percent of the population comprised the elite. The elite were those who were appointed by the ruler, and included officers, personal advisers to the

---

5. Gerhard Lenski, *Power and Privilege: A Theory of Social Stratification* (Chapel Hill, NC: University of North Carolina Press, 1994), 190–242.

6. Ibid., 210–96.

ruler, military leaders, priests, and local rulers. The elite typically held large landholdings that were granted to them by the ruler, who technically possessed all of the territory of the empire. The elite were rich, but in agrarian societies, the rich were not necessarily elite. Due to issues of honor and collectivism, some people who were able to amass fortunes lacked the social and political connections to turn their fortunes into influence. For this reason, these people were not able to secure a place among the elite. Often in the Bible, the elite are considered those who pervert justice and otherwise make life miserable for the peasants (1 Sam. 8:11–18; Prov. 17:5; Isa. 1:15–17; Amos 6:3–7; Mic. 3:9; 7:3; Matt. 19:23–24; Mark 12:40–44; Luke 16:19–31; 1 Tim. 6:9–10; Rev. 18:1–18). The letter of James addresses this theme extensively (James 1:9–10; 2:1–7; 5:1–5).

Just below the elites on the pyramid were a group of "retainers" who served the elites. These retainers comprised about 5 percent of the population. The duties, rights, and responsibilities of the retainers varied greatly depending upon which of the elite they served and what position they occupied within that service (Matt. 8:9; Luke 7:8). Retainers could include soldiers (sometimes as a full-time occupation, but more frequently in limited campaigns), household servants, and slaves who were responsible for seeing to all of the daily activities of the household and advising the elites (Luke 12:42). The services of the retainers as a class were especially important to maintaining the elites' grip on power, but the individual members of the retainer class were, for the most part, replaced easily (Matt. 25:24–30; Luke 16:2).

The vast majority of people in agrarian societies were the peasants who worked the land. Owing largely to the increased technology of production, agrarian societies were able to produce a surplus of food and goods. The elites extracted this surplus from the peasants through rents and taxes. Estimates for rents and taxes in agrarian societies range from 10 percent to 70 percent of the total production of peasant farms. The tax system in first-century Galilee was extractive, and Herod took between 23 and 35 percent of the crops grown in his territory as tribute.[7] The production of food was the lifeblood of agrarian societies, and the elites needed it

---

7. K. C. Hanson and Douglas E. Oakman, *Palestine in the Time of Jesus: Social Structures and Social Conflict,* 2nd ed. (Minneapolis: Fortress, 2008), 105–8.

to feed themselves and their retainers and to provide food for areas in which droughts and famines made it impossible to maintain local populations without importing food from elsewhere.

In the absence of forced population shifts, peasants typically worked their ancestral lands, but during difficult times it was not uncommon for peasants to have to sell their lands and go to work as tenant farmers (Mark 12:1–9). These tenant farmers worked on the estates of the elite, and they were paid a percentage of the crops, or sometimes wages from which they had to purchase the crops that they themselves had grown. When peasants were unable to produce enough food or earn enough money to feed themselves, elites might offer them patronage. Though in most agrarian societies the elites showed negligible interest in the needs and desires of the peasant class, the elites also recognized that, if a large segment of the population of any part of their territory were to starve, it might be harder to produce enough in future years to maintain their control.

In addition to elites, retainers, and peasants, there were also artisans, those who produced goods other than food. Artisans in agrarian societies were typically lower in social status than peasants because they were often displaced peasants who had lost their land. Overlapping with the artisans were merchants, people who made their living from trade. It sometimes happened that a merchant would amass quite a large fortune, but, as noted above, it was much harder to translate that fortune into elite status.

Beneath the artisans in social status were classes of people who were unable to care for themselves and lacked the requisite safety net of family or friends to care for them. This group included chronically ill people with no access to health care (Mark 10:46–52; John 5:5–7).

One of the characteristics of agrarian societies is urbanization, the building of cities. The elites in Mediterranean agrarian societies typically had two residences. One was located within the city walls, and the other was usually some type of countryside villa or estate. These two residences served different functions. Ancient cities, in most respects, were unlike modern cities.[8] The cities were populated

---

8. Eric C. Stewart, "The City in Mark," in *In Other Words: Essays on Social Science Methods and the New Testament in Honor of Jerome H. Neyrey*, ed. Anselm C. Hagedorn, Zeba A. Crook, and Eric Stewart (Sheffield, UK: Sheffield Phoenix, 2007), 202–20, at 204–11.

almost exclusively by elites, their retainers, and those who served them in other capacities. The vast majority of the population of agrarian societies lived in villages located outside of the cities. Cities functioned as places of retreat for elites, especially during times of warfare. The cities were also the places in which the elite attended to public matters: the city was the province of politics. It is estimated that no more than 10 percent of the population of any agrarian society ever lived within cities. During the growing season, the elites usually lived in their countryside estates, overseeing the production of crops by their slaves and clients. These countryside villas could offer respite from the endless attempts to maintain and improve one's honor rating in the city, and they also provided a place to flee should epidemics of illness break out in the cities.

There was no social safety net in the ancient Near Eastern, Hellenistic, or Roman cultures. When people found themselves unable to work due to disease, old age, or physical or mental disability, they were at the mercy of others to provide care for them. In such societies that have marked social inequality, systems of exchange are needed in order to ensure that those at the lower ends of the social spectrum have access to needed goods and services. The family was the first line of support for people unable to care for themselves. This familial reciprocity, or exchange, was open-ended; aid was provided even if the recipient was unable to reciprocate.

Among neighbors and friends, balanced reciprocity was most common. Balanced reciprocity involves even exchange and the immediate discharge of debts so that people would not have outstanding obligations to one another. Generalized reciprocity is characterized by unequal exchange among unequal parties. Patronage is a form of generalized reciprocity in which those who are able provide access to first-order goods like food or land for clients who receive such benefactions and reciprocate loyalty to their patrons. Patrons and clients are bound by the ability of the patron to supply the goods and the willingness of the clients to offer praise to the patron. When patrons do not supply goods, clients may seek new sources of patronage, while patrons who are not honored are not likely to continue to provide patronage. Jesus teaches his disciples a prayer that appeals to God's patronage (Luke 11:2–4). Women offer patronage to Jesus (Luke 8:2–3), and Jesus' followers were commonly patrons to early Christian missionaries (Acts 15:4; Rom. 16:1–5).[9] Where those among the lower strata of society were unable to access patrons directly, brokers who had established relationships with patrons could arrange for patronage, usually for a price.[10] Perhaps one factor that attracted people to join with Jesus' followers was the meeting of their material needs (Luke 14:12–14; Acts 2:37–45; Rom. 15:25–27; Gal. 2:10).

Kinship

Kinship refers to the whole range of relationships based on ethnicity and the household. One's kin group extended beyond the household to include all of those to whom one was related by blood. Within the household, kin could include multiple generations as well as friends, guests, and slaves of the owner of the house.

Most of the biblical texts describe the ideal family similarly. A powerful male figure rules and directs the family's affairs. Such father figures are responsible for raising sons (Eph. 6:4), for blessing them, for protecting daughters (Sir. 42:9–14) and finding them suitable marriage partners, and for maintaining the relationships of the family with other groups.

Children obey their parents (Eph. 6:1), and failure to do so is punishable by death. First Timothy 3:4–5 suggests that a man incapable of maintaining his own household is unfit to serve as a bishop for a local community of Christians. Ideal women manage the affairs of the household, contribute to the good name of their husbands (Jth. 8:1–8), and raise children (Titus 2:3–5; 1 Pet. 3:1–6).

These idealized versions of family relationships, especially those contained in the Wisdom literature, ought to be read prescriptively rather than descriptively.[11] Many families did not fit this ideal due to a variety of factors. Early deaths among marital relationships were common enough to merit attention in the story of Ruth (Ruth 1:3–5). Widows were a distinct class among early

9. Carolyn Osiek and Margaret Y. MacDonald, with Janet H. Tulloch, *A Woman's Place: House Churches in Earliest Christianity* (Minneapolis: Fortress, 2006), 194–219.

10. Alicia Batten, "Brokerage: Jesus as Social Entrepreneur," in *Understanding the Social World of the New Testament*, ed. Dietmar Neufeld and Richard E. DeMaris (London: Routledge, 2010), 167–77.

11. Osiek et. al., *A Woman's Place,* 118–43.

communities of Jesus' followers, and contention about their status is evident in some cases (1 Tim. 5:9–16). In other cases, in-fighting among family members might lead to the death of one or more of the members of the family or other problematic situations (1 Cor. 5:1–5). Jesus imagines a time of infighting among family members that will accompany the persecution of his followers (Matt. 10:21–22).

Households varied considerably. The households of the peasants who farmed the land were located mostly within village contexts. These villages were most often populated by extended kinship networks. Within these villages a small number of families, frequently from the same tribe or ethnic group, lived in close proximity to one another. Families within the village structure were sometimes composed of more than two generations. The oldest male in the household ran the household, at least from a legal perspective. Generally speaking, the ancestral lands were passed on to the eldest son (or the majority of the land was so passed on), and the other children either continued to live within the village structure, subservient in some ways to the eldest son, or else were forced to leave the ancestral land due to the size of the land relative to the consumption needs of the family. Those who left the land might become servants of the elites in cities, artisans, or clients for elites, or they might be forced into slavery due to mounting debts.

Slaves were part of the kinship structure of families. There are relatively few restrictions on the treatment of slaves by their masters within the biblical texts, though for Hebrew slaves, some restrictions were mandated, such as freedom after a six-year period of enslavement (Exod. 21:2–9; Deut. 15:12–18). The New Testament says nothing about the enforcement of these restrictions, and treats slavery as a normal part of life (Matt. 10:24; 24:45–51; Acts 10:7–8; 1 Cor. 7:21; Eph. 6:5).

Slaves in ancient Near Eastern and Mediterranean contexts were teachers for children, cooks, launderers, field hands, and wet nurses. Children of slaves grew up alongside the children of their owners. Slaves had no legal rights within these societies, and they could be bought and sold at the whim of their owners. Slave marriages were not legally recognized. Many slaves in the Roman world in particular were granted freedom at some point in their lives. These freedmen and freedwomen had legal and ethical obligations to act as clients of

Slaves attend their mistress in this Roman bas-relief. Slavery was a given in Greco-Roman society, and all large households included a sizeable staff of slaves.

their former masters.[12] Both male and female slaves were considered sexually available to their masters. This fact makes especially challenging the New Testament admonition that slaves should obey their masters (Eph. 6:5; Col. 3:22; Titus 2:9–10).

Though the social contexts of the Bible are varied, these cultures shared some commonalities, including a collectivist orientation, a concern for honor, marked social stratification, and kinship patterns that incorporated more than just biological, nuclear families. Basic knowledge of these cultural features help modern western readers of the Bible to understand the cultural codes of the biblical texts.

Discussion Questions

1. How do the social contexts of ancient Mediterranean societies differ from twenty-first-century, western societies?

---

12. Zeba A. Crook, "BTB Readers Guide: Loyalty," *Biblical Theology Bulletin* 34 (2004): 167–77, at 170–71.

2. Some Christians argue that certain biblical injunctions should not be taken at face value—for example, that wives should submit to their husbands—because the cultural expectation in biblical times was very different from that of modern western society. Others express concern that such an argument could be used to negate any moral injunction the modern reader happens to dislike. What do you think, and why?

3. In what ways is the role of honor in biblical societies similar to the role of wealth in modern, western society? In what ways is it different?

4. How does the social reality of patronage shape the ways in which these authors address issues related to wealth and poverty?

5. What does it mean that the authors of the New Testament use kinship language to describe the groups to which they write and belong? What obligations within these groups are implied by this use of kinship language?

FOR FURTHER STUDY

Glancy, Jennifer A. *Slavery in Early Christianity.* Minneapolis: Fortress, 2006.

Neufeld, Dietmar, and Richard E. DeMaris, eds. *Understanding the Social World of the New Testament.* London: Routledge, 2010.

Oakes, Peter. *Reading Romans in Pompeii: Paul's Letter at Ground Level.* Minneapolis: Fortress, 2009.

Osiek, Carolyn. *What Are They Saying about the Social Setting of the New Testament?* Rev. and exp. ed. New York: Paulist, 1992.

Stegemann, Ekkehard W., and Wolfgang Stegemann. *The Jesus Movement: A Social History of Its First Century.* Trans. O. C. Dean, Jr. Minneapolis: Fortress, 1999.

Internet Resources

virtualreligion.net/iho

A collection of resources exploring the political, social, intellectual, and cultural climate out of which Christianity emerged.

18

New Testament Christologies

Seán Charles Martin

The periodic intervention of God into human history is a foundational conviction of Jewish and Christian traditions. The call of Abraham (Gen. 12:1–3), the commissioning of Moses (Exod. 3:1–10), and the raising up of prophets like Isaiah (Isa. 6), Jeremiah (Jer. 1:4–10), Ezekiel (Ezek. 2:1–3:15), or Amos (Amos. 7:14–15) represent privileged instances in which the divine plan comes to light in the words and deeds of particular people living in specific times, places, and cultures. Christians claim that the birth, ministry, suffering, death, and Resurrection of Jesus signify a new moment in the relationship between God and humanity (John 1:14; Phil. 2:6–11; Heb. 1:1–2). A sustained reflection upon the significance of the life, suffering, death, and Resurrection of Jesus is called Christology. Since the New Testament presents a number of such reflections, one may say that the New Testament presents a number of Christologies.

The New Testament and Jesus

The principle sources for the deeds and sayings of Jesus are the Gospels according to Matthew, Mark, Luke, and John. The four Gospels do not purport to be biographies of Jesus in the contemporary sense of the term. The Gospels, instead, should be understood as narrative Christologies—reflections on the significance of Jesus' life arranged in story form.

While the New Testament documents agree on the basics of Jesus' life, they frequently differ with respect to the manner in which he is depicted. He appears in the likeness of Moses in the Gospel of Matthew, or as a high priest in Hebrews, as a suffering servant in 1 Peter, or even as a lamb with horns in Revelation. This diversity of images reflects the diversity of the earliest communities in which the stories about Jesus were originally preserved. But as ethnically and geographically diverse as these earliest communities of believers were, their members were typically conversant with the Torah, the Prophets, and the Writings—what Christians today call the Old Testament. Members of these communities would have used these earlier Scriptures, probably in Greek translation, in public worship, communal study, and private prayer. Thus these first believers in Jesus, reflecting upon the wealth of concepts and images found in Israel's sacred literature, came to understand Jesus as the new Adam, or the new Moses, or the new Melchizedek, or the new Passover, or the new covenant.

Typology

There were good reasons for looking to Israel's Scriptures in order to understand the ministry of Jesus. Jesus was born a Jew and brought up in a Jewish household. His earliest followers were all Jews. With few exceptions (Matt. 8:5–13; Mark 7:24–30), Jesus ministered exclusively among his own people. His name—*Yeshua'* in Aramaic, or *Yehoshua'* in Hebrew—is a traditional Jewish name (more conventionally transliterated into English as Joshua), indicating that he was named after the successor of Moses (Josh. 1:1–9), just as his mother Mary was probably named after Miriam, the sister of Moses (Exod. 15:20), and her husband Joseph was probably named after Joseph, the eleventh of the patriarch Jacob's twelve sons (Gen. 37–50). As a Jew living in first-century Galilee, Jesus would have been circumcised eight days after his birth as a sign of the covenant between God and the descendants of Abraham and Sarah (Luke 2:21); he would have studied the Hebrew Scriptures (Luke 2:41–52); he would have taught in the synagogue (Matt. 4:23; Mark 1:21; Luke 4:15); he would have observed the rhythm of the Jewish liturgical seasons by participating in periodic pilgrimages to the Jerusalem Temple (Matt. 21:1; Mark 11:1; Luke 2:41–51; John 2:13, 23; 5:1;

270 ANSELM COMPANION TO THE BIBLE

7:10; 10:22–23; 12:12); and he would have abided by the dietary restrictions that were prescribed in the Torah and required of his people. Apart from the faith and traditions of his people, Jesus cannot be understood.

So it is no wonder that Jesus' earliest followers turned to their Jewish religious traditions and sacred literature to make sense of his life. One way by which they sought to understand Jesus was through typology, or the interpretation of Jesus in the light of his resemblance to figures from the Scriptures. In this interpretative approach, the earlier figure is the "type" or foreshadowing (Greek: *typos*, "dent," "mark," or "original form"). Thus Paul uses typology when he calls Adam "a type of the one who was to come," meaning Jesus (Rom. 5:14). Similarly, the Letter to the Hebrews makes use of typological comparisons in associating Jesus with the figure of Melchizedek, who appears in Genesis 14 (Heb. 7:1–10), and the Gospel according to Matthew uses typology in relating Jesus to the figure of Moses (Matt. 2:16–18; 5:1–7:29).

Typological readings of Israel's Scriptures were intended to illustrate the unity of salvation history. The resemblance between Jesus and persons like Adam, Melchizedek, or Moses was thought to indicate the consistent plan of God.

Titles for Jesus in the New Testament

One of the most important ways by which New Testament authors present their understanding of the significance of Jesus is by attributing to him various titles. These titles, principally Son of Man, Son of God, and Messiah or Christ, are also found in Israel's Scriptures, and like the typological presentation of Jesus in the likeness of Adam, Moses, or Melchizedek, depict Jesus in terms that would have been familiar to his earliest followers.

Son of Man

In all four Gospels Jesus uses the phrase "Son of Man" to refer to himself (see, e.g., Matt. 8:20; Mark 10:45; Luke 7:34; John 5:27). In Israel's Scriptures, the phrase "son of man" (Hebrew: *ben 'adam*) occurs 107 times, 94 of which appear in Ezekiel. Originally the term seems to have designated any human being (see Num. 23:19; Ps. 8:4; 144:3), much as the expression "every mother's child" in English can refer to any human being. "Son of man" can also connote the frailty of the human condition, especially the brevity of human life in view of the inevitability of death, as in Psalm 144:4, where men and women are said to be "but a breath; their days are like a passing shadow."

In Ezekiel (ca. 623–571 BCE), the phrase takes on the added connotation of a person called to be a prophet, and to act as an intermediary between human beings and God. God addresses Ezekiel as son of man throughout the book (e.g., Ezek. 2:1–8; 6:2; 37:3).

This prophetic usage is taken up in the book of Daniel, a work composed around 165 BCE, in which one like a son of man is presented before the Ancient of Days and rewarded with "dominion and glory and kingship" (Dan. 7:13–14). This book appears to have been written during the Maccabean revolt (167–160 BCE) to encourage Jews to remain faithful despite persecution under the administration of Antiochus IV Epiphanes (ca. 215–164 BCE), the Seleucid king who ruled over Judaea, and who had outlawed Jewish practices like circumcision and Sabbath observance (2 Macc. 6:1–11). In Daniel, the phrase connotes fidelity to God in spite of persecution, a faithfulness God recognizes and rewards.

Jesus' use of "the Son of Man" as a self-designation, especially in Mark's Gospel, builds upon all of these previous usages. Like the composer of Psalm 144, he is conscious of the brevity of human life. Like Ezekiel, he stands as an intermediary between God and human beings. Like the figure in Daniel 7, he remains faithful despite persecution. Nine of the fourteen times in which the expression is found in Mark indicate the inevitability of Jesus' suffering and death (8:31; 9:9, 12, 31; 10:33, 45; 14:21a, 21b, 41). In Mark's Gospel, as in the other Gospels, it is clear that Jesus knows that he will suffer for what he has been saying and doing.

The remaining five Son of Man sayings in Mark's Gospel (2:10, 28; 8:38; 13:26; 14:62) reflect Jesus' sense of his authority. In the first two, the Son of Man exercises powers in the present ordinarily associated with God: the forgiveness of sins (2:10) and regulation of Sabbath practices (2:28). The remaining three speak of the Son of Man who "comes in the glory of his Father with the holy angels" (8:38), or who comes "in the clouds with great power and glory" (13:26), or who will be "seated at the right hand of the Power, and 'coming with the clouds of heaven'" (14:62).

Son of God

In the Synoptic Gospels, Jesus is identified as the Son of God by others: the angel Gabriel at the annunciation of Jesus' birth (Luke 1:35), the disciples after they witness Jesus walking on the water (Matt. 14:33), Simon Peter at Caesarea Philippi (Matt. 16:16), a Roman centurion immediately after Jesus' death (Matt. 27:54//Mark 15:39). Even the devil (Matt. 4:3, 6//Luke 4:3, 9) and unclean spirits (Matt. 8:29; Mark 3:11//Luke 4:41) call him the Son of God.

In John's Gospel, the title "Son of God" is similarly applied to Jesus by others: John the Baptist (1:34), Nathaniel (1:49), and Martha (11:27). But John's Gospel also includes the title as a term of self-designation by Jesus himself (5:25; 10:36; 11:4).

The term as Jesus uses it with respect to himself signifies a privileged relationship with God and, like the expression "Son of Man," has deep roots in Israel's Scriptures. Israel is called God's son in Exodus: "Israel is my firstborn son. . . . Let my son go that he may worship me" (Exod. 4:22–23). In a similar way, Hosea (ca. 780–725 BCE) uses the language of sonship in reference to God's choice of Israel: "When Israel was a child I loved him, and out of Egypt I called my son" (Hos. 11:1). Jeremiah (ca. 655–586 BCE) refers to the nation as the son of God: "For I have become a father to Israel, and Ephraim is my firstborn" (Jer. 31:9). This understanding of divine sonship is closely linked to that of divine election, so that in calling Israel God's son, the authors of Exodus, Hosea, and Jeremiah point to the relationship the nation enjoys with God.

Divine sonship also appears in Israel's Scriptures to signify the relationship between God and the House of David. Nathan's oracle (2 Sam. 7:4–16) describes the king who will succeed David as God's son: "I will be a father to him, and he shall be a son to me" (2 Sam. 7:14//1 Chron. 17:13). Here, as in Exodus and Hosea, the image of divine sonship indicates divine election, though the one identified here as the son of God is an individual—a royal figure—and not the nation as a whole. This royal usage is also reflected in Psalm 2:7, probably originally intended for use at an enthronement ceremony for a Davidic king, and in Psalm 89:27–38, another psalm celebrating the status of the house of David.

In John's Gospel, Jesus' own use of the term "Son of God" always has a singular reference, like Nathan's oracle and Psalms 2 and 89. But the title denotes, in addition to the notions of election and privileged relationship found in the earlier Scriptures, a complete identification of Jesus' mission with that of God: "Can you say that the one whom the Father has consecrated and sent into the world is blaspheming because I said, 'I am God's Son'? . . . The Father is in me and I am in the Father" (John 10:36–38). Similarly, in describing Lazarus' illness, Jesus says, "This illness does not lead to death; rather it is for God's glory, so that the son of God may be glorified through it" (11:4). This complete identification with God thus allows Jesus to exercise divine powers: "The hour is coming, and is now here, when the dead will hear the voice of the Son of God, and those who hear will live. For just as the Father has life in himself, so he has granted the Son also to have life in himself; and he has given him authority to execute judgment, because he is the Son of Man" (5:25–27). Both of the two major titles by which Jesus refers to himself—Son of God and Son of Man—are united in this saying, identifying Jesus as the one who gives life to the dead (cf. Isa. 26:19; Ezek. 37:12) and exercises divine judgment (see Ps. 7:11; Isa. 2:4).

Son of God in the Pauline Literature

The use of the title "Son of God" in Paul's letters constitutes a unique witness to the person and mission of Jesus in the first several decades after his death and Resurrection. In the letter to the Romans, Paul makes use of an early creedal statement, probably originating among Torah-observant Christians, when he asserts that Jesus was "descended from David according to the flesh and was declared to be Son of God with power according to the spirit of holiness by resurrection from the dead" (Rom. 1:3–4). The contrast between David and God, as well as that between flesh and "spirit of holiness," signifies the contrast between the human and the divine, and stresses the dual role of Jesus who simultaneously represents the human race to God, and God to the human race. "Son of God" in the letter to the Romans expresses faith in the transformation wrought by the

Resurrection, in which the human ancestry of Jesus, however distinguished it might have been thanks to his family connection to the house of David, is nevertheless eclipsed when God raises him from the dead.

The point cannot have been lost on Torah-observant believers in Jesus who constituted, at least in part, the original audience to whom Paul addressed the letter to the Romans. These believers would have claimed that their own family connections to Abraham, ancestor of the chosen people, gave them privileged access to God, thanks to the covenant God had made with Abraham and his descendants (Gen. 17). But for Paul, no one's ancestry, no matter how distinguished or how faithful, counts for anything in the aftermath of the Jesus event: "Then what becomes of boasting? It is excluded" (Rom. 3:27). Depicting Jesus as Son of God thus diminishes anyone's claim on God apart from that afforded the believer by Jesus himself. To call Jesus Son of God, as Paul does here, is to make a claim that Jesus alone opens the way to God.

Second Corinthians addresses converts from Greco-Roman polytheism. In this letter, probably an anthology of letter fragments preserved by the Corinthian congregation after Paul's death, Paul describes Jesus as the Son of God specifically in connection with Paul's preaching: "For the Son of God, Jesus Christ, whom we proclaimed among you, Silvanus and Timothy and I, was not 'Yes' and 'No'; but in him it is always 'Yes'" (2 Cor. 1:19). The subject of preaching in the Pauline mission, whether by Paul or by assistants like Silvanus or Timothy, was always Jesus. The task was difficult: (1) Paul and his assistants had to persuade their Gentile audiences to abandon their polytheism and commit themselves to the one God, the Father of Jesus Christ; and (2) the Pauline preachers had to demonstrate that Jesus of Nazareth, crucified and raised from the dead, offered these Gentiles exclusive access to God. "Son of God," in this context, indicates Jesus' own fidelity, a faithfulness that took him through the cross to the Resurrection. Such fidelity becomes in Paul's view a model that can inspire these Corinthian Christians to become ever more faithful to their new religious commitments.

In the letter to the Galatians, Paul describes Jesus as the Son of God in extraordinarily personal terms: "I have been crucified with Christ; and it is no longer I who live, but it is Christ who lives in me. And the life I now live in the flesh I live by faith in the Son of God, who loved me and gave himself for me" (2:19–20). For Paul, the death of Jesus is not merely a historical event, the way one today might view any tragic death—an event to be mourned and chronicled for posterity. In his own radical identification with the crucified and risen Jesus ("Christ lives in me"), Paul sees the hope of his own transformation, and, by extension, the transformation of any believer who likewise identifies with the crucified and risen Jesus. Paul's characterization of Jesus as "Son of God" thus denotes a self-sacrificing love that transforms even the most unlikely persons— like Paul himself.

In Paul's thought, to call Jesus the Son of God is to present him as the one who alone gives people access to God; the one who alone gives a witness of faithfulness unto death; the one who alone transforms humanity through self-sacrifice. So persuasive was Paul's presentation of the person and mission of Jesus that the title "Son of God" has become the church's norm against which every other understanding of Jesus is measured.

Christ

In contemporary usage, Christ is a virtual surname for Jesus. To the earliest believers in Jesus, however, the title "Christ" signified the unique identity and mission of Jesus, including the necessity of his suffering (Luke 24:26). Derived from the Greek *christos*, which translates the Hebrew *mashiach*, or "messiah," meaning "the anointed one," the title is rooted in Israel's scriptures. Rulers (1 Sam. 10:1; 16:13) and priests (Exod. 28:41) were anointed with oil when they assumed their respective offices. In some passages from the Old Testament (1 Sam. 24:6; 2 Sam. 1:14; Ps. 2:2), "the Lord's anointed" seems to be a royal title that signifies a privileged relationship with Israel's God.

Even though Matthew entitles his work "an account of the genealogy of Jesus the Messiah" (Matt. 1:1) and Mark calls his "the good news of Jesus Christ" (Mark 1:1), Jesus himself is reluctant to be identified as the Messiah in the Synoptic accounts. When Jesus asks his disciples, "Who do people say that I am?" Simon Peter replies "You are the Messiah." Then Jesus warns the disciples not to tell anyone about him (Matt. 16:13–20//Mark 8:27–30//Luke 9:18–21). In the Johannine account, by contrast, he accepts Martha's identification of him as the Messiah without comment (John 11:27).

This reluctance on the part of Jesus to be identified as the Messiah can be puzzling to a contemporary reader of the Gospels, especially since in the Pauline Letters, as well as in James, 1–2 Peter, 1–2 John, Jude, and Revelation, Jesus is ordinarily referred to as Christ. The "messianic secret," as this narrative phenomenon is sometimes called, may reflect Jesus' ambivalence at being celebrated for his wonder-working (Matt. 8:4; 9:30; Mark 1:44; 5:43; 7:36; Luke 8:56), but it also is tied to the question of his suffering, and the disciples' failure to understand its necessity. Immediately after Peter identifies Jesus as the Messiah, he rejects the necessity of Jesus' suffering, a rejection which occasions a stern rebuke from Jesus (Matt. 16:21–23//Mark 8:31–33). Indeed, in all four Gospels, Jesus frequently predicts the inevitability of his suffering (Matt. 16:21; 17:22–23; 20:17–20; Mark 8:31; 9:31; 10:32–34; Luke 9:21–22, 44; 18:31–33; John 3:14; 8:28; 12:32). For Jesus, his suffering and his identity are integrally linked.

Jesus the Wonder-Worker

In his own day, Jesus was regarded as a wonder-worker. The Gospels report that he cast out demons (Matt. 15:21–28; Mark 1:21–28; Luke 8:26–39), healed the sick, especially people afflicted with leprosy (Matt. 8:1–4; Mark 1:40–45; Luke 17:11–19), and raised the dead (Luke 7:11–17; John 11:1–44). His followers specifically cited his capacity to work wonders in their preaching about his Resurrection (Acts 2:22).

In Israel's Scriptures, the capacity to work miracles is imputed to the prophets, especially Elijah (1 Kings 17:8–24) and Elisha (2 Kings 4:1–37). Likewise, the Acts of the Apostles portrays Peter and John (Acts 3:1–10) as well as Paul of Tarsus (Acts 20:7–12; 28:7–9) as wonder-workers. The capacity to work wonders is not, then, an unambiguous sign of divine status.

What distinguishes Jesus' wonder-working from both that of his predecessors and that of his followers is its connection to the reign of God, the central theme of his preaching according to the Synoptic Gospels. In the Gospels of Matthew and Mark, Jesus' first public speech calls people to repentance (or "conversion," *metanoia* in Greek) because the reign of God is at hand (Matt. 4:17; Mark 1:15).

© Scala / Art Resource, NY

Jesus heals a woman suffering from bleeding in this fourth-century fresco from the catacombs of Rome (see Mark 5:25–34). In the Gospels, the healing miracles serve to illustrate Jesus' message of the coming kingdom of God; they also make a statement about Jesus' identity and authority.

And while nowhere in the four Gospels is the reign of God defined, Jesus' wonder-working gives a glimpse into what it is like, especially since his miracles respond to human suffering.

Whether he is expelling an unclean spirit (Mark 1:21–28), curing a person with leprosy (Matt. 8:1–4), restoring life to a widow's only son (Luke 7:11–17), or feeding the hungry multitude (Matt. 14:13–21; 15:32–39; Mark 6:34–44; 8:1–9; Luke 9:11–17; John 6:1–15), Jesus confronts suffering at its most concrete: hunger, disease, and death. In feeding, healing, and restoring life, he manifests the power and the presence of God to the very people who would have had the greatest reason to wonder whether God had abandoned them. Jesus' miracles indicate, then, that efforts to relieve suffering are signs of the in-breaking of God's reign. The Gospels, in record-ing the typically joyful reaction to these wonders—"God has looked favorably on his people!" (Luke 7:16)—indicate that the bystanders see the connection between wonder-working and the reign of God.

But not everyone reacts so positively to Jesus' miracle-working in the Gospel accounts. Some people accuse him of being in league with the demonic (Matt. 9:34; 12:24//Luke 11:15); the Gospels depict Jesus as replying logically that, in such a scenario, evil defeats itself (Matt. 12:25b–26//Luke 11:17b–18). The Gospel authors then press the point home: "But if it is by the finger of God" (or "Spirit of God," in the Matthean version) "that I cast out the demons, then the kingdom of God has come upon you" (Matt. 12:28//Luke 11:20). According to the Gospels, therefore, Jesus' miracles herald the advent of God's reign; they give a foretaste of a world in which God allevi-ates all pain and suffering (cf. Rev. 21:4).

The Aphorisms of Jesus

An aphorism is a brief and memorable saying. In the Gospel accounts, Jesus' aphorisms reveal his thoughts about morality ("Do to others as you would have them do to you," Matt. 7:12//Luke 6:31) and the paradox of self-sacrifice ("Those who find their life will lose it, and those who lose their life for my sake will find it," Matt. 10:39; 16:25//Mark 8:35//Luke 9:24; 17:33//John 12:25). They also indi-cate what Jesus thinks about himself ("The Son of Man came not to be served but to serve, and to give his life a ransom for many," Matt. 20:28//Mark 10:45).

One of the most striking aspects of Jesus' aphorisms as presented in the Gospels is their tone of authority. For example, Jesus expects his followers to withhold judgment: "Do not judge, and you will not be judged; do not condemn, and you will not be condemned. For-give, and you will be forgiven" (Luke 7:37//Matt. 7:1). The use of the so-called "divine passive" in these sayings ("you will be forgiven") indicates that the one who refrains from condemnation, and who thus forgives, is God. The fact that Jesus speaks on behalf of God here gives an important indication of the way the Gospels depict Jesus as understanding himself. Israelite prophets had also spoken on behalf of God, but their speeches were typically prefaced by the formula, "Thus says the Lord" (see, for example, Amos 1:3, 6, 9, 11). In the Gospels, Jesus uses no such formula.

This assumption of the voice of God is particularly apparent in the Antitheses (Matt. 5:21–48), found in the Sermon on the Mount in Matthew's Gospel (Matt. 5:3–7:29). Jesus recalls some important stipulation in the Torah ("You have heard that it was said to those of ancient times"), and then counterpoises it to some new teaching ("But I say to you"). In some examples, the new teaching internalizes the values that are protected by the prohibition in the Torah. So, for instance, the law forbidding adultery (Exod. 20:14//Deut. 5:18) is internalized when Jesus prohibits looking at someone with lust (Matt. 5:27–28). But more frequently the new teaching reinterprets the Torah, as when Jesus prohibits divorce (Matt. 5:31–32), the taking of oaths (Matt. 5:33–37), violent retaliation (Matt. 5:38–42), and hatred for one's enemies (Matt. 5:43–48). Here, too, the Gospels depict Jesus as adopting a tone of authority that bespeaks an awareness of his own capacity to revise the provisions of Torah.

Jesus in New Testament Hymnody

Two important early Christian hymns depict Jesus in terms that move beyond a narrative description of his teaching and wonder-working in Galilee and Judaea. Instead, they convey an understanding of Jesus in terms of his divine origin. These two hymns were probably originally composed for use in liturgies, and were subsequently incorporated into Paul's letter to the Philippians and the Gospel of John.

The hymn in Philippians 2:6–11 comprises two stanzas. In the first (vv. 6–8), Jesus is said to empty himself, to enter into the human condition, and accept the inevitability of death, even the most painful, shameful death imaginable in the first century, death on a cross (v. 8b). Yet, according to the second stanza (vv. 9–11), that willing acceptance of suffering and death is precisely the reason God raises him from the dead: "Therefore God also highly exalted him and gave him the name that is above every name" (v. 9), an exaltation that is hailed by all of creation (those "in heaven and on earth and under the earth" v. 10), in both gesture ("every knee should bend," v. 10) and acclamation ("and every tongue should confess that Jesus Christ is Lord, to the glory of God the Father," v. 11).

The primary contrast in the Philippians hymn is between the self-emptying of Jesus described in the first stanza and his exaltation described in the second. But the first stanza also depicts a contrast between the "form of God" (v. 6a; Greek: *morphē theou*) and the "form of a slave" (v. 7b; Greek: *morphēn doulou*). The hymn's depiction of Jesus as one initially "in the form of God," which may imply all the attributes typically associated with divinity (immortality, immutability, and omniscience) makes his willing embrace of humanity all the more striking. The language of slavery in verse 7 probably alludes to the Septuagint translation of the Suffering Servant songs in Isaiah (Isa. 42:1–4; 49:1–7; 50:4–11; 52:13–53:12), especially Isaiah 49:3, 5, and 53:11, where the Servant is said to be God's slave (Greek: *doulos*). By characterizing Jesus as a slave like the Suffering Servant, the hymn introduces the theme of divine vindication for the one who shoulders such suffering (see Isa. 49:6–7; 52:13; 53:12).

The Philippians hymn ascribes a descending and ascending pattern to Jesus. He empties himself of any privilege to which he has claim, endures suffering and death, and returns to God with "the name that is above every name" (2:9b).

A descending pattern can be detected in the Prologue to John's Gospel (1:1–18). This Prologue depicts Jesus as the Word made flesh (v. 14) who reveals God to humanity (v. 18). Like the Philippians hymn, the Johannine Prologue makes reference to Israel's Scriptures, especially Genesis, Exodus, Psalms, and Proverbs. The opening words, "In the beginning," echo the opening of Genesis and describe Jesus as the Word through whom the universe was made: "All things came into being through him" (v. 3). To speak of the Word as present at the moment of creation is to situate that Word outside of time, in eternity, the technical term for which is pre-existence. This understanding of Jesus as the pre-existent Word of God alludes to the description of Wisdom in the Book of Proverbs: "When he established the heavens, I was there. . . . When he marked out the foundations of the earth, then I was beside him, like a master worker" (Prov. 8:27, 29b–30a).

The Word is described in the Prologue initially as light (vv. 4, 9), a probable allusion to Psalm 119:105, which celebrates the power of God to save the afflicted. The descending action appears in verses 9–11: "The true light, which enlightens everyone, was coming into the world." The Prologue neatly summarizes Jesus' suffering and death: "The world did not know him . . . his own people did not accept him" (v. 10c, 11b).

Unlike the Philippians hymn, which posits an ascending exaltation to counterbalance the descending self-emptying, John's Prologue depicts a Word that became flesh "and lived among us" (literally, "pitched his tent among us," v. 14) a probable allusion to Exodus 25:8. Just as the tent of meeting in Exodus was the privileged place of encounter between God and Israel, so, according to the Prologue, the person of Jesus becomes the meeting place between God and humanity. It is precisely in becoming flesh that the Word reveals God, according to the Prologue: "We have seen his glory, the glory as of a father's only Son, full of grace and truth" (v. 14b).

The Risen One

Paul of Tarsus provides the earliest written witness to the Resurrection of Jesus. He asserts, first, that Jesus had been raised from the dead by the power of God (1 Cor. 15:3–28), and second, that

© Mordechi Meiri / www.shutterstock.com

This first-century tomb near Nazareth, with its rolling stone for a door, is similar to the tomb of Jesus as described in the Gospels. The claim that Jesus' tomb was found empty—that Jesus had risen from the dead—was crucial to early Christianity.

Paul had personally encountered the risen Christ and had received a mandate to preach about Jesus "among the Gentiles" (Gal. 1:16). For Paul, Jesus' death by crucifixion was only comprehensible in light of his ultimate triumph over death. Jesus' Resurrection becomes the basis for Paul's understanding of discipleship. He argues, for example, that were Christ not raised, the Christian's faith would be "in vain" (1 Cor. 15:14), and that the believer's life consists in conformity to Jesus' death, symbolized in baptism, so as to have conformity to his Resurrection (Rom. 6:1–11).

The Gospel narratives of the empty tomb (Mark 16:1–8 // Luke 24:1–11), of the appearances of the risen Jesus to the women (Matt. 28:9–10; John 20:11–18), and of the subsequent appearances to the larger groups of disciples (Matt. 28:16–20; Luke 24:13–53; John 20:19–21:25), augmented by Paul's reference to multiple post-Resurrection appearances (1 Cor. 15:5–8), likewise testify to a widespread conviction among the early followers of Jesus that Jesus' Resurrection was the basis upon which their faith rested.

The New Testament documents assert that Jesus' words and deeds conveyed the in-breaking of the reign of God. Through these words and deeds, he presented insights into what the reign of God is like; he also presents himself as the one who alone has authority on earth to inaugurate it. The New Testament writings also assert that, in Jesus, the power of God is fully present in the world, and that his distinctive claims to authority are vindicated by God in his Resurrection from the dead. For Christians, the words and deeds of Jesus thus permit them to appropriate the hope of the reign of God and to deepen their understanding of the one who proclaims it with such authority.

DISCUSSION QUESTIONS

1. Explain what is meant by typology, and cite an example. What are some advantages to using typology to construct a theological understanding of Jesus? What are some disadvantages?

2. Describe the background of the titles "Son of Man" and "Son of God." How do the meanings of these titles overlap? How do their meanings differ?

3. Explain the origins of the title "Christ." What is there about this title that caused it to become so closely associated with Jesus that, for many people, it is virtually Jesus' last name?

4. In the Gospels, what is the relationship between Jesus' miracles and his message? What is the relationship between his miracles and his identity?

5. Describe the two hymns to Christ in John 1 and Philippians 2. What themes do they share? In what ways do they differ?

6. Discuss the significance of Jesus' Resurrection to his early followers, according to the New Testament accounts.

FOR FURTHER STUDY

Fredrikson, Paula. *From Jesus to Christ: The Origins of the New Testament Images of Christ.* 2nd ed. New Haven: Yale University Press, 2000.

O'Collins, Gerald. *Christology: A Biblical, Historical, and Systematic Study of Jesus.* New York: Oxford University Press, 2009.

Rausch, Thomas. *Who Is Jesus: An Introduction to Christology.* Collegeville, MN: Liturgical Press, 2003.

White, L. Michael. *From Jesus to Christianity: How Four Generations of Visionaries and Storytellers Created the New Testament and Christian Faith.* New York: HarperOne, 2005.

19

Early Christian Apocrypha

François Bovon

The first Christians were not a unified body of believers; several different communities are known to have existed. Their common denominator was that they lived with the Old Testament as scripture and the apostolic preaching as good news. Around the year 50 CE the first letters were written; then the first Gospels, called "memoirs" in the second century by Justin Martyr, were composed. To minimize divisiveness, the different Christian groups established bonds of faith and love, bringing to the common table their first writings. The grouping of the Gospels according to Matthew, Luke, and Mark in the first half of the second century CE gives evidence of an attempt to reach unity. A little later, in the second half of the second century CE, the Gospel of John was added.

Before going further one must make a distinction: the grouping of texts does not constitute canonization, that is, an official collection of books as scripture. Even though the three, then four, Gospels were brought together, they were not immediately considered to be sacred. When Polycarp of Smyrna, writing around 115–125, mentions the Pauline Epistles (*To the Philippians* 3.2), he still considers them to be simply a corpus of documents, authoritative but not yet part of the canon of Holy Scripture. The passage, however, from a corpus to a canon then occurred relatively rapidly; in the time of Irenaeus, around 180 CE, the four Gospels had received the status of canonical writings.

Noncanonical Gospels and Epistles

Not all of the texts in circulation became part of this process from corpus to canon, however, because not all of the groups who produced such literature were connected with the Christian communities that would eventually form the orthodox church. An ancient gospel that did not make it into the canon is the *Gospel of Peter*. In this gospel, a long passage tells of Jesus' passion, while smaller fragments, especially some verses of Jesus' missionary speech, relate to his ministry in Galilee. Therefore this was not only a gospel of Jesus' passion, as is commonly accepted, but a full gospel of the genre and the age of the Synoptic Gospels. In his *Ecclesiastical History* (6.12.3–6), Eusebius of Caesarea preserved the opinion of Serapion, Bishop of Antioch in Syria, about this gospel in the second half of the second century CE. Serapion at first looked favorably upon the *Gospel of Peter*, for he considered that, since the readers of that Gospel were good, orthodox people, their holy writings should be acceptable. The same sympathy was not shown toward all noncanonical gospels: the early church disapproved of the *Gospel of Philip* (among the Nag Hammadi Codices), the *Gospel of Mary* (Mary Magdalene; in the Berlin Codex 8502), and the *Gospel of Judas* (in the Tchacos Codex), all recently discovered.

The death of the apostles and of Jesus' family, Nero's persecution in 64–65 CE, the fall of Jerusalem in 70 CE, and the delay of Jesus' second coming brought new problems to the forefront. Faithful to the origins of their faith, early Christian leaders tried to find new solutions by digging into the old traditions. Generally they declared that the works on which they drew were of apostolic origin when in reality they were post-apostolic responses. For example, some of Paul's disciples tried to address the problems of their day by generating new works in Paul's name. An exchange ostensibly between Paul and the Corinthian community, known as *3 Corinthians*, was actually written in the middle of the second century CE—as was an *Epistle to the Laodiceans*. These documents came too late to be integrated into the canon of the New Testament.

The same motives that led Christians to write letters in Paul's name pushed other believers to write in the name of Peter or James. Most of these epistles are of an ethical nature, and recommend strict

286 ANSELM COMPANION TO THE BIBLE

but generous attitudes. For example, besides the two letters of Peter in the New Testament, there is a Coptic *Epistle of Peter to Philip* and a Greek *Epistle of Peter to James* (a preface to the *Pseudo-Clementine Homilies*). The author of an enigmatic *Epistle of Titus* argues in favor of an ascetical tendency and tries to impose sexual abstinence.

The Term *Apocryphal*

The term *apocryphal* does not appear to have been used before the second century for Christian documents. Literally, it means "hidden." Humans "hide" either what they cherish or what makes them ashamed. Agreeing with other believers on the elementary core of the Christian faith, some spiritual groups—rapidly condemned as gnostics because they tried to earn salvation through knowledge (*gnōsis*)—claimed with pride to possess additional teachings that they preferred to hide and to reveal only to the happy few. They called these secret writings "apocryphal" (in a positive sense) and often used the period after the Resurrection as a literary trope to develop their esoteric teachings. Modern scholars call such writings "dialogues with the Savior." Such treatises as *The Book of Thomas the Contender* are particularly abundant among the Nag Hammadi Codices. The *Gospel of Thomas*—in its present form a second-century CE document—claims from its very beginning to offer a secret, an "apocryphal" (again, in the positive sense) path to eternal life. This claim can also be heard in other writings of the Nag Hammadi Codices, for example the *Apocryphon of James* and the *Apocryphon of John*.

About the same time, writers from the emerging orthodox church began to condemn what they considered heretical teachings, rejecting the documents that their adversaries collected with respect. Justin Martyr, Irenaeus, and Tertullian, and later Eusebius and Jerome, describe these condemned documents as "false," "corrupt," "bastard," or "apocryphal" (in the negative sense).

Nevertheless, writings that paralleled the four Gospels and the Pauline Epistles continued to exist and even develop. In the second century CE, different Jewish-Christian congregations in Judea and Galilee, Egypt, and Transjordan, still practicing the Mosaic law but believing in Jesus as the Messiah, had preserved their own memories of Jesus. Their gospels are lost, but references to them and even a few quotations have survived. Among these were a *Gospel of the Nazarenes*, a *Gospel of the Hebrews*, and a *Gospel of the Ebionites* (a title assigned by modern scholars).

While the faith of the first Christians in Jerusalem was oriented more toward the end of Jesus' life and the end of history, an interest in Jesus' birth and the origin of the world arose a few years later among Christian Hellenists, particularly in Antioch in Syria. This interest appears in the two canonical infancy narratives, Matthew 1–2 and Luke 1–2. It then developed into two forms that arrived too late to be integrated into the New Testament canon. This does not mean that they were rejected immediately as "apocryphal."

The first form is related to *time*, to the past in the life of Jesus and his family: the most ancient witness, written in the second century CE, is the Greek *Birth of Mary*, claiming to have been written by James, the brother of the Lord. It is known by its modern title, *Protevangelium of James*. This book was never declared apocryphal in the Greek Orthodox world, even if it remained outside the canon and

Saint Anne appears in this illumination from a twelfth-century Greek codex. The identification of Mary's mother as Saint Anne can be traced back no further than the second-century *Protevangelium of James*.

was considered a historical document. It has been condemned in the West since the time of Jerome but survived for a time in Latin translations. It was then rewritten in an orthodox way to avoid further condemnations. This Latin rewriting, called the *Gospel of Pseudo-Matthew* (sixth–eighth centuries CE), was soon eclipsed by the *Birth of the Virgin Mary* (ninth–tenth centuries CE). The names of Anne and Joachim for Mary's parents come ultimately from the *Protevangelium of James*.

The second form speculates on *space* and imagines Christ's incarnation: the descent of the preexistent Son through seven levels of heaven. Such a speculation is attested in three documents, the *Ascension of Isaiah*, the *Epistle of the Apostles*, both from the second century CE, and the *Pistis Sophia*, probably from the third century.

Later in the fifth century CE, when theologians and bishops gathered for a council at Ephesus and meditated on Mary as the "Mother of God," Christian writers generated stories of the Virgin Mary's death and bodily assumption into heaven. At least sixty-seven parallel versions of that story—called the *Transitus Mariae* (*Mary's Crossing*) or the *Dormitio Mariae* (*Mary's* [*Last*] *Sleep*)—are known.

Noncanonical Acts of Apostles

In the first half of the second century, the Johannine community split (see 1 John 2:19). While one wing tried to give what became the orthodox understanding of Jesus and favored the canonization of the Fourth Gospel, another wing developed independent traditions, some of which are preserved in the *Acts of John*. This writing was condemned by the church at an early stage because a section of it denied the reality of Jesus' incarnation and death. The *Acts of Andrew* faced a similar fate. Because of these drastic condemnations these literary pieces were destroyed and only fragments or revised sections survive.

Stories told in the oral tradition of Peter, Paul, Thecla, Thomas, Philip, and Matthew were gathered into large written tomes on the lives, miracles, and martyrdoms of these apostles. These writings—the *Acts of Peter*, the *Acts of Paul* (including the story of Thecla), the *Acts of Thomas*, the *Acts of Philip*, and the *Martyrdom of Matthew*—focus on one apostle each and present his martyrdom after a ministry marked by ascetical recommendations and miraculous acts. This literary form is closer to the canonical Gospels than to the Acts of the Apostles. Because these noncanonical acts were not so different from the Gospels and not antagonistic to the canonical book of Acts, they were at first accepted by certain theologians. Teachers in theological schools as well as monks liked these noncanonical works more than bishops and priests in the cities. While Origen knew and appreciated the *Acts of Paul*, Tertullian disliked it because it conferred a ministerial role on a woman; for others, the excessive ascetic tendency attested in several sections of the *Acts of Andrew*, the *Acts of Thomas*, and the *Acts of Philip* was despicable.

Noncanonical Apocalypses

The New Testament book of Revelation elaborates its visions in a cosmic framework and describes the end of the world through large symbolic frescoes. The same is true of another apocalypse, the *Apocalypse of Peter*. Written probably a generation after the Johannine book of Revelation, in association with the second Jewish revolt of 132–135 CE, the *Apocalypse of Peter* also is oriented toward the end of the world with an apocalyptic perspective. Although the original form of this apocalypse was amazingly preserved in Ethiopic, it is also partly known in a revised form in a long Greek fragment. In this fragment the context is no longer the end of the world but death. This *Apocalypse of Peter* was very popular in Antiquity, even though the author knows of others who refused to read it in church. Building on 2 Corinthians 12:1–4, several writers created apocalypses of Paul. One is present in the Nag Hammadi Library and another in the Greek apocryphal literature. This latter *Apocalypse of Paul* was never condemned, and it circulated widely in the Middle Ages. Dante knew one of its versions.

The Reception of the Apocryphal Literature

Apocryphal literature had an impact on many aspects of Christian life in late antiquity, the Byzantine period, and the Middle Ages—on liturgy, Christian art, literature, history, and theology. At

© Peter Mathews / Eric Jump / www.petermathews.net

This tympanum from the church of Notre-Dame at Semur-en-Auxois shows scenes from the life of Saint Thomas, some of which are found only in the apocryphal *Acts of Thomas*. A tympanum is the decorative wall space within an arch and above a doorway.

Notre-Dame at Semur-en-Auxois (Burgundy, France), for example, the tympanum of the north doorway to the transept relates Saint Thomas's doubts at the Resurrection and his later travels to India as narrated in the *Acts of Thomas*.

How was it possible that such works continued to be influential after being condemned in the fourth–fifth centuries CE by major theologians like Eusebius and Amphilochius in the East and Jerome and Augustine in the West? To explain this paradox one has to recognize two contradictory forces among early Christian thinkers. On the one side, there is the tendency to close the canon and to remain, thereafter, as biblical as possible. On the other, there are new liturgical, pastoral, and monastic needs requiring noncanonical texts. One solution was to revise, to purify, and finally to select noncanonical documents in addition to the biblical canon. So rewritten, these documents became part of the tradition. Gregory, bishop of Tours in the sixth century, preserved the plot of the *Acts of Andrew*. In his preface to his *Life of Andrew* he reports finding a book, probably a Latin version of the old apocryphal *Acts of Andrew*. He liked the narrative but felt that several of the speeches of the apostle in it were heretical in many respects. (Diplomatically he says that they were too long.) Therefore he rewrote the book, respecting the narrative but eradicating the speeches.

Without becoming canonical these revised apocryphal texts nevertheless ceased to be despicable, heretical, and rejected. They became part of the Christian tradition. But their identity did not exactly correspond to the definition of the apostolic tradition set forth at the Council of Trent in the sixteenth century. While the council asserted that the Catholic Church has control over Scripture and tradition, the historians and theologians of today believe that these documents, neither canonical nor apocryphal, were composed by the spontaneous needs and desires of local communities. They were not written by powerful church authorities but by local Christian leaders. Later they were revised by theologians eager to reach church people and curious to discover unusual but respectable documents. In their new versions these books were considered by some to be profitable and useful for the soul.

DISCUSSION QUESTIONS

1. What does "canonical" signify? What can be inferred about the early Christian communities on the basis of the scriptures they generated and the acceptance of some scriptures as canonical and the rejection of others as noncanonical?

2. Why do you think the noncanonical Christian literature remained popular in spite of official attempts to eradicate it?

3. What role does religious imagination play in the composition and use of this material?

FOR FURTHER STUDY

Ehrman, Bart. *Lost Scriptures: Books that Did Not Make It into the New Testament.* Oxford and New York: Oxford University Press, 2005.

Ehrman, Bart, and Zlatko Plese. *The Apocryphal Gospels: Texts and Translations.* New York: Oxford University Press, 2011.

Foster, Paul. *The Apocryphal Gospels: A Very Short Introduction.* Oxford; New York: Oxford University Press, 2009.

Klauck, Hans-Josef. *The Apocryphal Gospels: An Introduction.* London; New York: T & T Clark, 2004.

Schneemelcher, Wilhelm, and R. M. Wilson, eds. *New Testament Apocrypha.* Translation edited by R. McL. Wilson. Rev. ed. 2 vols. Louisville: Westminster John Knox, 1990–1992.

20

The Christian Bible and the Jews

Erica L. Martin

Just as there are several different types of "Christian Bible,"[1] there are a variety of attitudes toward Jews and Judaism in Christian texts. To understand the depiction of Jews in the Christian Bible and Christian interpretation it is helpful to begin with the New Testament. Not only does the New Testament contain texts that are formative for and unique to Christianity, it also acts as a lens through which Christian readers understand the meaning of Old Testament texts. This "lens" or interpretive filter often provides Christian readers with a dramatically different understanding of Old Testament/Hebrew Bible texts than the understanding of Jewish readers, who utilize different lenses. It is ironic that the New Testament is often accused of being the most influential anti-Jewish text in history; almost all of its authors were Jews, it is packed with quotes from Jewish scriptures, and focuses on the life, death, and significance of a Jewish Messiah and his Jewish followers. How did this happen? Is the New Testament really anti-Jewish? The answer to these questions is as complex as the New Testament itself.

The New Testament and the Jews

The New Testament is a collection of writings by a variety of different authors, composed over the span of roughly one hundred years. Readers should not be surprised, then, that New Testament

---

1. See the chart "Canons of Scripture" in the additional study aids section.

texts display a wide range of opinions, information, and assumptions regarding Jews and Judaism.

Jesus, the Apostles, Paul, and the vast majority of people depicted in the Gospels were Jewish. Earliest Christianity (which was not called "Christianity" until somewhat after the time of Jesus) was one of many kinds of Judaism that existed in Roman-occupied Judea during the first century of the Common Era. Differing sects and movements within first-century Judaism sometimes overlapped and intermingled, and sometimes maintained distinct boundaries. In the time of Jesus, for a Jew in Roman-occupied Judea to become a Jesus-follower did not imply conversion from Judaism. Many first-century Jews expected a Messiah, or anointed one. Many candidates for this Messiah-figure appeared, including Jesus of Nazareth. First-century Jews who became Jesus-followers, therefore, added a belief in Jesus as Messiah to their pre-existing Judaism, rather than abandoning their Judaism for a new religious system.

In the first century of the Common Era, significant numbers of Gentiles (non-Jews) also participated in Jewish life and observances.

The "Conversion" of Paul

Paul of Tarsus, a Jew who persecuted followers of Jesus after the Crucifixion, experienced a visual and auditory revelation, which caused him to accept Jesus as the Messiah, or Christ, and begin defending and furthering the Jesus Movement. According to Acts, he received this vision while travelling to Damascus (Acts 9). Although Paul's visionary experience is commonly referred to as his conversion, that term is misleading. Paul did not cease to be Jewish and become a Christian at this moment or at any point in his lifetime; in fact, there was no "Christianity" separate from Judaism to which one might convert. Paul went from being a Jew who did not believe that Jesus was the Jewish Messiah to a Jew who did believe that Jesus was the Jewish Messiah. Paul then began to teach his new understanding of Jesus and its implications for both Jews and non-Jews (Gentiles).

According to Acts, Paul received his vision on this road from Jerusalem to Damascus. Though traditionally termed Paul's "conversion," his experience more closely resembles a prophetic call narrative. Paul remained a Jew throughout his life.

Gentiles attended and funded Jewish synagogues and observed many Jewish holidays and customs, often without fully converting to Judaism. Conversion to Judaism required circumcision for men (the removal of part of the genital foreskin) and the observation of Jewish dietary requirements, both of which ran the risk of estranging the potential converts from their family and wider Gentile society. Many Gentiles, known as God-fearers, did not fully convert to Judaism but maintained a peripheral presence in their local Jewish communities.

Early Jewish-Christian leaders differed significantly regarding the requirements for Gentiles who became Jesus-followers. Many felt that Gentiles who wished to follow Jesus needed to fully convert to

Judaism and follow the Torah, the Jewish Law. Some New Testament authors, like Paul and the writer of Luke-Acts, insisted that although *parts* of Torah were indeed incumbent upon Gentile Jesus-followers, many facets of the Torah (circumcision, dietary regulations, etc.) did not need to be followed by Gentile Christians. This approach toward Gentile inclusion eventually won out, and helped to make earliest Christianity an attractive option for God-fearers and other Gentiles. By the mid-first century, earliest Christianity consisted of both Jewish Christians and Gentile Christians, with significant geographical and ideological variety in each community.

The Pauline Epistles and the Jews

The earliest preserved Christian texts are the letters either written or dictated by Paul, a highly educated Jew from Tarsus, and a Roman citizen according to Luke's account.[2] Paul was not a participant or eye-witness to the ministry of Jesus, and in fact was violently opposed to Jewish Christianity until a visionary experience changed his mind. Paul's self-description as "apostle to the Gentiles" (Rom. 11:13) defines his mission: to spread the news of Jesus among the Gentile inhabitants of the Roman Empire. Paul was not the sole Jewish-Christian missionary to Gentiles. References to others occur often in the course of his letters; some of them won Paul's enmity for taking a different approach to Gentile inclusion.

Paul's letters contain many statements that seem to vilify Judaism. For example:

- But Israel, who did strive for the righteousness that is based on the law, did not succeed in fulfilling that law. (Rom. 9:31)
- But their minds were hardened. Indeed, to this very day, when they hear the reading of the old covenant, that same veil is still there, since only in Christ is it set aside. Indeed, to this very day whenever Moses is read, a veil lies over their minds; but when one turns to the Lord, the veil is removed. (2 Cor. 3:14–16)
- For all who rely on the works of the law are under a curse. (Gal. 3:10)

---

2. See chapter 23, "Introduction to Pauline Literature."

In the history of New Testament interpretation, quotations like these gave rise to the idea that Paul taught Judaism as a cursed, corrupt, and failed religion. Christian and Jewish readers alike have assumed that Paul believed that the Torah was now null and void and that God had rejected Judaism and replaced it with Christianity. The problem with this interpretation is that Paul's letters also contain numerous positive statements regarding Judaism, such as:

- Then what advantage has the Jew? Or what is the value of circumcision? Much, in every way. (Rom. 3:1)
- They are Israelites, and to them belong the adoption, the glory, the covenants, the giving of the law, the worship, and the promises; to them belong the patriarchs, and from them, according to the flesh, comes the Messiah. (Rom. 9:4–5)
- Is the law then opposed to the promises of God? Certainly not! (Gal. 3:21)

The tension between negative and positive portrayals of Judaism in Paul's letters requires explanation. Was he inconsistent? Confused? Christian interpretation has tended to subordinate the positive statements to the negative ones, implying that the negative statements vilifying Judaism are more normative, more indicative of Paul's true position. However, since the late twentieth century, many scholars have accepted some form of the "new perspective on Paul,"[3] holding that Paul did not deny the ongoing efficacy of Judaism. Rather, Paul criticized *some* Jews—primarily those Christian Jews who argued, against Paul, that Gentiles could not be full participants in the Jesus movement without converting to Judaism.

The study of Paul's letters as *occasional literature*—messages written in a specific historical context to a specific audience about a specific problem—reveals that Paul was, for the most part, neither confused nor inconsistent, though he did sometimes state his case in an exaggerated manner. The appearance of inconsistency stems from the fact that he was discussing different things with different people at different times. Paul absolutely advocated that Jesus was the Jewish Messiah, and presumably wished that all of his fellow Jews would

---

3. The advent of the "new perspective" is usually traced to E. P. Sanders, *Paul and Palestinian Judaism* (Philadelphia: Fortress, 1977).

acknowledge Jesus as such. But Paul did not ask them to abandon their Judaism. One the contrary, he argued that Jesus completed their Judaism: Christ is "the end of the law" (Rom. 10:4), not in the sense of terminating it, but of being the completion and goal of the law.

For Gentiles, on the other hand, Paul offered the good news of "justification" (righteousness in the sight of God) without following the Torah. Paul was adamant that Gentiles did not need to follow Torah. In fact, Paul considered Gentile conversion to Judaism not simply unnecessary but offensive, an affront to Paul's authority as an apostle of Christ and an affront to the grace of God, because it

Anti-Semitism or Anti-Judaism?

There is a thin line differentiating anti-Judaism, the opposition to Judaism as a religion and Jews as its adherents, and anti-Semitism, prejudice against or hatred of Jews as a race or people. Anti-Judaism was certainly present in the Roman Empire and evident in some New Testament literature, notably works written later in the canonical process. In earlier New Testament writings it is more difficult to label negative rhetoric anti-Judaistic because the invective there (at times quite harsh) is generally directed by Jews against other Jews—specifically, by Jesus-following Jews against non-Jesus-following Jews. Like squabbling factions within one modern political party, these New Testament voices are often not opposed to Judaism itself, but rather to forms of Judaism that do not match their own. As the Jewishness of earliest Christianity was forgotten in the history of Christian interpretation, however, the crucial understanding that these arguments are internal debates was lost. Often influenced by later anti-Semitic notions of the inferiority of Jews as a race, subsequent generations of Christian interpreters read these passages in an anti-Judaistic light. In this way, anti-Judaism and anti-Semitism were mutually reinforcing and exponentially more harmful, leading to political and economic repression of Jews, expulsion of Jews from their home countries, pogroms (massacres), and even attempted genocide.

This depiction of the crossing of the Red Sea adorned the second-century synagogue of Dura-Europos in Syria. Some Syrian Christians attended both church and synagogue as late as the fourth century. Christianity's separation from Judaism began early but took centuries to finalize.

© Zev Radovan / www.biblelandpictures.com

amounts to setting conditions upon God's offer of salvation to the Gentiles through Jesus. In Galatians 5:4 he admonishes, "You who want to be justified by the law have cut yourselves off from Christ." Most of Paul's seemingly anti-Judaistic statements occur in instances when he is angry with other apostles who are undermining his teaching by insisting that Gentile members of Paul's congregations become circumcised and begin following other Jewish customs (see, e.g., Gal. 3). These seemingly anti-Judaistic statements are part of an internal debate over the method of Gentile inclusion, and must be understood in that context and not as blanket assertions regarding the nature and validity of Judaism.

The Gospels and the Jews

The Gospels of Matthew, Mark, Luke, and John tell the story of Jesus in remarkably distinct ways. Mark's Jesus is a man of action; Matthew's Jesus is given to long speeches, and strongly resembles Moses; Luke's Jesus more closely resembles other Old Testament prophets like Samuel and Elijah. Mark's Jesus is achingly human; John's Jesus exudes divinity and otherness. The communities that received and preserved the Gospels were equally diverse. One trait the Gospels share, however, is that they depict Jesus as having been opposed by Jewish religious authorities. In the Gospel of John,

Jesus' opponents are often identified simply as "the Jews," as in these examples:

- Therefore the Jews started persecuting Jesus, because he was doing such things on the Sabbath. . . . For this reason the Jews were seeking all the more to kill him. (John 5:16, 18)
- Then the Jews began to complain about him because he said, "I am the bread that came down from heaven." (John 6:41)
- After this Jesus went about in Galilee. He did not wish to go about in Judea because the Jews were looking for an opportunity to kill him. (John 7:1)
- Yet no one would speak openly about him for fear of the Jews. (John 7:13)

It should be noted that the word in question (*Ioudaios*) was flexible in meaning, and the author clearly does not mean "all Jewish people" every time he uses it. Sometimes it means "Judeans" (a geographical reference), sometimes the Jewish authorities (a political reference), and sometimes Jews who rejected Jesus and his followers (a theological reference). This last use is complicated by the fact that the community for which John's Gospel was written appears to have experienced rejection by a Jewish community, and the Gospel seems to read this later conflict back into the time of Jesus.

The Synoptic Gospels (Matthew, Mark, and Luke) tend to be more specific—but no less harsh—in their depiction of Jesus' opponents, often naming the Pharisees and scribes as the chief offenders.

- "But woe to you, scribes and Pharisees, hypocrites! For you lock people out of the kingdom of heaven. For you do not go in yourselves, and when others are going in, you stop them. Woe to you, scribes and Pharisees, hypocrites! For you cross sea and land to make a single convert, and you make the new convert twice as much a child of hell as yourselves." (Matt. 23:13–15)
- The Pharisees went out and immediately conspired with the Herodians against him, how to destroy him. (Mark 3:6)
- Meanwhile, when the crowd gathered by the thousands, so that they trampled on one another, he began to speak first to his disciples, "Beware of the yeast of the Pharisees, that is, their hypocrisy." (Luke 12:1)

Texts such as these pit Jesus and his followers against the Pharisees, who are depicted as hypocritical and murderously conspiratorial. Conflict drives narrative, and the Gospels are narratives. Much of this conflict is likely anachronistic, however, built into the text of the Gospels in the generations following Jesus' life. The Pharisees were one of several Jewish sects (groups) active in the first century. Pharisaic beliefs differed from other Jewish sects of the time by, among other things, their strong affirmation of resurrection, the afterlife, and adherence to the Oral Torah (ongoing discussion of Jewish law outside of the writings attributed to Moses). An important precursor to Rabbinic Judaism, Pharisaic interpretation created a "fence around Torah," protecting essential commandments through the addition of safeguards that prevent the accidental violation of the commandment.

When compared to all known first-century Jewish groups, the teachings and statements of Jesus preserved in early Christian literature are markedly similar to Pharisaic teachings and beliefs. In the Gospels, Jesus speaks of resurrection, the afterlife, and builds fences around Torah: "You have heard that it was said, 'You shall not commit adultery.' But I say to you that everyone who looks at a woman with lust has already committed adultery with her in his heart" (Matt. 5:27–28). By forbidding lust, the commandment against adultery is protected. Jesus also protects the commandments against murder and false oaths with fences in a remarkably Pharisaic manner (Matt. 5:21–26, 33–37). This observation should not downplay the apparent differences between Jesus and some Pharisees on questions such as healing on the Sabbath. Is it appropriate to heal a chronic illness on the Sabbath, as Jesus does (Mark 3:1–6), or is it only appropriate to heal an acute, or life-threatening one, as the Pharisees believed? Despite the fervor of the argumentation, the difference between Jesus and "the Pharisees" is slim.

Along with the scribes, Pharisees are cast in the Gospels as an overwhelming religious and political force. Pharisees held varying degrees of power in the Jewish community at different times, but the sect did not attain authority until the generations following the Roman destruction of the Jerusalem Temple in 70 CE—decades after Jesus' Crucifixion. Although the Gospels undoubtedly contain much material that originated in the time of Jesus, the Gospels were not written until decades later. The intermittent antagonism depicted

Varieties of Judaism in the First Century CE

When the followers of Jesus began, after his death, to form a recognizable movement, they took their place alongside several other expressions of Judaism in first-century Palestine, the most important of which were the Sadducees, the Essenes, the Pharisees, and the armed resistance movements. It is likely that most first-century Jews did not consider themselves to be members of any of these groups, although they might have been favorably disposed toward one or another of them.

The Sadducees consisted primarily of the chief priests, their extended families, and their supporters. Their understanding of Judaism focused upon worship in the Temple. They were theological conservatives, accepting only the Torah as inspired scripture, and rejecting belief in a resurrection of the dead or the coming of a Messiah.

The Essenes appear to have coalesced around a group of priests who were deprived of their positions of authority within the Temple hierarchy. They opposed the Sadducees, whose authority they regarded as illegitimate, and adopted a strongly dualistic, apocalyptic worldview.

The Pharisees were non-ordained scholars who promoted the implementation of Torah standards of purity in everyday life. To that end, the Pharisees developed traditions regarding the correct way to put into practice the Torah's commandments. One important principle was that of building a "fence" around the law. For example, because work on Shabbat (the Sabbath) is forbidden, "fences" around this commandment are erected forbidding one to hold objects on Shabbat that are connected to work, such as tools, money, and writing utensils. By avoiding these objects, the individual is less likely to perform work accidentally. Classical rabbinic Judaism has its roots in the Pharisees.

Armed resistance movements sprang up periodically across first-century Palestine. The most prominent of these was the Zealots, who were active in the Jewish War (66–73). Such groups were both military-political and religious: their leaders sometimes claimed messianic status.

in the Gospels between the followers of Jesus and the wider Jewish community likely reflects sporadic and specific conflict between Jesus-following Jews and non-Jesus-following Jews at the time of the Gospel's writing, rather than in the time of Jesus. The Gospel narratives sometimes retroject the concerns of their audiences back onto the time of Jesus, anachronistically incorporating post-70 CE social and religious turmoil into their tales of Jesus' life and teaching.

In the history of Jewish-Christian relations, however, it has made little difference whether or not Jesus actually uttered statements against "the Jews" like that in John 8:44—"You are from your father the devil, and you choose to do your father's desires. He was a murderer from the beginning and does not stand in the truth, because there is no truth in him. When he lies, he speaks according to his own nature, for he is a liar and the father of lies." When taken out of its original context as an intra-Jewish conflict, it was easy for subsequent generations of Christians to interpret such a statement—incorrectly—as a blanket condemnation of the Jews as a people, with disastrous consequences for Jewish-Christian relations.

The Jewish and Christian Bibles

Although Jews and Christians seem to share at least part of a Bible, the differences are more than just the number of books included. While the books of the Bible's New Testament are seen as Scripture only by Christians, the writings found in the Jewish Tanak comprise all or part of various Christian Old Testaments. Even so, the Christian Old Testaments differ from the Hebrew Bible in terms of content, order, categorization, and interpretive lens. Differences in categorization influence the way that the contents are understood; several books such as Joshua, Judges, Samuel, and Kings are labeled as "Prophetic" books in the Jewish canon, whereas Christian canons label them "Historical" books.[4]

The Hebrew Bible and Christian Old Testaments begin with the same stories: Creation, the Patriarchs and Matriarchs, Israelite enslavement and deliverance from Egypt, and the giving of the

---

4. See chapter 1, "The Formation of the Bible," and the chart "Canons of Scripture" in the additional study aids section.

Torah. This initial agreement is short-lived. The Jewish canon follows the history of its people through conflicted monarchies, foreign invasions, prophetic chastisement and caution of imminent doom, and then destruction and exile in a foreign land. The Hebrew Bible closes with the return of the Jews to their homeland and reestablishment of the Jewish community in the books of Chronicles.

Unlike the Hebrew Bible, the Christian Old Testaments do not conclude quietly. The Christian canon understands the life, death, and Resurrection of Jesus as the culmination of all Jewish history, the destination toward which, Christians claim, Old Testament texts have always been pointing. Placing the return and reestablishment of the Jewish community in the middle of the canon and moving the prophetic chastisement and caution to the end, Christian Old Testaments end on a note of crisis.[5] The resolution of this Old Testament crisis is found in its intended continuation, the New Testament.

The Christian past-as-prologue approach to Old Testament writings means that Jews and Christians will understand ostensibly "shared" texts quite differently. A classic example of this phenomenon, Isaiah 7:14, reads, "Therefore the Lord himself will give you a sign. Look, the young woman is with child and shall bear a son, and shall name him Immanuel." First, there is an issue of translation; the Hebrew text, like the English version above, refers to the expectant mother as an *almah*, "young woman." However, the Greek (Septuagint) version reads "the *parthenos* will conceive." *Parthenos* means "unmarried" or "virgin." *Almah* can also be used to mean "virgin," but that is almost certainly not the intended meaning here, given the historical context of the verse. In this chapter, the prophet Isaiah is giving King Ahaz advice about a looming military threat. The length of the child Immanuel's gestation and weaning is longer than the length of time required for the crisis to resolve: "He shall eat curds and honey by the time he knows how to refuse the evil and choose the good. For before the child knows how to refuse the evil and choose the good, the land before whose two kings you are in dread will be deserted" (Isa. 7:15–16). In the context of this child as a comforting sign of divine protection, the virginal state of the mother-to-be is

___
5. The Orthodox Old Testament uses a different order of the prophetic books than the Catholic and Protestant canons and places several apocryphal books in this category.

illogical; Jewish interpretation holds that the young woman in question was the wife of either Isaiah or Ahaz.

For the author of the Gospel of Matthew, writing in Greek and quoting Greek versions of Israelite prophetic texts, the young woman's virginity was a given. Add the early Christian assumption that Jesus' life was the interpretive key to Jewish history, and the identity of mother and child is clear to this author: some eight hundred years before his birth, Isaiah prophesied the Advent of Jesus. As the author states: "All this took place to fulfill what had been spoken by the Lord through the prophet: 'Look, the virgin shall conceive and bear a son, and they shall name him Emmanuel,' which means, 'God is with us'" (1:22–23).

From a Jewish perspective, the two markedly different readings of Isaiah 7:14, as referring either to the immediate future (the woman is the wife of Ahaz or Isaiah) or the distant future (she is the mother of a much later figure), are not necessary mutually exclusive; Jewish interpretive tradition holds that biblical texts are polysemous, possessing multiple, divergent, yet equally valid meanings.[6] The use of Jewish texts by New Testament authors, including the insistence that ancient texts prophesied the events of their days, is completely within the tradition of Jewish interpretation. Such interpretive techniques demonstrate how thoroughly *Jewish* these authors were.

Over time, however, Christian interpreters and audiences became distanced from Christianity's formative ties with Judaism and the historical contexts of Israelite prophetic criticism. The abundant prophetic critique and caution of the Hebrew Bible was written over many centuries to address specific problems and chastise particular groups or individuals in those periods. In Christian interpretation, the historical and social specificity of the Old Testament prophets was collapsed; it was assumed that the prophets' condemnations were directed against *all* Jews in *all* times. In this way, the sacred texts of Judaism became a scriptural weapon in Christian hands, used as justification for Christian vilification of Jews.

Conflict between differing Jewish groups in the first-century context of Roman occupation is indelibly etched into formative

---

6. The rabbinic phrase *elu ve-elu divrei Elohim hayyim*, "both *this* and *that* are the words of the living God," concedes that there is usually not one "correct" interpretation, but several correct interpretations implicit in the text.

Christian texts, as is debate over the proper methods of induction for the rapidly growing numbers of Gentiles taking their place beside the earliest Jesus-followers, who understood themselves as thoroughly and faithfully Jewish. The historical core of Christian anti-Judaism is an internal quarrel; Judaism and Christianity at the time of the New Testament's writing were not separate religions, but sister movements. Much of the infighting to which the text bears witness constitutes a sort of sibling dispute, a record of communities in the slow and painful process of differentiating one from another.

Other internecine Jewish arguments are attested in nonbiblical ancient texts. Some of the Jewish sectarian literature found in the Dead Sea Scrolls demonstrates one Jewish group vilifying other Jewish groups to whom they stand opposed. These texts, from the century before the time of Jesus, express their community's wrath at fellow Jewish groups and leaders. Their invective is every bit as harsh as that which we find in New Testament texts; they deride their opponents as "seekers of smooth things" (4Q169) and disparage the "man of lies" (Cairo Damascus document).

When we encounter these sectarian disputes in ancient literature, it is important to remember that we are outsiders listening in on the conversations of communities from the distant past. It is difficult to reconstruct exactly what they are arguing about, and dangerous to assume that their strife has anything to do with relationships between modern groups that may or may not bear the same names. In the case of the Dead Sea scrolls, there is little possibility that the ancient animus will bear modern consequences, simply because the texts preserving this rhetoric are not a part of any modern people's scriptures. The canonization of New Testament texts creates an environment in which the ancient struggle for Christian identity is continually renewed, detrimentally affecting the Christian understanding of Jews and Judaism.

Most mainline Christian denominations have taken steps in recent decades to recognize, contextualize, and condemn anti-Judaistic interpretations of the Christian Bible, but old habits die hard. It is essential to understand the sources and dynamics of anti-Judaism in Christian biblical texts and interpretation in order to avoid perpetuating this prejudice in the modern day.

DISCUSSION QUESTIONS

1. Traditionally, Christians have tended to overlook the Jewishness of Jesus, but in recent decades biblical scholars have emphasized that Jesus himself was a Jew. Does this understanding of Jesus make a difference in the interpretation of New Testament texts that refer to the Jews?

2. Although an understanding of the historical context of New Testament texts that are critical of Judaism changes our understanding of their meaning, do such texts remain problematic regardless of their original context? Why or why not?

3. Like the New Testament, the Hebrew Bible contains many passages that are highly critical of the Jewish people for being disobedient to God—especially in the writings of the prophets. Does it make a difference when such criticism comes from co-religionists rather than from persons who do not share the same faith? Does it make a difference to see such criticisms in the New Testament as also coming from co-religionists?

4. How do Anti-Judaistic ideas originating in Christian biblical interpretation continue to have influence in the modern world?

FOR FURTHER STUDY

Galambush, Julie. *The Reluctant Parting: How the New Testament's Jewish Writers Created a Christian Book.* New York: Harper One, 2006.

Levine, Amy-Jill. *The Misunderstood Jew: The Church and the Scandal of the Jewish Jesus.* New York: Harper One, 2007.

Levine, Amy-Jill, and Marc Brettler, eds. *The Jewish Annotated New Testament: New Revised Standard Version Translation.* Oxford: Oxford University Press, 2011.

Sanders, E. P. *Paul and Palestinian Judaism: A Comparison of Patterns of Religion.* Philadelphia: Fortress Press, 1977.

Sandmel, Samuel. *A Jewish Understanding of the New Testament.* Woodstock, VT: Skylight Paths Publishing, 2005.

Stendhal, Krister. *Paul among Jews and Gentiles.* Minneapolis: Fortress Press, 1976.

Internet Resources

The following websites provide official statements on Jewish-Christian relations:

www.bc.edu/dam/files/research_sites/cjl/texts/cjrelations/resources/ documents/catholic/french_repentance.htm

> The Catholic Bishops of France's "Declaration of Repentance," promulgated December 1997 on the fifty-seventh anniversary of the passage of anti-Semitic laws by the collaborationist Vichy government during the Nazi occupation of France.

www.elca.org/en/Faith/Ecumenical-and-Inter-Religious-Relations/ Inter-Religious-Relations/Online-Resources

> The Evangelical Lutheran Church in America Churchwide Assembly's "Declaration," adopted on April 18, 1994, which repudiates Luther's anti-Jewish writings, expresses deep regret for their historical consequences, and reclaims the desire to live in "love and respect for Jewish people."

www.ccjr.us/dialogika-resources/documents-and-statements/ protestant-churches/na/presbyterian

> Presbyterian statements regarding Judaism spanning from 1987 to 2011.

www.jcrelations.net/Dabru+Emet+-+A+Jewish+Statement+on+ Christians+and+Christianity.2395.0.html?L=3

> *Dabru Emet*: A Jewish Statement on Christians and Christianity (2000). This document, concerning the relationship between Jews and Christians, was signed by more than 220 rabbis and scholars, representing all branches of Judaism.

21

Introduction to the Synoptic Gospels and Acts of the Apostles

Susan Calef and Laurie Brink, OP

The Synoptic Gospels

Susan Calef

The twenty-seven documents that comprise the New Testament all reflect upon the significance of Jesus for Christian faith. Of those documents, only the four that stand at the head of the collection—the Gospels of Matthew, Mark, Luke, and John—narrate Jesus' life and work. The arrangement of the New Testament canon does not reflect the chronological order in which the texts were composed. Rather, placement of the Gospels at the front of the collection affirms the historical priority of Jesus of Nazareth for Christian faith and the theological primacy of his story.

Texts are composed and interpreted according to conventions of form and content that determine their nature; familiarity with the conventions associated with a particular genre is necessary for proper interpretation of a piece of literature. Serious study of the Gospels therefore requires that one consider what type of writing they are. The nature of the canonical Gospels has been illumined by biblical scholars in two ways: by comparison of the Gospels to ancient literary types or genres known from roughly contemporaneous literature, and by means of close examination and comparison of the Gospels themselves. Both procedures clarify the nature of canonical Gospel literature, and thus how these texts ought to be read and interpreted.

The Nature of the Gospels

Present-day readers often view the Gospels as a uniquely Christian genre, but would these texts have been viewed so by ancient audiences? In seeking to understand biblical texts in relation to their original historical and cultural contexts, biblical scholarship has sought to illumine the nature of the canonical Gospels by comparison to various genres known from ancient Greek, Roman, and Jewish literature. Since at least the time of Aristotle the study of literature has classified works in three principal categories—narrative, drama, and poetry—each of which includes various subgenres based on differences of form or content. In their focus on the life, death, and Resurrection of Jesus, the Gospels may be classified as a form of narrative literature. But what is the precise nature of these narratives? Are they strictly accurate historical accounts? Are they fictional? A combination of the two?

Literary Genre: The Search for Parallels

Scholars have compared the Gospels to subgenres of ancient narrative, including aretalogies, epics, biographies, and novels, and in so doing, have revealed resemblances. There are obvious similarities, for example, to stories that told of humans who possessed a divine power confirmed by their miracle-working activity, some even including a physical union between a mortal and a deity.

To persons in the ancient world familiar with the literary culture of the times, the Gospels probably looked more like biographies than anything else. The various types of biography (Greek: *bios*; Latin: *vita*) written in the centuries immediately before and after Jesus afford fruitful comparisons: Diogenes Laertius' *Lives of the Ancient Philosophers*, Plutarch's *Lives of Famous Greeks and Romans*, and Suetonius' *Lives of the Caesars*, among others. These works present an overarching narrative of a life, beginning with the subject's birth or arrival on the public scene and ending with his death. Within this narrative framework a variety of shorter forms—anecdotes, speeches, maxims—conveyed the character of the subject. Similarly, the narrative frame of the Gospels extends from Jesus' birth or emergence on the public scene (his baptism) to his death, with a variety of short forms—sayings, genealogies, pronouncement stories, parables, miracle stories, etc.—filling the frame. This resemblance to the biographical genre does not mean, however, that the Gospels provide the degree of historical accuracy required by the canons of modern historiography.[1] The ancient *bios* may be considered a subgenre of historical narrative, but while modern biography tends to emphasize the subject's individuality and historical particularity, the ancient form treated its subjects as stylized types (for example, as philosophers, statesmen, or emperors), presenting them in terms of a typecast role and attributing to them the stereotypical virtues and vices associated with that role. The resemblance of the Gospels to the ancient biographical genre, then, does not ensure the historical accuracy of the Gospels.

Moreover, these comparisons reveal that the Gospels do not match the ancient biographies exactly. The most obvious difference is that Greco-Roman biographies, in addressing a social and literary elite, were written with literary pretensions and an appropriately high stylistic level; this is lacking in the Gospels. In this regard, the Gospels more closely resemble the biographical aspects of prophetic literature, sharing with the latter a number of elements, including a simpler Hebraic style. The book of Jeremiah, for example, opens with a report of the prophet's call that includes reference to God's plan before he was born (Jer. 1:4–5), followed by an account of his speeches and prophetic actions, including words and acts in the Temple (Jer. 7), warning of impending doom for Jerusalem, and reports of the prophet's suffering (Jer. 26, 37–38). Similarly, in the Gospel of Mark, Jesus' baptismal call in accord with God's plan (Mark 1:2–11) is followed by an account of a public ministry of proclamation and mighty deeds (Mark 1:14–10:52), culminating in Jerusalem with critical words and actions in the Temple (Mark 11:15–18), warnings of trials and tribulations to come (Mark 13), and the events of Jesus' passion, death, and burial (Mark 14–15). The frequent use of Old Testament quotations and allusions in all the Gospels suggests a conscious effort to set the story of Jesus in relation to the story of

---

1. It should be noted that no ancient literary genre—not even history—aimed at the degree of factual accuracy required by the canons of modern historiography.

312 • ANSELM COMPANION TO THE BIBLE

God's relationship with ancient Israel; therefore, it is likely that the biographical elements of the prophetic books exerted a more direct influence on the Gospel portrayal of Jesus than did Greco-Roman biographies of emperors, philosophers, and orators.

The search for generic parallels has demonstrated that the Gospels are similar to ancient biographies but not an exact match. Consequently, most scholars grant that the Gospel narratives may be classified as a singularly Christian subtype of biographical narrative. A fuller understanding of these narratives and their distinct nature and purpose is gained by close comparison of the Gospels and by investigation of the process by which they came to be written.

The Synoptic Gospels

Those who read all four Gospels in their entirety soon discover that while the basic outline of the story of Jesus is similar, many of the episodes, figures, and details in the Gospel accounts differ significantly. Close inspection of their contents reveals that some traditions about Jesus are found in three Gospels (the "triple tradition"), others in only two (the "double tradition"), and others in only one (the "single tradition").

The three Gospels that are most similar—Matthew, Mark, and Luke—tell the same general story in much the same way with more or less the same chronology, and so are referred to as the "Synoptic Gospels," from the Greek *synoptikos*, meaning "seen together." Indeed, reading any one of them with an eye to the other two enlightens the process of interpretation. That these Gospels repeat many of the same stories in nearly identical wording suggests some kind of literary interdependence, even actual copying. But who copied from whom? Was the shortest Gospel, Mark, written first, and then copied and expanded by Matthew and Luke? Or was the shorter Mark an abridged version of Matthew or Luke? Were Matthew and Luke written independently of each other, or was one of them used in writing the other?

The problem of accounting for the multiple similarities and differences among the three Synoptic Gospels is known as "the Synoptic Problem." Based on centuries of painstaking analysis, scholarship has proposed two basic solutions to the problem. The first, offered by

J. J. Griesbach in the late eighteenth century, is a variation of Augustine's view. Augustine argued that Matthew was written first, then abbreviated by Mark; Luke then drew upon them both in the writing of his Gospel. Griesbach agreed that Matthew was composed first (what scholars refer to as "Matthean priority"), but concluded that Luke came next, and Mark used and abridged both. Despite the strengths of this "Two Gospel Hypothesis," its proponents find it difficult to explain satisfactorily why Mark left out so much of the other two. Because it is much easier to explain why Matthew and Luke would expand Mark than why Mark would delete so much of Matthew and Luke, the majority of scholars subscribe to the second solution, the "Two Source Theory," also known as the "Two Document Hypothesis."

According to this theory, Mark was composed first, then the authors of Matthew and Luke, independently of each other, incorporated most of Mark into their own compositions. Noting that Matthew and Luke also contain nearly identical sayings and parables not found in Mark (e.g., the temptation of Jesus, the Beatitudes, the Lord's Prayer, the parable of the Lost Sheep), scholars further hypothesize that both borrowed from a second source, which they designate "Q" (from the German *Quelle*, "source"). The discovery in 1945 of the *Gospel of Thomas*, a collection of sayings that includes some overlaps with the Q material, added plausibility to the Q theory. To explain the material found

The *Gospel of Thomas* consists of a collection of sayings of Jesus. Scholars believe a similar collection, which they designate "Q," was used by Matthew and Luke in the writing of their Gospels.

solely in Matthew or solely in Luke, some scholars posit the existence of two additional documents, designated "M" (for Matthean) and "L" (for Lukan) respectively.

The Gospel of John is not included in this theory, since it is by far the most distinctive of the Gospels. Although John resembles the Synoptics in telling of Jesus' ministry with the same basic elements—preaching, teaching, and healing that provokes controversy and culminates in his passion, death, and Resurrection—the material of which it is constructed differs in striking ways from that contained in the Synoptics. In view of these differences, it is not clear whether the author of John had access to the Synoptic Gospels in written form. It is apparent, however, that he was familiar with some of the traditions incorporated into the Synoptics (such as the cleansing of the Temple, the multiplication of the loaves, the walking on the sea, and the entry into Jerusalem).[2]

The similarities and differences between the Synoptic Gospels, then, are best explained by concluding that a later Gospel develops an earlier one—that is, Matthew and Luke develop Mark and additional sources. Readers of the Gospels can discover this development for themselves by using a synopsis or "Gospel parallels," a tool of biblical research that aligns the Synoptic Gospels (sometimes John also) in parallel columns for ease of comparison. Viewing the Gospels laid out side by side discloses how Matthew and Luke develop their source Mark by means of additions, deletions, or simply changing the placement or wording of a particular pericope (a complete thought unit in the Gospels).

According to the Two Document Hypothesis, the author of Matthew's Gospel drew upon Mark, Q, and traditions known only to him ("M"). The author of Luke's Gospel used Mark, Q, and traditions known only to him ("L").

© 2014 Anselm Academic

2. See chapter 22, "Introduction to Johannine Literature," for a fuller discussion of the Gospel of John.

Stages of Gospel Tradition

In addition to studying the literary interrelationship among the Gospels, modern biblical scholarship has also addressed the triple question: how, when, and why were the Gospels composed? There is general agreement that the Gospels are the end product of a three-stage process of formation, spanning roughly seventy years, in which material about Jesus was passed on and developed by the earliest generations of Christians in light of their understanding of his Resurrection. This broad consensus on the history of the Gospel tradition is widely accepted by Christian interpreters of various confessional backgrounds.

Stage 1: The Public Activity of Jesus of Nazareth and His Disciples

The origin of the Gospel tradition may be traced to the public activity of Jesus of Nazareth late in the first third of the first century CE. That public activity, which focused on the renewal of his people Israel by proclamation of the nearness of the reign of God, was witnessed by a band of disciples. These disciples observed what Jesus said and did, what and whom he taught, how he responded to people in need, and how he came to be arrested and crucified. The first stage of tradition consisted of the words and deeds of Jesus living on in the memories of the disciples. This was the raw Jesus material that was passed on and developed in subsequent stages.

Stage 2: Christian Preaching about Jesus

The second stage of Gospel tradition consisted of what Christians preached about Jesus in roughly 30–65 CE. It began shortly after the death of Jesus, when the disciples' experience of post-Resurrection appearances (1 Cor. 15:5–7) formed the conviction on which Christian faith is based: that Jesus had been raised from death and was now the living Lord. Because this original generation of preachers understood themselves as sent forth by the risen Christ, they are referred to as apostles, from the Greek *apostellein*, "to send forth." Initially the apostolic preaching focused not on what Jesus said and did during his public ministry but on what is known as the primitive *kerygma* (the Greek word for "proclamation"): the good news of Jesus' death and Resurrection in which his followers perceived the fulfillment of God's promise of salvation. Gradually, as the mission expanded and a network of Christian communities spread throughout the Mediterranean, memories of Jesus' words and deeds and his conflicts with opponents (stage one material) were utilized to address the emerging needs of Christians and the struggles that arose in community and mission. Thus, in the decades of oral transmission that stretched from Jesus' death to the composition of the Gospels, the raw Jesus material of stage one was shaped by preaching, catechetical needs, worship practices, and internal and external controversies.

Stage 3: Composition of the Gospels by the Evangelists

The third stage of Gospel tradition consists of the four narratives about Jesus that were being written about 65–100 CE, some thirty-five to seventy years after the death of Jesus. As in the preceding stage of oral transmission, their composition involved a process of selection, editing, and enhancement of tradition, guided by the community's needs and a belief in the continuing presence of the risen Christ. Each of the four Gospel writers, or "evangelists," gathered traditions that had developed in the preceding decades, some of which had been committed to writing but are now lost (e.g., Q), then selected, shaped, and arranged them within an overall narrative framework of the life of Jesus. The scholarly consensus is that Mark was completed first, just before or after 70 CE, Matthew and Luke in the eighties. The differences between the three suggest that the purpose of the evangelists in composing these quasi-biographical narratives was not simply to report the verifiable "facts" of Jesus' past historical existence, but to express the meaning and significance of Jesus for their present communities (cf. Luke 1:1–4).

The Gospels, then, are a composite of materials from all three stages: the words and deeds of Jesus as witnessed and remembered by his disciples (stage one), which were subsequently reflected upon and developed in the preaching, catechesis, and worship of Christian communities in the decades after his death (stage two), then further developed by the Gospel writers (stage three). Thus they contain earlier and later layers of material: the original Jesus layer, the layer of early Christian preaching, and the layer of the evangelists. Or to put it differently, the Gospels contain multiple voices: the remembered voice of Jesus, the voices of apostolic preachers, and the voices of the evangelists. Together they preserve for future generations the original disciples' *past* experience of Jesus of Nazareth and the early Christians' *present* experience of him as their risen Lord. Reading and interpreting the Gospels properly, then, requires an appreciation of this combination of memory and testimony.

The Question of Authorship

Christians generally assume that the authorship of the Gospels is indicated by their traditional titles: "Gospel according to Matthew," "Gospel according to Mark," and so on. However, because the original manuscripts of the Gospels (i.e., the *autographs* or signature copies) no longer exist, it is difficult to ascertain whether the texts originally bore these titles. Based on intensive study of the ancient manuscripts, scholars conclude that the traditional names of the Gospels first appeared as headings of the Greek manuscripts, the oldest of which are dated to around 200 CE, more than a hundred years after the writing of the latest Gospel, John. The earliest titles in these manuscripts consisted of just two words, *kata*, "according to," followed by the name of the evangelist. Since such a naming convention (*kata* + author's name) is unknown among ancient literary works, it seems unlikely that four authors would have arrived, independently, at the exact same mode of designation; therefore, most scholars conclude that these stereotypical titles were affixed to them only after all four had been collected together and accepted as authoritative. Consequently, New Testament scholars conclude that none of the Gospels originally bore any attribution of authorship.

Early tradition attributes two Gospels to apostles who were eyewitnesses of Jesus' ministry (Matthew and John) and the other two to "apostolic men" (i.e., companions of apostles, with Mark thought to be a companion of Peter, and Luke a companion of Paul). This tradition now appears dubious. The striking differences among the Gospels and the evidence for borrowing among them suggest that the Gospels are not eyewitness reports; why, for example, would Matthew, an eyewitness, borrow so much of his account from Mark, who was not an eyewitness? For the sake of convenience, New Testament scholars continue to refer to the authors of the Gospels by their traditional designations, but their true identity is irretrievably lost.

Use of the Word *Gospel*

The word "gospel," derived from the Anglo-Saxon *godspell*, meaning "good news," translates the New Testament Greek noun *euangelion* (Latin *evangelium*), which still survives in "evangelist" and related English words. For most Christians, "gospel" is, first and foremost, a designation for the four canonical texts that bear the names Matthew, Mark, Luke, and John, and so, a familiar genre of canonical Christian literature. Use of the word "gospel" (*euangelion*) for a written text, however, represents a late and secondary development. In the cultural matrix of the first century, the term refered to various forms of messages. In the Greek translation of the Hebrew Bible (the Septuagint), for example, the noun *euangelion* was used in the plural to translate the Hebrew term for "good news" (e.g., 2 Sam. 4:10). Especially pertinent, in view of its later usage in the New Testament, the related Greek verb, *euangelizesthai* ("to proclaim good news"), occurs multiple times in Isaiah in reference to the good news of the advent of God's reign (e.g., Isa. 40:9–11; 52:7–10; 61:1). *Euangelion* was also part of the vocabulary of Roman propaganda, referring, for example, to the public proclamation of significant imperial events such as the emperor's birthday, a Roman military victory, or the ascent of a new emperor to the throne.

The term first appears in Christian literature in the letters of Paul, who uses it in formulaic phrases such as "the gospel of God" (Rom. 1:1; 15:16), "the gospel of Christ" (Rom. 15:19; 1 Cor. 9:12; 1 Thess. 3:2), and "the gospel of his Son" (Rom. 1:9). In Paul both "gospel" (*euangelion*) and the related verb "to proclaim the gospel" (*euangelizethai*) are technical terms for, respectively, the Christian message of salvation that focused on the death, Resurrection, and exaltation of Jesus (Rom. 1:2–4; 1 Cor. 15:2–5) and for the proclamation of that message. Only two of the canonical Gospels use the noun "gospel" (Mark and Matthew). Mark introduces his account, "The beginning of the good news (*euangelion*) of Jesus Christ, the Son of God" (Mark 1:1). Here the term *euangelion* does not designate the literary genre of Mark's work, but the primary message of his narrative, namely, that Jesus is the Christ, the Son of God. Similar to Paul, in Mark, "gospel" refers both to the message Jesus preached as the "gospel of God" (Mark 1:14–15) and to the message that disciples must preach to all the nations (Mark 8:35; 13:10). Although Matthew qualifies the noun, most often as "the gospel of the kingdom" (Matt. 4:23; 9:35; 24:14), his use of *euangelion* is consistent with Mark's, referring to the good news of salvation preached first by Jesus, then by the church. It was not until the mid-second century that the noun "gospel" was used for a literary work, when Justin Martyr writes, "The Apostles in their memoirs, which are called gospels, have handed down what Jesus ordered them to do" (*First Apology* 66.3).

From this point onward the narratives about Jesus became known as "the Gospel according to Matthew," "the Gospel according to Mark," and so on. Recent discoveries, however, reveal that several writings not in the biblical canon, some of a totally different content and aim, were also designated as "gospels," such as *Gospel of Thomas*, *Gospel of Mary*, and *Gospel of Philip*. Unlike the canonical Gospels, these extracanonical or "apocryphal" gospels come in a variety of forms: *Gospel of Thomas*, for example, is a collection of sayings, while *Gospel of Mary* narrates post-Resurrection conversations between the risen Christ and his disciples.[3] The fact that writings of such diverse aims were all designated "gospels" suggests that even at this later stage of usage, the term retained its original and primary referent (i.e., the message of salvation associated with Jesus), and that Christian writers of the first four centuries chose to convey that message for their communities in various forms or genres.

Acts of the Apostles

Laurie Brink, OP

A few generations after the Easter event, on the eve of the turn of the century, Christian believers pondered about the origins of their own faith. They asked the question, "After the Resurrection, then what happened?" How did the faith spread beyond Jerusalem where the apostles are last seen?

---

3. See chapter 19, "Early Christian Apocrypha."

Penned by the same hand that wrote the Gospel of Luke, the Acts of the Apostles became one attempt to address those growing questions. The Holy Spirit promised in Luke 24:49 descends in Acts 2 and inspires the preaching and proclamation of the Gospel "to the ends of the earth" (Acts 1:8). Thus Acts of the Apostles picks up where the Gospels leave off.

Genre and Authorship

Is Acts simply the creative answer to the question of how the faith spread? Or is it a compilation of historical facts verifying that movement? Is it a story or a theology? Various scholars have proposed that Acts of the Apostles best fits the genre of history, romance novel, or biography, or some hybrid version of these. When describing Acts of the Apostles as "history," one should realize that the modern definition, which assumes the use of verifiable facts and eyewitness accounts, doesn't quite fit. Ancient historians portrayed actual events and peoples, but they were not concerned with absolute factual accuracy. Rather, their goal was to provide what was useful and "true" in a deeper sense, so that people could learn from the past.

Acts shares literary motifs with ancient romance novels or adventure tales, including travels to foreign places (Acts 13–14; 16–19), miraculous prison breaks (Acts 12:6–11; 16:25–34), and harrowing shipwrecks (Acts 27:39–44). Another generic contender is biography. If the Gospel of Luke is viewed as a biography of Jesus, the Acts of the Apostles could be seen as a biography of Jesus' disciples. Such a second volume would demonstrate that the authority and status of the founder continued unabated in his followers.

Whether one views Acts of the Apostles through the generic lens of history, novel, or biography, one is nonetheless confronted with a text that was written two thousand years ago, a text that does not perfectly fit modern categories. One can only say that the author of Acts demonstrates a knowledge of various literary conventions and is purposefully using them to portray the movement of Christianity from Jerusalem to points beyond.

As noted in regard to the Gospel of Luke, the identity of the author is lost to us. Tradition has named him "Luke," a presumed co-worker with Paul (Col. 4:14; 2 Tim. 4:11; Phlm. 24). The author is generally thought to be a well-educated Gentile Christian (though some suggest a Hellensitic Jewish Christian), perhaps writing in the large urban city of Antioch.

Purpose and Theology

The author of Acts may intend his work to be a defense of the faith—or apology (*apologia* in Greek)—meant to persuade Romans that Christians are not a threat to the good order of the state. The work may also serve to encourage Christians that they can remain faithful and still be part of the empire.

Another purpose may be to provide a counter to mystery religions and the use of magic. The apostles run into several magicians in their travels, but they best them in each encounter (Acts 8:9–24; 13:6–12; 19:13–20).

Several theological concerns are evident throughout the work. Luke's two volumes clearly establish the importance and presence of the work of the Holy Spirit. A major theme in Acts is the spirit-directed growth of the church and its expansion from Jerusalem. But this Spirit-directed mission is not limited to the Jews. It is universal and includes the Gentiles as well (Luke 2:29–32; 24:45–48; Acts 10:34–35, 44). Luke is also concerned with the appropriate use of resources within the community, a theme introduced in the Gospel and expanded on in Acts. The early community in Jerusalem held all things in common (Acts 2:44–45; 4:32–35), and gifts of the Spirit could not be purchased (Acts 8:18–20).

Within its twenty-eight chapters, the reader can follow the timid disciples (ch. 1) as they are imbued with the Holy Spirit (ch. 2) and emboldened to proclaim the Gospel to Samaria (ch. 8), the Hellenistic cities on the coast (chs. 9–10), Antioch (ch. 11), Asia Minor (chs. 13–15), Greece (chs. 16–20), and finally Rome, the heart of the empire (ch. 28). In the first half of Acts, Peter emerges as the leader among the Apostles. After his baptism of Cornelius the Centurion (ch. 10) and the subsequent Jerusalem Council (ch. 15), the "Way" (Luke's preferred term for believers; e.g., Acts 9:2) is officially opened to the Gentiles. The second half of Acts depicts the preaching of Paul and his co-workers, as they traverse the eastern Mediterranean world. Acts of the Apostles ends with Paul under house arrest awaiting trial in Rome, "proclaiming the kingdom of God and teaching about the Lord Jesus Christ with all boldness and without hindrance" (Acts 28:31).

DISCUSSION QUESTIONS

1. The expectations of ancient biography are different from those of modern biography. As a modern reader, what do you not find in the Gospels that you would expect to find in a biography of Jesus? What do these differences tell you about the interests of the Gospel authors?

2. Which of the three stages of Gospel development do you find most interesting and why?

3. Given that the Gospels do not agree perfectly with each other, would it not have been simpler for the early Christians if they had adopted only one as the "correct" version, and rejected the other three? Why do you think the early church did not take this step?

4. How would the Gospels have been "good news" for the people for whom they were written?

5. What are some possible genres for the Acts of the Apostles and how does the question of genre affect how the book is understood?

6. Of the four canonical Gospels, only one, the Gospel of Luke, continues the story after the life of Jesus. How is one's understanding of the Gospel of Luke affected by seeing it as the first part of a two-part story? How is one's understanding of Acts affected by seeing it as the continuation of the Gospel of Luke?

FOR FURTHER STUDY

Aune, David E. *The New Testament in Its Literary Environment*. Philadelphia: Westminster, 1987. See especially 17–157.

Burridge, Richard A. *What Are the Gospels? A Comparison with Graeco-Roman Biography*. 2nd ed. Cambridge: Cambridge University Press, 1992.

Hengel, Martin. *The Four Gospels and the One Gospel of Jesus Christ.* London: SCM Press, 2000.

Koester, Helmut. *Ancient Christian Gospels: Their History and Development.* Harrisburg, PA: Trinity Press International, 1990.

Miller, Robert, ed. *The Complete Gospels.* San Francisco: Harper San Francisco, 1994.

The Bible Today, 52, no. 3 (2014). The theme for this issue is "The Acts of the Apostles in the Twenty-First Century."

Throckmorton, Burton H., Jr. *Gospel Parallels: NRSV Edition: A Comparison of the Synoptic Gospels.* Nashville: Thomas Nelson, 1992.

Internet Resources

www.utoronto.ca/religion/synopsis

This site sets the four canonical Gospels and the *Gospel of Thomas* in parallel columns.

Introduction to the Gospel of John, Johannine Letters, and Revelation

Henry W. Morisada Rietz

This chapter introduces the literature in the Christian Scriptures attributed to people named "John": the Gospel of John, the Johannine Letters (1–3 John), and Revelation. There are questions about the authorship of each of these documents. The Gospel of John and the Johannine Letters were probably produced within the same community of early followers of Jesus; scholars call this the Johannine community. While the language of Revelation overlaps to a small degree with the language of the other documents (e.g., the emphasis on Jesus as the "Lamb of God"), the author of Revelation was not closely related to the Johannine community. Therefore, Revelation will be treated on its own terms in a separate section of this chapter.

The Johannine Community (Gospel of John, 1–3 John)

Authorship

From the second century, some early Christian writers identified the author of the Gospel of John with the Apostle John, the son of Zebedee and brother of James. At least in its final form, the Gospel of John, along with the letters, reflects a period at some distance from the historical Jesus. The Gospel does not identify its author by name. The Gospel does privilege one of Jesus's disciples, whom it identifies as the "disciple whom Jesus loved" (13:23; 19:26–27, 35; 20:1–10; 21:7, 20–24). This "Beloved Disciple" may have been the founder of the Johannine community and one of the original sources of its traditions. The identity of the "Beloved Disciple" remains unknown, although some scholars have attempted to identify him as John, Thomas, Lazarus, or even Mary Magdalene.

The language, theology, and situation being addressed in 1–3 John provide evidence that they are related to the community that produced the Gospel of John, and may have been written by the same person. The author of 2 and 3 John, which are written in the form of a letter, identifies himself as "the elder." While traditionally this author was also identified with the author of the Gospel of John, the historical situation addressed in these letters suggests that they come from a later period in the community's history.

Relationship to the Synoptic Gospels

While the author of the Gospel of John may have relied on some sources that were also used by the Synoptic Gospels (Mark, Matthew, and Luke), John reflects different traditions. This Gospel does not narrate John baptizing Jesus (1:19–34) and there is some debate within the Gospel whether Jesus himself baptizes people (3:22; 4:1; but cf. 4:2). In contrast to the Synoptic Gospels, where the adult Jesus makes only one trip to Jerusalem, Jesus journeys there several times in John. The cleansing of the Temple scene is narrated at the beginning of Jesus' ministry rather than at the end (John 2:13–25; cf. Mark 11:15–19 and parallels). In this Gospel, Jesus dies on the eve of Passover (John 19:14) rather than the day of Passover (Mark 14:12). Jesus in John does not narrate a memorial meal at his last supper (although knowledge of the ritualizing of bread and wine may be implied, for example, at John 6:30–59); instead, Jesus washes the disciples' feet (John 13:1–20). In the Synoptic Gospels, Jesus speaks about the "kingdom of God" (Mark and Luke) or the "kingdom of heaven" (Matthew). In John, Jesus emphasizes his identity and his relationship with the Father, employing in particular a series of "I am" sayings (e.g., John 10:1–16; 15:1–10).

Structure and Themes of the Gospel

The narrative of John can be divided into several different movements. After the introductory prologue (1:1–18), the first half of the Gospel comprises Jesus' public ministry (to chapter 12:36a). This section looks forward to the "hour [which] has not yet come" (2:4; cf. 7:30; 8:20). In 12:23 Jesus announces that the "hour has come for the Son of Man to be glorified" (cf. 13:1; 17:1), and in 12:36b he withdraws from the public, beginning a private ministry with his disciples that continues through chapter 17. Chapters 18–19 narrate the arrest, trial, Crucifixion, and burial of Jesus. The narrative concludes with accounts of Jesus after the Resurrection (20–21).

This Gospel uses dualistic imagery of light against darkness and above versus below to situate the various characters in the narrative (e.g., 3:17–21). Jesus is portrayed as a pre-existing being—"the Word"—who was at creation in the beginning with the Father (1:1–5), Jesus "comes from above" (3:31; cf. 3:13) and is the "light of the world" (8:12; cf. 1:4–5). The Gospel's dualism provides the basis for the Gospel's use of irony and the characters' misunderstanding of Jesus. For example, in 3:1–21 Nicodemus misunderstands Jesus' question about being born "from above" as being born "a second time" (the word in Greek can mean either "from above" or "anew").

Jesus is portrayed as having a unique relationship with God as the Father's only son (John 3:16; cf. 1:14, 18). Jesus provides the only access to God the Father (e.g., 14:6–7). Jesus claims to be united with God: "I am in the Father and the Father is in me" (14:11; cf. 14:8–14). This is a unity not only of substance but of will: Jesus shares the Father's will. Thus Jesus prays for his disciples and their disciples "that they may all be one" (17:20–21; cf. 17:22–24). As Jesus was sent from God (16:27–28; 17:8), he in turn is sending the disciples into the world (17:18).

Throughout this Gospel, Jesus is portrayed as powerful and in control, especially at the Crucifixion. This Gospel emphasizes that Jesus is not killed, but allows his life to be taken: "I lay down my life in order to take it up again. No one takes it from me, but I lay it down of my own accord. I have power to lay it down, and I have power to take it up again" (10:17–18). At the climactic death scene, he asks for a drink, and "when Jesus had received the wine, he said, 'It is finished.' Then he bowed his head and gave up his spirit" (19:30).

The Gospel of John emphasizes the physicality of Jesus' body both before and after his Resurrection. In this sixth-century mosaic, the risen Christ invites "doubting" Thomas to touch the wounds inflicted upon him in his crucifixion (see John 20:27).

Despite the very elevated portrayal of Jesus, the Gospel also emphasizes the physical body of Jesus. The prologue states explicitly that "the Word became flesh and lived among us" (1:14). Moreover, this Gospel stresses that Jesus experienced a bodily Resurrection. Jesus invites Thomas, "Put your finger here and see my hands. Reach out your hand and put it in my side" (20:27). Later Jesus is portrayed as having breakfast with his disciples (21:12–14), demonstrating that his post-Resurrection body was physical, given that, according to the belief of that time, spiritual bodies could not eat material food.

Composition of the Gospel

While the Gospel of John may be read as a continuous narrative in its final form, many readers detect literary seams and discern different sources or editorial layers. Occasionally there are abrupt changes in the setting and scene. For example, in 5:1 Jesus is said to be going up to Jerusalem. Then in 6:1, Jesus goes "to the other side of the

Sea of Galilee." In 14:31, Jesus seemingly concludes a speech by telling his disciples, "Rise, let us be on our way." However, Jesus then
launches into a very long speech (chapters 15–16) followed by a
prayer (chapter 17), before the narrator describes Jesus and his disciples leaving in 18:1.

Several of the miracles—called "signs" in this Gospel—are numbered. Changing water into wine at Cana (2:1–11) is called "the first
of his signs" (2:11). The healing of an official's son (4:46–54) is called
"the second sign." This has led some scholars to suggest that one of
the sources for this Gospel may have been a hypothetical "Semeia
Source" or "Sign Source" (*sēmeia* is Greek for "sign"). The function and
value of "signs" or miracles is debated within this Gospel. On the one
hand, they are often viewed positively as leading to belief (e.g., 2:11,
23–25; 20:30–31). On the other hand, the crowd's desire for signs is
criticized (4:48), and believing without seeing is commended (20:29).

The purpose of the Gospel is expressed in 20:30–31: "Now Jesus
did many other signs in the presence of his disciples, which are not
written in this book. But these are written so that you may come to
believe that Jesus is the Messiah, the Son of God, and that through
believing you may have life in his name." Many scholars think this
passage served as the original ending of the book and the material in
chapter 21 is a later addition. The prologue (1:1–18) is also considered to be a late addition.

The Historical Situation
of the Johannine Community

Three historical situations are discernable in the Johannine community: (1) a conflict with some other "Jews," (2) the death of the
Beloved Disciple, and (3) a conflict within the community over
whether Jesus had come in the flesh. The Gospel evinces concern
with all three situations, while the Johannine letters reflect the third.

Conflict with other "Jews"

Throughout this Gospel, Jesus and his disciples are portrayed as
being in conflict with the "Jews." In some places (e.g., chapter 7, see
especially 7:1, 52; chapter 11, see especially 11:7–8), "Judeans" might
be a better translation (*Ioudaios* can mean either "Jew" or "Judean"),

reflecting a conflict between Jesus and his followers from Galilee and the Judean religious leaders in and around Jerusalem. Elsewhere, however, the term is anachronistic (reflecting a later time in history) since Jesus and his followers during his lifetime were all Jews; the inclusion of the Gentiles into the movement only occurs after Jesus' death, as is evidenced by controversy reflected in Matthew, Luke-Acts, Romans, and Galatians over whether and how to include them.

Some of the stories in the Gospel seem to reflect the Johannine community's conflict with Jewish leaders in their region. For example, the story of the Pharisees investigating the healing of the man blind from birth in chapter 9 probably addresses this conflict. That passage asserts that "the Jews had . . . agreed that anyone who confessed Jesus to be the Messiah would be put out of the synagogue" (9:22). Later in the account, some believers are afraid to confess their belief that Jesus was the Messiah "for fear that they would be put out of the synagogue" (12:42–43). Jesus privately warns his disciples, "They will put you out of the synagogues" (16:1–2). Implicit in these passages is the Johannine community's desire to worship in the synagogue.

Some scholars suggest that this threat of expulsion led some followers within the Johannine community to keep their belief in Jesus a secret. Thus, for example, Joseph of Arimathea is identified as "a disciple of Jesus, though a secret one because of his fear of the Jews" (19:38). Similarly, the character of Nicodemus may have been composed to reflect such people. In chapter 3, the reader is introduced to Nicodemus as "a Pharisee," "a leader of the Jews" who "came to Jesus by night"— perhaps a euphemism for "in secret" (3:1–2). Later, when Nicodemus tries to defend Jesus to his fellow Pharisees, he is accused of being one of his followers; the phrasing of the rhetorical question implies they do not believe that he actually is a follower of Jesus (7:45–52). Finally, Nicodemus appears in this Gospel for the last time at Jesus' burial along with Joseph of Arimathea. This time, however, Nicodemus is identified as one "who had at first come to Jesus by night" (i.e., secretly), implying that Nicodemus now comes openly (19:39).

Death of the Beloved Disciple

A second discernible situation addressed in the Johannine literature is the death of the Beloved Disciple. As discussed earlier, it is thought that the Beloved Disciple was the founder and original leader of the Johannine community. The ending identifies the Beloved Disciple as the source of the Gospel's traditions: "This is the disciple who is testifying to these things and has written them, and we know that his testimony is true" (21:24). As previously noted, the Gospel originally ended with 20:30–31, with the material in chapter 21 being a later addition. Included in that additional material is the strange conversation between Peter and the risen Jesus concerning the Beloved Disciple; in response to Peter's question about the Beloved Disciple, Jesus says, "If it is my will that he remain until I come, what is that to you?" (21:22). The passage explains that "the rumor spread in the community that this disciple would not die. Yet Jesus did not say to him that he would not die, but, 'If it is my will that he remain until I come, what is that to you?'" (21:23). This passage was probably added to the Gospel after the Beloved Disciple had died, and was intended to counter the belief that Jesus had said he would not die.

Conflict about Jesus Having Come in the Flesh

A third discernible situation is a conflict within the community. First and Second John inveigh against opponents who are identified as "antichrists." The author warns, "It is the last hour! As you have heard that antichrist is coming, so now many antichrists have come" (1 John 2:18). Rather than representing an external threat, the author of 1 John clarifies that these opponents originated within the Johannine community and the conflict reflects an internal dispute: "They went out from us, but they did not belong to us; for if they had belonged to us, they would have remained with us. But by going out they made it plain that none of them belongs to us" (1 John 2:19; cf. 2 John 7). While 1 John says that these "false prophets" were "denying Jesus is the Christ" (1 John 2:22; cf. 4:1), the dispute was specifically about whether Jesus had a fleshly body or was spirit only, merely appearing to have a body of flesh.[1] Second John clarifies, "Those who do not confess that Jesus Christ has come

---

1. The idea that Jesus only *appeared* to be corporeal would develop in the second and third centuries into a doctrine called Docetism (from a Greek root meaning "to seem" or "appear"). In 325 the First Council at Nicea rejected Docetism as a heresy.

in the flesh; any such person is the deceiver and the antichrist!" (2 John 7; cf. 1 John 4:2–3). The later editorial layers of the Gospel of John also seem to be responding to this internal conflict. The prologue to the Gospel (John 1:1–18), while it affirms that Jesus is the preexistent "Word," insists, "The Word became flesh and lived among us" (1:14). Similarly, Jesus' bodily existence is highlighted in the Resurrection scenes with Thomas (20:26–29) and Jesus' other disciples (21:12–14).

DISCUSSION QUESTIONS: GOSPEL OF JOHN AND JOHANNINE LETTERS

1. How does the portrayal of Jesus in this Gospel compare to his portrayal in the Synoptic Gospels (Matthew, Mark, and Luke)?

2. How do the interactions of characters and groups in the Gospel of John reflect situations faced by the Johannine community a generation or two after the time of Jesus. What does this suggest about the way the retelling of stories of the past can be meaningful to a later community?

3. How does irony—the difference between what the reader knows and misunderstandings by characters in the narrative— function? To what end does the author of John's Gospel use irony?

4. John's Gospel employs imagery (e.g., the dualism of light and darkness, above and below) and metaphor (e.g., the "I am" sayings); how do these figures of speech function to convey John's message?

5. It seems clear that members of the Johannine community wanted to continue to worship God in the synagogue; what does this say about the relationship between the early followers of Jesus and other Jews? How might this situation be used in interreligious dialogue?

6. What were some of the internal debates that troubled the Johannine community? What information do these debates provide about the early followers of Jesus in the first few generations after his death?

7. Discuss the importance of the Gospel of John portraying Jesus as a pre-existing, divine figure. Why do the Gospel and the Letters also emphasize that Jesus came "in the flesh"?

FOR FURTHER STUDY: GOSPEL OF JOHN AND JOHANNINE LETTERS

Carter, Warren. *John and Empire: Initial Explorations.* London: T & T Clark, 2008.

Charlesworth, James H. *The Beloved Disciple: Whose Witness Validates the Gospel of John?* Norcross, GA: Trinity Press, 1995.

Culpepper, R. Alan. *The Gospel and Letters of John.* Interpreting Biblical Texts. Nashville: Abingdon, 1998.

Kysar, Robert. *John, the Maverick Gospel.* 3rd. ed. Louisville: Westminster John Knox Press, 2007.

Levine, Amy-Jill, with Marianne Bickenstaff, eds. *Feminist Companion to John.* 2 vols. Feminist Companion to the New Testament and Early Christian Writings. New York: Pilgrim Press, 2003.

Martyn, J. Louis. *History and Theology in the Fourth Gospel.* Rev. and exp. ed. New Testament Library. Louisville: Westminster John Knox, 2003.

Reinhartz, Adele. *Befriending the Beloved Disciple: A Jewish Reading of the Gospel of John.* New York: Continuum, 2001.

Schneiders, Sandra. *Written That You May Believe: Encountering Jesus in the Fourth Gospel.* Rev. and exp. ed. New York: Crossroad, 2003.

Smith, D. Moody. *First, Second, and Third John.* Interpretation Commentary. Louisville: Westminster John Knox, 1993.

Smith, D. Moody. *John.* Abingdon New Testament Commentaries. Nashville: Abingdon, 1999.

Revelation

The title of Revelation comes from its first word, *apokalypsis*, (from which we get the English word "apocalypse"), meaning "uncovering" and therefore a "revelation." According to the opening sentences of

Definition of *Apocalypse*

Scholars situate Revelation within a genre of first Jewish and then Christian writings they call apocalypses. John J. Collins provides a widely accepted definition of apocalypse that here is expanded by A. Yarbro Collins: "Apocalypse is a genre of revelatory literature with a narrative framework, in which a revelation is mediated by an otherworldly being to a human recipient, disclosing a transcendent reality which is both temporal, insofar as it envisages eschatological salvation, and spatial, insofar as it involves another supernatural world intended to interpret present, earthly circumstances in light of the supernatural world, and of the future, and to influence both the understanding and the behavior of the audience by means of divine authority."[2] This genre is thought to have its origins in the prophetic and also wisdom traditions of post-exilic Israel.

the "book" (1:11), this is "the revelation of Jesus Christ, which God gave him to show his servants what must soon take place; he made it known by sending his angel to his servant John, who testified to the word of God and to the testimony of Jesus Christ, even to all that he saw" (1:1–2).

For a Specific Time

Revelation also identifies itself as "words of . . . prophecy" (1:3; 22:7, 10, 18–19). Prophecy here does not refer to predicting events far into the future. Rather, like the prophets of the Hebrew Bible, this author seeks to provide an exhortation—a word on target—addressing his community's immediate situation. Indeed, what is being revealed

---

2. J. J. Collins, "Apocalypse: The Morphology of a Genre," *Semeia* 14 [1979]: 9, and A. Yarbro Collins, "Introduction: Early Christian Apocalypticism," *Semeia* 36 [1986]: 7; cf. J. J. Collins, "Genre, Ideology and Social Movements in Jewish Apocalypticism," in *Mysteries and Revelations: Apocalyptic Studies since the Uppsala Colloquium*, ed. J. J. Collins and J. H. Charlesworth, JSOP Supplement Series 9 (Sheffield: Sheffield Academic Press), 19.

John of Patmos

Revelation claims to have been given to "John" on Patmos (1:1, 4, 9–11; 22:8). There is no reason to doubt that a person named John wrote Revelation, but there is debate over who this John was. Some early Christian writers identified this John with the apostle named John, and some also associated him with the Gospel of John and the Johannine letters. The language and theology of Revelation point away from a relationship with the other Johannine literature. John of Patmos, moreover, does not identify himself as a disciple or apostle of Jesus. In fact, the reference in 21:14 to "the twelve names of the twelve apostles of the Lamb" inscribed in the foundation of the new Jerusalem reflects a time after the first generation of followers of Jesus. John (in Hebrew, *Yochanan*) was a common Jewish name in the first century. The Greek of Revelation uses a number of Semitic constructions, suggesting that John may have been originally from the land of Israel, but his detailed knowledge of the churches in Asia Minor suggests that he worked among them.

"must soon take place" (1:1; cf. 1:3; 22:7, 10, 12, 20). Revelation is addressed to those suffering persecution (1:9; cf. 2:10, 13; 6:9–11; 12:17; 13:7, 15; 17:6; 18:24; 20:4) as well as internal conflict (2:2, 14–15, 20–25). Following historical clues in the text, scholars typically date Revelation to the end of the reign of the Roman Emperor Domitian, who ruled from 81 to 96 CE, although an increasing number of scholars see the work as dating earlier, to the end of the First Jewish Revolt against Rome (ca. 66–73).

For a Specific Place

Revelation is addressed "to the seven churches that are in Asia" (1:4). The Roman province of Asia—in what is now the western part of Turkey—was bounded by the Aegean Sea to the West, Bithynia to the North, Galatia to the East, and the Mediterranean Sea and Lycia to the South. The seven churches are those at Ephesus, Smyrna, Pergamum, Thyatira, Sardis, Philadelphia, and Laodicea (1:11). All of these cities are within one hundred and fifty miles of each other. Chapters 2 and 3 contain a series of letters, each one addressed to "the angel" of one of these churches, and includes references to certain people, such as the "Nicolaitans" (2:6, 15) and a "prophetess" (2:20). All this indicates that Revelation was written for a specific place at a specific time, the Roman province of Asia in the second half of the first century.

Revelation addresses the challenges of persecution and internal conflict. The letters to the seven churches, which emphasize judgment, reveal conflicts within the movement. Coded references to people within those churches—those who hold to the teaching of Balaam in 2:14 (cf. Num. 22–24) and Jezebel in 2:20 (cf. 1 Kings 18–19)—assume familiarity with the Hebrew Bible and attest to the author's conviction that the evildoers thus identified will be punished. Consistently throughout Revelation, judgment is based on "works" (e.g., 2:2, 5; cf. 20:12).

The Roman imperial system is the target of Revelation's critique, despite the fact that persecution of followers of Jesus in the first century was only intermittent and localized. As a subversive text opposing imperial forces in the late first-century Mediterranean world, Revelation employs fantastic imagery as coded language hiding the referents of its critique. For example, Israel's ancient oppressor Babylon represents the Roman Empire. Unmasking the lie of the imperial *Pax Romana*—the "peace" established and violently enforced by the Roman Empire—Revelation reveals it to be a reign of violence and death. In stark contrast to the violence of the empire is the "Lamb standing as if it had been slaughtered" (5:6). Nevertheless, Revelation revels in the violent overthrow of the empire. This upcoming war against the empire also takes place in heaven (12:7); its course and its outcome already decided and written on a heavenly scroll (5:1). The war culminates in Satan being bound for a thousand years (20:2–3) while Christ and the resurrected martyrs reign unopposed (20:4). At the end of that thousand years—a millennium—Satan is released for a final battle and defeat (20:7–10). Then follows the resurrection of the rest of those who have died and a final judgment in which even death will be destroyed (20:11–15; cf. 21:3–4).

The archangel Michael battles Satan in this fifteenth-century illumination (see Rev. 12:7–9). In apocalyptic literature, events such as this, taking place in the spiritual world, determine the course of events in the mundane world.

Despite the fantastic visions of heavenly battles, Revelation should not be misunderstood as strictly otherworldly. Rather, the rhetorical force of the heavenly visions is to provide assurance and confidence in the face of persecution that God's will and reign will be done "on earth as it is in heaven." Indeed the final vision is of a new heaven and a new earth, with a new Jerusalem descending from heaven (21:1–2; see 21:9–22:5). For Revelation, ultimately "the home of God is among mortals" (21:3); there will be "no temple in the city, for its temple is the Lord God the Almighty and the Lamb" (21:22).

While the author cannot be positively identified, certain features of the audience can be inferred. The coded language of the book assumes familiarity with the Jewish traditions preserved in the Torah and the Prophets. Envisioned is a reconstitution of Israel—the chosen 144,000 comprise twelve thousand from "every tribe of the people of Israel" (7:1–8; 14:1–5). It is only after these are "sealed" that the "great multitude that no one could count, from every nation, from all tribes and peoples and languages" appear "before the throne and before the Lamb" (7:9). Similarly, the center of the envisioned new earth is Jerusalem, to which the "nations will walk by its light, and the kings of the earth will bring their glory into it" (21:24; cf. 21:26).

The Ambiguous Specificity of Imagery

Some religious readers understand Revelation as miraculously predicting accurately events of the present time. These "prophecy believers" reject the evidence that Revelation was addressing a

666

According to Revelation 13:18, "This calls for wisdom: let anyone with understanding calculate the number of the beast, for it is the number of a person. Its number is six hundred sixty-six." Beginning in early Judaism, letters of the Hebrew alphabet were assigned a numerical value. The first letter (*aleph*) was one, the second letter (*bet*) was two, the eleventh letter (*kaph*) was twenty, the twelfth letter (*lamed*) was thirty, the nineteenth letter (*qoph*) was one-hundred, the twentieth letter (*resh*) was two-hundred, and so forth. The number 666 is most likely a reference to the Emperor Nero (54–68)—*Neron Caesar*—with the letters represented by "n", "r", "o", "c"/"k," and "s" having the following value: n=50 (times 2), r=200 (times 2), o=6, c/k=100, s=60. The phrase *Nero Caesar*—without the final "n" on *Nero*—provides the most likely solution for the number 616, which is a variant reading found in some of the ancient manuscripts of Revelation. Nero was noted for his particularly violent reign, and after his death a legend (called *Nero redivivus*) arose that he would return (cf. 13:3; 17:11).

THE

ATLANTIC MONTHLY.

A MAGAZINE OF LITERATURE, ART, AND POLITICS.

VOL. IX.—FEBRUARY, 1862.—NO. LII.

BATTLE HYMN OF THE REPUBLIC.

MINE eyes have seen the glory of the coming of the Lord :
He is trampling out the vintage where the grapes of wrath are stored ;
He hath loosed the fateful lightning of His terrible swift sword :
        His truth is marching on.

I have seen Him in the watch-fires of a hundred circling camps,
They have builded Him an altar in the evening dews and damps ;
I can read His righteous sentence by the dim and flaring lamps :
        His day is marching on.

I have read a fiery gospel writ in burnished rows of steel :
" As ye deal with my contemners, so with you my grace shall deal ;
Let the Hero, born of woman, crush the serpent with his heel,
        Since God is marching on."

He has sounded forth the trumpet that shall never call retreat;
He is sifting out the hearts of men before His judgment-seat :
Oh, be swift, my soul, to answer Him ! be jubilant, my feet !
        Our God is marching on.

In the beauty of the lilies Christ was born across the sea,
With a glory in his bosom that transfigures you and me :
As he died to make men holy, let us die to make men free,
        While God is marching on.

The "Battle Hymn of the Republic" offers one example of how the vivid imagery of the book of Revelation has been appropriated and reinterpreted to apply to later crises.

specific situation in Asia Minor in the first century of the Common Era. Other readers—some religious and others not—make Revelation meaningful as a social critique of systems of imperialism, violence, and death that exist in the present world.

Although it was originally written for specific places in a particular situation in history, Revelation has sparked the imagination of readers for two millennia, at times inspiring courageous resistance to imperial forces of destruction and at other times inciting violence, replicating evil. It is, perhaps, the most powerful, but most dangerous book in the Bible. One of the reasons for its enduring meaningfulness and varied interpretations is the ambiguous specificity of its imagery. As an apocalyptic vision, Revelation is replete with extremely detailed images that give the impression that actual people and events are represented there—and indeed they are. Babylon is the Roman Empire and the "beast" is the Roman Emperor. The ambiguity of the details, however, enables Revelation to be made meaningful at different times and different places.

DISCUSSION QUESTIONS: REVELATION

1. This introduction points out that Revelation emphasizes "works," a "this-worldly" orientation, and the centrality of Jewish traditions. How do those emphases affect the interpretation of Revelation? How might Revelation be used in interreligious dialogue?

2. Find an example of a passage from Revelation used in a different literary and historical context (e.g., Revelation 19 in "The Battle Hymn of the Republic" by Julia Ward Howe, 1861). How is imagery and language being used? How does the new context create a new meaning?

3. How might Revelation's social critique of imperial forces of violence and death be appropriated today for both religious and non-religious communities?

FOR FURTHER STUDY: REVELATION

Blount, Brian K. *Revelation: A Commentary*. Louisville: Westminster John Knox, 2009.

Collins, John J. *The Apocalyptic Imagination: An Introduction to Jewish Apocalyptic Literature*. 2nd ed. Biblical Resource Library. Grand Rapids: Eerdmans, 1998.

Koester, Craig. *Revelation and the End of All Things*. Grand Rapids: Eerdmans, 2001.

Levine, Amy-Jill, with Maria Mayo Robbins. *A Feminist Companion to the Apocalyse of John*. Feminist Companion to the New Testament and Early Christian Writings. London and New York: T & T Clark, 2009.

Metzger, Bruce M. *Breaking the Code: Understanding the Book of Revelation.* Nashville: Abingdon, 2003.

Rhoads, David, ed. *From Every People and Nation: The Book of Revelation in Intercultural Perspective.* Minneapolis: Augsburg Fortress, 2005.

Richard, Pablo. *Apocalypse: A People's Commentary on the Book of Revelation.* Maryknoll, NY: Orbis, 1995.

Schüssler Fiorenza, Elizabeth. *Revelation: Vision of a Just World.* Proclamation Commentaries. Minneapolis: Fortress, 1991.

23

Introduction to Pauline Literature

Laurie Brink, OP

Twenty–one of the twenty-seven books of the New Testament are called "letters"; they comprise nearly a third of the New Testament texts. Traditionally, fourteen of these letters are collectively known as Pauline Literature. The remaining seven are classified as Catholic Epistles. While Pauline Literature is identified by the community or the individual addressed, the Catholic Epistles are identified by their authors. The traditional list of Pauline Literature includes the "Letter" to the Hebrews, which is neither a true letter nor written by Paul.

The canonical order of the Pauline Letters is not based on chronology but arranged according to the length of each letter. Longer letters come before shorter ones. Letters addressed to churches (Romans, 1 and 2 Corinthians, Galatians, Ephesians, Philippians, Colossians, and 1 and 2 Thessalonians) are placed ahead of those written to individuals (1 and 2 Timothy, Titus, and Philemon). Hebrews does not state in its text that it was written by Paul, though its mention of Timothy (Heb. 13:23) led Christians of the third and fourth centuries to surmise Pauline origin. It is placed after the Pauline Letters in the canonical order.

Paul's authorship of only seven of the thirteen letters is undisputed: Romans, 1 and 2 Corinthians, Galatians, Philippians, 1 Thessalonians, and Philemon.

The Apostle Paul

Less than two decades after the Resurrection of Jesus, an unlikely apostle proclaimed the folly of the cross as the very wisdom of God (1 Cor. 1:18–25). In the first-century Mediterranean world where religion defined one's ethnicity and one's patriotism, this foolhardy preacher was himself a living paradox. A Hebrew, a Pharisee, a zealous Jew, and an admitted persecutor of the church (Phil. 3:5–6), Paul came to regard his religious roots as "loss because of Christ" (Phil. 3:7).

Not since the books of the prophets had the individual's voice sounded in Scripture. In the New Testament, the Gospels and the Acts of the Apostles, which are located before the letters from Paul, report the teachings and deeds of Jesus and his apostles. But beginning with the Letter to the Romans, the reader hears the actual voice of the writer, not mediated through narrative, but directed to the church of that day. The result is a personal, somewhat provocative, and always cross-centered view of the developing faith in Christ.

Paul did not intend to be an apostle to the Gentiles (Rom. 11:13; Gal. 2:8). By his own admission, he was a persecutor of the church (1 Cor. 15:9; Gal. 1:13; Phil. 3:6), zealous for his Jewish faith (Gal. 1:14). Like the prophet Jeremiah before him, he had been called while in his mother's womb (Gal. 1:15), but through a revelation from God he recognized his mission to proclaim the gospel to the Gentiles (Gal. 1:12, 16). Three years following his initial revelation, Paul went to Jerusalem to meet with Cephas (Aramaic equivalent of *Petros*, Peter; both names mean "rock") and remained with him for fifteen days. At that time, he also met James, the Lord's brother (Gal. 1:18–19). Fourteen years later, Paul returned to Jerusalem and met with James, Cephas, and John, who approved of Paul's mission to the Gentiles (Gal. 2:9), requiring only that the Gentile converts "remember the poor" (Gal. 2:10). Sometime later in Antioch, Paul chastised Cephas for refusing to eat with Gentiles after the arrival of persons from the "circumcision faction" (Gal. 2:11–12).

Paul's remarkable revelation cost him dearly. He was imprisoned, suffered beatings by lashes and rods, was stoned, thrice shipwrecked, and was adrift at sea for a night and a day (2 Cor. 11:24–25). He enumerated the multiple dangers he endured, including hunger, thirst, cold, and exposure (2 Cor. 11:26–27).

The Acts of the Apostles characterizes Paul from the lens of the late first-century author known as Luke. Paul's "conversion"[1] is dramatically told in three separate accounts (Acts 9:1–19; 22:3–21; 26:9–20). He identifies himself as a citizen of Tarsus (Acts 21:39; 22:3) and a Roman citizen (Acts 22:25). He received a strict religious education at the feet of Gamaliel, a leading figure in the Sanhedrin (Acts 22:3). His family included a sister and a nephew, who warned him about a planned ambush (Acts 23:16). Though Paul was critical of his oral abilities (1 Cor. 2:1–4) or was criticized for them (2 Cor. 10:10), Luke presents him as a persuasive speaker (Acts 17:34). Paul is said to have possessed the ability to heal (Acts 14:8–10; 19:11–12) and to cast out demons (Acts 16:18). The Acts of the Apostles concludes with Paul in Rome under house arrest. The second-century apocryphal *Acts of Paul* narrate Paul's martyrdom in Rome at the behest of the emperor Nero.

The early church father, John Chrysostom (ca. 349–407), readily admitted that of all the saints, he loved Paul the most.[2] Few are lukewarm when it comes to an evaluation of this apostle-come-lately. On issues of gender and sexuality, his proponents call him a "proto-feminist," citing Galatians 3:28, while detractors argue that he is a misogynist who thought it better if women kept quiet in church (1 Cor. 14:33b–36). His apparent pro-Gentile stance gains him the title "marginal Jew," while his apocalyptic perspectives place him in good stead with other apocalyptic Jews of his day. Romans 13 is cited as demonstrating Paul's conservative political views. But others see his creation of communities and encouragement to refrain from participating in public religion (the eating of meat sacrificed to idols) as examples of his anti-imperial attitude. He is seen as anti-slavery when he supports the runaway slave, Onesimus, in the Letter to Philemon. However, this stance is hard to support when reading 1 Corinthians 7:21–24.

An overview of Paul's first-century Mediterranean world will provide a context in which to read the archive of letters left to us by this irascible preacher.

---

1. Many think that Paul "converted" from Judaism to Christianity, but this is not so. He remained a faithful Jew, but also acknowledged Jesus as the Messiah of Israel and the savior of the nations. In these early years, Jews and Christians were not yet distinct.

2. Margaret M. Mitchell, *The Heavenly Trumpet: John Chrysostom and the Art of Pauline Interpretation* (Louisville: Westminster John Knox, 2002), 1.

The Religious Marketplace

Paul uses a variety of terms to talk about the Christian community. The earliest nomenclature appears to be *ekklēsia* (e.g., 1 Thess. 1:1), a term also utilized by Matthew (Matt. 16:18; 18:17) and Acts (Acts 5:11; 8:1, 3; 9:31; 11:22, 26; 14:23, 27; 15:3, 4, 22, 41; 16:5; 18:22; 20:17, 28). *Ekklēsia* is the Greek term for an assembly or gathering. The term is nearly synonymous with *synagōgē* ("synagogue"), the Jewish assembly. *Ekklēsia* is translated as "church," though the connotations of the term in Paul's time differ significantly from the present meaning of that word. By the turn of the century when Acts was written, this *ekklēsia* appears to have a formal structure, as indicated by Acts 14:23, where the churches appoint elders at Antioch of Pisidia, and by Acts 15:4, where the *ekklēsia*, apostles, and elders gather to meet Paul in Jerusalem. Other terms used by Paul include "those called" (*klētoi*, e.g., Rom. 1:1; 1 Cor. 1:1), often paired with "the saints" (*hagioi*, e.g., Rom. 1:7; 1 Cor. 16:1); "the elect" (*eklogē*, Rom. 11:7), "the believers" (*pisteuontes*, e.g., 1 Thess. 1:7; 2:10), and "brothers/sisters" (*adelphoi*, e.g., 1 Cor. 1:10; 1 Thess. 1:4).

This *ekklēsia* was just one of many religions competing for attention in the religious marketplace of the first century. One need only read the Acts of the Apostles to hear about the religious competition: Zeus and Hermes in Lystra (Acts 14:11–13), the nameless gods in Athens (Acts 17:22–23), and the great goddess Artemis in Ephesus (Acts 19:23–41). In addition to the temples that encircled the forum of any Greco-Roman city in the East—the locale of much of Paul's mission work—the hospital was dedicated to the healing god Asclepius, the meat sold in the market most often had originally been sacrificed in a pagan temple, and the daily visit to one's patron often meant participating in the worship of their household gods.

Romans tolerated the practice of various religions as long as the state gods were not ignored. In fact, Rome often adapted and adopted the divinities they found in other parts of the empire. The Egyptian Isis became "Romanized" and redressed as a more modest matron. Another religious ritual with strong ties to the state was the worship of the emperor as a god, though only in its infancy during Paul's lifetime. By the end of the first century, the imperial cult would become a serious challenge to Christian faith. Even in Paul's day, the

In ancient Ephesus, Artemis was worshipped as a fertility goddess. According to Acts, a mob of incensed Ephesian citizens rioted against Paul and Christian converts for undermining devotion to the city's patron diety (see Acts 19:23–41).

emperor claimed the title "lord" and "savior," so Paul's use of these titles for Jesus Christ (e.g., Rom. 1:4; 4:24; 16:2; Phil. 2:11; 3:20) stands in direct opposition to Caesar.

Snapshots of the Society

The Corinthian correspondence provides a unique glimpse into some of the social concerns of the Pauline *ekklēsia*. Though a bit like listening to half a conversation, the letters show Paul's response to questions about immorality (1 Cor. 5), law suits (1 Cor. 6), marriage (1 Cor. 7), food (1 Cor. 8), and women's roles (1 Cor. 11:2–16).

Paul believed that Christ would return imminently and that the community of believers was living in the last days. This sense of eager expectation is part of his eschatology and informed his social teachings. Salvation would be completed (1 Cor. 5:5; 1 Thess. 5:1–11) with Christ's return (*parousia*), but those who were in Christ had already begun their new life. They were a new creation (2 Cor. 5:17). As such, they had a different set of moral expectations.

The term that is often translated as "immorality" is *porneia* in the Greek, used for an array of illicit sexual activities. Paul responds to a report he has received that a man is living with his father's wife (1 Cor. 5:1). Paul declares such behavior appalling—even the Gentiles would not engage in such acts. The context suggests that the man may have married his stepmother either after his father's death or after the couple's divorce. Marriage between a stepson and stepmother was illegal by both Jewish and Roman standards.[3] The members of the *ekklēsia* were not to associate with a fellow member who was immoral, greedy, an idolater, a reveler, a drunkard, or a robber (1 Cor. 5:11).

Catalogues of virtues and vices were common in Greco-Roman writings (Plutarch, *De Stoicorum repugnantiis* 1034c; Epictetus, *Diatribai* 2.16.11–17; Cicero, *Tusculanae disputationes* 4.3.5) and Hellenistic Jewish literature (Wisdom of Solomon; Philo, *Who Is the Heir?* 168–73). These lists were used to demonstrate clear boundaries of good moral behavior. In the undisputed Pauline letters, catalogues are found in Romans 1:29–31; 13:13; 1 Corinthians 6:9–10; 2 Corinthians 12:20–21; and Galatians 5:19–21. The ethical behavior expected of members extended to their legal affairs as well. Paul chastises the Corinthian community for using the civic legal system to work out their own disagreements (1 Cor. 6:6–8).

As members of the body of Christ (Rom. 12:5), believers were to refrain from participating in cultic practices that would damage the "body": (1 Cor. 10:20–21). Since meat was often sacrificed to the gods then sold in the meat market, a Christian had a moral dilemma. Should he or she eat the meat or not? Paul offers two responses, one

---

3. Hans Conzelmann, *1 Corinthians* (Philadelphia: Fortress, 1975), 96.

concerned with the conscience of weaker believers (1 Cor. 8:10–11), and the other concerned with witnessing to non-believers (1 Cor. 10:27–29).

In the first-century world, Paul's statement that is it well for a man not to touch a woman (1 Cor. 7:1) would have seemed anti-social. Legislation enacted under Caesar Augustus provided incentives for women to have children. Judaism saw marriage and the procreation of children as a holy command (Philo, *On the Special Laws* 3.1–82). But Paul's sense of imminent eschatology (1 Cor. 7:31) meant that the believers were living in an "already and not yet" reality. The reign of God was already in process but not yet complete. In this context, Paul offers his "concession" to the Corinthians' questions about marriage.

Paul claims that wives as well as husbands have the right to sexual gratification (1 Cor. 7:3–4). But gender equality does not seem to extend to the case of public worship. Women who prophesy are to cover their heads (1 Cor. 11:5). Women should keep silent in the churches, and ask their husbands at home if they have questions (1 Cor. 14:34–35). However, some scholars argue that 1 Corinthians 14:34–35 is an interpolation inserted later to create conformity with 1 Timothy 2:11–12. Or it may have been misinformation to which Paul is responding like that found in 1 Corinthians 7:1 ("Now concerning the matters about which you wrote: 'It is well for a man not to touch a woman.'")

The roles of women in the first-century Mediterranean world were far from uniform from region to region. In general, Roman women exercised more authority than their Greek sisters. Roman women could own property, inherit, and in some cases be independent of a male guardian. The extent to which Roman gender customs spread to the Greek East is unknown. Paul names women as active participants in the church. Of the twenty-four names listed in Romans 16, ten belong to women who are variously titled as *diakonos* ("deacon" or "minister"; Phoebe, v. 1), fellow worker (Prisca, along with her husband Aquila, v. 3), hard workers (Mary v. 6, Tryphaena, Tryphosa, and Persis, v. 12), relative and fellow prisoner and "prominent among the apostles" (Junia, v. 7), Rufus' mother (v. 13), and saints (Julia, and Nereus' sister, v. 15).

Letter-Writing and the Ancient Postal Service

The books of the New Testament are remarkable for their content, which is made all the more amazing given the vagaries of history. One wonders how many other letters from the apostles were penned but never preserved, sent but never received. A brief excursus into letter-writing and delivery in the first century serves to accent the extraordinary existence of the Pauline corpus.

The originals of the letters that appear in the New Testament were likely written by reed pens on papyrus rolls. The scribe would select a length of papyrus depending on the anticipated contents. The message would be written on the inside of the scroll with delivery instructions on the outside. Since a secretary or a professional letter-writer (an *amanuensis*) penned most letters, Paul's epistles were probably not written by his hand. In fact, one such amanuensis added his own personal note in Romans 16:22: "I, Tertius, the writer of this letter, greet you in the Lord." On occasion, Paul does add his own postscript (1 Cor. 16:21; Philem. 19), and in Galatians 6:11 Paul notes his penmanship: "See what large letters I make when I am writing in my own hand!" Personal interjections in the author's own hand may have served to authenticate the letter.

While Paul appears to be the mastermind behind the content of the letters,

© Randal Stegmeyer / University of Michigan

Paul's epistles follow the basic format of ancient letters. In this second-century letter, one Apollinarius, a new recruit to the Roman military, writes to his mother in Egypt to reassure her that he has arrived safely in Rome and to urge her not to worry about him.

he is not alone. In 1 Thessalonians 1:1 (cf. 2 Thess. 1:1), he includes Silvanus and Timothy as co-senders. 1 Corinthians is written by Paul and Sosthenes. Timothy is identified as the co-sender of 2 Corinthians, Philippians, and Philemon (also the deuteropauline Colossians). The Letter to the Galatians is sent by Paul "and all the members of God's family [i.e., fellow Christians] who are with me" (Gal. 1:2).

The postal system of the Roman Empire was restricted to governmental agents, so private correspondence had to be sent by couriers or trusted travelers. The cache of papyri discovered in the trash heaps of Egypt testifies to the happenstance of much personal correspondence. Letters were sent home when one happened upon a traveler going that direction. Paul's letters give only occasional indications of who his courier may have been. Chloe's people brought a report to Paul (1 Cor. 1:11), which may have been in letter form or oral. Perhaps these same people carried Paul's earlier letter to the Corinthians (1 Cor. 5:9). The tearful letter that Paul mentions in 2 Corinthians 2:4 was likely carried to the church of Corinth by Titus, whose return Paul anxiously awaited (2 Cor. 7:6–13). Delicate details concerning the business or controversy under discussion were often left to the trusted emissary.

> For this reason I sent you Timothy, who is my beloved and faithful child in the Lord, to remind you of my ways in Christ Jesus, as I teach them everywhere in every church. (1 Cor. 4:17)

Paul follows standard epistolary form when dictating his letters. Most ancient epistles included a prescript and greeting, followed by a health wish or thanksgiving section, the body of the letter, greetings, and a closing formula. Paul adds his personal touch to the standard *chairein* (greetings). He incorporates the Jewish formula of shalom, so that that the greeting becomes grace (*charis*) and peace (shalom, *eirēnē* in Greek). All of Paul's genuine epistles include the various parts of a standard letter, save the Letter to the Galatians, which lacks the usual thanksgiving. Paul is furious, so he has nothing to be thankful about in his chastising letter to the churches of Galatia. Romans 16 closes with an extensive greetings section in which Paul sends his regards to numerous individuals and groups.

Paul's Undisputed Letters

Scholarly consensus attributes to Paul (and his co-senders) seven letters: Romans, 1–2 Corinthians, Galatians, Philippians, 1 Thessalonians, and Philemon. By reconstructing Paul's itinerary from his genuine letters and the Acts of the Apostles, approximate dates and places of origin of these letters can be mapped.[4]

First Thessalonians is believed to have been written early in Paul's apostolic career when he resided in Corinth (approximately 50–51 CE). The Corinthian correspondence followed in 54–56 CE. Acts of the Apostles records Paul's two-year stay in Ephesus (Acts 19:10), following his preaching in Corinth (Acts 18:1–17). Given his lengthy stay, Paul may have penned several letters there, including 1 and 2 Corinthians and Galatians (55–56 CE). Paul wrote the Letter to the Romans from Corinth (56–57 CE). Determining the date and place of origin for Philippians and Philemon depend on the location of Paul's imprisonment at the time of writing. If Paul is writing from Ephesus, the letters could have been composed between 53–55 CE. If Paul is in the custody of Felix and then Festus in Caesarea, he may be writing shortly before he is taken to Rome. If Paul writes from Rome, then Philippians and Philemon become the last letters preserved from the Apostle Paul. According to Eusebius, the fourth-century church historian, Paul was martyred under Nero, who reigned from 54–68 CE.

Letters Written In the Name of Paul

The Pauline corpus found within the New Testament includes letters that were attributed to Paul but actually written long after his death. The deuteropauline letters of 2 Thessalonians, Colossians, and Ephesians appear to have been written between 70–100 CE, though some scholars argue that one or more of these are genuinely Pauline. First and Second Timothy and Titus, also known as the Pastoral Epistles because of their concern about matters of church management, demonstrate by their vocabulary and content a late first-century to

4. Hans-Josef Klauck, *Ancient Letters and the New Testament* (Waco, TX: Baylor University Press, 2006), 299–408.

The first church buildings were simply private homes that were also used for Christian worship services, like this second-century example from Dura-Europos, in Syria. Buildings constructed specifically for use as churches were rare until the late third or early fourth century.

© Zev Radovan / www.biblelandpictures.com

early second-century date. While 1 Timothy and Titus appear to be from the same hand and address similar concerns, 2 Timothy is markedly different and may have another author.

In the time of Paul and the earliest Christian communities, the churches gathered in the households of members (Rom. 16:5; 1 Cor. 16:19). The church anticipating the end time ("our citizenship is in heaven," Phil. 3:20) had no need for structures or even developed ministries beyond "apostles"—those sent to preach the coming reign of God. Hence, little source material is found in Paul's own letters concerning the internal functioning of the churches. Intra-church differentiation of ministries includes apostles (2 Cor. 8:23; Phil. 2:25), prophets (Rom. 12:6; 1 Cor. 12:28; 14:1–5; 1 Thess. 5:20), teachers (Rom. 12:7; Gal. 6:6), overseers and deacons, both male and female (Phil. 1:1; Rom. 16:1), and leaders (Rom. 12:8; 1 Cor. 12:28; 1 Thess. 5:12). Those members who had the means to host the Lord's Supper rose in responsibility and authority in the early communities. Some of these house church patrons were women (1 Cor. 16:19; Col. 4:15).

As time went on, the delay of the parousia (Jesus' return) and the growing number of believers led to the development of institutional elements. For the next generation of Pauline communities, the church that met in the household of a Christian patron readily developed into the "household of God" (Eph. 2:19). Like other households of the time, order and proper management were vital for the welfare of the members of that household. Codes of behavior were common in the Greco-Roman world and provided directives for ethical behavior as well as good order among social classes. These "household codes" were adapted to fit the growing Christian communities and are found in Ephesians 5:21–6:9; Colossians 3:18–4:1; 1 Timothy 2:8–15; 5:1–2; 6:1–2; and Titus 2:1–10; 3:1 (cf. 1 Pet. 2:11–3:12). What distinguishes the New Testament household codes is their emphasis on "compassion, kindness, humility, meekness, and patience" (Col. 3:12). The model for behavior is Christ, whose example all members are to follow: "And whatever you do, in word or deed, do everything in the name of the Lord Jesus, giving thanks to God the Father through him" (Col. 3:17).

By the time of the Pastoral Epistles (1–2 Timothy and Titus), the "household of God" had developed a hierarchical ministry of bishops (1 Tim. 3:1–7; Titus 1:7–9), presbyters (1 Tim. 5:17–22; Titus 1:5), deacons (1 Tim. 3:8–13), and widows (1 Tim. 5:3–16), with set standards for their selection and their behavior.

Issues Addressed in the Letters

A quick survey of the life of the Apostle Paul and his religious and social context provides the backdrop for reading the Pauline corpus found in the New Testament. None of the letters in the canon are "notes" meant simply to send greetings to acquaintances at a distance, although they do perform that function as well. Each letter, whether genuinely authored by Paul or in the tradition of Paul, is addressed to a specific community with specific concerns and questions. The Thessalonians are worried that their beloved dead will be left behind when Jesus returns (1 Thess. 4:13–18). The Corinthian correspondence includes myriad questions about right behavior within a polytheistic urban environment. The Letter to the Galatians shows Paul's temper as he chastises the churches for their fickle faith: "You foolish Galatians! Who has bewitched you? It was before your eyes that Jesus Christ was publicly exhibited as crucified!" (Gal. 3:1).

The Philippians seem to have been favored by Paul; he is effusive in his praise of them (Phil. 1:3–11), but he does admonish two of their leaders to resolve their differences (Phil. 4:2–3). The shortest of the genuine letters is addressed not to a church but to an individual. Paul attempts to mediate between Onesimus, the runaway slave, and his owner, Philemon, both of whom are believers. And finally, Paul's Letter to the Romans is addressed to a community he did not establish. It summarizes and expands his theological thinking to date, particularly with respect to the question of Israel and God's righteousness to Jews and Gentiles. Many scholars sense that one major reason for Romans was Paul's concern to mediate between Gentile believers and Jews who were returning after Nero lifted Claudius' edict that expelled some of the Jews from Rome about 49 CE (see Acts 18:2).

The disputed letters of Paul are so-called because many scholars believe that Paul is not the actual author; rather, anonymous writers have taken on the persona of Paul in order to address emerging concerns for a later church. Differences in vocabulary, writing style, and content suggest that these letters may have been written by different authors between 80–110 CE. Ephesians and Colossians provide direction for believers who wonder how to live in the time between Jesus' ascension and his eventual return. Although the letters claim to have been written by Paul during one of his imprisonments (Eph. 3:1; Col. 4:3–4), many scholars assert that Ephesians and Colossians are likely pseudonymous and were meant to provide a general summary of Paul's genuine letters for the churches in southwest Asia Minor.

Like Ephesians and Colossians, the authorship of 2 Thessalonians is debated. It claims to be authored by Paul, Silvanus, and Timothy (2 Thess. 1:1), who write to encourage a community that is undergoing intense persecution for their faith (1:4–6). Additionally, some members are announcing that the end has already arrived (2:1–2), but the author advises, "Let no one deceive you in any way; for that day will not come unless the rebellion comes first and the lawless one is revealed, the one destined for destruction" (2 Thess. 2:3).

The Pastoral Epistles, 1 and 2 Timothy and Titus, reflect an early second-century community that is developing both ecclesial structures and theological understanding. Attributed to Paul, these

354 • ANSELM COMPANION TO THE BIBLE

letters were likely the result of a "Pauline school" that reflected
on Pauline theology in light of the church's developing needs and
concerns.

The Letter to the Hebrews, likely a sermon in letter form,
attempts to encourage believers whom the author fears are in danger
of apostasy—renouncing one's faith (Heb. 2:1–4). Hebrews reflects
on the death of Jesus as a saving act and finds support and direction
from Old Testament texts.

Specific issues and local concerns notwithstanding, the undisputed Pauline letters and those attributed to Paul share much
common ground. They are attempts to shore up the faith of new
believers, correct the misunderstandings created by false apostles, and
encourage a virtuous life. They are Christocentric, or more correctly,
cross-centric (1 Cor. 1:18; Gal. 6:14; Phil. 2:8), focused on the saving
act of Christ Jesus.

> For I handed on to you as of first importance what I in turn
> had received: that Christ died for our sins in accordance
> with the scriptures, and that he was buried, and that he
> was raised on the third day in accordance with the scrip-
> tures. (1 Cor. 15:3–4)

DISCUSSION QUESTIONS

1. How might the religious context of the first century Greco-
   Roman world have affected Paul's mission?

2. What are the implications of becoming a member of "the body
   of Christ" while still living in a Greco-Roman polytheistic
   society?

3. How did letter-writing facilitate the development of the early
   church?

4. What are some of the issues addressed in Paul's undisputed
   letters? What can be learned from these problems—and Paul's
   responses—about the early Christian communities?

5. What are some of the issues addressed in the disputed Pauline
   letters? What can be learned from these problems—and the
   authors' responses to them—about the Christian communities

in the generation after Paul? How is their situation similar to that in Paul's day? How is it different?

FOR FURTHER STUDY

Collins, Raymond F. *The Power of Images in Paul.* Collegville, MN: Liturgical Press, 2008.

Klauck, Hans-Josef. *Ancient Letters and the New Testament.* Waco, TX: Baylor University Press, 2006.

Murphy-O'Connor, Jerome. *Paul: His Story.* New York: Oxford University Press, 2006.

Scholz, Daniel J. *The Pauline Letters: Introducing the New Testament.* Winona, MN: Anselm Academic, 2013.

Still, Todd D., and Bruce W. Longenecker. *Thinking through Paul: A Survey of His Life, Letters, and Theology.* Grand Rapids: Zondervan, 2014.

Taylor, Walter F. *Paul, Apostle to the Nations: An Introduction.* Minneapolis: Fortress, 2012.

Introduction to the Catholic Epistles and Hebrews

Aliou Cissé Niang

Catholic Epistles, also known as General Epistles, were written by Christian authors to fellow Christians living somewhere in the Roman Empire. The word *catholic*, meaning general or universal, describes writings addressed to the whole church instead of specific churches or persons.[1] They include Hebrews, James, 1 and 2 Peter, 1, 2 and 3 John,[2] and Jude. They share certain characteristics—including a context in the eastern Roman Empire, unknown date of origin, and anonymous or pseudonymous authorship—but their content differs widely. Their authors read scripture, including texts now considered apocrypha or pseudepigrapha, and were influenced by Greco-Roman literary traditions.

Though termed "epistles," the Catholic Epistles are not letters in the real sense. Some of the Catholic Epistles share a number of literary and theological characteristics with Paul's letters, while others have less in common with that corpus. Rather than treating the Catholic Epistles in their canonical order, this essay will begin with

---

1. "Such is the story of James, whose is said to be the first of the Epistles called Catholic. It is to be observed that its authenticity is denied, since few of the ancients quote it, as is also the case with the Epistle called Jude's, which is itself one of the seven called Catholic; nevertheless we know that these letters have been used publically with the rest in most churches" (Eusebius, *Ecclesiastical History* 2.23.25.2).

2. The Johannine Epistles are discussed in chapter 22, "Introduction to the Gospel of John, Johannine Letters, and Revelation."

3. See M. Eugene Boring, *An Introduction to the New Testament: History, Literature, Theology* (Louisville: Westminster John Knox, 2012), 400–66.

the letters that show the greatest literary influence of Paul (1 Peter) and proceed to those with the least similarity to Paul.[3]

1 Peter

The author of 1 Peter claims to be "Peter, an apostle of Jesus Christ" (1 Pet. 1:1), "an elder myself and a witness of the sufferings of Christ" (1 Pet. 5:1). Peter was a prominent figure among Jesus' disciples in the Gospels and the Acts of the Apostles, and was known as one of the "pillars" of the church (Gal. 2:9). Whereas some scholars maintain Petrine authorship, most think the Greek of the letter is too polished for a Galilean fisherman, and conclude that the work is pseudonymous, written between 70 and 90 CE.

The author claims to be writing from "Babylon" (1 Pet. 5:13), probably a metaphor for Rome. The intended recipients appear to have been a mixed but predominantly Gentile Christian group in northern Asia Minor suffering persecution from their non-Christian neighbors (1:1; 3:8–17). The author characterizes them metaphorically as "aliens and exiles" (2:11). They were socially shamed, persecuted, and alienated for their new-found faith and practices—an estrangement with possible economic ramifications. The author begins his message with a greeting formula similar to greetings in Paul's letters, then moves to advice on Christian life (1:1–2:10), followed by a discussion of Christian responsibility (2:11–5:11), and ending with encouragement and final greetings (5:12–14).

First Peter's readers are landless "exiles" (1:1–2), chosen by God to be saved from their former non-Christian identities (1:14, 18; 2:10; cf. Deut. 26:5) and lifestyle (1 Pet. 4:2–4). Whereas some scholars think the unique expression "exiles of the Dispersion" (1:1) was a non-political way to refer to God's people throughout the ages, others insist that it held political ramifications, in view of imperial demands. Although the recipients' suffering does not stem directly from imperial policy, their neighbors, who appear to be responsible for the addressees' problems, were influenced by imperial ideology, especially allegiance to imperial cultic practices.

The author uses the birth metaphor to speak of his readers' new identity in Christ (1 Pet. 1:3, 23), and exhorts them to live a distinct life, exercising mutual love, developing both into the spiritual building, whose capstone is Christ, and a royal priesthood to serve God (2:4–5). As children of God, they are encouraged to exercise an exemplary lifestyle. Specifically, they are to be good citizens (2:15, 17) and uphold the kind of household relations that reflect Greco-Roman norms (2:13–4:11). The admonition to fear God, honor the emperor (2:13–17), and suffer as innocents (4:15–16) implies that some readers did otherwise. Scholars often cite assimilation, resistance, or "polite resistance"[4] as alternative responses that some of this letter's readers might have adopted to adjust to harsh imperial demands.

These readers are encouraged to emulate God and Jesus Christ by enduring hardships from their oppressors (1 Pet. 2:20–23), leading a lifestyle free from licentiousness, meeting their suffering with good deeds (3:13–4:11), especially toward their persecutors (cf. Matt. 5:11–12; Rom. 12:16–21). Although they sometimes need to assimilate, their Christian identity also requires them to reject some features of their Greco-Roman culture. Representing himself as an elder and eyewitness of the sufferings of Jesus Christ, the author advises elders to exercise proper oversight without being domineering. He reminds them that, in the present context of unjust suffering, they are not to assert themselves, but to rely upon God to vindicate them (4:12–5:11). The letter ends with greetings from the author and from Mark and Silvanus, probably referring to the Pauline co-workers (1 Thess. 1:1; Acts 12:12–17).

Hebrews

The Letter to the Hebrews is a literary gem crafted by an unknown writer.[5] The author uses Jewish and Greco-Roman literary traditions to argue for both discontinuity and continuity between the Old and

---

4. David G. Horrell, *Becoming Christian: Essays on 1 Peter and the Making of Christian Identity*, ed. John Barclay and Mark Goodacre, LNTS 394 (New York: Bloomsbury; T & T Clark, 2013).

5. "If I were to state my own opinion, I should say that the thoughts are the apostle's, but that the style and composition belong to one who called to mind the apostle's teachings. . . . But who wrote the epistle, in truth God knows" (Eusebius, *Ecclesiastical History* 6.25.13–14, quoting Origen).

New Testaments. The continuity rests solely on faith in the uniqueness of Jesus over the Mosaic and Levitical sacred institutions (Heb. 7:27–28) and biblical figures (Heb. 1:1; 3:3), with the exception of Melchizedek (Heb. 7, especially 7:27–28; cf. Gen. 14:18–24). Readers and hearers of Hebrews are called to a peculiar and exclusive life of faith in Jesus Christ as their new identity marker.

The author characterizes the letter to the Hebrews as an exhortation (Heb. 13:22); scholars classify the work as either a sermon or a theological tractate. The author introduces the work with salutations (1:1–4), moves to the uniqueness of Jesus Christ over angels (1:5–2:18), the uniqueness of the priesthood of Jesus (3:1–5:10), the eternal priesthood and sacrifice of Jesus (5:11–10:39), and exhortations about endurance (chs. 11–12) and remaining faithful (ch. 13).

There is no scholarly consensus on the date of Hebrews but clues from the letter lead some scholars to place it between 60 and 95 CE. The provenance of Hebrews is as unknown as the location of its recipients. The author of Hebrews writes to encourage persecuted Christians who are teetering between faithfulness to Christ or reverting back to their former religious practices within Judaism.

Hebrews passionately argues that past divine revelation is now completed in Jesus Christ, who is the ultimate aim of all previous divine communications. Similar to Paul, Hebrews reads key biblical texts (from Torah, prophets, and wisdom literature) creatively to maintain that the once indirectly mediated revelation of God is now made fully manifest through Jesus. God's revelation through Jesus Christ is unique—a theme that serves as the theological anchor of Hebrews. Jesus is God's heir, the divine priest who purifies from sin, the agent through whom God made and sustains creation, who manifests God's image, glory, and effective word (1:1–4).

Hebrews' Jesus is the *charactēr*, "exact imprint, image" of God's self (1:3), the unmediated divine revelation of God (2:5–3:6). Since the term "impress, image" also describes the emperor's priestly function as mediator in the imperial cult system, the addressees would have readily understood that Hebrews was implicitly arguing for the final, unique, and incomparable revelation of God in Jesus. This argument echoes the author's keen familiarity with Paul's Christology (Rom. 3:21–26; Phil. 2:5–11) and his view of human and angelic agents of divine revelation (Gal. 3:19–20).

360 • ANSELM COMPANION TO THE BIBLE

Hebrews 5:11–10:39 develops further the author's initial argument for the uniqueness of Jesus. Hebrews encourages spiritual maturity and insists that those who have fallen away from faith in Jesus Christ cannot be restored. Jesus is the unique and eternal

Melchizedek

Though there are few references to Melchizedek in Scripture, they provided the basis for increasing speculation about this mysterious figure in the first century, as the following sequence of passages illustrates:

"And King Melchizedek of Salem brought out bread and wine; he was priest of God Most High." (Gen. 14:18)

"The Lord has sworn and will not change his mind, 'You are a priest forever according to the order of Melchizedek.'" (Ps. 110:4)

"Melchizedek; f[or He will cast] their [lot] amid the po[rtions of Melchize]dek, who will return them there and will proclaim to them liberty, forgiving them [the wrong-doings] of all their iniquities. . . . And the Day of Atonement is the e[nd of the] tenth [Ju]bilee, when all the Sons of [Light] and the men of the lot of Mel[chi]zedek will be atoned for." (11Q13)

"This 'King Melchizedek of Salem, priest of the Most High God, met Abraham as he was returning from defeating the kings and blessed him'; and to him Abraham apportioned 'one-tenth of everything.' . . . Without genealogy, having neither beginning of days nor end of life, but resembling the Son of God, he remains a priest forever. See how great he is! . . . It is even more obvious when another priest arises, resembling Melchizedek, one who has become a priest, not through a legal requirement concerning physical descent, but through the power of an indestructible life. For it is attested of him, 'You are a priest forever, according to the order of Melchizedek.'" (Heb. 7:1–4; 15–17) priest in the lineage of Melchizedek (5:1–10; 7), a priest with no human ancestry, to whom Abraham paid tithes. He is a true human with a true divine nature whose suffering is salvific (Heb. 2:5–18; cf. Ps. 8:4–6). In contrast to the yearly sacrifices officiated by priests (Lev. 16) in the Levitical and imperial cults, Jesus is the high priest whose self-sacrifice is final. Hebrews' Jesus is the perfect priest and mediator of the new covenant (Heb. 9, esp. vs. 15; cf. Jer. 31:31–34) in the heavenly sanctuary.

The author's sharp contrast between the heavenly and the earthly emphasizes the eternal role of Jesus. The earthly is a "shadow" of that which is genuinely heavenly (Heb. 8:1–10:18). Hebrews 11–12 illustrates faith by appealing to biblical figures whom the author considers worthy of emulation because of their heroic faith. They lived faithfully as "strangers and foreigners on the earth," setting their sight on God's promised homeland, a heavenly "city" (11:13–16). The author of Hebrews asserts that God fulfilled this promise in Jesus. The faithfulness of God, and especially of Jesus, is an empowering presence that enables human agents to exercise faith and endure persecution, which inspires and sustains hope for the unseen. The author claims that Scripture tells how faithful Jewish men and women persevered through trials by faith even without experiencing the fulfillment of the divine promise (ch. 11). This promise is now empirically fulfilled in the unique revelation of God, Jesus Christ, in whom they find their new identity.

Chapters 12 and 13 include further exhortations for the addressees to stay faithful by imitating Jesus Christ, who overcame suffering and death and was vindicated by God. They should accept their suffering as an act of God who is disciplining them (12:7–11). The letter ends in a Pauline style that includes a prayer request and benediction.

James

The work claims to be written by "James, a servant of God and of the Lord Jesus Christ" (James 1:1). Most scholars, however, ascribe it to an unknown writer, well versed in the Septuagint, Greco-Roman rhetorical traditions, the sayings of Jesus, and Pauline Letters, sometime between 70 and 130 CE.

Echoes of Scripture, other Jewish texts, and Greco-Roman literature pervade the work, which consists of impassioned exhortations
to a community of predominantly poor members living either in Palestine or Rome. Scholars debate whether the expression "the twelve
tribes in the Dispersion" (1:1) limits the intended audience to Jewish
Christians outside Palestine or includes all followers of Jesus. The
work expresses a deep concern for active faith that is morally attuned
to others in the community and directs interpersonal relations.

The structure of this letter is problematic. James introduces his
work with salutations (1:1), then discusses the practice of Christian
faith amid trials (1:2–27), enacting their faith (ch. 2), developing
instruction and wisdom (ch. 3), avoiding unwise living and other
evils (4:1–12), and exercising faith wisely (4:13–5:20).

James weaves together exhortations and wise sayings drawn
from Jewish and Greco-Roman literary traditions. He is fully
immersed in the world that shaped his ideas but from which he is
assiduously trying to distance his audience. For instance, like Stoic
philosophers, James uses questions, answers, and expressions such as
"show me . . . and I will show you" (2:18) and "come now" (4:13;
5:1) to argue his position and discredit his opponents. Scholars call
this argumentation *diatribe*.

James symbolically advises his addressees to pray for true wisdom from God to endure temptations in order to attain mature faith.
In chapter 2, James reminds them of the importance of translating
their words into concrete actions with deference for widows and
orphans—a pure exercise of faith. Some scholars argue that James is
using the term "pure" (1:27 and 3:17) to construct the identity of his
readers because he does not want them to accommodate to the values
of their Diaspora context (1:1), in contrast to the position of Paul, as
this author sees it. Others, however, think James agrees with Paul and
adapts his teachings.

Like Paul, James appeals to the Abrahamic stories to substanti-
ate his arguments. Paul, however, reads Genesis 15:6 (Rom. 3:28–4:3;
Gal. 3:6) but ignores Genesis 22, whereas James finds both texts
operative (James 2:21, 23), suggesting that James builds on and
innovates Pauline traditions for his readers.

James' concern for the poor and defenseless runs deep (2:5–7;
4:13–5:5). He dissuades the poor from extending preferential

Diatribe

Examples from Chrysostom and Epictetus illustrate the style of argumentation known as diatribe, which is also employed by James. Scholars have noted Paul's use of elements of diatribe in some of his correspondence as well (e.g., Rom. 2:1–5; 6:1–5; Gal. 3:1–9).

> "And so, you ridiculous fellow, are you attempting to make use of the god when you are incapable of using a slave? Or does not the latter strike as less difficult and dangerous than the former for those who are incapable of using things properly? Besides, what is your object in hunting for the boy? Was he not a bad slave?"
>
> (Dio Chrysostom, *Servants* 10.2, quoting Diogenes)

> "Aren't you ashamed to be more cowardly and ignoble than a runaway slave? How do they, when they run off, leave their masters? In what estate or slave do they put their confidence? Don't they steal just a little bit to last them for the first few days . . . ?"
>
> (Epictetus, *Diatribai* 3.26)

> "Has not God chosen the poor in the world to be rich in faith and to be heirs of the kingdom that he has promised to those who love him? But you have dishonored the poor. Is it not the rich who oppress you? Is it not they who drag you into court? Is it not they who blaspheme the excellent name that was invoked over you?"
>
> (James 2:5–7; cf. 3:2–12)

treatment to the wealthy, a practice he thinks exploits and oppresses them. As for the wealthy, James calls them to exercise the law by caring for the poor, God's elect and "heirs" (2:5), and thus imitate God. Community members, especially teachers, should not slander or judge (3:1–4:12) because it is unwise and destructive to the community. The wealthy will be punished for their mistreatment of the poor (James 1:9–11; 4:13–5:6; cf. Exod. 3:7; Ps. 73:8–11, 16–20). He encourages the poor to exercise patience like a "farmer" and endure like "Job" (James 1:2–4; 5:7–11). The author reemphasizes the practical dimension of prayer and of a lifestyle that reflects one's faith. James' Diaspora requires not only wise living but also a quest for a place to stand and make a home (cf. Jer. 29:4–7). James emphasizes purity as a boundary marker lest his readers try to acculturate to Roman imperial values.

Jude

The author claims to be "Jude . . . brother of James" (Jude 1). Although there is some debate about whether the author is a sibling of James and Jesus (Matt. 13:55; Mark 6:3; Acts 15:13; Gal. 2:6–9, 12), most scholars conclude that "Jude" is a pseudonym, partly because the text's Greek is too polished for a rural Palestinian Jew. The author is an unknown second-generation Jewish Christian who was influenced by Pauline traditions. He wrote during the postapostolic era (v. 17), probably between 125 to 150 CE. The work is silent about its provenance but may have been authored by a Hellenized Jew. He begins with salutations and the reason for the letter (vv. 1–4), moves to false teachers and their fate (vv. 5–16), an exhortation against false teachers (vv. 17–23), and a doxology (vv. 24–25).

Textual similarities between Jude 4–16 and 2 Peter 2:2–17 suggest a literary dependence and similar theological concern. Jude wrote to address a competing understanding of faith (v. 3) introduced by individuals he characterizes as "intruders" (v. 4). He engages in a vigorous, one-sided, in-house debate. His understanding of the apostolic tradition is now competing with that of his opponents. Faith, as Jude understands it, is being assaulted by some of his community members. What they are actually teaching is difficult to ascertain, since it can only be reconstructed from Jude's own invectives. He writes to persuade his readers to hold on to the faith transmitted by the apostles, to warn them about his opponents' fate, and to denounce their falsehood.

Jude begins in line with traditional Pauline epistolary style, identifying himself as "Jude, a servant of Jesus Christ and brother of

James to those who are called" (vv. 1–2). The omission of the geographical location of his addressees makes their identification difficult. He asserts that he had meant to write about his community's shared experience of salvation, but must instead address the problem of the scandalous behavior of some unnamed intruders (vv. 3–4). His ire is explicit, and like Paul (Gal. 1:1–6), he omits the customary epistolary thanksgiving and proceeds to encourage them "to contend for the faith that was once for all entrusted to the saints" (v. 3), an exhortation that presumes that "faith" has evolved into a body of teachings to be preserved and transmitted to the next generation of believers. Jude's intruders are perverse individuals who spurn angels and disrespect authority, especially that of Christ and some Mosaic traditions (vv. 4–10).

Jude 5–13 reads Genesis 6:1–4 and 19:4–11 through the lens of later Jewish literature, such as the *Assumption of Moses* and *1 Enoch* 1.9; 6–19, to warn readers that divine punishment would befall the intruders. Jude shares some characteristics of apocalyptic literature.[6] Apocalypses were written to address crises like those generated by imperial domination; they enshrine messages of resistance to imperial religious repression, economic exploitation, and assimilation policies. Assimilation, acculturation, accommodation, and resistance are ways colonized people or groups negotiated life amid imperial domination. Jude opposes this process by appealing to *1 Enoch* and accusing his opponents of propagating false teachings and leading a licentious lifestyle.

Jude's intruders are false shepherds intent on self-gain (Jude 12, echoing Ezek. 34:2, 10) possibly by deceptive means (Jude 16). Economic exploitation is implied in these critiques; these individuals may have been unscrupulous itinerant preachers (cf. 2 and 3 John). This is not an entirely new phenomenon, Jude insists; the disobedience, false teaching, and depravity in their midst comes as no surprise because apostolic traditions foretold of such a proliferation of "scoffers, indulging their own ungodly lusts" (Jude 18), a theme attested in Acts 20:21–31 and 2 Timothy 3:1–9.

---

6. See the discussion of Revelation in chapter 22, "Introduction to the Gospel of John, Johannine Letters, and Revelation."

Denouncing rather than debating these intruders, Jude exhorts his addressees to uphold the tradition and to ensure that those community members who were duped by the intruders be restored. Jude closes with a doxology rather than a formal epistolary ending (vv. 24–25).

2 Peter

Although 2 Peter identifies its author as "Simon Peter, servant of Jesus Christ and apostle" (2 Pet. 1:1), most scholars think an unknown author wrote the letter after Jude, between 140 and 150 CE. The work

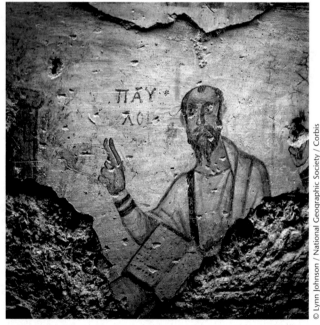

Paul holds one of his epistles in this fourth-century fresco. Christians came to accept Paul's letters as inspired literature at an early date: Second Peter provides the earliest evidence of Paul's writings being accepted as Scripture (2 Peter 3:15–16).

7. Most scholars believe that 2 Peter draws upon Jude.

is occasional, that is, written to respond to a specific issue. The author acknowledges Paul's letters as Scripture (2 Pet. 3:15–16), and knows Matthew's transfiguration story (2 Pet. 1:17–18; cf. Matt. 17:1–8) and 1 Peter (2 Pet. 3:1–2). Textual similarities between 2 Peter and Jude (2 Pet. 2:2–17; cf. Jude 4–16) lead to a debate regarding which author used which, or whether they were written by the same author, or by independent authors who shared a common source.[7] Greek rhetorical traditions permeate the work, including distinctive terms found also in the Apostolic Fathers and Jewish authors.

If 1 and 2 Peter were written by the same author, then 2 Peter was probably intended for the same readers, namely Christians in northern Asia Minor. Second Peter appeals to apostolic traditions (2 Pet. 3:2), Pauline correspondences (2 Pet. 3:15–16), and Jude's polemical warnings (Jude 4–16) to dissuade Christian leaders from following false teachings and to affirm both Christ's return (2 Pet. 3:4), which the intruders deny, and divine punishment. The theme of the "knowledge" of God or of Jesus Christ runs throughout 2 Peter (1:2–3, 5–6, 8; 2:20; 3:18).

Second Peter begins with salutations (1:1–2), moves to the development of Christian faith (1:3–21), discusses false teachers and their fate (ch. 2), and the second coming of Jesus Christ (3:1–17), ending with a doxology (3:18). Although 2 Peter begins like one of Paul's letters, it fails to mention a specific community as addressee. The author wants his readers to know that genuine "knowledge of God" inspires righteous living (1:3–11) but the knowledge of the false teachers leads to corrupt conduct (2:20–22). Scholars disagree as to whether 2 Peter's false teachers reflect gnostic beliefs or simple assimilation of Greek thought forms. In 2 Peter 1:12–2:21, the author draws upon Scripture and apostolic witness to counter his opponents' charge that belief in Christ's return is a deceptive ploy.

The false teachers, in turn, characterize the author's reading of Scripture as shrewdly orchestrated "myths" (1:16). Second Peter then interprets and revises Jude's wording for his addressees, illustrating how the dangers they face are not an entirely new phenomenon. For 2 Peter's false teachers, the redemptive work initiated by Jesus Christ warrants neither a second coming nor divine judgment. In other words, there is no basis for belief in divine involvement in human affairs. Such a conviction suggests that 2 Peter's false teachers might have been influenced by Epicureans instead of Gnostics.

Second Peter also adapts Jude's apocalyptic references to resist and discredit the false teachers' denial of the second coming of Jesus Christ. This faulty teaching, 2 Peter argues, is a pretext for libertine deportment based on a serious distortion of the Pauline traditions (2 Pet. 3:15–16) and dangerous rejection of divine governance. The delay of the parousia, as far as he is concerned, is an act of divine grace, not, as his opponents charged, manipulative myths. Therefore his readers should take care not to be misled but remain firmly faithful to the tradition (3:14–18).

The Catholic Epistles reflect various trends within Christianity with dense in-house conversations over the nature of faith in Jesus Christ and Christian life under the empire—for Christians, a transitional state. They recall much of the Pauline in-house debates. Like Paul, authors of the Catholic Epistles read and wrote alongside other readers and authors. Reading Scripture and Jewish traditions in a context influenced by Greco-Roman thought naturally engendered the polemical interpretative innovations found in Hebrews, James, 1–2 Peter, and Jude. Each epistle reflects a process of adjusting to culture while maintaining a distinctively Christian belief, identity, and practice. These emergent Christian groups appropriated Scripture as well as other Jewish and Greco-Roman literary traditions as they deemed necessary.

DISCUSSION QUESTIONS

1. How does 1 Peter connect Christian faith and suffering to God, Jesus, and Jesus' return?

2. How does Hebrews explain the unique function of Jesus Christ in divine revelation?

3. Describe Hebrews' use of the Jewish Scriptures and their regulations regarding worship and sacrifice. How does the author use these traditions to make a case for the uniqueness of Jesus Christ?

4. What relationship does James establish between faith and law, faith and speech, faith and wealth, and faith and the needy?

5. In their characterization of their opponents' teachings, what key issues do Jude and 2 Peter raise about religious tradition, faith, and theological innovation?

FOR FURTHER STUDY

Batten, Alicia J. *What Are They Saying about the Letter of James?* New York: Paulist Press, 2009.

Boring, M. Eugene. *An Introduction to the New Testament: History, Literature, Theology.* Louisville: Westminster John Knox, 2012.

Harner, Philip B. *What Are They Saying about the Catholic Epistles?* New York: Paulist Press, 2004.

Horrell, David G. *Becoming Christian: Essays on 1 Peter and the Making of Christian Identity.* Library of New Testament Studies 394. Edited by John Barclay and Mark Goodacre. New York: Bloomsbury; T & T Clark, 2013.

Kittredge, Cynthia Briggs. "The Second Letter of Peter." In *A Postcolonial Commentary on the New Testament Writings*, edited by Fernando F. Segovia and R. S. Sugirtharajah, 404–12. New York: T & T Clark, 2007.

McCruden, Kevin B. "2 Peter and Jude." In *The Blackwell Companion to the New Testament*, edited by David E. Aune, 596–612. Malden, MA: Wiley-Blackwell, 2010.

Punt, Jeremy H. "The Letter to the Hebrews." In *A Postcolonial Commentary on the New Testament Writings*, edited by Fernando F. Segovia and R. S. Sugirtharajah, 338–68. New York: T & T Clark, 2007.

Ringe, Sharon H. "The Letter of James." In *A Postcolonial Commentary on the New Testament Writings*, edited by Fernando F. Segovia and R. S. Sugirtharajah, 369–79. New York: T & T Clark, 2007.

Internet Resources

www.enterthebible.org/resourcelink.aspx?rid=1111
A map showing Asia Minor in the first century.

Part 4

Additional Study Aids

Time Line of Biblical History

The history of the Israelite tribes begins in the Late Bronze Age with the settlement of the central highlands in the southern Levant. The Merneptah Stele indicates that there was a socioethnic group called "Yasir'il" (Israel) in that region around 1230–1205 BCE. Thus a "historical timeline" for Israel can begin with the thirteenth century BCE. The first truly datable event in the history of Israel is the fall of Jerusalem in the sixth century. *Any dates assigned to figures or events prior to that time are approximate.*

PREHISTORY	2000 BCE	1900 BCE	1800 BCE	1700 BCE

Jacob's descendants settle in Egypt. (1750)

Abraham and Sarah arrive in Canaan. (1850)

FOUNDATION FIGURES

Adam and Eve
Cain and Abel
Noah

SPIRITUAL ANCESTORS OF THE MONOTHEISTIC FAITHS

Abraham and Sarah
Isaac and Rebekah
Jacob, Leah, and Rachel
Joseph and Asenath

Prophets of Israel and Judah (All dates are BCE.)

Ahijah (10th cen.)	Shemaiah Jehu (10th cen.)	Eliezer (9th cen.)	Elijah (9th cen.)	Micaiah, son of Imlah (9th cen.)	Zedekiah (9th cen.)	Elisha (9th cen.)	Amos (8th cen.)	Jonah (8th cen.)

Kings of Judah (All dates are BCE.)

Rehoboam (931–913)	Abijam (Abijah) (913–911)	Asa (911–870)	Jehoshaphat (870–848)	Jehoram (Joram) (848–841)	Ahaziah (841)

Kings of Israel (All dates are BCE.)

Jeroboam (931–910)	Nadab (910–909)	Baasha (909–886)	Elah (886–885)	Zimri (885)	Omri (885–874)	Ahab (875–854)

A Few Key Dates in Human History

- ca. 3800 BCE—City-states and river-valley civilizations begin with Bronze Age.
- ca. 3000 BCE—First pharaohs rule Egypt. Hieroglyphic writing is invented.
- ca. 2500 BCE—Great pyramids are built.
- ca. 1792 BCE—Hammurabi develops code of law in Babylon.
- ca. 1550 BCE—Canaanites invent alphabet.

- ca. 563 BCE—Buddha is born in India.
- ca. 551 BCE—Confucius is born in China.
- 500 to 300 BCE—Height of golden age of Greece.
- 43 BCE—Roman Empire is established.
- 476 CE—Roman Empire falls.
- 622 CE—Muhammad founds Islam in Arabia.

1600 BCE	1500 BCE	1400 BCE	1300 BCE	1200 BCE	1100 BCE

Judges lead Israelite tribes in Canaan. (1200)

Moses leads Exodus from Egypt. (1290)

Joshua invades Canaan. (1250)

TIME IN EGYPT AND THE EXODUS

Important Biblical Figures
Moses
Aaron
Miriam

TIME OF THE JUDGES

Important Biblical Figures
Deborah
Gideon
Samson
Samuel

Hosea (8th cen.)	Isaiah of Jerusalem (8th cen.)	Micah (8th cen.)	Nahum (7th cen.)	Zephaniah (6th cen.)	Jeremiah (7th–6th cen.)	Uriah (7th cen.)	Hananiah (6th cen.)	Ezekiel (6th cen.)

Athaliah (841–835)	Joash (Jehoash) (835–796)	Amaziah (796–767)	Azariah (Uzziah) (767–740)	Jotham (740–732)	Ahaz (732–716)

Ahaziah (853–852)	Jehoram (Joram) (852–841)	Jehu (841–814)	Jehoahaz (814–798)	Jehoash (Joash) (798–782)	Jeroboam II (782–753)

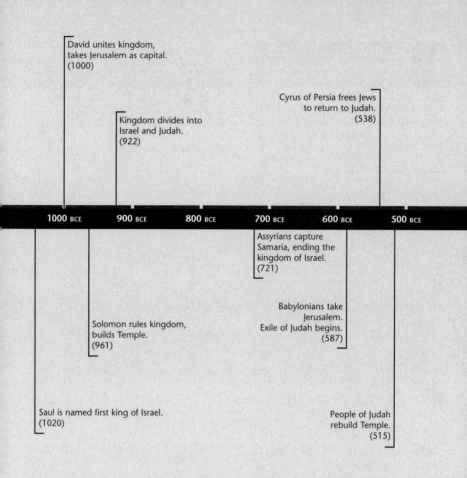

David unites kingdom, takes Jerusalem as capital. (1000)

Kingdom divides into Israel and Judah. (922)

Cyrus of Persia frees Jews to return to Judah. (538)

1000 BCE   900 BCE   800 BCE   700 BCE   600 BCE   500 BCE

Assyrians capture Samaria, ending the kingdom of Israel. (721)

Babylonians take Jerusalem. Exile of Judah begins. (587)

Solomon rules kingdom, builds Temple. (961)

Saul is named first king of Israel. (1020)

People of Judah rebuild Temple. (515)

KINGDOMS OF
ISRAEL AND JUDAH

BABYLONIAN/PERSIAN
DOMINATION

Prophets after Exile of Judah by Babylonians	*(All dates are BCE.)*					
Obadiah (6th cen.)	Second Isaiah (6th cen.)	Zechariah (6th cen.)	Haggai (6th cen.)	Third Isaiah (6th cen.)	Malachi (5th cen.)	Joel (5th cen.)

Kings of Israel	*(All dates are BCE.)*				
Zechariah (753–752)	Shallum (752)	Menahem (752–742)	Pekahiah (742–740)	Pekah (740–732)	Hoshea (732–721)

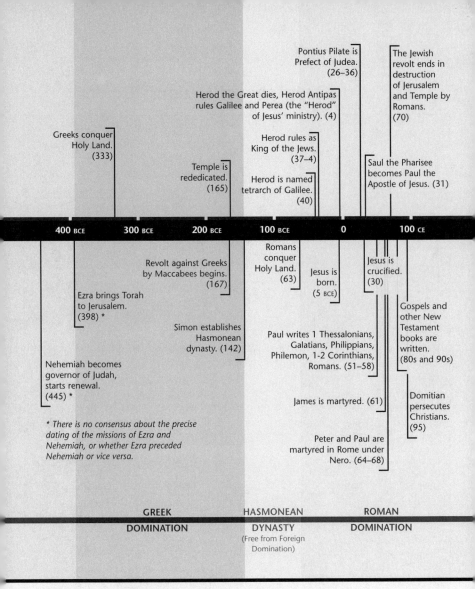

Greeks conquer Holy Land. (333)

Temple is rededicated. (165)

Herod the Great dies, Herod Antipas rules Galilee and Perea (the "Herod" of Jesus' ministry). (4)

Herod rules as King of the Jews. (37–4)

Herod is named tetrarch of Galilee. (40)

Pontius Pilate is Prefect of Judea. (26–36)

The Jewish revolt ends in destruction of Jerusalem and Temple by Romans. (70)

Saul the Pharisee becomes Paul the Apostle of Jesus. (31)

400 BCE   300 BCE   200 BCE   100 BCE   0   100 CE

Revolt against Greeks by Maccabees begins. (167)

Romans conquer Holy Land. (63)

Jesus is born. (5 BCE)

Jesus is crucified. (30)

Ezra brings Torah to Jerusalem. (398) *

Simon establishes Hasmonean dynasty. (142)

Paul writes 1 Thessalonians, Galatians, Philippians, Philemon, 1-2 Corinthians, Romans. (51–58)

Gospels and other New Testament books are written. (80s and 90s)

Nehemiah becomes governor of Judah, starts renewal. (445) *

James is martyred. (61)

Domitian persecutes Christians. (95)

There is no consensus about the precise dating of the missions of Ezra and Nehemiah, or whether Ezra preceded Nehemiah or vice versa.

Peter and Paul are martyred in Rome under Nero. (64–68)

GREEK   **HASMONEAN**   **ROMAN**

DOMINATION   **DYNASTY**   **DOMINATION**
                         (Free from Foreign
                         Domination)

Kings of Judah: Post-Destruction of Israel	*(All dates are BCE.)*						
Hezekiah (716–687)	Manasseh (687–642)	Amon (642–640)	Josiah (640–608)	Jehoahaz (608)	Jehoiakim (609–597)	Jehoiachin (Jeconiah) (597)	Zedekiah (Mattaniah) (597–586)

375

MAP 1

The Table of Nations

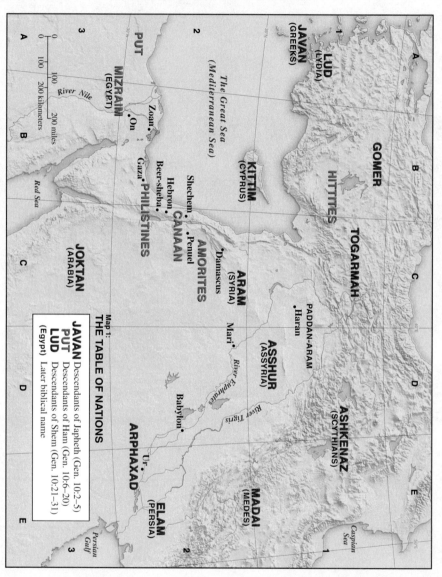

Map 1:
THE TABLE OF NATIONS

JAVAN Descendants of Japheth (Gen. 10:2–5)
PUT Descendants of Ham (Gen. 10:6–20)
LUD Descendants of Shem (Gen. 10:21–31)
(Egypt) Later biblical name

MAP 2
The Tribal Territories

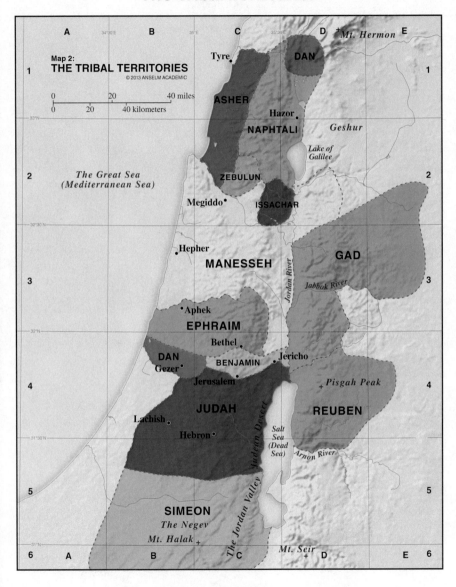

Map 2:
THE TRIBAL TERRITORIES
© 2013 ANSELM ACADEMIC

Tyre

DAN

ASHER

Hazor

NAPHTALI

Geshur

Lake of Galilee

The Great Sea (Mediterranean Sea)

ZEBULUN

Megiddo

ISSACHAR

Hepher

MANESSEH

GAD

Jordan River

Jabbok River

Aphek

EPHRAIM

Bethel

DAN
Gezer

BENJAMIN

Jericho

Jerusalem

+ Pisgah Peak

JUDAH

Lachish

Hebron

Judean Desert

Salt Sea (Dead Sea)

REUBEN

Arnon River

SIMEON

The Negev

Mt. Halak +

The Jordan Valley

Mt. Seir +

+ Mt. Hermon

MAP 3

The Kingdom Years

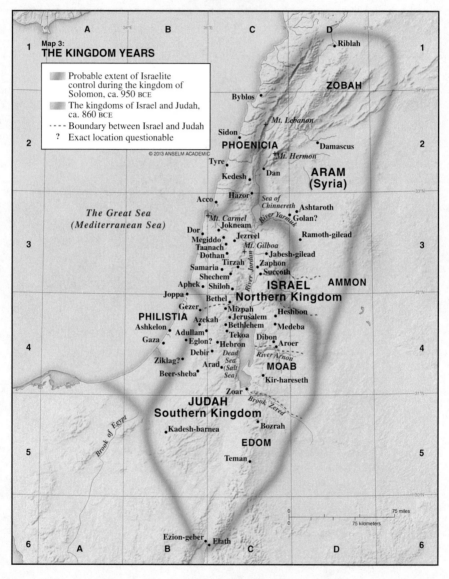

Map 3:
THE KINGDOM YEARS

- Probable extent of Israelite control during the kingdom of Solomon, ca. 950 BCE
- The kingdoms of Israel and Judah, ca. 860 BCE
- ---- Boundary between Israel and Judah
- ? Exact location questionable

© 2013 ANSELM ACADEMIC

Riblah

ZOBAH

Byblos

Mt. Lebanon

Sidon

PHOENICIA

Damascus

Tyre

Mt. Hermon

Kedesh

Dan

ARAM (Syria)

Acco

Hazor

Sea of Chinnereth

Ashtaroth

The Great Sea (Mediterranean Sea)

Mt. Carmel

Jokneam

River Yarmuk

Golan?

Dor

Megiddo

Jezreel

Ramoth-gilead

Taanach

Mt. Gilboa

Dothan

Jabesh-gilead

Tirzah

River Jordan

Zaphon

Samaria

Succoth

Shechem

Aphek

Shiloh

ISRAEL
Northern Kingdom

AMMON

Joppa

Gezer

Bethel

Mizpah

Heshbon

PHILISTIA

Azekah

Jerusalem

Ashkelon

Adullam

Bethlehem

Medeba

Gaza

Eglon?

Tekoa

Dibon

Aroer

Debir

Hebron

Ziklag?

Arad

Dead Sea (Salt Sea)

River Arnon

MOAB

Beer-sheba

Zoar

Kir-hareseth

JUDAH
Southern Kingdom

Brook Zered

Brook of Egypt

Kadesh-barnea

Bozrah

EDOM

Teman

0   75 miles
0   75 kilometers

Ezion-geber

Elath

MAP 4
The Assyrian Empire

Map 4:
THE ASSYRIAN EMPIRE (ca. 700 BCE)

→ Exiles from Israel into Assyrian captivity (721 BCE)

© 2013 ANSELM ACADEMIC

MAP 5
The Babylonian Empire

Map 5:
THE BABYLONIAN EMPIRE (ca. 600 BCE)

→ Exiles from Judah into Babylonian captivity (605, 597, 587 BCE)
→ Return of exiles under Shesbazzar and Zerubbabel (538 BCE)
→ Return of exiles under Ezra and Nehemiah (445 BCE)

© 2013 ANSELM ACADEMIC

MAP 6

The Ministry of Jesus and
Acts of the Apostles

Map 6:
**THE MINISTRY OF JESUS AND
ACTS OF THE APOSTLES**

| *(1,742)* | Elevation, in feet |
| ? | Exact location questionable |

© 2013 ANSELM ACADEMIC

Sidon

Damascus

Zarephath

Mt. Lebanon (11,000)

Mt. Hermon (9,200)

ITUREA

Tyre **PHOENICIA**

Panias (Caesarea Philippi)

TRACHONITIS

GALILEE

Ptolemais

Chorazin Bethsaida

Capernaum

The Great Sea (Mediterranean Sea)

Magdala Gergesa

Cana *Lake of Galilee*

Tiberias

Mt. Carmel (1,742)

River Kishon

Nazareth *River Yarmuk*

Gadara?

Mt. Tabor (1,843)

Nain

Esdraelon *R. Jezreel*

Caesarea Scythopolis

Mt. Gilboa (1,696) **DECAPOLIS**

SAMARIA

Samaria Gerasa

Sychar *River Jordan* *River Jabbok*

Mt. Gerizim (2,890)

Joppa **PEREA**

Antipatris

Gadara?

Arimathea Ephraim

Philadelphia

Emmaus? Jericho

Jerusalem

Bethabara

Azotus Bethany

Ashkelon Bethlehem

Herodium

JUDEA Machaerus

Gaza Hebron

Dead Sea (Salt Sea) (-1,300) *River Arnon*

IDUMEA

Masada

0 30 miles

0 30 kilometers

Beer-sheba

MAP 7
The Levant in Modern Times

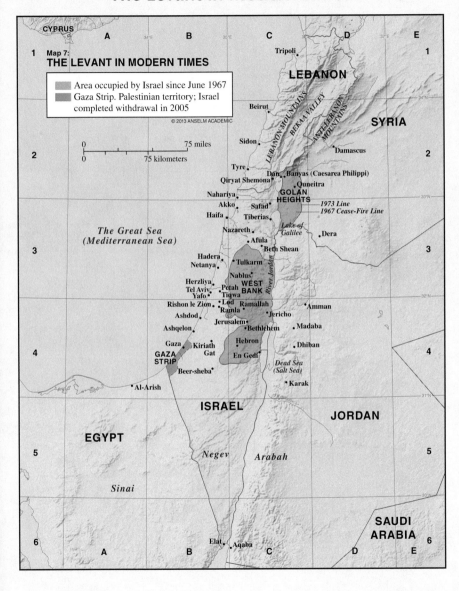

Canons of Scripture
Old Testament (Hebrew Scriptures)

Jewish	Protestant	Roman Catholic	Orthodox
Torah (Law)	Pentateuch	Pentateuch	Pentateuch
Genesis	Genesis	Genesis	Genesis
Exodus	Exodus	Exodus	Exodus
Leviticus	Leviticus	Leviticus	Leviticus
Numbers	Numbers	Numbers	Numbers
Deuteronomy	Deuteronomy	Deuteronomy	Deuteronomy
Nevi'im (Prophets)	Historical Books	Historical Books	Historical Books
Former Prophets	Joshua	Joshua	Joshua
Joshua	Judges	Judges	Judges
Judges	Ruth	Ruth	Ruth
1 and 2 Samuel	1 and 2 Samuel	1 and 2 Samuel	1-4 Kingdoms (same
1 and 2 Kings	1 and 2 Kings	1 and 2 Kings	as 1 and 2 Samuel
Later Prophets	1 and 2 Chronicles	1 and 2 Chronicles	and 1 and 2 Kings)
Isaiah	Ezra	Ezra	1 and 2 Chronicles
Jeremiah	Nehemiah	Nehemiah	1 Esdras
Ezekiel	Esther (short	Tobit	2 Esdras (same as Ezra
Hosea	version)	Judith	and Nehemiah)
Joel		Esther (long version)	Judith
Amos		1 and 2 Maccabees	Tobit
Obadiah			Esther (long version)
Jonah			1, 2 and 3 Maccabees
Micah			4 Maccabees (as an
Nahum			appendix, if included)
Habakkuk			
Zephaniah	Wisdom Books	Wisdom Books	Wisdom Books
Haggai	Job	Job	Job
Zechariah	Psalms	Psalms	Psalms (includes
Malachi	Proverbs	Proverbs	Psalm 151)
	Ecclesiastes	Ecclesiastes	Proverbs
Kethuvim (Writings)	Song of Solomon	Song of Solomon	Ecclesiastes
Psalms		Wisdom	Song of Solomon
Proverbs		Sirach (Ecclesiasticus)	Wisdom
Job			Sirach (Ecclesiasticus)
Song of Solomon			Prayer of Manasseh
Ruth			
Lamentations	Prophets	Prophets	Prophets
Ecclesiastes	Isaiah	Isaiah	Isaiah
Esther	Jeremiah	Jeremiah	Jeremiah
Daniel	Lamentations	Lamentations	Lamentations
Ezra	Ezekiel	Baruch	Baruch
Nehemiah	Daniel (short	Ezekiel	Ezekiel
1 and 2 Chronicles	version)	Daniel (long version)	Daniel (long version)
	Hosea	Hosea	Hosea
	Joel	Joel	Joel
	Amos	Amos	Amos
	Obadiah	Obadiah	Obadiah
	Jonah	Jonah	Jonah
	Micah	Micah	Micah
	Nahum	Nahum	Nahum
	Habakkuk	Habakkuk	Habakkuk
	Zephaniah	Zephaniah	Zephaniah
	Haggai	Haggai	Haggai
	Zechariah	Zechariah	Zechariah
	Malachi	Malachi	Malachi
24–39 Books	**39 Books**	**46 Books**	**48–49 Books**
(Some collections treat the following as single books: Samuel, Kings, the twelve Minor Prophets, Chronicles, Ezra-Nehemiah.)	(Protestant canon follows the Hebrew canon.)	(Roman Catholic canon follows the Septuagint, which includes seven books not in the Hebrew canon.)	(Orthodox canon follows an expanded version of the Septuagint.)

© 2014 ANSELM ACADEMIC

(continued)

New Testament

Roman Catholics, Orthodox, and Protestants have the same twenty-seven books within the canon of the New Testament.

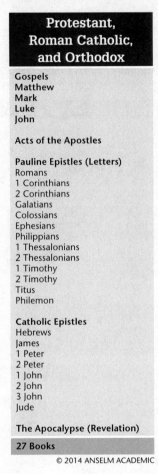

Protestant, Roman Catholic, and Orthodox

Gospels
Matthew
Mark
Luke
John

Acts of the Apostles

Pauline Epistles (Letters)
Romans
1 Corinthians
2 Corinthians
Galatians
Colossians
Ephesians
Philippians
1 Thessalonians
2 Thessalonians
1 Timothy
2 Timothy
Titus
Philemon

Catholic Epistles
Hebrews
James
1 Peter
2 Peter
1 John
2 John
3 John
Jude

The Apocalypse (Revelation)

27 Books

Biblical Genres

The literature of the ancient world utilized different genres, or types of literature, from those of modern works. Many misunderstandings of biblical texts arise when readers do not understand the genre of the literature that they are reading. For example, although a book like 1 Kings seems to be a history of Israel, the ancient conventions of history writing were not the same as they are today. Ancient historians felt quite free to rearrange events, create speeches, and embellish stories in order to make their point.

The following chart lists the major genres found in the Old and New Testaments. Some of the genres, such as parables, can be found in both collections, but most are found in specific texts or sections of the Bible. The methods of studying the Bible that are most concerned with genre are form criticism, literary criticism, and rhetorical criticism.

Genre	Description	Features	Example
Law Code	Collections of laws used throughout the community	Most laws are either apodictic or casuistic in form	**Apodictic:** "You shall not steal" (Exod. 20:15). **Casuistic:** "If you take your neighbor's cloak in pawn, you shall restore it before the sun goes down" (Exod. 22:26).
Prose Narrative	Found in historical books and fictional narratives	Reads like a story, with plot development and characterization	The book of Ruth
Prophecy	Statement, often in poetic form, that is presented as a message from God; often called "oracles"	Often introduced by the words, "Thus says the LORD . . ." or some other stock prophetic phrase	"Thus says the LORD, for three transgressions of Damascus, and for four, I will not revoke the punishment" (Amos 1:3).
Proverb	Short, pithy statement that encapsulates general wisdom from the community	Often written in parallel lines with matching or mirroring images. Also includes riddles and metaphors from nature	"The way of the lazy is overgrown with thorns, but the path of the upright is a level highway" (Prov. 15:19).
Psalm	Words to sacred music; poetic in form; most are several verses long	Usually can be classified as laments, praise, or thanksgiving	Lament: Psalm 42 Praise: Psalm 8
Apocalyptic literature	Report of a vision or revelation that looks forward to a change in human history, sometimes involving the end of this world	Uses mythic images; highly dualistic in worldview	Daniel 7 Revelation
Gospel	Prose accounts of the life of Jesus, often focusing on his death and Resurrection	Contains other genres, such as miracle stories and parables	Gospel of Mark
Epistle	Letter, often written by an ancient Christian leader to a specific community	Often contains the stock elements of ancient letters, including a greeting, ethical exhortation, and praise to God	1 Thessalonians

There are also smaller genres within larger texts, such as genealogies (usually listing only heads of households), prayers (which often resemble psalms but do not follow the strict outline of a psalm), parables (extended metaphors written as narratives that make a point about a larger concept), miracle stories (usually told of prophets to demonstrate their connection to God), and sermons or speeches (often including exhortations by a leading character to a particular community).

Sacred Time: Festivals, Feasts, and Fasts of Judaism Practiced by Jesus, the Apostles, and Their Contemporaries

Festivals include feasts to celebrate fertility, happiness, commitment, births, marriages, or victories. Times of fasting include penance and periods when feasting is forbidden.

Event	Significance and Reference
Sabbath	The seventh day is a day of rest to honor God and family. No work is permitted (Exod. 20:8–11; Lev. 23:1–3; Deut. 5:12–15). In the New Testament period, synagogue attendance on the Sabbath is typical (Mark 1:21; 6:2; Luke 4:16; Acts 15:21; 18:4). Jesus often engages in disputes about how to honor the Sabbath (Matt. 12:1–12; Mark 2:23–28; 3:2–4; Luke 13:10–16; John 5:10–18). Christians celebrate Sunday instead of the Sabbath to honor the Paschal mystery of Christ's life, death, and Resurrection (Matt. 28:1–10; Mark 16:1–8; Luke 24:1–12; John 20:1–23; 1 Cor. 16:2; Heb. 4:9).
New Year	Rosh Hashanah marks the New Year with prayers and rest. It is a day of trumpets (Num. 29:1–6).
Yom Kippur or Day of Atonement	Ten days after the New Year, the Day of Atonement honors ancestors and is a day of repentance, symbolized by a scapegoat driven into the wilderness (Lev. 16; 23:26–32; Num. 29:7–11).
Sabbatical year	Every seven years the land rests, slaves are freed, and all debts are suspended or erased (Exod. 21:2; 23:10–11; Lev. 25:1–7; Deut. 15:1–6).
Jubilee (fiftieth year)	The seventh sabbatical year is honored with compassion to the poor, the freedom of slaves, erasure of debts, the return of property to its original owner, and resting the land (Lev. 25:8–22; 2 Chron. 36:21; Isa. 61:1–2). Jesus draws on this tradition in the synagogue at Nazareth (Luke 4:16–22).
Feast of Passover or Unleavened Bread	The memorial of the Exodus from Egypt is honored in a seder meal in which prayers and blessings are offered for Jews across the world (Exod. 12:1–28; 34:18, 25; Lev. 23:4–14; Num. 9:1–14; 28:16–25; Deut. 16:1–8; Ezek. 45:18–24). It is also a time of pilgrimage to the Temple. Jesus gave new meaning to Passover when he offered himself as the bread of life in the Eucharist (Matt. 26:17–19, 26–29; John 6:4–14, 22–59; 1 Cor. 10:1; 11:23–26).
Feast of Weeks (Shavuot or Pentecost)	Shavuot ("weeks") concludes a period of seven weeks after the rite of Omer (the second day of Passover, on which the first sheaf of wheat is offered in thanks for the harvest). The Greek name for this feast, Pentecost ("fifty"), derives from the fact that the feast falls fifty days after Passover (Exod. 23:16; 34:22; Lev. 23:15–22; Num. 28:26–31; Deut. 16:9–10). Pentecost, for Christians, marks the descent of the Holy Spirit and the beginning of the church (Acts 2:1–11; 20:16; 1 Cor. 16:8).
Feast of Tabernacles or Booths (Succot)	Autumn feast; gathering of the harvest on the fifteenth to the twenty-first days of the seventh month. The feast recalls Israel's experience of living in the wilderness during the Exodus (Lev. 23:33–43; Num. 29:12–39; Deut. 16:13–17; Ezek. 45:25; Zech. 14:16–19). Jesus attended the feast of Tabernacles (feast of Booths) in the Temple (John 7:2–14, 37).
Purim	Holy day that marks the defeat of Haman of Persia by Esther and honors Mordecai's faith. The feast includes drama, fasting, feasting, and prayers for Israel (Esther 9:20–32).
Hanukkah	The dedication of the Second Temple and the defeat of Antiochus IV (167 BCE) in the Maccabean War is the mythic source of Hanukkah. The festival includes feasting and celebrations (1 Macc. 4:1–59; 2 Macc. 10:1–8; John 10:22).

Contributors

John J. Ahn is assistant professor of religious studies at St. Edward's University in Austin, Texas.

Stephen J. Binz is an independent scholar specializing in biblical pedagogy; founder and author of Ancient-Future Bible Study, Lectio Divina Bible Study, and Threshold Bible Study, in Baton Rouge, Louisiana.

François Bovon (d. 2013) was Frothingham Research Professor at Harvard Divinity School in Cambridge, Massachusetts.

William P. Brown is the William Marcellus McPheeters Professor of Old Testament at Columbia Theological Seminary in Decatur, Georgia.

Laurie Brink, OP, is associate professor of New Testament Studies at Catholic Theological Union in Chicago and Associate Editor for *The Bible Today*.

Susan Calef is assistant professor of New Testament Studies at Creighton University in Omaha, Nebraska.

Corrine L. Carvalho is professor of theology at the University of St. Thomas in St. Paul, Minnesota.

Carol J. Dempsey, OP, is professor of theology (biblical studies) at the University of Portland in Oregon.

John C. Endres, SJ, is professor of sacred Scripture at the Jesuit School of Theology of Santa Clara University and the Graduate Theological Union in Berkeley, California.

Leslie J. Hoppe, OFM, is professor of Old Testament Studies at Catholic Theological Union in Chicago.

John Kaltner is associate professor of religious studies at Rhodes College in Memphis, Tennessee.

Joel S. Kaminsky is professor in the Department of Religion at Smith College in Northampton, Massachusetts.

Amy-Jill Levine is university professor of New Testament and Jewish Studies, E. Rhodes and Leona B. Carpenter Professor of New Testament Studies, professor of Jewish Studies at Vanderbilt Divinity School and College of Arts and Sciences in Nashville, Tennessee, and affiliated professor in the Centre for the Study of Jewish-Christian Relations at Woolf Institute in Cambridge, United Kingdom.

Erica L. Martin is professor of Hebrew Scripture at the School of Theology and Ministry, Seattle University in Seattle, Washington.

Seán Charles Martin is associate professor of biblical studies at the Aquinas Institute of Theology in St. Louis, Missouri.

John L. McLaughlin is associate professor of Old Testament/ Hebrew Bible in the faculty of theology, University of St. Michael's College, and associate member of the graduage faculty, Department of Near and Middle Eastern Studies, University of Toronto in Ontario, Canada.

Younus Mirza is professor of Islam at Allegheny College in Meadville, Pennsylvania.

Aliou Cissé Niang is assistant professor of New Testament, Union Theological Seminary in New York.

James Chukwuma Okoye, CSSp, is director of the Center for Spiritan Studies at Duquesne University in Pittsburgh and adjunct professor of Old Testament at Catholic Theological Union in Chicago.

Henry W. Morisada Rietz is professor of Religious Studies at Grinnell College in Grinnell, Iowa.

Claudia Setzer is professor of Religious Studies at Manhattan College in New York, NY.

Eric Stewart is associate professor of Religion at Augustana College in Rock Island, Illinois.

Marvin A. Sweeney is professor of Hebrew Bible, Claremont School of Theology in Claremont, California.

Patricia K. Tull is the A.B. Rhodes Professor Emerita of Old Testament at Louisville Presbyterian Seminary in Louisville, Kentucky.

Gale A. Yee is the Nancy W. King Professor of Biblical Studies at Episcopal Divinity School in Cambridge, Massachusetts.

Index

Special features are indicated using lower case letters after page numbers: i (illustrations), m (maps), c (charts), cap (captions) and n (footnotes).